W9-CDB-753

Politics and International Relations of Southeast Asia

GENERAL EDITOR

George McT. Kahin

Indonesian Foreign Policy and the Dilemma of Dependence

FROM SUKARNO TO SOEHARTO

Indonesian Foreign Policy and the Dilemma of Dependence

FROM SUKARNO TO SOEHARTO

FRANKLIN B. WEINSTEIN

Cornell University Press | ITHACA AND LONDON

First published 1976 by Cornell University Press.
Published in the United Kingdom by Cornell University Press Ltd., 2-4 Brook Street, London W1Y 1AA.

International Standard Book Number 0-8014-0939-X
Library of Congress Catalog Card Number 75-36998
Printed in the United States of America by York Composition Company, Inc.
Librarians: Library of Congress cataloging information appears on the last page of the book.

For my mother and father

Contents

Foreword

That broad area lying between China and India which since World War II has generally been known as Southeast Asia is one of the most heterogeneous in the world. Though it is generally referred to as a region, the principal basis for this designation is simply the geographic propinquity of its component states, and the fact that collectively they occupy the territory between China and the Indian subcontinent. The fundamental strata of the traditional cultures of nearly all the numerous peoples of Southeast Asia do set them apart from those of India and China. Beyond that, however, there are few common denominators among the states that currently make up the area except for roughly similar climatic conditions and, until recently at least, broadly similar economies and economic problems.

The political systems presently governing the lives of Southeast Asia's 300 million inhabitants have been built on considerably different cultures; the religious component alone embraces Buddhism, Confucianism, Christianity, Hinduism, and Islam. Except in the case of Thailand, the politics of all these countries have been conditioned by periods of colonial rule—ranging from little more than half a century to approximately four—each of which has had a distinctive character and political legacy. Even the nature of the Japanese wartime occupation, which covered the entire area, varied considerably among the several countries and had different political consequences. And after Japan's defeat, the courses to independence followed by these states diverged widely. Only through revolutionary anticolonial wars were two of the most populous, Indonesia and Vietnam, able to assert their independence. Although the others followed routes that were peaceful, they were not all necessarily smooth, and the time involved varied by as much as a decade.

Moreover, subsequent to independence the political character of these states has continued to be significantly affected by a wide range of relationships with outside powers. In a few cases these have been largely harmonious, attended by only relatively minor external efforts to influence the course of local political developments. However, most of these countries have been the object of interventions, covert and overt, by outside powers—particularly the United States—which have been calculated to shape their political life in accordance with external interests. Thus the range of contemporary political systems in Southeast Asia is strikingly varied, encompassing a spectrum quite as broad as the differing cultures and divergent historical conditionings that have so profoundly influenced their character.

This series, "Politics and International Relations of Southeast Asia," stems from an earlier effort to treat the nature of government and politics in the states of Southeast Asia in a single volume. Since the second, revised edition of that book, *Governments and Politics of Southeast Asia,* was published in 1964, interest in these countries has grown, for understandable reasons especially in the United States. This wider public concern, together with a greater disposition of academics to draw on the political experience of these countries in their teaching, has suggested the need for a more substantial treatment of their politics and governments than could be subsumed within the covers of a single book. The series therefore aims to devote separate volumes to each of the larger Southeast Asian states. All the books are to be written by political scientists who have lived and carried out research in one or more of the countries for a considerable period and who have previously published scholarly studies on their internal politics.

Presumably one no longer needs to observe, as was the case in 1964, that the countries treated "are likely to be strange to many of our readers." But even though the increased American interaction with most of the countries has clearly obviated that proposition, many readers are still likely to be unacquainted with their earlier histories and the extent to which their pasts have affected the development of their recent and contemporary political character. Thus all these volumes will include substantial historical sections as well as descriptions of the salient features of the present social and economic setting. In order to provide as much similarity of treatment as is compatible with the range of cultures and political systems presented by these states, the authors will follow a broadly similar pattern of organization and analysis of their political history, dynamics, and processes. This effort to achieve some basis of comparability may appear rather modest, but to have attempted any greater degree of uniformity would have militated against the latitude and flexibility required to do justice to the differing characteristics of the political systems described.

Although each of these volumes will include a section on the foreign policy of the country concerned, the increased importance of Southeast Asia in international relations that transcend this area has suggested the need for a few studies focused on the foreign relations of its major states. The series will include this additional component. The present volume, the first in the series, is one of these. As is true elsewhere, of course, the foreign policies of these countries are heavily influenced by their own domestic politics. Hence all contributors to the volumes that are primarily concerned with international relations are also specialists on the internal politics of the country, or countries, about whose foreign policy they write.

This book, by Franklin Weinstein, is, I believe, the most substantial and perceptive account of Indonesia's foreign policy yet to appear. It rests on the author's intimate knowledge of that country's internal politics and provides important insights into the ways in which domestic factors have influenced Indonesia's role in international affairs. Drawing upon depth interviews with the foreign policy elite, Professor Weinstein shows how these leaders have been affected by the pressures of indigenous political competition in their attempts to resolve the dilemma of securing outside resources for their country's development without compromising its independence. This is a dilemma that is not, of course, confined to Indonesia. Thus the value of this book is not limited to the understanding it gives of Indonesia's foreign policy and the domestic and international factors that have conditioned it. The conclusions reached are also relevant for other underdeveloped countries and the problem of dependence in general.

GEORGE MCT. KAHIN

Ithaca, New York

Preface

This book is the product of research conducted in Indonesia from 1968 to 1970 and during the first quarter of 1973. I have relied heavily on interviews with Indonesian leaders; without the cooperation of numerous individuals who gave generously of their time this study would have been impossible. Since many of the interviewees were willing to speak frankly only with the assurance that they would not be cited by name, I cannot list all of those to whom I am indebted. I would like, however, to express special thanks to some of those who went out of their way to assist me in my research: Aminuddin, Mohammad Choesin, Alwi Dahlan, Fuad Hassan, Lim Bian Kie, Abu Bakar Lubis, Isak Mahdi, Nono Anwar Makarim, Adam Malik, Nugroho Notosusanto, R. S. Poegoeh, Mohammad Roem, Selo Soemardjan, Subadio Sastrosatomo, the late Subchan, Sudjono Humardani, and Widjojo Nitisastro. As a research assistant, Karjoso Wirosuhardjo was outstanding and provided invaluable help in the compilation of documentary materials. For access to their materials, I am grateful to the Research and Documentation Sections of the Department of Foreign Affairs, and to the Documentation Sections of the Department of Information and the Antara News Agency. At every stage my research in Indonesia was facilitated by the Indonesian Council of Sciences (LIPI), particularly by Sjamsiah Achmad and Harbison Napitupulu.

I am fortunate to have undertaken the study of Indonesian politics at Cornell University, where the Modern Indonesia Project, under the directorship of George McT. Kahin, provided an extraordinarily supportive atmosphere for young scholars. Throughout the course of my graduate study at Cornell and the subsequent preparation of this book, Professor Kahin provided enlightenment, encouragement, and counsel without which this book would not have been written. It is impossible to express adequately my feelings of gratitude for the support he has given me over the last decade. I profited greatly from having had the opportunity to work with Benedict R. O'G. Anderson, whose vast knowledge of Indonesia, always challenging intellect, and personal friendship enriched my years at Cornell and saved me from some serious errors in this study. I also owe a great deal to John W. Lewis and David P. Mozingo, both of whom significantly influenced my approach to the study of Indonesian politics. I am indebted to several other colleagues who were kind enough to offer comments on portions of this study: Frederick P. Bunnell, Daniel S. Lev, Ruth T. McVey, and the late Wayne A. Wilcox. Donald K. Emmerson, Herbert Feith, Karl D. Jackson, and Martha G. Logsdon all made helpful suggestions while I was engaged in field research. Successive versions of the manuscript were typed with care by Roberta Ludgate and Patsy Tutsch.

I wish to acknowledge with gratitude the various organizations whose financial support made this book possible. The initial period of field research and writing was funded by the Foreign Area Fellowship Program and by Cornell University's Modern Indonesia Project, Southeast Asia Program, and Project on the International Relations of East Asia. An International Affairs Fellowship from the Council on Foreign Relations made it possible for me to return to Indonesia in 1973, and the National Fellows Program of the Hoover Institution on War, Revolution, and Peace provided financial support during the period when the initial manuscript was being revised for publication. Stanford University's Arms Control and Disarmament Program supported the final typing of the manuscript.

Finally, Linda Weinstein has made Indonesia as much a part of her life as it is of mine, has borne the frustrations of having a preoccupied husband, and has offered many criticisms that have improved this book. She knows how much her support has meant.

Of course, none of those whose help has been acknowledged bears responsibility for any deficiencies in this book.

Earlier versions of some of the arguments presented in this book have appeared elsewhere. I wish to thank the publishers for permission to draw upon portions of these works: "The Uses of Foreign Policy in Indonesia: An Approach to the Analysis of Foreign Policy in the Less Developed Countries," *World Politics,* vol. 24, no. 3 (copyright © 1972 by Princeton University Press); "World Politics and World Powers: The View from Djakarta," *Asia,* no. 27 (Autumn 1972), published by the Asia Society; "The Indonesian Elite's View of the World and the Foreign Policy of Development," *Indonesia,* no. 12 (Fall 1971), published by the Modern Indonesia Project, Cornell University; *The Meaning of Nonalignment: Indonesia's "Independent and Active" Foreign Policy* (Ithaca, 1974), published by the International Relations of East Asia Project, Cornell University; "The Foreign Policy of Indonesia," in James N. Rosenau, Kenneth Thompson, and Gavin Boyd, eds., *World Politics* (New York, 1976, copyright © 1976 by The Free Press, The Macmillan Publishing Company); and "Indonesia," in Wayne Wilcox, Leo E. Rose, and Gavin Boyd, eds., *Asia and the International System* (Cambridge, Mass., 1972), published by Winthrop Publishers.

This preface, like many others introducing books on Indonesia, ends with a note on the spelling of Indonesian names. Since gaining independence from the Dutch, most Indonesians have changed the spelling of their names, replacing the Dutch-derived *oe* with *u,* the latter being closer to the actual pronunciation. But some individuals, including President Soeharto, have chosen to retain the earlier form. In each case, I have followed the spelling most commonly used in recent years, except where names appear in titles published when the earlier form was in use. A new set of inconsistencies in spelling results from changes introduced in the early 1970s in order to create a single system of spelling for the Indonesian and Malay languages. Of these changes, the one which may be most confusing to readers of this book is the replacement of *dj* with *j* (Djakarta becoming Jakarta). Except for titles of works produced before the change and the names of individuals who have retained the older spelling, I have followed the new forms.

FRANKLIN B. WEINSTEIN

Stanford, California

Indonesian Foreign Policy and the Dilemma of Dependence

FROM SUKARNO TO SOEHARTO

1 | The Dilemma of Dependence

Indonesian foreign policy in recent years has displayed two sharply contrasting faces. Under Sukarno in the first half of the 1960s, Indonesia aspired to lead an international anti-imperialist front. Sukarno condemned the prevailing international system as an exploitative order in which the "old established forces" (OLDEFOS) of the world sought to keep the "new emerging forces" (NEFOS) in subjugation. Warning that aid from the OLDEFOS was but another device to limit the independence of the NEFOS, he exalted self-reliance and told the United States to "go to hell with your aid." As Indonesia's economy stagnated, Sukarno filled his people's ears with stirring oratory, hammering away at the theme that real independence was possible only through an all-out confrontation with the forces of exploitation.

Under Soeharto since 1966, however, Indonesian foreign policy has eschewed flamboyance and oriented itself to the search for Western economic aid and capital investment. The anti-imperialist crusade has been abandoned, and confrontation has been replaced by passivity and talk of regional cooperation. Where Jakarta's newspapers once carried headlines proclaiming Indonesia's determination to fight to the death against the OLDEFOS, since 1967 they have told of favorable evaluations of its economic performance by the International Monetary Fund (IMF) and of efforts to win ever larger aid commitments from the OLDEFOS. No longer do government leaders describe their foreign policy as a struggle to preserve Indonesia's independence in a world of powers intent on dominating their country. Unceasing confrontation has, it appears, been replaced by an equally ceaseless search for foreign aid.

This striking transformation is of more than historical interest. The contrasting policies of Sukarno and Soeharto represent very different ways of dealing with one of the most persistent, and often most painful, dilemmas confronting the underdeveloped countries: how to use outside resources without compromising independence. Should leaders permit the country to become dependent on foreign capital, or must independence be guarded even at the sacrifice of such resources? This dilemma of dependence has been a central concern of Indonesian policymakers since the proclamation of independence in 1945. Even Sukarno sought, and to some extent relied on, foreign aid; nor has Soeharto been wholly unconcerned about the dangers of excessive reliance on outsiders. Neither found the situation simple or easily resolved. The dilemma is painful precisely because Indonesia is an underdeveloped country: the economic and political deficiencies that make cooperation with the outside world appear indispensable also make it seem dangerous.

Although sometimes discussed as part of the psychological aftermath of colonialism, the nature of the choice between aid and independence has not received substantial analytic treatment. To be sure, a number of recent studies have drawn attention to the dependence of underdeveloped states on larger powers and have explored the nature, extent, and implications of their dependence.[1] But these studies rarely view the problem from the vantage point of the policymaking elite of an underdeveloped country. None has

1. The most comprehensive is Marshall R. Singer, *Weak States in a World of Powers: The Dynamics of International Relationships* (New York: Free Press, 1972), especially ch. 2. Apart from this, most of the work has been done on Latin America. Among the most interesting are Susanne Bodenheimer, "Dependency and Imperialism: The Roots of Latin American Underdevelopment," in K. T. Fann and Donald C. Hodges, eds., *Readings in U.S. Imperialism* (Boston: Porter Sargent, 1971), pp. 155–81; Theotonio Dos Santos, "The Structure of Dependence," in *ibid.*, pp. 225–36; and James D. Cockcroft, Andre Gunder Frank, and Dale L. Johnson, *Dependence and Underdevelopment: Latin America's Political Economy* (Garden City, N.Y.: Doubleday, 1972).

dealt with the relation of dependence to the making of foreign policy—specifically, the question of why some governments choose a foreign policy that maximizes independence at the expense of aid, while others accord top priority to the search for aid.

The reasons for this neglect are worth considering at some length because they point up a fundamental weakness in the literature on foreign policy in the new nations. Most studies fail to clarify how foreign policy relates to those political and economic problems defined as underdevelopment.

In most Western analyses the foreign policy of underdeveloped countries is pictured as having a peculiar irrelevance to the real concerns of those nations. It is often described as little more than a game played by an individual or a small group at the expense of the nation's real interests. Typically, Edward Shils observes of the new states: "Foreign policy is primarily a policy of 'public relations,' designed not, as in advanced countries, to sustain the security of the state or enhance its power among other states, but to improve the reputation of the nation, to make others heed its voice, to make them pay attention to it and to respect it."[2]

A related theme is the decisive influence of the personal idiosyncracies of the top leadership in the determination of policy.[3] The leaders of the new states are frequently said to engage in "reckless" conduct and to make decisions on the basis of "almost random"

2. "The Intellectuals in the Political Development of the New States," in John H. Kautsky, ed., *Political Change in Underdeveloped Countries: Nationalism and Communism* (New York: Wiley, 1962), p. 211.

3. See, for example, James N. Rosenau, "Pre-theories and Theories of Foreign Policy," in R. Barry Farrell, ed., *Approaches to Comparative and International Politics* (Evanston: Northwestern University Press, 1966), p. 48; Werner Levi, *The Challenge of World Politics in South and Southeast Asia* (Englewood Cliffs: Prentice-Hall, 1968), pp. 13–14; I. William Zartman, *International Relations in the New Africa* (Englewood Cliffs: Prentice-Hall, 1966), pp. 47, 53; Frederick P. Bunnell, "Guided Democracy Foreign Policy: 1960–1965," *Indonesia,* 2 (October 1966), 37–76; Bunnell, "The Kennedy Initiatives in Indonesia, 1962–1963" (Ph.D. dissertation, Cornell University, 1969); and W. Scott Thompson, *Ghana's Foreign Policy, 1957–1966* (Princeton: Princeton University Press, 1969).

pressures.[4] Foreign policy "at times has no other criterion than whim, emotion, or accident," writes one leading authority on the international relations of Africa; for the most part, he adds, foreign policy has "little to do with domestic needs or purposes."[5] Unfettered by the restraints of entrenched bureaucracies and large-scale organizations, these leaders can set policies which primarily express their personal ambitions, ideologies, and frustrations.[6] The inclination among political scientists to stress these factors is paralleled by a propensity in the press to apply such adjectives as "mercurial," "irrational," and "erratic" to the foreign policies of the less developed countries.

Even when long-range factors are adduced to explain or justify certain conduct, there is a tendency to see foreign policy in isolation from the nation's internal political processes. Some writers stress the importance of "pure" external goals like expansionism—"a struggle for external influence for its own sake."[7] Others allude to domestic political considerations and the role of parliaments, political parties, and interest groups, but the author's primary interest is often in showing that foreign adventures are being undertaken as a "distraction" from domestic difficulties, or as a means of fostering a heightened, if illusory, sense of national solidarity.[8] Several

4. Henry A. Kissinger, "Domestic Structure and Foreign Policy," *Daedalus* (Spring 1966), pp. 513, 523. The "erratic and unpredictable" nature of foreign policy in these countries is also stressed by Lucian W. Pye, *Politics, Personality and Nation Building: Burma's Search for Identity* (New Haven: Yale University Press, 1962), p. 295, and Fred W. Riggs, *Administration in Developing Countries: The Theory of Prismatic Society* (Boston: Houghton Mifflin, 1964), pp. 76, 89–95.

5. Zartman, *International Relations,* p. 53, refers specifically to the West African states.

6. The fullest formulation of the view that the lack of a multiplicity of "subsystems" encourages such idiosyncratic behavior is Bernard K. Gordon, *The Dimensions of Conflict in Southeast Asia* (Englewood Cliffs: Prentice-Hall, 1966), pp. 120–40. See also Levi, *Challenge of World Politics,* pp. 155–56, and Rosenau, "Pre-theories and Theories," p. 47n.

7. Zartman, *International Relations,* p. 53. See also Gordon's discussion of Indonesian foreign policy in *Dimensions of Conflict,* pp. 68–119.

8. For one of the best statements of this thesis, see Donald Hindley, "In-

writers emphasize the ways in which foreign policy is molded by size and location, historical and cultural background, industrial and military capabilities, and ideology.[9] Still others point out that the leaders of less developed countries face so many external constraints which they are powerless to control that they fall victim to a kind of "situational determinism."[10] This line of argument suggests that the intractable realities of world politics have repeatedly frustrated unrealistic foreign policies set by leaders who indulged their excessive personal ambitions and gave expression to their identity crises and other postcolonial psychological disorders. At last, it is said, the leaders of the new nations are learning to resist the "temptations" of foreign policy and have begun to concentrate instead on long-neglected domestic problems.[11]

Of course, analyses of the personal idiosyncracies of charismatic leaders have made their actions more comprehensible. The best of the other studies mentioned also make it clear that policies which appear to represent merely the eccentricities of present leaders often are grounded in longer-term considerations. Rarely, however, is

---

donesia's Confrontation with Malaysia: A Search for Motives," *Asian Survey,* 4 (June 1964), 904–13. See also Daniel Lerner's discussion of Nasser in *The Passing of Traditional Society: Modernizing the Middle East* (New York: The Free Press, 1958), pp. 247–48. A few studies have given attention to the role of interest groups, political parties, parliaments, public opinion and government structure. Zartman, *International Relations,* treats most of these briefly. Domestic politics is given greater emphasis in Claude S. Phillips, Jr., *The Development of Nigerian Foreign Policy* (Evanston: Northwestern University Press, 1964).

9. For example, William C. Johnstone, *Burma's Foreign Policy: A Study in Neutralism* (Cambridge: Harvard University Press, 1963); Roger M. Smith, *Cambodia's Foreign Policy* (Ithaca: Cornell University Press, 1965); and Phillips, *Development of Nigerian Foreign Policy.* Robert Curtis, "Malaysia and Indonesia," *New Left Review,* 28 (November-December 1964), 5–32, and George McT. Kahin, "Malaysia and Indonesia," *Pacific Affairs,* 37 (Fall 1964), 253–70, combine analysis of historical and sociological factors with discussion of domestic political considerations. Ideology is given particularly full treatment in Donald E. Weatherbee, *Ideology in Indonesia: Sukarno's Indonesian Revolution* (New Haven: Yale Southeast Asia Studies Monograph Series, 1966).

10. For example, see Zartman, *International Relations,* pp. 80–81, 144–48.

11. Levi, *Challenge of World Politics.*

foreign policy seen as a positive instrument in the promotion of the nation's development or the sustaining of its political system. The literature is dominated by a perception of foreign policy as primarily a diversion from efforts to deal with important problems, and in much of the writing, as an attempt to escape from reality. The manner in which foreign policy choices are defined and circumscribed by the economic and political conditions peculiar to less developed countries remains an unanswered, and for the most part unasked, question.[12]

This situation is partly a reflection of the fact that charismatic leaders engaged in "troublesome"[13] diplomacy have attracted most of the attention from students of foreign policy in the new nations. Understandably, scholars have tended to concentrate either on explaining their controversial policies or on demonstrating that the policies are unrealistic. There are, indeed, few studies of the foreign policy process in countries whose policies are not regarded as "troublesome." Nonetheless, scholars have shown a tendency to generalize about foreign policy in the less developed countries on the basis of the experience of those countries which have had flamboyant leaders and controversial policies.[14] As a result, foreign policy analysis in the less developed countries frequently takes on the appearance of pathology—an effort to explain why leaders act in such apparently irrational ways.

The principal reason, however, for our inadequate understanding of the relationship between foreign policy and underdevelopment is the paucity of analyses that explore the interaction among the factors that influence the formation of foreign policy. The studies

12. One of the few really enlightening discussions of this relationship is Robert C. Good, "State-Building as a Determinant of Foreign Policy in the New States," in Laurence W. Martin, ed., *Neutralism and Nonalignment: The New States in World Affairs* (New York: Praeger, 1962), pp. 3–12.

13. Roger Hilsman, *To Move a Nation* (Garden City: Doubleday, 1967), p. 365.

14. See, for example, Kissinger, "Domestic Structure and Foreign Policy," pp. 521–25: "The new nations, in so far as they are active in international affairs, have a high incentive to seek in foreign policy the perpetuation of charismatic leadership."

which stress idiosyncratic sources generally convey little sense of the policy's context and of the conditions which allow leaders to indulge their peculiarities. Why are some idiosyncracies tolerated but not others? Do certain fundamental constraints operate even in those states where strong charismatic leaders appear relatively unencumbered in their conduct of foreign policy? If so, how are these constraints expressed and what kinds of limits do they impose? How much choice does such a leader really have, if his charismatically-based power is to be preserved? And when the pivotal figure is removed, how can we know what basic factors remain at work that might help us understand what the new leaders are likely to do, if we have focused our attention overwhelmingly on the personality of the erstwhile leader?

Accounts that emphasize long-range factors, on the other hand, often do not explain sudden policy shifts which occur in the absence of any change in those long-term givens. Very few studies tell us how such factors as geography, economics, historical experiences, external pressures, domestic politics, and the personal likes and dislikes of leaders affect one another.

Rather than investigate such relationships, most analyses either simply list a series of factors which they say are interrelated, or they attempt to rank the variables, an enterprise likely to yield only inconclusive results. The preoccupation with ranking, which has dominated so much of the research in comparative foreign policy, obstructs any significant advance in understanding the policymaking process. It seems futile to hope that we can ever single out a particular variable as the dominant factor in a country's foreign policy. In a great many cases, it is simply impossible to discover which variable is most important; often the decision-maker does not even know. For example, did Sukarno choose to oppose the newly-formed state of Malaysia in 1963 mainly because of his personal dislike for Malaysia's prime minister, his recollection of British and Malayan assistance to anti-Jakarta rebels in 1958, his calculation of domestic political benefits, or for some other reason?

Even the author of one of the most comprehensive case studies of the foreign policy process found it "premature" to rank the variables on the basis of just one study.[15] But if it is impossible to rank the variables in one case, how can they be ranked with respect to many? A survey of many cases will tell us which factors appear most frequently, but this is not necessarily an accurate indicator of the importance of each variable. For example, geography may be the most frequent factor without ever being the decisive one. It would be meaningless to then assert that geography was the most important determinant of foreign policy.

Nor is it clear that knowing which factor is decisive, were it possible to obtain such information, would be very rewarding. Is the factor which provides the final impulse toward a decision more important than the influences which earlier set the stage? Instead of which straw broke the camel's back, what one really needs to know is the prior condition of the camel's back, how its load was distributed, and the motivation of the person who did the loading. It is not the last straw but the combination of preconditions that led to the camel's demise.

With respect to foreign policy, we need to ask, for example, not whether idiosyncracies are more important than politics or long-term factors like geography and history, but how geography and history encourage certain leadership pecularities and not others; how politics creates incentives to respond to some of the problems created by geography and history but not to all of them; and how a president's idiosyncracies may alter the political constellation, thus affecting the foreign policy attitudes of other leaders. Very little attention has been devoted to this more promising line of inquiry. Yet it is the answers to such questions that will explain the interactions through which the political and economic needs of the less developed country find expression in foreign policy.

This study explores the relationship between underdevelopment and foreign policy by focusing on the difficult choice between inde-

15. Bernard C. Cohen, *The Political Process and Foreign Policy: The Making of the Japanese Peace Settlement* (Princeton: Princeton University Press, 1957), p. 281.

pendence and reliance on foreign support. It begins with a recognition of the sense of weakness that prevails in Indonesia. Most informed Indonesians see their nation's problems as overwhelming and its capacity to deal with them as extremely limited. This kind of weakness is perhaps endemic to the state of underdevelopment, but Indonesia's potential—due to its size, natural resources, military capability, and highly developed culture—makes its weakness all the more depressing. Many sensitive, educated Indonesians have confidence in their individual capabilities and are convinced that their country is the natural leader of Southeast Asia. Precisely because of their aspirations and expectations, they find Indonesia's weakness especially frustrating, and in fact, humiliating.

Foreign policy in such a situation is bound to reflect the condition of weakness.[16] It should be stressed, however, that the less developed countries are not wholly without leverage in their relations with more powerful nations. Under certain circumstances underdevelopment can be advantageous. Could a modern state like Belgium have defied American military might as the Vietnamese did? North Vietnam's lack of a highly specialized economy undoubtedly helped to minimize the disruptive effects of American bombardment. The Saigon government too demonstrated an ability to work its will on the United States. If it is too much to say that the Vietnamese tail wagged the American dog, the tail at least displayed a capacity to cause the dog to stumble when it ran in a displeasing direction.

The same kinds of relationships can be observed with regard to Indonesia. In the past, Indonesia succeeded more than once in forcing its will on the "stronger" Dutch. At present, Indonesian officials worried about the influence of foreign agencies on policy-making in Jakarta take consolation from their knowledge that the foreigners' stake in Indonesia's development effort is now so great that to deny Indonesia's aid requests would be to invite unacceptable consequences.

16. For studies alluding to the importance of weakness, see Johnstone, *Burma's Foreign Policy*, pp. 248–49, and Michael Brecher, *India and World Politics: Krishna Menon's View of the World* (New York: Praeger, 1968), p. 306.

The real importance of weakness is not that it places a state at the mercy of stronger powers but rather that it dictates the chief concerns of policymakers. Indonesia's foreign policy, notwithstanding all the changes it has undergone in recent years, has consistently sought either to alleviate or to provide an explanation for the country's weakness. Under both Sukarno and Soeharto foreign scapegoats have been used to explain Indonesia's inability to solve its problems. For Sukarno, neocolonialist machinations were to blame; Soeharto has held international Communist subversion responsible, especially that emanating from China. Both leaders have promised that their foreign policies would help solve these problems. Sukarno's confrontation with Malaysia rested on the assumption that Indonesia could advance only if neocolonialism were smashed first. In Soeharto's Indonesia, the search for foreign economic aid has been seen as the key to the success of his development program.

Miles Copeland describes the choice: "In those countries where the economic and social conditions appear hopeless—or, at least, beyond the local resources of a government—the usual outcome is either for a local leader shouting 'freedom from imperialism' as his country goes to ruin, or for a practical type to take over the country with foreign aid and hold on, as a 'stooge of the imperialists' or an 'agent of Moscow,' with foreign protection."[17] But the dilemma, in reality, is considerably more subtle, and the possible responses much more varied. The real choice is not one of aid *or* independence, for everyone, even a Sukarno, desires both. The question is, rather, how much dependence on outside assistance should be accepted and how much foreign control tolerated. The relationship between aid and independence is by no means uncomplicated, and it is worthwhile clarifying just what is implied by the two terms and how they relate to one another.

In Indonesia emphasis on economic development has become synonymous with emphasis on foreign aid because it is so hard to conceive of development without aid, barring revolutionary changes

17. *The Game of Nations: The Amorality of Power Politics* (New York: Simon and Schuster, 1969), p. 27.

in the political and social systems. Indonesia's economy has experienced extraordinary difficulties, owing to a number of fundamental problems: overpopulation and underemployment, especially on Java, ubiquitous corruption and bureaucratic inefficiency, a dependence on world market prices for the several key export commodities, a lack of any substantial industrial capacity, a shortage of technical expertise, a sorely inadequate economic infrastructure, and until fairly recently, chronic inflation, often of runaway dimensions. Moreover, a key fact of Indonesian political life is the inadequacy of government power. Indonesia's political, military, and socio-religious groupings have been continually beset by internal disunity and by conflict with one another. The parties and the armed forces are fragmented by cliques which may reflect ethnic, regional, or in the case of the army, divisional associations, but often signify nothing more than a network of highly idiosyncratic personal relationships. Because no political group has had the capacity to mobilize domestic resources as, for example, the Chinese Communists have done, total self-reliance as an approach to economic development has never really been a viable alternative.

The Indonesian leaders' sharp awareness of their country's weakness thus dictates a foreign policy directed toward securing from abroad the funds and expertise needed to bring about economic development. It is the task of foreign policy to acquire government-to-government loans and credits, to attract foreign investment, and to negotiate favorable terms of trade. The need for aid is not, however, restricted to the economic sphere. The Indonesians are aware that an underdeveloped country can develop and maintain a modern armed forces establishment only with continuing foreign military assistance, encompassing both materiel and training. Moreover, at key points in the course of their conflicts with the Dutch, the Indonesians made strenuous efforts to win diplomatic aid from a broad range of countries in their efforts to gain and protect their sovereignty.

Independence, on the other hand, means more than the ending of colonial rule and the transfer of sovereignty to an indigenous administration. When we speak of defending the nation's independence, we are talking not merely about the preservation of sovereignty. Independence means, in the first instance, avoiding dependence. It is the task of foreign policymakers to assure that Indonesia does not rely so heavily on others as to jeopardize Jakarta's ability to determine its own policies. Many Indonesians regard neocolonialism as a fact of contemporary international life. They are convinced, at the very least, that they must remain ever alert to the danger of finding their formal independence a sham and their fate dictated by foreign forces. Some fear as well a kind of cultural neocolonialism that threatens to destroy Indonesia's national identity, and in so doing, to weaken her capacity to resist outside pressures.

For many Indonesian leaders, the definition of independence is broader still. Given their country's size, resources, and history, they see independence as entailing the "resumption" of Indonesia's rightful and natural position of leadership in Southeast Asia. Efforts by outside powers to dominate the region and to exclude Indonesia from deliberations about its fate are viewed as an infringement of this independence. To say that Indonesians are inclined to see independence as entailing a position of some authority and dignity in the region is not, however, to say that they have expansionist ambitions. Most of them are convincing in their denials of such aspirations. But they do feel that an Indonesia which is isolated, her influence curtailed, is not fully independent. Ultimately, it is a matter of self-respect.

The key assumption underlying the view that defense of Indonesia's independence must take highest priority is that the outside world is basically exploitative, dominated by forces seeking to subjugate the country. Every nation, of course, has its enemies. But those who perceive the outside world as hostile are worried about their friends as well. They are acutely sensitive to foreign penetration and to the likelihood that any economic relationship with a stronger foreign power will find them in a subservient position.

A foreign policy emphasizing defense of the nation's independence may assume a variety of forms. It may be a largely negative policy of avoiding dependent relationships and relying to the maximum extent possible on the nation's own resources. It may manifest itself as an attempt to minimize the effects of dependence by balancing against each other the forces that would dominate the country. Or it may be an effort to confront these forces directly and eliminate them from the region.

The aid-independence dilemma corresponds to the two sides of a more general problem in the less developed countries. Political scientists have for some time observed conflicts between problem-solvers and solidarity-makers in Indonesia, administrators and politicians in Burma, and "experts" and "reds" in China.[18] It is not surprising that this basic cleavage should find expression in foreign policy. To some extent, aid and independence have been defined in terms of opposition to each other. Thus, when Indonesia followed an independence-oriented foreign policy from 1962 to 1966, it was criticized for sacrificing the foreign aid needed to fulfill its developmental needs. Since 1966, with the government heavily emphasizing the acquisition of aid for development, a frequent criticism has been that the country is in danger of sacrificing its independence.

In some ways, however, aid and independence are complementary; in fact they feed on and stimulate one another. Aid is necessary for economic development, and development is a means of giving substance to independence. An underdeveloped state will always be dependent on others, Indonesians believe. Only a nation with substantial economic strength and a reasonable degree of self-sufficiency can realistically hope to act in accord with its own interests when they run contrary to the desires of more powerful states. Moreover, economic underdevelopment is considered a legacy of colonialism and thus remains a symbol of the limitations on Indonesia's independence. Insofar as development signifies a transformation of Indonesia's economic structure, from that of a colonial dependency geared to fostering the development of the metropolitan

18. See Herbert Feith, *The Decline of Constitutional Democracy in Indonesia* (Ithaca: Cornell University Press, 1962); Pye, *Politics, Personality and Nation Building;* and Franz Schurmann, *Ideology and Organization in Communist China* (Berkeley: University of California Press, 1966). "Expert" and "red" refer to professional and political elements respectively.

power to that of a viable national economic unit, it occupies a clear position in the process of moving from colonial domination to total independence. Additionally, development is associated with the longing for a position of leadership appropriate to Indonesia's self-image. Like independence, development is also a matter of self-respect. Many Indonesians feel that economic development is the only area in which Indonesia lags behind other countries in Southeast Asia; once this embarrassing failure has been rectified, Indonesia's leadership will surely be recognized and her independence assured. Finally, where military and diplomatic aid have been sought in order to enhance Indonesia's security or to press claims against the Dutch, aid has been explicitly conceived of as contributing to the attainment and preservation of independence.

On the other hand, it is widely believed that meaningful development is impossible without prior independence. This view is deeply rooted in the expectations aroused by the anticolonial struggle: the end of colonialism was expected to bring not only independence but prosperity and economic development. Independence and development remain inextricably linked in the minds of many members of the Indonesian elite. To the extent that Indonesia's independence is impaired, any economic development is likely to benefit the foreigners who control Indonesia's destiny more than it helps Indonesia.[19] This kind of development is seen as indistinguishable from colonialism. As one Indonesian leader put it: "What was the point of freedom? If all we wanted was the kind of development you get when outsiders hold control, we could have had that by staying under the Dutch."

Moreover, to those who defend the entry of foreign capital on

19. As Nkrumah described it, there is a "bridge of gold" between total independence and economic development (Pablo Gonzalez Casanova, "Internal and External Politics of Underdeveloped Countries," in Farrell, ed., *Approaches,* p. 135). Gonzalez, a Mexican scholar, adds: "Without independence there is no development. Underdeveloped countries that depend fundamentally on an external market for their development cannot industrialize themselves and are highly vulnerable. Unlike ancient empires, . . . new nations can only rely on the growth of their internal market and the protection of their products and imports to the outside market" (*ibid.,* p. 138).

the ground that it contributes to economic development and thus to real independence, others respond that severe restrictions on foreign capital are the surest spur to the establishment of indigenous economic institutions and thus the safest guarantee of independence in the long run. The problem, they point out, is that to seek economic development by relying on foreign aid and investment is to seek long-run independence by accepting greatly increased short-run dependence. But who can guarantee that this intensified short-run dependence will not perpetuate itself? Nor is real security believed possible if the search for military aid is permitted to restrict the country's independence by binding Indonesia to a military pact.

This interplay between aid and independence is not fully comprehensible without continuous reference to the political functions of foreign policy—that is, the uses foreign policy serves in domestic political competition.[20] The exploitation of foreign policy for political purposes is not, of course, peculiar to the less developed countries, but it does take a somewhat different form. The heavy degree of foreign penetration in many less developed countries automatically gives the foreign powers great influence on the domestic power struggle. Thus perhaps the most pointed criticism of foreign policy from 1962 to 1966 was that, by isolating Indonesia from the West, the policy would tip the internal balance in favor of the Indonesian Communist Party (PKI). Similarly, critics of foreign policy since 1966 often see it as creating foreign relationships which help the present ruling elite maintain its political dominance.

The political uses of foreign policy reflect the distinctive features of the country's political life. Political competition energizes Indonesian foreign policy, reshaping basic impulses like the desire for independence and development to fit the needs of each political actor and giving expression to limitations imposed by the nature of

20. For a broader discussion of this, see Franklin B. Weinstein, *Indonesia Abandons Confrontation: An Inquiry into the Functions of Indonesian Foreign Policy* (Ithaca: Cornell Modern Indonesia Project, 1969). See also W. Howard Wriggins, *The Ruler's Imperative: Strategies for Political Survival in Asia and Africa* (New York: Columbia University Press, 1969), pp. 221–38.

the Indonesian political system. Those who rule define independence and development in a way that fits their own political needs.

Indonesian foreign policy has often served to compensate for, or at least to mitigate the effects of, some of the key political deficiencies of the ruling elite. The anti-Western campaigns of Sukarno not only expressed deeply held feelings but also constituted a way in which a basically conservative elite could provide the illusion of revolutionary progress, without risking its own position in a real internal revolution. Similarly, by its heavy reliance on foreign aid, the Soeharto government has been able both to avoid the kinds of reforms that might endanger its own existence and to compensate for its inability to mobilize domestic resources for development. Moreover, resources acquired from abroad constitute an important political asset. Ruling groups have not infrequently diverted development aid to other purposes such as maintaining the cohesion of political parties or the armed forces.

An essential element in determining which political uses foreign policy can serve is the degree of competitiveness in the political system. In a highly competitive system foreign policy can be used to legitimize controversial political demands or to isolate one's domestic enemies from their foreign allies. In a less competitive polity, the views of potential critics can more easily be ignored because their capacity to use foreign policy to embarrass the government is limited.

The interaction among aid, independence, and political competition is complex. On the one hand, the dominant attitudinal pattern helps determine which political uses can profitably be exploited. For example, the prevalence of attitudes emphasizing threats to independence means that certain political uses will be especially exploitable. If the outside world is widely perceived as threatening, political capital can easily be made out of appeals for solidarity in the face of an ambiguous external danger. On the other hand, political needs can affect perceptions, and people may hold particular attitudes because it is in their political interest to do so.

In this analysis of the dilemma of dependence only minimal attention will be given the idiosyncratic sources of policy. There are two reasons. First, to the extent that a leader's psychological or ideological predispositions reflect the country's underdevelopment, they are likely to emerge in the view of the world of other leaders who have had similar experiences. Second, while idiosyncratic factors always have some influence on policy formation, and especially on its implementation, few leaders who care about their political future will express personal eccentricities which run counter to dominant attitudes and political realities.

In other words, to the extent that Sukarno's personal dislike for Malaysia's prime minister could be related to broader suspicions about Malaysia, Sukarno could allow himself to be influenced by his personal feelings toward the Malaysian leader. But he obviously could not have made a personal dislike of the ruler of Sweden the basis for a policy of opposition to the existence of that Scandinavian state, toward which Indonesians tend to be either apathetic or favorably disposed. Only those idiosyncracies which neither violate dominant attitudes nor radically alter the domestic political configuration are likely to find expression in foreign policy.[21]

This, then, is a study of attitudes and politics. It examines the Indonesian foreign policy elite's view of the world and the process by which these perceptions interact with the pressures of political competition to help determine the resolution of the aid-independence dilemma.

This elite's view of the world is based on a variety of relatively long-term internal and external conditions. Some policymakers interpret these long-term factors as requiring and justifying substantial reliance on outside support, while others see them as necessitating that dependence on outsiders be kept to a minimum. Taking geography as an example, Indonesia's strategic location and

21. On the limited capacity of a dictator to convert whim into foreign policy, see Werner Levi, "Ideology, Interests, and Foreign Policy," *International Studies Quarterly,* 14 (March 1970), 26: "[A dictator may be able] to go a bit farther than others, but he cannot go all the way." He too is bound by both internal and external constraints. A useful discussion of the conditions under which personal idiosyncracies can influence policy is found in Fred I. Greenstein, *Personality and Politics: Problems of Evidence, Influence, and Conceptualization* (Chicago: Markham, 1969), pp. 33–62.

wealth of natural resources can be seen as placing the country in an unusual state of jeopardy, because they encourage larger powers to seek to dominate Indonesia. Or alternatively, they may be perceived as important assets for development, and ultimately a source of strength which makes it unnecessary for the country to fear domination. Indonesia's history, if interpreted as full of attempts to subjugate the country, will generate suspicion of the motives of other countries; to the extent that the foreign policy elite's view of the world does not reflect such a reading of history, the leaders may be inclined to trust other nations.

A leader's view of the world, of course, is constantly evolving, as the environmental variables change and as the policies adopted meet with success or failure. Through this feedback the country's real capabilities, not just the elite's perceptions of them, are brought to bear on policymaking. Though leaders act on their perceptions, not necessarily on reality, repeated failures are likely to produce a change either in the perceptions or in the leadership itself. Moreover, foreign policy needs to be seen as an independent, as well as a dependent, variable. For example, prolonged adherence to a foreign policy involving heavy dependence on foreign aid may itself contribute to the rise of pressures for a more independent foreign policy, just as years of emphasizing the need to struggle against real or imagined threats to independence may bring weariness and an intensified desire to seek foreign aid for economic development.

The principal source of attitudinal data for this study was a series of depth interviews conducted by the author during 1969 and 1970 with members of the Indonesian foreign policy elite.[22]

22. Few other studies provide either methodological guidance or serve as a reliable data base. Most research on elite perceptions of the world has relied on content analysis of public statements. Examples include: Philip M. Burgess, *Elite Images and Foreign Policy Outcomes: A Study of Norway* (Columbus: Ohio State University Press, 1967); Harold D. Lasswell and Satish K. Arora, *Political Communication: The Public Language of Political Elites in India and the United States* (New York: Holt, Rinehart & Winston, 1969); Sheldon W. Simon, *The Broken Triangle: Peking, Djakarta, and the PKI* (Baltimore: Johns Hopkins University Press, 1969); and Michael Brecher, Blema Steinberg, and Janice Stein, "A Framework for Research on Foreign

This group was selected on a reputational basis, with the assistance of a panel of twelve prominent Indonesians representing a wide variety of political perspectives.[23] Of the 75 individuals rated most influential[24] on foreign policy matters, 64 were interviewed at least

---

Policy Behavior," *Journal of Conflict Resolution,* 13 (March 1969), 79–93. Without deprecating the value of content analysis as a supplementary technique, one can question whether that approach can provide a reliable, nuanced description of elite thinking and its origins. For the author's views on this subject, see "The Uses of Foreign Policy in Indonesia: An Approach to the Analysis of Foreign Policy in the Less Developed Countries," *World Politics,* 24 (April 1972), 361–62. An excellent overall critique of content analysis is Robert Jervis, "The Costs of the Quantitative Study of International Relations," in Klaus Knorr and James N. Rosenau, eds., *Contending Approaches to International Politics* (Princeton: Princeton University Press, 1969), pp. 177–217. Where interviews have been used, they have tended to involve narrowly focused, highly structured questionnaires, usually administered by hired interviewers to middle level officials. For a good example, see Karl W. Deutsch *et al., France, Germany and the Western Alliance* (New York: Scribner's, 1967).

23. The following procedure was used. First, a list of all Indonesians who could conceivably be regarded as influential in recent foreign policy was compiled. The names were drawn from newspapers; materials provided by the Information Department, Foreign Department, and Parliament; and conversations with a wide variety of Indonesians, foreign scholars, and diplomats. This list was restricted to Indonesians who were still alive, in Indonesia, and out of jail. (This means that no Indonesian Communist leaders were included.) The list contained 194 names. The panelists, chosen by the author, then individually inspected the list and selected those whom they regarded as genuinely important in foreign policy, adding any names they wished. The selections made by the panelists were subsequently combined to yield a single list, arranged according to frequency of mention. Finally, during the author's interviews with the members of the foreign policy elite, each respondent was asked to review the list of names and select those regarded as genuinely influential at present. This second set of selections, which served as a partial (because the question asked was not precisely the same) check on the panel of twelve, confirmed that no truly important figures had been omitted.

24. The panel's selections were not treated as binding. Several individuals just below the cut-off point were included, for one or more reasons: (1) the name was late in being added to the list and probably would have been chosen by some previous panel members had it been on the list earlier; (2) someone with special knowledge felt very strongly that an individual was important; (3) the individual belonged to a group that seemed underrepresented in the panel of twelve; (4) an individual was generally believed to represent the views of someone higher on the list who was unavailable for interviewing.

once, and 53 were interviewed in depth, averaging about seven and one-half hours. Two more foreign policy elite members made information concerning their attitudes available indirectly.[25] In addition, some 30 lower echelon leaders were interviewed to see if they would corroborate the views of particular groups and foreign policy elite members. Finally, a few foreign policy elite members from each political and generational group were interviewed again in early 1973 to determine whether attitudes had changed substantially in response to later developments. All but four of the interviews were conducted mainly in the Indonesian language.

It needs to be stressed that the group interviewed does not represent a random sample of any larger population. An effort was made to define the most influential leaders and to interview them all. Moreover, inasmuch as the top elite's experiences tend to differ significantly from those of Indonesians at the middle levels, it is quite conceivable that interviews with a random sample of middle level elite members would have revealed very different attitudes.

The depth interviews did not follow a rigid schedule and usually contained a mixture of historical and attitudinal questions, since most of the key sources of historical information were members of the foreign policy elite. Although the sequence, wording, and depth of the questions were kept flexible in order to encourage frankness, essentially the same areas were covered in all the depth interviews. After all the interviews were completed, the author drew up a questionnaire reflecting the points that had generally been covered. The

---

Likewise, a corresponding number just above the cut-off point were dropped: (1) an elder statesman from a group that seemed overrepresented and who was said to be too feeble to be interviewed; (2) someone with special knowledge of that group asserted emphatically that an individual was not influential in foreign policy matters. Also, although the author is confident that no important figures were omitted from the list of 75, the panel tended to include as well people regarded as authorities on foreign policy even if they were no longer influential.

25. One granted a written interview (in which he was surprisingly frank), and the other permitted his assistant to talk at length with the author. In a 1973 interview with the second elite member, the author was able to confirm the earlier information provided by the assistant.

66 questionnaires were then filled out by the author based on the individual's comments on each point, expressed in a variety of contexts, and on corroborative data provided by other Indonesians.[26] Besides the interviews, there were several supplementary sources of attitudinal data, including a wide range of Indonesian newspapers, government documents, and political party statements.

Some of the hazards of this method of collecting data are all too evident. In probing the origins and evolution of their attitudes the author asked some respondents to recall perceptions and experiences thirty or forty years in the past. One must assume a certain loss of accuracy due to faulty memory, and a certain amount of intentional distortion, motivated by political or personal considerations. The author's nationality presumably introduced some bias into the interview as well. Additionally, any survey is tied to a particular point in time, while attitudes are constantly changing. Some of the interviews were probably disproportionately influenced by then current issues.

Efforts were made, of course, to minimize the impact of these methodological problems. The interviews with each respondent generally stretched over a period ranging from several months to nearly a year, and key questions were asked again in different contexts at various stages; some respondents clearly became more candid after several sessions. Published writings of a few foreign policy elite members or their contemporaries, along with comments from others, were useful corroboration, especially in the case of recollections of times long past. The extensive questioning about past attitudes also made the results less static than they would otherwise be; the additional interviews in 1973 helped in this too. That the author's nationality was not too formidable a deterrent to candor is suggested by the ease with which respondents criticized the United States.

One final methodological question requires comment—the rela-

26. Though the same general areas were covered in all the completed interviews, it often proved impossible to say with confidence what a respondent's views were on a particular point. Thus, the number of respondents on each question fluctuated widely.

tionship between this study and the ongoing debate about how best to develop meaningful generalizations on the foreign policy process. Leading theorists have suggested that theory-building can advance only if researchers are willing to process their data through a common framework, thus channeling the masses of data compiled in case studies into categories that will render the data comparable. Faced with a growing number of case studies which by and large have not produced generalizations in a form conducive to the development of theory, these authors have created frameworks in the hope that the area specialists who write case studies would use them. Few have used them, however, and the reasons may reflect something more than mere orneriness on the part of area specialists.[27] The point is not that the models are without value for certain studies, but that it is neither feasible nor necessary for all researchers to use a common framework. In the first place, it is extremely hard to imagine a framework that all, or even many, foreign policy analysts would find appropriate. Moreover, though facts can always be stretched to fit a preconceived set of categories, the generalizations based on these distorted facts do not advance our understanding of political processes, however stimulating such "theories" may be.

The prospects for theorizing will be enhanced if each researcher devises an individual framework, assuring above all that it is suited to the researcher's own data and particular theoretical concerns. Such an approach is more likely to be fruitful than one which begins with general "pre-theories" and theories, seeks to force all research into a highly structured mold, stimulates endless arguments about whose definitions and categories are best, and runs a serious risk of culminating in sterile typologizing. The possibility of comparative analysis depends less on the use of a common framework than on the willingness of case study writers to put their conclusions in the form of general hypotheses, using well-known, loosely-defined variables capable of easy translation from one study

27. For an explanation of why none of the major frameworks proved applicable to this study, see Weinstein, "Uses of Foreign Policy: An Approach," pp. 358–63.

to the next. There does not seem to be any logical reason why theory-building cannot begin at such modest levels, close to the data, and then move upward as studies accumulate.

The present work will first discuss the origins and evolution of the Indonesian foreign policy elite's view of the world. Then those perceptions will be analyzed in some detail to see what they suggest about the issues of aid and independence. Finally, we shall return to the subject with which we began—the dramatic transformation of Indonesian foreign policy from Sukarno's administration to Soeharto's—and assess the way in which attitudes and politics interact to help determine the resolution of the dilemma of dependence.

2 | First Impressions of the International System

Early in the author's research, several Indonesian leaders suggested that their country's position in the world was analogous to that of a pretty maiden constantly being approached by men who wanted to take advantage of her. This analogy was subsequently presented to the foreign policy elite during the interviews. Because the discussion evoked by the analogy highlights several principal features of this group's view of the international system, it seems useful, before examining the sources of their perceptions, to dwell for a moment on what these leaders said when they were asked to compare their country to a harassed pretty girl.

The response to the analogy was one of overwhelming agreement. Of the 50 leaders who expressed an opinion, 40 saw at least some truth in it, and 26 asserted that it had a great deal of validity. These sentiments were by no means confined to "old order" adherents. Substantial agreement was found among practically every important element, with strongest agreement coming from the top levels of the army and the foreign ministry, as well as from leaders of the PNI (Indonesian Nationalist Party) and PSI (Indonesian Socialist Party).[1] Young and old alike supported the analogy, although the

1. Of 10 generals, 9 saw some truth in the analogy, 8 saw much truth in it; of 6 foreign ministry officials, 5 saw much truth, the sixth saw none; of 9 PNI leaders, 8 saw some truth, 6 saw much; of 5 PSI respondents, 4 saw much truth; the fifth saw no truth. (The PSI, banned by Sukarno, was never formally rehabilitated, but a small group of its leaders met regularly in 1968–1970.) As for the other major groups, 5 of 7 technocrats saw truth in the analogy, but only 3 saw much truth; 3 of 4 Catholic leaders saw truth in it, but none saw much; and 3 of 5 leaders of the Islamic parties saw some truth, but only one saw much.

youngest generation was reluctant to embrace it with enthusiasm.[2]

Those who agreed with the pretty girl analogy offered a number of explanations for their country's predicament. A common line of reasoning, particularly among military officers, emphasized geopolitical factors. Indonesia's strategic location and wealth of natural resources were said to place the country in an unusual state of jeopardy because they constitute incentives for larger powers to intervene.[3] "Our wealth makes us vulnerable," asserted several leaders. There is, certainly, a strong belief that these material advantages represent a long-run asset, but as long as Indonesia remains weak and underdeveloped, its resources are considered a liability.

This view is, of course, the product of Indonesia's history as well as a reflection of its leaders' analysis of the current situation. The Indonesians feel that Dutch colonial rule was motivated primarily by a desire to exploit Indonesia's natural wealth. After independence, this belief was extended to the Cold War experience of the 1950s, in which Jakarta was wooed and pressured by both sides. Though the Americans and British are seen as withdrawing from Southeast Asia, these leaders fear a new scramble for influence, led this time by the Japanese and the Chinese.[4]

2. In the oldest generation, 6 of 8 saw some truth, 4 saw much. Of 36 members of the intermediate generation, 29 saw some truth, 21 saw much. As for the youngest, 5 of 6 saw some truth but only one saw much. One young leader who accepted the essential validity of the analogy nonetheless characterized it as "something the older generation told itself in order to boost its self-image."

3. This idea occasionally emerges in public pronouncements on the subject of national defense. For examples, see *"Tjatur Darma Eka Karma": Doktrin Pertahanan-Keamanan Nasional dan Doktrin Perdjuangan Angkatan Bersendjata Republik Indonesia* (Jakarta: Staf Pertahanan-Keamanan, 1967), pp. 12–19; General Panggabean, "Peranan AD Dalam Pertahanan Keamanan Nasional," *Karya Wira Jati,* no. 23 (February 1967), pp. 23–24; the statement of Foreign Minister Adam Malik at the Foreign Ministry's 1968–69 "Senior Course," reported in *Dasar-dasar Pegangan untuk Pengolahan/Pengetrapan Kebidjaksanaan Politik Luar Negeri atas Masalah-Masalah Internasional* (Jakarta: Departemen Luar Negeri, 1969), p. 24; *Berita Yudha,* 25 November 1966; and *Gotong Rojong,* 24 May 1967.

4. This picture of an Indonesia besieged on all sides is displayed with un-

Many leaders doubted that the industrialized nations of the world really wish to see Indonesia develop economically. They pointed out that much of the foreign investment taking place in Indonesia is "exploitative," that is, investors export raw materials without building local refineries, lumber mills, and other processing facilities. They complained also about the strings attached to economic aid. As a strongly anti-Communist army officer explained:

> Sukarno said we were surrounded by imperialists. We said yes, but also by Communists. . . . I don't know whether I would use the term surrounded today, but we must accept as reality the fact that colonialism and imperialism still exist, both from the non-Communist side and the Communist side. . . . Take, for example, the United States. We are trying to sell our tin, it is very important to us, and the US exerts its influence to lower the price of tin. That may be in the economic interests of the US, but we see it as imperialism. The US is trying to protect the interests of General Motors, but it is very damaging to us. The case of Japan is even more obvious. They are dependent on imports for 85% of their energy supply. There can be no question that they are going to continue to depress prices, to keep control of the situation. This is exploitation. . . . I am very suspicious of the motives of these countries. Maybe I am too suspicious, but I can't help it. It is the result of our experience. We have been stabbed in the back so many times.

In some cases, agreement with the pretty girl analogy clearly derived from a Marxist ideology, but in others the influence of Morgenthauian realism was evident: strong nations always seek to dominate and exploit weaker ones. Recognition of the basically exploitative character of the outside world is simply a sign of political maturity.

A more subtle but still important consideration is race. All of the powers which threaten to dominate Indonesia are either yellow or

---

usual clarity by Major General Sajidiman Surjohadiprodjo, "The Defence of Indonesia," in K. K. Sinha, ed., *Problems of Defence of South and East Asia* (Bombay: Manaktalas, 1969), pp. 219–40. A much milder version is Sajidiman's "The Future of Southeast Asia," *Indonesian Quarterly,* 1 (January 1973), 38–49.

white. Though talking to an American, several of the elite expressed bluntly their conclusion, rooted in the colonial experience, that the white Western powers felt racially superior. As for the Chinese and Japanese, they were frequently described as the "yellow peril." Closely tied to the race problem is the fear of cultural invasion and the loss of national identity. This concern is especially strong in Islamic circles but is certainly not confined to them.

Those who failed to see any validity at all in the pretty girl analogy felt that it simply reflected the inferiority complex of certain individuals. One preferred to compare Indonesia to a person walking in the street: a pedestrian must always be alert but need not assume that most drivers are out to run pedestrians down.

Even some of those who thought the pretty girl analogy accurate voiced concern that others who shared their view might be motivated by an inferiority complex. Whether or not the predatory designs of the outside world pose a serious danger to Indonesia depends on Jakarta's response, they argued. An inferiority complex was dangerous because it could push Indonesia into an isolationist or "supernationalist" posture. Indonesia, warned a technocrat, "must not be like the pretty girl who never goes out because she is afraid of getting raped, and thus never gets married." A leader of the younger generation pointed out that it is quite possible for "the girl to maintain high principles and use her attractions to her own advantage."[5]

Thus, while the situation is by no means viewed as totally without advantages, the foreign policy elite members believe that their country is besieged by forces that will exploit Indonesia for their own purposes. How have the Indonesians leaders come to hold such a view? How does this perception manifest itself in their analysis of the international system in the 1970s? And how does it affect the way they perceive the aid-independence dilemma?

5. An army officer compared Indonesia to the mousedeer (*kancil*) which must defend itself by its wit. See Philip Frick McKean, "The Mouse-Deer (Kantjil) in Malayo-Indonesian Folklore: Alternative Analyses and the Significance of a Trickster Figure in South-East Asia," *Asian Folklore Studies,* 30 (1971), 83–84.

The Indonesian leaders interviewed were drawn from three age groups, divided according to the descriptions of political generations employed by the Indonesians themselves.

Of the 66 members of the foreign policy elite about whom data is available, 11 are men of the Generation of 1928, so named because of its identification with the "youth oath" of 1928 and the commitment to a unified, independent Indonesia. Members of the 1928 Generation were born prior to 1910. They virtually all have been leaders of political parties, specifically the Masjumi (an Islamic party banned by Sukarno in 1960), the PNI, the Catholic Party, and the Christian (Protestant) Party. All 11 have held cabinet posts, 4 having served as prime minister and 3 as minister of foreign affairs.

By far the largest component of the foreign policy elite is the Generation of 1945, which came of age politically during the "physical revolution" from 1945 to 1949. The 46 leaders in this group were born between 1910 and 1935. They differ significantly from their elders in their political and occupational associations. Besides PNI and Catholic Party figures, they include members of political parties not represented in the 1928 Generation, such as the PSI and the NU (Nahdatul Ulama), an Islamic party that has been a bitter rival of the Masjumi. In addition, many of the 1945 Generation leaders are not politicians. Rather, they are army generals, several of whom have been key advisers to President Soeharto; technocrats, mainly American-trained economists who hold high government positions; and foreign ministry officials, including virtually all of the top officeholders during the period of the interviews.

The smallest segment of the elite is the Generation of 1966, consisting of 9 leaders of the group that gained its political identity from the struggle to depose Sukarno. Born after 1935, they do not represent a cross-section of the future leaders of Indonesia; they are merely those who, because of their leadership of student organizations, have emerged as spokesmen for the young generation. They include no young army officers, foreign ministry officials, or technocrats. Though only a few have formal ties to nonstudent groups, the

1966 Generation leaders as a whole are closest to the PSI, Islamic, and Catholic party leaders.

The foreign policy elite may also be divided according to the members' political and occupational associations. Among those interviewed were at least four representatives of each of seven major groups: the army (12), foreign ministry (9), technocrats (9), PNI (9), Islamic political parties (8), PSI (6), and Catholic Party (4).[6]

The chief sources of the Indonesian leaders' first impressions about international relations were their formal schooling, participation in study clubs and other student associations, and casual conversations with friends and relatives. Early impressions were modified or reinforced by travel and residence abroad, by the course of Indonesia's relations with the major powers, and by direct experience in diplomatic negotiations. This exposure has led to a mixture of trust and suspicion in which the latter is dominant. To a remarkable degree, given the diverse conditions under which they acquired their views, the three generations have come to share a perception of the world as a threatening place.

The 1928 Generation

The 1928 Generation leaders were beneficiaries of the excellent educational system established by the Dutch colonial government and opened to a small segment of the Indonesian elite in the early twentieth century. Practically all of these leaders successfully completed their secondary education at these elite schools and went on to receive university degrees, several at universities in the Netherlands.[7]

6. The foreign ministry figure includes only those who were officials at the time they were interviewed in 1969 and 1970. The total number of people is 50, but 7 people fit into two groups (for example, army generals who served in the foreign ministry). The 16 leaders not affiliated with any of the major groups include: 6 leaders of the 1966 Generation not yet clearly linked to any group: 3 navy officers; 2 independent newspaper editors; 2 eminent politicians of the 1928 Generation not identified with any particular political party; one leader of the Christian party; one leader of a minor political party; and one high-ranking civil servant.

7. Of the 11 members of the 1928 Generation, 10 graduated from elite

The elite schools offered comprehensive courses in European history and geography, with only cursory mention of such "remote" areas as China or the United States; nor was the history of Indonesia given any substantial treatment. Coverage of the Netherlands, on the other hand, was so thorough that some leaders recall their surprise on discovering in their travels that certain towns which had loomed so large in their studies were such small and insignificant places.

Learning in depth about the history and government of the Netherlands did, however, generate a heightened awareness of Indonesia's lack of independence. The students could easily see the difference between the authority of the Dutch parliament and the limited powers of their colonial legislature. Even more important, perhaps, was the realization of the racial basis of Indonesia's inferior status.[8] While attendance at such elite schools, some of which had a student body that was over 90 percent Dutch,[9] was a source of considerable prestige for an Indonesian, it could also be an unsettling experience. It was not unusual for Indonesian students to be harassed as "inlanders" (natives) by their Dutch classmates, and

---

Dutch secondary schools; 9, of whom 4 studied in the Netherlands, received university degrees. For a discussion of the colonial education system, see Paul W. Van der Veur, *Education and Social Change in Colonial Indonesia* (Athens, Ohio: Ohio University Center for International Studies, Southeast Asia Program, 1969), vol. 1; Ruth T. McVey, "Taman Siswa and the Indonesian National Awakening," *Indonesia,* 4 (October 1967), 128–68; Bernhard Dahm, *Sukarno and the Struggle for Indonesian Independence* (Ithaca: Cornell University Press, 1969), pp. 28–31; *Sukarno: An Autobiography as Told to Cindy Adams* (Indianapolis: Bobbs-Merrill, 1965), pp. 22–68; George McT. Kahin, *Nationalism and Revolution in Indonesia* (Ithaca: Cornell University Press, 1952), pp. 31–33; and Robert Van Niel, *The Emergence of the Modern Indonesian Elite* (The Hague: Van Hoeve, 1960).

8. Mohammad Hatta claimed in 1928 that even in the elite Dutch primary schools Indonesians could feel the "lashing blows" of racial conflict ("Indonesia Free," in *Portrait of a Patriot: Selected Writings by Mohammad Hatta* [The Hague: Mouton, 1972], p. 209).

9. See Van der Veur, *Education and Social Change,* pp. 11, 14a, and *Sukarno: An Autobiography,* p. 43.

some Indonesians felt discriminated against in grading.[10] In certain cases, socializing with Dutch girls brought to the surface latent insecurities and produced a sharpened sensitivity to racial intolerance.

Several 1928 Generation members recalled that a few of their Dutch teachers favored independence for Indonesia and gave their Indonesian students a sense of self-respect. Some were even Marxists or at least permitted discussion of Marxist writings.[11] But the first intensive exposure to nationalist and Marxist ideas was experienced by those educated in Holland, especially at Leiden. There they learned of the glories of Indonesia's past empires. To their surprise, they discovered that Indonesian mariners were sailing far across the seas at a time when the Greeks and Romans were confined to the Mediterranean. They remembered their professors as "inspiring," "great men," who instilled in them an awareness of the greatness of their own culture and history and a belief in the legitimacy of their claim to equality and independence. And of course, in this time of intellectual ferment and social unrest in Western Europe, they were equally influenced by what was happening outside the classroom.

By the middle 1920s study clubs and student associations had become a significant forum for ideological debate and nationalist agitation. Of the 11 leaders in the 1928 Generation, 9 participated in study clubs. All four who studied in Holland were active in the Perhimpunan Indonesia (PI), an association of Indonesian students there.[12] By 1923 the PI had become an unequivocal spokesman for radical nationalism, espousing "noncooperation" with the Dutch colonial authorities.

In their discussions, the PI members delved into Marxist litera-

10. See, for example, *Sukarno: An Autobiography,* pp. 43–47.

11. Dahm, *Sukarno and the Struggle,* pp. 30–31.

12. The PI was established in 1908 as the nonpolitical organization Indische Vereeniging. For its history, see Sunario, "Perhimpunan Indonesia dan Peranannja Dalam Perdjuangan Kemerdekaan Kita" (paper presented at Seminar Sedjarah Nasional II, Jogjakarta, 26–29 August 1970); Hatta, "Indonesia Free," pp. 216–21; and James Bruce Amstutz, "The Indonesian Youth Movement, 1908–1955" (Ph.D. diss., Fletcher School of Law and Diplomacy, 1958), pp. 56–71.

ture and the revolutionary experiences of other nations. Though few of them were Communists, they met with leaders of the PKI, such as Semaun, who lectured them on Marxism and sought to work out a cooperative arrangement with them. The PI members devoted considerable attention to the experiences of India, Egypt, China, Turkey, and Ireland, and especially to the Sinn Fein movement in Ireland.

They also traveled to Paris, Brussels, and other European cities to meet with nationalists from India, Vietnam, and other Asian and African countries, as well as with European anticolonialists. They attended anti-imperialist conferences, such as the 1926 International Democratic Congress for Peace, in which the name Indonesia was used for the first time in international politics, and the 1927 Congess of the League Against Imperialism and Colonial Oppression, held in Brussels. Through their contacts with other nationalist leaders, as well as their reading, the Indonesian students developed a sense of common purpose with other Asians and Africans, and came to recognize that Indonesia's experience was but one manifestation of an exploitative international order that had subjugated most of Asia and Africa.[13]

Colonialism, in fact, came to be seen as an inevitable consequence of the international system. According to Mohammad Hatta, chairman of the PI in the latter 1920s, colonialism was the "use of the rapacity and greed of the stronger nations in order to satisfy their economic and commercial interests at the expense of the weaker nations." It was rooted in the insatiable need of the advanced countries for food, raw materials, and markets, and in the doctrine of racial superiority. At no point, Hatta claimed, did the interests of the strong and the weak run parallel, and it was naive to expect any generosity. Even the Western socialists had proved untrustworthy supporters of

13. For more detail, see the following articles in Hatta's *Portrait of a Patriot:* "Indonesia in the Middle of the Asian Revolution" (1923), pp. 20, 24; "The Economic World Structure and the Conflict of Power" (1926), pp. 54–56; "The Anti-Colonial Congress in Brussels in the Light of World History" (1928), p. 196; and "The Objectives and Policy of the National Movement in Indonesia" (1930), pp. 105–6, 113, 141.

Indonesia's cause.[14] Thus, Hatta concluded, only by self-reliance could Indonesia achieve independence.[15]

Still, if their exposure to the Europe of the 1920s made the Indonesian students more sharply aware of colonialism as an inevitable product of the international system, they also had the exhilirating experience of being treated with a degree of respect and equality unknown in Indonesia. "We were treated as free men," recalls one leader.[16] Contacts with European anticolonialists, as well as an awareness of the United States commitment to self-determination as expressed in Wilson's Fourteen Points, did inspire hopes, however fragile, of foreign assistance for Indonesia's struggle. The belief that the outside world contained potential allies was evident in the PI's 1925 platform, which laid special emphasis not only on self-help and noncooperation, but also on the need for increased efforts to attract international attention to the Indonesian problem.[17]

14. The Second International (August 1928) classified Indonesia as not ready for independence or even self-determination. Hatta's resentment led him to declare that the colonized nations would "wage war against *any* colonial imperialism, whether it is called capitalist or socialist!" ("The Second International and the Oppressed Peoples" (1928), in *Portrait of a Patriot,* pp. 358–60). See also "The Colonial Resolution of the Second International" (1928), in *ibid.,* pp. 364, 370–72, in which the Dutch socialist party is sharply criticized. Another target was the British Labour government, which Hatta accused of trampling underfoot the rights of self-determination "for which their own organization . . . has stood up with tenacity." The history of the twentieth century, Hatta concluded in 1930, testifies that "Western socialism gradually passes from the defender to the rapist of the right of self-determination, from ally to oppressor of the coloured people" ("Non-cooperation," in *ibid.,* pp. 341–42).

15. See, in *Portrait of a Patriot,* "Indonesia and Her Independence Problem" (1927), pp. 168, 179; "Economic World Structure," pp. 41–43, 45, 49–52; "Anti-Colonial Congress," pp. 189–91, 196–98; "Drainage" (1923), pp. 28–33; "Objectives and Policy of the National Movement," pp. 105–6, 111–12; "Indonesia Free," pp. 213–14, 221, 245–46; "National Claims" (1924), pp. 314, 317–18; and "Colonial Resolution of the Second International," p. 362. See also Amstutz, "Indonesian Youth Movement," pp. 56–57.

16. See also Hatta's "Indonesia Free," pp. 211–13. Hatta claimed that living in Holland made the Indonesian students aware that the Dutch were really quite ordinary people, thus smashing the myth of the superiority of the white race.

17. Sunario, "Perhimpunan Indonesia," pp. 18–19.

Foreign propaganda was "an indispensable element in the struggle for national independence."[18]

Hatta's inconsistency in first dismissing hopes of foreign support and then calling for stepped-up efforts to win such support reflected the sometimes subtle ambivalence that characterized the 1928 Generation leaders' view of the outside world. Even as they moved toward a determination that the colonial tie had to be severed, the young Indonesians increasingly looked to the West for intellectual sustenance. A good description of this paradox comes from the diary of Soetan Sjahrir, the socialist leader who became Indonesia's first prime minister in 1945.[19]

Sjahrir, whose stay in Holland had instilled in him a deep admiration for the discipline and rationalism of the West, was dismayed to find that most of his comrades were more anti-Western than before. But, he noted, even as the Indonesians came to reject the Dutch, they did so increasingly within a Dutch, or at least a Western, framework. For Sjahrir, the Indonesians' hatred of their Western exploiters was, compared to the hatred of the Chinese, Arabs, Indians, or Japanese, "only superficial, because the haters themselves have actually assimilated the patterns of living and thinking of the whites." Indonesian intellectuals were "much closer to Europe or America than . . . to the Boroboedoer or Mahabharata or to the primitive Islamic culture of Java and Sumatra." They had become so "nationally characterless" as to preclude their espousal of the kind of "fanatical nationalism" which other Asians had displayed. Sjahrir contended that Indonesian nationalist leaders who advocated militant opposition to the Dutch were, in their hearts, merely members of the "loyal opposition," whose boldness hid an underlying respect for the Dutch.

18. "Propaganda" (1926), in *Portrait of a Patriot,* pp. 145–46. See also "The Brussels Congress against Imperialism and Colonial Oppression and our Foreign Propaganda" (1927), in *ibid.,* pp. 161–64.

19. *Out of Exile,* trans. Charles Wolf, Jr. (New York: Greenwood, 1949), pp. 2–3, 67, 85, 124–26, 202–6. These observations were made between 1934 and 1938.

Upon returning home the PI members sought to transmit the ideological perspectives they had acquired in Holland to students who had remained in Indonesia. One of the principal means of doing so was the establishment of study clubs to replicate the PI experience.[20] Between 1924 and 1927, politically-oriented study clubs were founded in a number of Indonesia's principal cities, and former PI members were among the leaders of the new clubs. In the proliferating study clubs and youth organizations, the 1928 Generation leaders held lengthy debates on subjects that included Marxism, capitalism, and the applicability to Indonesia of the American, French, Russian, and other revolutionary experiences.[21]

Of special note is the enthusiasm with which the 1928 Generation leaders initially responded to Marxist writings. All eleven had read at least some Marxist materials before reaching the age of twenty-five. Of the seven who said they could remember their first reaction to Marxism, all but one recalled being favorably impressed with at least the anti-imperialist aspects of the doctrine. The lone dissenter was a Catholic who said his initially hostile reaction, based mainly on Catholic sources, was later moderated when he read more widely and discovered that there was "some truth to Marxism, at least on economic matters." Some of the leaders of Islamic parties remember thinking that Marxism had some relevance to Indonesia's problems, though they were repelled by the idea of class struggle.

Other writings also had a strong influence on the 1928 Generation leaders, including the works of writers on Islam like Snouck Hurgronje, and nationalists from Thomas Jefferson to Ataturk. Ernest Renan particularly impressed the Indonesians with his argument that in building a nation a sense of national unity was more important than such attributes as a common language or a shared

20. Kahin, *Nationalism and Revolution in Indonesia,* pp. 88–90; Sunario, "Perhimpunan Indonesia," pp. 47–48; and Amstutz, "Indonesian Youth Movement," p. 68. See also Dahm, *Sukarno and the Struggle,* pp. 54–55.

21. The American revolution was said to be the most relevant because it had been directed against a foreign country.

cultural heritage. But the dominant influence clearly was Marxism.

In sum, the education of the 1928 Generation leaders generally made them more aware of their inferior status, more conscious that this was the consequence of the prevailing international order, and more strongly committed to the termination of foreign domination. At the same time, the Western origin of the nationalist and Marxist ideas that fortified their determination to work for independence, as well as the encouragement given by European anticolonialists and Dutch teachers, inevitably raised hopes that the outside world would lend support to Indonesia's struggle.

The 1945 Generation

The education of the 1945 Generation was much more diverse than that of the older generation. Whereas virtually all of the 1928 Generation leaders had had either a university education abroad or an elite Dutch secondary education in Indonesia, only about 60 percent, or 28 of the 46 leaders of the 1945 Generation received such training. The rest were educated either in lesser Dutch schools, traditional *pesantren* or modern Muhammadijah schools maintained by the Islamic community, missionary-run Catholic schools, nationalist Taman Siswa schools, or secondary schools established by the Indonesian government following independence.[22]

Those who had neither a foreign university education nor elite Dutch secondary schooling were virtually unanimous in asserting that their formal education played very little part in forming their view of the world. Though education in the nonelite schools was sometimes of high quality, most recalled their world history and geography courses as superficial; one leader, now an army general close to President Soeharto, declared that he was never taught about any other countries.

22. The lesser Dutch schools were predominantly agricultural, primary, or lower secondary schools. For the Taman Siswa schools, see McVey, "Taman Siswa," pp. 128–49. The Muhammadijah schools offered a curriculum "equivalent to that of the colonial schools system, with religious instruction in addition" (*ibid.*, p. 133). Students who attended Catholic schools, as well as those in Indonesian government-run schools in the Jogjakarta area during the revolution, recall their teachers as generally of high competence.

Even an elite Dutch secondary education did not have the same impact it had on the 1928 Generation leaders. Students of the 1930s probably already possessed a sharpened awareness of the exploitative character of the colonial system. Also, the atmosphere in the schools themselves had changed, for the nationalist movement's development in the direction of noncooperation had made the Dutch less permissive than they had been in the 1920s. As for those 1945 Generation leaders who went on to university-level study in Indonesia during the 1930s and early 1940s, they did find the experience influential in molding their view of the world, but mainly because of what they learned outside the classroom.

Classroom experiences were more influential in the case of younger members of the 1945 Generation who studied at the University of Indonesia in the 1950s. They were exposed in their political science and economics courses to writings that led them to view the outside world with suspicion. They read Hans Morgenthau's *Politics Among Nations* and came away impressed with his "realist" interpretation of international politics as a struggle for power.

In economics, they came to see how classical theory, or at least certain parts of it, served the special interests of the industrialized nations. Professor Sumitro Djojohadikusumo, the most influential teacher of economics in Indonesia, criticized the comparative cost theory of international trade on the ground that it was detrimental to the interests of the less developed countries.

In Sumitro's view, specialization in production on the basis of comparative advantage only perpetuated existing disparities. Moreover, he contended that international trade was strongly influenced by monopolistic elements in the industrialized countries to the detriment of the less developed. Nor did classical theory explain the chronic tendency for the prices of raw materials to decrease relative to prices of industrial products. Classical theory also failed to take into account the fact that countries specializing in raw materials production were basically in a weaker position than industrialized countries, because productivity tends to increase more rapidly in industrial products than in primary goods. Finally, he argued, there was no reason to assume that benefits from productivity increases in the industralized countries would be passed on to the less developed.[23]

More than a third of the 1945 Generation members in the foreign policy elite studied at universities abroad and several more went abroad for advanced military training, but most did not go until the 1950s or early 1960s.[24] Those who went were mainly holders of Indonesian university degrees undertaking graduate work in the United States, though there were Indonesian students in Holland, Canada, and England as well.

American universities in the 1950s and early 1960s were, of course, very different places from the Dutch universities which older Indonesian leaders had attended in the 1920s. The 1945 Generation members, especially the substantial group studying economics, were exposed to an optimistic ideology of capitalist-based economic development as an alternative to the Communist model. There were high expectations that through the use of economic aid the Western powers could successfully foster economic development in the third world and thereby counter the threat of Communism. Indonesian students could not help acquiring, or becoming strengthened in, a view of development that reflected prevailing American thinking.

Some, however, found their classroom experiences unsettling. Studying in America at times brought about a face-to-face confrontation with power politics and its implications for a weak nation. For example, one leader told of his experiences at Harvard's International Seminar, a summer program in which many foreign students participated. Henry Kissinger's stimulating lectures had aroused his interest in international relations, but some of Kissinger's remarks had been disturbing. When Kissinger argued that the doctrine of limited war was a sound one for the United States be-

23. Robert Rice, "Sumitro's Role in Foreign Trade Policy," *Indonesia,* 8 (October 1969), 183–85.

24. Of 46 leaders, 17 attended universities abroad, while another 7 received foreign military training. Only one went abroad in the 1930s, and that was to Holland. In the 1940s, two more studied in Holland, and one took a law degree in Iraq.

cause it enabled Americans to fight their wars on other people's soil, this leader protested that he did not want the United States to fight its wars in Indonesia. In response, he said, Kissinger just laughed, and stated that he, as an American, evaluated the limited war doctrine in terms of American national interests.

Like university study, advanced military education had a mixed effect on the 1945 Generation members' view of the world. The basic component in the formal education of Indonesian army officers for higher command was a course at the Staff and Command School in Bandung. The study of international politics there has traditionally focused on strategic appraisals of various countries as potential threats. Morgenthau has long been used as a basic text, and the comments of several army generals made it clear that his concept of realism had a significant influence on them.

This view was partly a matter of role; there is a natural inclination to search for external threats in order to justify not only an expanded military budget but also the very existence of the armed forces and the social importance of a military career. As one lecturer at the army school explained: "If you don't talk about threats and dangers, they have no use for you."

As for military training abroad, the effect was different. The military members who went abroad received primarily technical training. But like the economists who acquired Western models of economic development, they tended to conceive of a modern armed forces establishment as one conforming to Western, particularly American, standards, and to think in terms of American equipment, techniques, and assistance. Still, experiences outside the classroom tended to counteract the subtle binds being forged by their formal military training (see below, pp. 75–82).

Most of the 1945 Generation leaders recall their participation in study clubs and other student associations as having played a decisive role in the formulation of their initial impressions of the outside world. Of the 37 for whom information is available, 70 percent either were active in study clubs (15) or took part in other groups that provided an equivalent experience (11). This is where they received their initiation into political life. Some asserted that their study club discussions had been far more meaningful than any they ever had in school.

The clubs to which the 1945 Generation leaders belonged ranged from sophisticated associations of well-read university students to gatherings of pupils at nonelite secondary schools in central Java which had difficulty obtaining books to read. The various clubs usually met in groups of eight to fifteen students, at least once a month, but sometimes weekly or more often.

Like their predecessors, they mainly discussed anticolonial literature, including Marxist writings. They debated the programs of the political parties, studied the constitutions and revolutionary experiences of other countries, and sometimes argued about the kind of country they would have if Indonesia were independent. Considerable attention was also given to the speeches and writings of Indonesian nationalist leaders like Sukarno and Hatta. There were frequent lectures by 1928 Generation leaders, and groups that had difficulty getting books thus became acquainted with nationalist and Marxist literature from abroad.

Study clubs at universities tended to concentrate much more heavily on Marxist materials than did clubs at the secondary school level. Before the Japanese occupation, students at the university in Jakarta also discussed such issues as the role of Japan in Asia and the applicability to Indonesia of the American plan for giving independence to the Philippines. During the occupation they especially emphasized Marxist literature. The few who studied abroad during those years received the most intensive exposure to Marxism.

The younger members of the 1945 Generation, still in secondary school at the outbreak of the revolution in 1945, had few opportunities to join formal study clubs. Several foreign policy elite members in the Jogjakarta area recall belonging to such groups, sometimes led by their professors, but meetings were irregular. One future general received a complete Marxist indoctrination when he enrolled in the "short course" offered by Marx House in Jogjakarta. The course, which met daily for one and one-half months, was used, he claims to have discovered later, by the PKI to train cadres.

Participation in such formal groups was the exception, but most of the younger 1945 Generation leaders did engage frequently in informal debates on ideology and the revolutionary struggle. Especially during the first two years of the revolution, schoolmates and members of student army regiments had a good deal of time for such discussions, which, in the emotionally and ideologically heated climate of the struggle for independence, took on added urgency.

The chief materials for study and debate were the proliferating pamphlets and brochures distributed by newly formed political parties, especially Marxist ones. The most influential pamphlets, according to the leaders interviewed, were those of Tan Malaka, a longtime Communist who had broken with Moscow in the 1930s, and of the socialist leader Sjahrir. The latter held out hope that the United States would bring pressure on the Dutch to leave Indonesia, but Tan Malaka dismissed such hopes and called for an all-out struggle. Both men, however, agreed that the capitalist and imperialist powers dominant in the world would permit Indonesia "independence in name only."[25] The speeches of Sukarno and Hatta also continued to be widely read and discussed.

Clearly, the influence of Marxist and anticolonialist writings on the 1945 Generation's view of the world was at least as strong as it had been in the case of the 1928 Generation.[26] Of those with whom the subject was discussed, the overwhelming majority (30 of 32) indicated that they had read Marxist writings, and most (23 of 28) said that, initially at least, they had responded favorably. Like their elders, the 1945 Generation leaders were especially impressed with Lenin's interpretation of imperialism as the inevitable highest stage

25. Sjahrir, "The American Orbit," in Herbert Feith and Lance Castles, eds., *Indonesian Political Thinking, 1945–1965* (Ithaca: Cornell University Press, 1970), p. 444.

26. Asked to name the writings that had most influenced their impressions of the outside world, 23 named Marxist or nationalist writers (the most frequently mentioned were Marx, Lenin, Jan Romain, Trotsky, Mao, Tan Malaka, Sjahrir, Nehru, Gandhi, and Sukarno), 3 named Morgenthau, 3 mentioned religious writings (such as the speeches of Masjumi leaders Mohammad Roem and Mohammad Natsir, and the Bible), 7 named western non-Marxist writers (such as Schumpeter, John Gunther, MacIver, and Latourette), and 3 singled out no particular books.

of the capitalist system, the survival of which depended on the exploitation of colonies. In the words of an economist with an American Ph.D., this was "something that could be made use of" in the struggle for independence. Though many who found Marxism's anticolonial aspects attractive were repelled by its antireligious doctrine and rejected the idea of class conflict as damaging to the solidarity of the nationalist movement, others recalled being impressed by Marxism's concern for social justice. Even some strongly anti-Communist Catholic and Protestant leaders recalled having viewed Marx as the originator of a basically humanitarian philosophy.

The foreign policy elite members who probed most deeply into Marxist literature were the 1945 Generation leaders who joined Sjahrir's Socialist Party (PS—it subsequently split, with the Sjahrir faction forming the PSI). Several PSI leaders declared that they had been "almost Communists" during the revolution. Besides being attracted to the works of the European Marxists such as Jan Romain, they had become "great admirers" of Mao, and in some cases, Trotsky. Edgar Snow's book on Mao became "a kind of handbook." According to one PSI leader, Sjahrir's way of thinking was so close to Mao's that some people were certain they had met. He recalled that Sjahrir's *Our Struggle* was often compared to Mao's *On New Democracy,* and claimed that "people in the Communist world accepted *Our Struggle* as a contribution on the same level as Mao's."[27]

The 1945 Generation's initial view of the international system, then, was essentially similar to that of the 1928 Generation: the dominant capitalist powers sustained themselves by exploiting Asia and Africa. For the younger 1945 Generation leaders, there was a subsidiary theme: any strong nation would inevitably seek to expand its power at the expense of the weak. But both generations retained a measure of hope that some outside forces would lend

27. For evidence of Sjahrir's admiration for Mao, see *Out of Exile,* pp. 146–51.

support to their efforts to realize Indonesia's political and economic aspirations.

The 1966 Generation

In contrast to their elders, most of the 1966 Generation leaders felt that their formal secondary education did not significantly influence their thinking about the outside world. Nearly all of them (7 of 9) were educated entirely in Indonesian secondary schools and universities during the 1950s and 1960s. Of the various Indonesian schools, only the Catholic ones appear to have had much impact on their students' view of the world; their explanations of Marxism and descriptions of the horrors of life in Communist countries instilled a strong anti-Communism in the students. Though political indoctrination was made a part of the high school curriculum after 1959, and various pamphlets, including certain Sukarno speeches, were made required reading, none of the 1966 Generation leaders described those materials as influential.[28]

The 1966 Generation leader whose view of the world was most influenced by his secondary education was the only one who studied at an elite Dutch school. Being part of a miniscule number of Indonesians among the children of remaining Dutch businessmen, in a school where the Indonesian revolution was treated "in a rather cynical manner," he became much more conscious of his nationalism than other Indonesians of his generation. Several of the university-educated leaders also considered their training an important influence on their perceptions of the international system. They particularly recalled their Western political science texts, especially Morgenthau's *Politics Among Nations,* which remained basic reading in courses on international relations throughout the 1960s.

Two-thirds of the 1966 Generation leaders felt that participation in study clubs or similar groups had helped to mold their view of the world. Discussions in these clubs generally lacked the conspira-

28. Stephen A. Douglas, *Political Socialization and Student Activism in Indonesia* (Urbana: University of Illinois Press, 1970), pp. 69–70, reports that his interviewees also lacked enthusiasm for these materials.

torial atmosphere of the colonial period or the sense of urgency of the revolutionary years. But a lively interest in debating alternative models for Indonesia was fostered by the contentious years of parliamentary democracy from 1950 to 1957, and by Sukarno's radical nationalist ideology between 1957 and 1965.

Some 1966 Generation leaders took part in study clubs associated with their secondary schools, meeting about once a week. Others joined university-level study clubs or student organizations affiliated with the major political parties. The groups sometimes split into pro-Soviet and pro-American factions. Members of an informal circle of young anti-Communist intellectuals avidly discussed recent issues of *Encounter* magazine, published by the Council of Cultural Freedom, and those sessions made a deep impression.

As a group, these leaders were much less favorably disposed toward Marxism than the 1928 and 1945 Generation leaders had been in their youth. All the young leaders had read Marxist writings by the age of twenty-two, and all had been intensively exposed to the quasi-Marxist ideology expounded by Sukarno, especially after 1959. But whereas an overwhelming majority of the older leaders had recalled generally positive first impressions, two-thirds of the 1966 Generation leaders had completely negative initial reactions to Marxism, which they found difficult to distinguish from the PKI. Family background and religious training had a lot to do with this. For example, one leader was the son of a village chief constantly under attack by the PKI. Another remembered that his class in school used to pray for fellow Catholics suffering persecution at the hands of the Chinese Communists.

But half of the young leaders who initially disdained Marxism subsequently modified their views. Readings and study club discussions played an important role in bringing them to view Marxism as a partial explanation of the problems faced by Indonesia. There was, then, a Marxist strain in the thinking of the 1966 Generation. But where Marxist writings, along with nationalist literature, had been of paramount importance for the older generations, the young leaders, asked to name the writings that most influenced their view of the world, mentioned no nationalist works and gave roughly equal mention to Marxists, non-Marxist Western authors ranging from Morgenthau and Kissinger to MacIver and John F. Kennedy, and Western journals such as *Encounter,* the *Economist,* and the *Far Eastern Economic Review.*

The most distinctive characteristic of the 1966 Generation leaders' developing view of the world was their exaltation of pragmatism. By 1966 most of them had come to see themselves above all as hardheaded men, committed to the economic, social, and political modernization of Indonesia, and prepared to accept the reality of a world dominated by big powers practicing power politics. They recall that they had grown disillusioned with the empty promises of ideologues and were convinced that a preoccupation with ideology would only waste time and lead to dogmatism. One leader described his feelings this way: "Freedom has been won—now it is time to enjoy life. I don't think ideology is very important. I never read anything normative. . . . The only thing that counts is power."

The 1966 Generation's pragmatism embodied two not entirely consistent elements. On the one hand, the international system was perceived as an arena in which power politics was the guiding principle. This view had some of its roots in their reading of Morgenthau, as well as Marx. It also reflected something of their own experience. The young group had grown up with great-power intervention in Indonesia's affairs, and they could and did explain it in both Marxist and Morgenthauian terms.

On the other hand, their generation came of age politically at a time of severe economic distress. Many of the less wealthy young leaders saw rising prices and diminishing job opportunities in more personal terms than did the generally more secure older leaders. Having argued that Sukarno's neglect of economic development had destroyed his legitimacy to rule, they committed themselves to improving economic conditions. To be pragmatic was not merely to be aware that the world was an inhospitable place for small powers, but also to recognize that only with the assistance of the big powers, however untrustworthy, could Indonesia improve its economy. Pragmatism required on Indonesia's part substantial flexibility in accommodating the expectations of those who could help. Indonesia would have to "regain the confidence" of an international community in which the Indonesians themselves had little confidence.

The youngest generation's pragmatism should not, however, be permitted to obscure the rather considerable, if sometimes subtle, influence that Sukarno had on their view of the world. That Sukarno had a profound impact on the thinking of Indonsian leaders of all generations is suggested by their retrospective evaluation of his foreign policy. A majority of all three generations felt that he had "put Indonesia on the map," winning for the country a respected position as an independent, self-reliant leader among nations. Many leaders, including 6 of 9 members of the 1966 Generation, stated that Sukarno's foreign policy had aroused in them feelings of national pride: "The world knows about Indonesia because it knows about Sukarno."[29]

Criticism of Sukarno had less to do with the fundamentals of his foreign policy than with the extremes to which he carried it. Nearly half of the foreign policy elite members felt that his sole error lay in his failure to build a base of domestic economic strength sufficient to support a policy of self-reliance and international leadership; as a general expressed it: "The roof was too heavy for the structure." Most of the others objected to what they regarded as excessively close relations with China at the expense of relations with other powers. Several thought Sukarno's foreign policy flawless.[30]

Though some of them might be unaware of it or reluctant to

29. Twenty-five leaders acknowledged feelings of pride. Even a bitterly anti-Sukarno Catholic leader proudly recalled the Games of the New Emerging Forces held in Jakarta—"all those flags, with Indonesia's at the center." Of 48 leaders who discussed Sukarno's accomplishments in foreign policy, 29 mentioned his success in giving Indonesia a leading international role as his greatest achievement; 9, the Bandung conference of 1955; 5, other achievements, such as the West Irian triumph; and 5 said that there was nothing good about Sukarno's foreign policy. Praise was especially strong among PNI, army, foreign ministry, and PSI leaders, but it was also voiced by technocrats, Catholics, and Islamic party leaders.

30. Of 50 leaders, 22 faulted Sukarno only for neglecting the economy, 25 criticized the relationship with China as excessively close, 3 thought he had made no mistakes in foreign policy.

admit it, most 1966 Generation leaders have absorbed Sukarno's conception of Indonesia as a leader of those nations struggling for independence in a world dominated by exploitative powers. Their reluctance to challenge Sukarno's foreign policy goals stood in sharp contrast to their all-out attack on his inattention to economic problems and his cooperation with the PKI. Furthermore, over half (5 of 9) of the young leaders echoed Sukarno's strong concern about protecting Indonesia's national identity from erosion due to excessive foreign influence, though not all of them linked that concern to Sukarno personally.

In effect, Sukarno took the conception of an exploitative international system which foreign policy elite members had derived from a diversity of sources and articulated an Indonesian response to the challenge of life in such a world—a response that could give many Indonesian leaders a sense of pride and self-respect. Pulling together perceptions and emotions developed over many years, Sukarno distilled them and hurled them back in a way that tightened their hold on the thinking of the Indonesian leaders.

3 | Perceptions of the Major Powers

If the Indonesians came to see the international system as an arena where the strong seek to exploit the weak, what did they see when they looked at the four major powers with which their country has had to deal? How did they acquire their first impressions of the United States, the Soviet Union, China, and Japan, and how have those images coalesced with recent experiences?

The United States

The oldest members of the foreign policy elite began to form their impressions of the United States during the 1920s and 1930s. Eight of the nine 1928 Generation leaders recall those views as positive. Most of them attribute this to a belief that America was more inclined to support independence than were the other colonialists. They were impressed by Wilson's support of self-determination and drew inspiration from the fact that the country had won its own independence only after years of struggle.[1]

Most impressive of all was America's behavior in the Philippines. Several of the 1928 Generation leaders felt that the United States was "not a real colonialist," and "wished that the Dutch could be more like the Americans." The 1936 pledge of independence for the Philippines within ten years especially led the Indonesians to distinguish sharply between the United States and the other colonialist powers.[2]

1. See Hatta, "Indonesia and Her Independence Problem," p. 179; "Colonial Resolution of the Second International," p. 362; and "Anti-Colonial Congress," p. 189.

2. This pledge inspired the introduction of the Sutardjo Petition, asking for

America's image, however, was not quite as unblemished as it is now recalled. In 1928 PI leader Hatta wrote that Central and South America were threatened by "the claws of modern imperialism." "The modern Yankees are very clever at exploiting the Monroe Doctrine in the interests of their own economic expansion drive." Sukarno, who greatly admired Jefferson, declared in 1927 that the "great problem of the time" was "how Asia could shake off the yoke of England and America."[3]

In any case, it would be misleading to suggest that the United States impinged very heavily on the consciousness of these Indonesian leaders as youths. Several, in fact, stressed that it had seemed "very far away, just beyond the scope of our thinking."

Most members of the 1945 Generation had gained some impressions of the United States by the end of World War II, though some of the younger ones say they had no real image until the revolution or later. Like their elders, leaders of this generation generally recall their first impressions as favorable.[4] As with the 1928 Generation leaders, study club discussions of the American Revolution and America's relatively favorable disposition toward self-determination for the colonial areas played an important role in creating that positive image.

American films reinforced the image of the nation as idealistic and democratic. Young Indonesians recognized and admired American movie stars.[5] While most realized that the westerns, musicals, and gangster movies they saw in the 1930s did not accurately represent life in America, the films nonetheless conveyed an image of courageous fighters for truth and justice. For example, an Islamic leader declared that he had been greatly influenced by the "cowboy's code of honor," which led him to view the United States as a supporter of the underdog in the Robin Hood tradition.

---

dominion status for Indonesia within ten years, in the Volksraad (the colonial parliament which had limited Indonesian representation).

3. Hatta, "Anti-Colonial Congress," p. 190; *Sukarno: An Autobiography,* p. 39; Dahm, *Sukarno and the Struggle,* pp. 115–16.

4. Of 31 leaders, 23 were positive; 2, mixed; 6, negative.

5. Note the detailed recollections of American film stars in *Sukarno: An Autobiography,* pp. 27, 63.

The same virtues were perceived in America's wartime role, and particularly in Franklin D. Roosevelt. A substantial number of 1945 Generation leaders claim that their first impression of the United States was as the leader of the antifascist allies of World War II, the defender of democracy and freedom against German and Japanese tyranny. Roosevelt was admired not only as a man who had triumphed over physical adversity, but as the spokesman for the Four Freedoms and an opponent of the restoration of colonialism after the war.

The few 1945 Generation leaders who recall negative feelings about America before the Indonesian revolution expressed a variety of concerns. One remembered that cowboy movies had represented to him the exploitation of dark-skinned people by whites: "We always rooted for the Indians." Others mentioned U.S. domination of Latin America and the sacrifice of human values for the sake of technological advance. Army generals who had taken their initial military training under the Japanese army of occupation recalled Japan's intensive campaign of anti-American propaganda: "We found ourselves hating the United States, but by the end of the war it was all reversed because we were anti-Japan." Several suggested, however, that the growth of hostility toward Japan did not completely eradicate the anti-Western prejudices so assiduously fostered by the Japanese.

When the independent Republic of Indonesia was proclaimed in 1945, many Indonesian leaders looked to the United States for support; they were greatly disappointed at the meagerness of that support. Some felt betrayed, and in their disillusionment concluded that none of the big powers could be relied on to help them. An army general who had been close to the army commander during the revolution recalled: "We had the feeling that Indonesia was fighting against the whole world."

To be sure, a majority of the 1928 and 1945 Generation leaders say they felt that the United States had helped the Republic more than it had aided the Dutch.[6] American backing was of two kinds. After

6. Allowances must be made, of course, for the fact that they were talking to an American at a time of cordial Indonesian-American relations. Of 39

the Dutch had launched a military offensive in 1947, the United Nations appointed a three-nation Good Offices Committee, consisting of American, Australian, and Belgian representatives, to assist in negotiations. The American delegate, Frank Graham, deeply impressed a number of the foreign policy elite members with his sympathy for the Republic. They remembered his words, "you are what you are," as important encouragement when they were uncertain about the status of the Republic under the ceasefire agreement of January 1948. Graham is warmly remembered as a symbol of the support which individual Americans gave the Indonesian independence struggle. A more concrete form of backing was received in 1949, when Washington for the first time exerted real pressure on the Dutch to yield on some of the Republic's key demands. This intervention contributed to the final agreement.

Along with those manifestations of American support, however, the Indonesians remembered other, unfulfilled hopes. Some, including an American-trained technocrat, believed that Washington sympathized with the Dutch, and many more were dismayed because the support offered Indonesia fell so far below expectations.[7] They were disappointed to discover that Washington's declared policy of neutrality usually seemed to work in favor of the Dutch. The United States, they felt, repeatedly pressed the Republic to accept unfavorable terms, while refusing to exert equal leverage on the Dutch. When Indonesians protested in the UN against Dutch actions, it was usually the Russians and the Australians, not the Americans, who supported them. They even found Dutch soldiers using American weapons and wearing American-supplied uniforms.

---

leaders, 24 saw Washington as more helpful to the Republic than to the Dutch, 8 were unequivocally on the Dutch side, 7 on neither side. The eight who felt that Washington had clearly supported the Dutch included 2 army generals, 2 technocrats, and one each from the PSI, foreign ministry, PNI, and Islamic parties.

7. For an account of this disillusionment by a scholar who was in Indonesia during the revolution, see Kahin, *Nationalism and Revolution in Indonesia,* especially pp. 215, 477–78. See also Kahin, "Indonesian Politics and Nationalism," in William L. Holland, ed., *Asian Nationalism and the West* (New York: Macmillan, 1953), pp. 169–71.

A sharp distinction was drawn between the friendliness of individual Americans and the policies of their government. As one leader recalled: "Cochran [Graham's successor on the Good Offices Committee] used to send me *Time* and *Newsweek* when I was in jail, but he always sided with the Dutch in negotiations."

Even the American pressure finally brought to bear on Indonesia's behalf in the last year of the revolution was viewed with skepticism by foreign policy elite members who considered the terms of the transfer of sovereignty far too generous to the Dutch. PSI leaders, who recall their initially favorable image of the United States already being undermined by Marxist literature, were especially annoyed by Washington's attempt to portray itself as Indonesia's benefactor. When the United States started to "shout to high heaven that they gave us independence," their disappointment turned to disgust and even hatred. Another source of resentment was the feeling that Washington had finally pressed the Dutch to compromise not because of any American interest in Indonesia's independence. It had done so because the Indonesians had proved themselves anti-Communist by putting down a PKI rebellion in 1948 and had demonstrated that the Dutch could not win an easy military victory.

In sum, American support for the Republic during the revolution was sufficiently inconsistent and far enough below expectations to raise doubts in the minds of many foreign policy elite members about the reliability of the United States.

In the course of the decade and a half from the end of the revolution to the fall of Sukarno in 1966, goodwill toward the United States continued to erode. This was especially influenced by three American actions: efforts to draw Indonesia into alignment with the West in the early 1950s; support of anti-Jakarta rebellions in 1958; and failure to back Indonesia's claim to West Irian (Western New Guinea) until 1962. Trips to the United States for education or diplomatic assignment were also important.

When the Indonesian leaders talk about their feelings in the early 1950s, some tell of their admiration for America as a land of wealth and modernization. As one 1945 Generation leader said: "The definition of modernization was the United States." Its image as "the most modern country" was also a central element in the perceptions of the 1966 Generation leaders, who acquired their first impressions during the 1950s and like their elders began with largely favorable impressions.[8] From films, history books, and conversations with friends and relatives, the youngest generation gained an initial view of a pragmatic, modern, rich, and free country—and they assumed a connection among those attributes. Above all, the 1966 Generation leaders, especially Catholics and devout Muslims, viewed the United States as the leader of the anti-Communist world: "All I knew was that the United States was anti-Communist and that was good. . . . We were so blindly anti-Communist in those days that we even thought Dien Bien Phu was a victory for Communist aggression. We didn't have the vaguest idea about the independence struggle going on there." A few older leaders, however, recall being worried by the eagerness of American (and other foreign) firms to re-establish a strong position in Indonesia after the revolution.

By far the most common recollection of the early 1950s, though, was of the 1952 agreement that Washington would extend aid to Indonesia contingent on the latter's contribution to the defense of the "free world." Most of the foreign policy elite members, even the most pro-American, recalled their dismay at learning of this agreement, which became a symbol of the American effort to "push Indonesia into its corner."

Nothing did more to arouse the Indonesian leaders' suspicions than American involvement in the anti-Jakarta rebellions that broke out on the islands of Sumatra and Sulawesi in early 1958. Though the United States never officially acknowledged its role as a military backer of the anti-Communist, anti-Sukarno rebels, the foreign policy elite members had no doubt about it.[9] Those who had been

8. Of 8 leaders, 6 were positive, one negative, one mixed.

9. Of 46 leaders, 37 said that the United States had actively supported the rebels; 6 more were men who had either led or sympathized with the rebellions, and they criticized the inconsistency of American support for the rebels. Only 3 could not say what the American position had been.

army officers and cabinet ministers in 1958 talked of having seen proof that the United States had supplied arms to the rebels. They also recalled the use of Clark Air Force Base in the Philippines by rebel pilots and the shooting down of an airplane piloted by an American.

Generals, technocrats, foreign ministry officials, 1966 Generation leaders, PNI and PSI leaders—all recalled their disillusionment at discovering how far the United States was prepared to go "to impose its will on others." In many cases, the revelation of America's role in the rebellions was of decisive importance in reshaping their view of the country.[10] The army leaders seem to have been particularly shocked. One spoke of his "feeling of betrayal" on learning of the American involvement, adding: "I couldn't understand why the United States wanted to destroy our national unity." Another general remarked that it was "a miracle that Indonesia had survived as a nation in spite of the stupidity of the United States in supporting the rebellions."

The few who did not think less of the United States for its role in the rebellions were mainly Islamic and Catholic party leaders who sympathized with the rebels. But the rebel leaders did charge Washington with opportunism in deserting them as soon as difficulties were encountered.[11] Many other leaders who shared the rebels' goals were also upset at the U.S. role. Secretary Dulles, whose initial statements were interpreted as clear evidence of American backing for the rebels, was remembered with derision. He was characterized as "a terrible man" and a foolish one as well, because he erroneously equated nationalism and Communism, thus inadvertently helping to smooth the way for Indonesia's leftward turn. American backing of the rebellions facilitated the rise of the PKI because it

10. Of 38 leaders, 28 had lower estimates, and 16 of the 28 said their impression had deteriorated drastically. Only 10 maintained that their view was unaffected.

11. These leaders grew even more disillusioned after 1960, when Washington "did nothing to indicate its disapproval" of what they saw as a "pro-PKI trend." The American ambassador's "acquiescence" in Sukarno's banning of the Masjumi and PSI in 1960 "really upset" their faith in the United States.

embarrassed those whose sympathies lay with the West, while presenting the Communists with proof of America's unwillingness to respect Indonesia's independence. There was, then, a consensus among the foreign policy elite that the U.S. role in the 1958 rebellions had been "tragic, America's worst mistake."

The impact of Washington's attitude toward Indonesia's West Irian claim was not quite as profound as in the case of the rebellions. The 1949 agreement on Indonesia's independence had provided that the status of West Irian should be resolved through negotiations within a year. It was Jakarta's contention that all territories which had been part of the Dutch East Indies should be incorporated into the new Indonesian state. Negotiations failed, and the Indonesians ultimately brought the issue to the UN, where the lack of U.S. support doomed their efforts. The official American position was one of neutrality, but neutrality constituted an effective endorsement of the status quo, which meant continued Dutch occupation of the disputed territory. Only in 1962, after the Indonesians mounted a military threat to West Irian with Soviet military assistance, did Washington reverse its position and bring pressure on the Dutch to make a settlement favorable to Indonesia.

How did the Indonesian leaders weigh America's ultimate assistance on the Irian question against the years of de facto support of the Dutch? About half of those who discussed the issue felt that on balance the United States had helped the Dutch more than it had helped Indonesia, and most of those who held that view said that Washington's attitude had made their impression of the United States significantly worse.[12] No one felt that America's image had been improved by its stance.

The long years of disappointment with Washington's Irian policy accelerated the dissipation of goodwill toward the United States. Those who had been top government officials during those years stressed that they had counted on American support and had

12. Of 37 leaders, 18 said the United States had mainly helped the Dutch, 15 felt Washington's last minute assistance outweighed its earlier lack of support, 4 could not say. Of the 18, 10 said their view of the United States had deteriorated because of this issue.

been stunned by Washington's failure to back Indonesia in the UN. Even leaders who admit they were never particularly interested in the Irian question remember their resentment at America's de facto support of the Dutch.[13] PNI, PSI, and Islamic party leaders felt that Washington's Irian policy, like its support of the rebellions, had aided the PKI by "cutting the ground out from under the nationalists." They suggested that Sukarno's perspective on the United States might have been very different if the Americans had supported the West Irian claim from the beginning. There was, in fact, a tendency on the part of a number of leaders, including Islamic figures generally sympathetic to the United States, to discount the importance of its intervention on Jakarta's behalf in 1962 because it came so late.

Still, the backing given Indonesia in 1962 does appear to have generated some goodwill, much of it focused directly on the Kennedys. Leaders who were otherwise highly critical of the United States expressed in glowing terms their admiration for President John Kennedy and for Robert Kennedy, who played a role in the West Irian settlement. Repeatedly, President Kennedy was referred to as "a great man" and "a truly progressive leader" who "really understood" Indonesia. "Even Sukarno admired the Kennedys," it was frequently asserted. A Kennedy initiative which favorably impressed the army leadership was the "civic mission" program, in which the United States provided aid to the Indonesian army for infrastructure projects such as road building and repair.

The period of good feelings, however, was brief. When Indonesia declared its opposition to the proposed Federation of Malaysia in 1963, Indonesian-American relations again became tense, and the Indonesian leaders found themselves under pressure from Washington to abandon their confrontation with Malaysia. That attitudes toward the United States would not improve was assured by President Kennedy's assassination and by the cessation of American aid

13. See Hatta's 1958 article in *Foreign Affairs,* "Indonesia between the Power Blocs," reprinted in *Portrait of a Patriot,* pp. 564–65, and his 1961 article in *Asian Survey,* "Colonialism and the Danger of War," reprinted in *ibid.,* pp. 574–75.

to Indonesia in 1964. Nor was America's image helped by the escalating involvement in Vietnam or by the personal unpopularity of President Johnson, who was as scorned by the foreign policy elite as Kennedy was revered.[14] Johnson was "a crude Texas cowboy," not "a man of peace like Kennedy."

If U.S. policy during the 1950–1966 period resulted in a gradual erosion of confidence, direct exposure to the United States did little to halt the erosion. Contrary to the common assumption that travel and study abroad usually leave people more favorably inclined than before,[15] firsthand knowledge has tended to make Indonesians less sure about their country's relationship to the United States.

In response to a question about the influence of their travels in America, half of the leaders claimed that their impressions had not been affected, while the remainder divided almost evenly between those who said the trip had improved their image and those who thought less of the country.[16] But when asked specifically what they had learned about America during their sojourn, the response was considerably more negative. A clear majority named essentially negative characteristics, while less than a third recalled specific positive impressions, and the rest were neutral.[17] Typical was the

14. For a full discussion of Indonesian attitudes on the Vietnam question, see Chapter 4.

15. Singer, *Weak States in a World of Powers,* p. 151. Bryant M. Wedge concludes that Africans and Latin Americans visiting the United States under the State Department's foreign leader program generally find conditions, especially with respect to racial and economic matters, better than expected (*Visitors to the United States and How They See Us* [Princeton: Van Nostrand, 1965], pp. 6–10, 26, 63–67). An interpretation closer to the author's own findings is suggested by an aphorism attributed to F. Houphouet-Boigny: "If you want a man to be a good bourgeois, send him to Lumumba University in Moscow, but if you want to radicalize him, send him to the Sorbonne" (Henry Bienen, "Foreign Policy, the Military, and Development: Military Assistance and Political Change in Africa," in Richard Butwell, ed., *Foreign Policy and the Developing Nation* [Lexington: University of Kentucky Press, 1969], p. 110).

16. Of 30 leaders, 8 said their impressions had improved, 15 had not been affected, 7 thought less of the country.

17. Of 26 respondents, 16 gave negative characteristics, 7 gave positive ones, and 3 neutral.

response of an army general who had studied at Fort Leavenworth. He said that his impression of the United States had improved as a result of his stay, but when asked what had impressed him most, he named racism and unemployment.

Most frequently cited by the foreign policy elite members were the prevalence of racism and the existence of slums and poverty. The gravity of the race problem was clearly the most upsetting discovery. Some were shocked by visits to Harlem and by the intimidation of Negroes in the South. A few recalled experiences of racial discrimination themselves. The extent of poverty, slums, and unemployment also came as a surprise to some Indonesians, who had assumed that all Americans were rich. One recalled that the slums in Boston would be considered slums even "by Indonesian standards," though it was amazing to find that those houses had refrigerators inside and automobiles parked in front. Another expected that all kitchens in the United States would be like those in *Better Homes & Gardens*. Several years in New Haven changed that impression.

Other negative impressions included ignorance about Indonesia, rudeness, and excessive materialism. The ignorance of many Americans about Indonesia was insulting. An army general was among those who were appalled to discover that Americans had a hard time distinguishing between Indonesia and Indochina. A foreign ministry official, on his first trip to New York City, encountered so much rudeness that he decided the United States was "a barbaric country." And a 1966 Generation leader, an outspoken advocate of pragmatism and modernization, found buying cigarettes from a machine a dehumanizing experience; he much preferred to buy them at a stall where he could bargain on the price and chat with the vendor.

A few said they had encountered "imperialist thinking," and one 1966 Generation leader recalled conversations with Indonesians studying in America that convinced him of the dangers of becoming economically dependent on the United States. But even the negative impressions not directly related to foreign policy symbolized Indonesia's problems with America. In viewing what they saw as the exploitation of the dark-skinned by the light and of the poor by the rich, Indonesians could easily see the parallel between their own country's problems and those of the American underprivileged. Similarly, ignorance about Indonesia and rudeness were sometimes taken as analogous to the highhanded, arrogant treatment which some Indonesians, especially those who went abroad in the late 1950s and early 1960s, felt their country had received at the hands of the United States.

The chief positive impressions gained by travelers to the United States resulted from the friendliness of its people. Even sharp critics of Washington's policies described the American people as "the friendliest in the world." Many found their contacts with American intellectuals especially satisfying, but those personal bonds of friendship tended to produce more negative feelings about the country, since these intellectuals were the sharpest critics of American intervention abroad and racism at home. Visiting the United States in the 1960s was a good deal more like being in Europe in the 1920s than in America in the 1950s.

The visiting Indonesians also recalled having observed an atmosphere of freedom and democracy, and they were deeply impressed by the fact that "everyone, even farmers, felt they had certain rights." A few Indonesians found the United States even more industrially advanced than they had expected. Neutral impressions included the unanticipated diversity of nationalities and opinions and the discovery that many Americans were "just simple people," not nearly as sophisticated as the Americans encountered in Indonesia.

Of course, perceptions of American policies toward Indonesia and of life in the United States were not the only considerations that affected the foreign policy elite's attitudes. As already noted, studying in the United States often had the effect of instilling in Indonesian economists or army officers American models of economic development and military professionalism. This often resulted in the creation of subtle, but by no means insignificant, affinity for the United States. Domestic politics also influenced feelings about the country. Negative perceptions could undoubtedly be counterbalanced by the knowledge that good relations with the United States would help circumscribe the role of the PKI. Such relations would also increase the possibility of carrying out domestic policies that would enable American-trained economists and generals to make use of their training and foreign contacts.

Thus it was certainly possible for an Indonesian leader to be highly critical of the United States, and at the same time to hope for good relations with Washington, even to be regarded as pro-American, because of an interest in policies that would weaken the PKI. But this does not alter the fact that, at the level of conscious perceptions, the more the Indonesian leaders saw of American life and foreign policy, the more skeptical they became about the reliability of the United States.

The foreign policy elite's discussion of the United States in the late 1960s and early 1970s made it clear that the deep suspicions instilled over many years had not been overcome by the recent period of highly cordial Indonesian-American relations. There was, of course, a good deal of admiration for America, centered on the country's image as a model of democracy and individual liberty. When asked what they considered best about the United States, nearly two-thirds cited democracy or freedom.[18] The same characteristics were most often mentioned when the leaders were asked to list attributes of American life worthy of emulation[19] and to name the term best describing what the United States represented to them.[20] Also cited with some frequency were wealth and techno-

18. Of 44 respondents, 27 mentioned characteristics grouped under democracy and individual liberty; 12, wealth and technological prowess; 6, the strength and stability of executive leadership; 3, dynamism and a capacity for hard work; 2, idealism; 2, the frankness and directness of Americans (some named more than one characteristic).

19. With 29 respondents, 12 mentioned democracy and freedom; 9, technological and managerial skills; 5, the presidential or party system; 1, the capacity of Americans for hard work; and 5 declared that there was nothing that could serve as a model for Indonesia. It is noteworthy that some admirers of American democracy were quick to emphasize its inappropriateness for Indonesia.

20. The question was asked in roughly this form: What is the term that

logical-managerial skill. America's image as a rich nation is such that, in the words of a technocrat, people think that if Indonesians go there they will automatically become rich. To those laudatory perceptions can be added the belief, expressed by more than 75 percent of the interviewees, that the United States would like to see Indonesia become as strong as possible, at least so long as Jakarta retains its present anti-Communist posture.[21]

But despite this admiration, three-quarters of the leaders voiced at least some doubt that the United States really understands and sympathizes with Indonesia's aspirations as a nation.[22] Even though talking to an American, only a bit more than half cited clearly positive characteristics when asked to name the term that most accurately describes the country.[23] The most frequently mentioned pejorative was imperialist or interventionist. Furthermore, when asked what they considered worst about America, half the respondents, including at least two from every major group except the Catholics, mentioned imperialism or interventionism.[24] Typical was the complaint of an army general: "The United States is always throwing

best describes the essence of the United States—that is, when you think about the United States, what is the first thing that comes to mind? Of 47 leaders, 18 mentioned democracy or freedom; 10, wealth and technological prowess; 8, imperialism or interventionism; 7, decadence; 3, idealism; 2, racism; 2, dynamism or progressivism; 2, generosity; 1, too much in a hurry; 1, strength; 1, friendly giant.

21. Of 50 leaders, 38 asserted that the United States wants Indonesia to become strong, with the rest expressing various degrees of doubt. The only major group with a majority of doubters was the army (4 of 7).

22. Of 55 respondents, only 14 stated without equivocation that the United States understands and sympathizes with Indonesia's national aspirations. Doubts were expressed by 7 of 8 technocrats, 5 of 6 PSI leaders, 4 of 5 foreign ministry officials, 7 of 9 PNI leaders, 7 of 9 army leaders, and 5 of 8 Islamic politicians. None of the 3 Catholic leaders had any doubt about the United States. There were virtually no differences among the three generations.

23. Of 47 respondents, 25 used positive adjectives; 13, negative; 9, mixed or neutral. "Rich" was considered neutral in 4 cases.

24. The breakdown is as follows: 4 each, PNI and technocrats; 3 each, foreign ministry and Islamic parties; 2 each, army and PSI; and no Catholics. With respect to age groups, there were 3 of 8 from the 1928 Generation, 14 of 26 from the 1945 Generation, and 4 of 8 from the 1966 Generation.

its weight around. The Americans assume that money can buy anything." A young PNI leader complained even more vigorously: "The worst thing about the United States is that awful American arrogance. It is disgusting the way the United States thinks it has the right to intervene anywhere it wishes in order to protect its own security or other interests. . . . That is precisely what imperialism is all about."

The United States was specifically assailed for its domination of Latin America, and army generals joined with technocrats and PNI leaders in hoping that the Americans would not seek the same kind of hegemony in Southeast Asia. Attention was also drawn to alleged subversive activities; the operations of the CIA were a matter of intense concern to some, especially PSI and PNI leaders. Muslim leaders were bitter at the inability of American officials to comprehend their resentment of Christian missionaries in Indonesia.

Particularly pointed attacks were leveled at U.S. economic imperialism. Technocrats, PNI leaders, and Islamic politicians all displayed apprehension that America's enormous economic power would overwhelm Indonesia if given a free hand. Moreover, the United States was said to be more concerned about keeping Indonesia anti-Communist, stable, and open to American investment than about encouraging economic self-sufficiency. One disillusioned Indonesian leader recalled learning from his studies in the United States the kind of economic policies a developing country should carry out, but, he claimed, those were not the policies that the Americans were encouraging Indonesia to adopt.

Some Indonesians were not critical of American interventionism as such; rather, they complained that the United States exerts pressure "in the wrong ways, for the wrong causes." Pressure to follow a democratic course, or to root out corruption, would be more than welcome, according to PSI, Islamic, and 1966 Generation leaders. Nor should criticism of American intervention be taken to mean that most Indonesian leaders want the United States to cease completely its involvement in Southeast Asia. So long as other big powers are active in the region, a minimal American presence is desired as a balancing force; and American dollars, of course, are still welcome. But few really were worried about a complete withdrawal from Southeast Asia. As a technocrat pointed out, commenting on predictions of a lowered American profile in Asia: "After all, an elephant can go only so low."[25]

Almost as widespread as America's interventionist image was a picture of the United States as a decadent country losing its sense of national purpose. Representatives of every major group talked of America's decadence, but concern was strongest among technocrats and Catholic and Islamic politicians.[26] American democracy was said by some to have grown ineffective. They pointed to the series of assassinations in the 1960s as a sign of the political system's impending collapse. Technocrats and army generals were amazed that such things could happen in a modern country. "We thought the United States was a place where there was order, safety, and a strong government," observed an American-trained technocrat. "But any system that permits such killings must have something wrong with it." Student protests and urban riots were taken as further testimony on the system's advanced state of decay.[27] Even the successful moon landing cast doubt on the viability of American democracy, it was argued, because it reflected an allocation of resources that did not serve the interests of the majority.

There was also a cultural dimension to this perception of a decaying society. Islamic leaders were particularly critical of the hedonism

25. Judging from the 1973 interviews, events that have occurred since 1970 have not significantly altered this belief. Also, see Sayidiman, "The Future of Southeast Asia," p. 48. After the collapse of America's allies in Cambodia and South Vietnam, there was some talk of a U.S. withdrawal to a strengthened "blue water defense line," but there was virtually no mention in the Indonesian press of a complete American retreat from Southeast Asia. See *Kompas,* 13 and 14 May 1975, and *Merdeka,* 25 April 1975.

26. Characteristics that signified decadence were cited by 43 percent of the interviewees. The group breakdown is as follows: 4 technocrats, 3 each from the Catholic and Islamic parties, 2 each from the army and PNI, and one each from the foreign ministry and PSI. Also included were 4 leaders of the 1928 Generation, 11 from the 1945 Generation, and 3 from the 1966 Generation.

27. There were some, particularly among the 1966 Generation leaders, who expressed sympathy for the New Left, but most were puzzled or disturbed by it.

of American society. "When I read about how many millions of American young people have smoked marijuana," declared one Muslim politician, "I wonder what is to become of that country. Perhaps they are searching for something to believe in. I only hope they find it in time." Other foreign policy elite members decried the "emptiness" of American culture and the decline of morality, specifically the toleration of hippies, nudism, and sex films. A naval officer expressed his utter revulsion for "wild dances and music" and yearned for the "big band sound—the Dorseys, Benny Goodman, Glenn Miller, and dancing with politeness."

Besides imperialism and decadence, the foreign policy elite members sharply criticized racism[28] and the existence of a wide gap between the rich and the poor.[29] These concerns were strongest among Indonesians who had lived at least a year in the country, which confirms the earlier findings on the impact of trips.

It seems fair to conclude, then, that despite their genuine admiration, the Indonesian leaders retain a strong belief that the United States is a country which exploits its own downtrodden and seeks to dominate other countries as well. Few see it as a country that can be relied on to assist Indonesia.

The Soviet Union

Most of the oldest members of the foreign policy elite (6 of 8) remember their first impressions of the Soviet Union as negative.

28. Racism was mentioned by 21 percent: 2 each from the technocrats and Islamic parties; one each from the army, PSI, and PNI; and no Catholics or foreign ministry officials. There were 2 leaders of the 1928 Generation, 5 from the 1945 Generation and 2 from the 1966 Generation. One PNI leader who bitterly criticized U.S. racism did concede that Indonesians themselves were prejudiced against Chinese and Japanese. In fact, he added, he himself did not like the color of Negro skin, but, on the other hand, he did admire the fact that Negroes were so tall.

29. Social injustice was cited by 14 percent, including 2 each from the army and foreign ministry, and one each from the technocrats, Catholics, and PSI. There were 4 from the 1945 Generation and 2 from the 1966 Generation, but none from the 1928 Generation. Another 7 percent mentioned other characteristics, including "Middle America" and the impersonal nature of life.

The Soviets were "emotionally not differentiated" from the PKI, which was regarded as Moscow's instrument. The 1928 Generation members, especially Islamic and Catholic leaders, distrusted the PKI and found the Soviet revolution, with its doctrine of class struggle, uninspiring. Nor did most of them recall the USSR as a reliable supporter of Indonesia's independence struggle in the early years. Rather, they argued that whatever faith Indonesians had had in Moscow during the 1920s was destroyed when the Soviets forced PKI leader Semaun to repudiate an agreement pledging the party's cooperation in a common drive for independence. Though they did accept key elements of the Marxist perspective on the nature of international relations, the 1928 Generation leaders looked mainly to the West for outside support.

Those who spent a lengthy period in Europe in the 1920s and 1930s, however, generally gained more favorable impressions of the Soviet Union. One recalled being inspired because, contrary to Marx, the Communist revolution had occurred first in a backward country. The 1929 and 1930 writings of Hatta confirm that PI leaders did indeed perceive the Soviet revolution as an inspiration to Indonesia's struggle. Hatta contended that even anti-Communists in the suppressed nations should look with favor on the Soviet Union, since it posed "a continuous threat" to the European colonialists.[30]

The few 1945 Generation leaders who can recall having had any impressions of the USSR before World War II perceived the country as negatively as had the 1928 Generation members.[31] They thought of the Soviet Union mainly as "dangerous, forbidden, . . . Communist and therefore bad." A few others, however, asserted that by the war's end they had come to think of the USSR as a

30. "A Retrospective Account of the Second Congress of the League against Imperialism and for National Independence Held in Frankfurt" (1929), in *Portrait of a Patriot,* pp. 202–3, and "Objectives and Policy of the National Movement," p. 113.

31. Of 11 leaders, 7 were negatively disposed, 3 positive, one neutral. It should be emphasized that the foreign policy elite includes no members of the PKI.

pioneer in the anticolonial struggle and a heroic fighter against fascism.

Moscow's behavior during the revolution seems generally to have improved the foreign policy elite's assessment of the USSR, although the Russians' identification with the PKI rebellion of 1948 did much to negate this. Most of those who discussed the USSR's role in the revolution felt that on balance the Soviets had helped the Republic.[32] Thus 1945 Generation leaders, most of whom formed their first impressions of the USSR during the revolution, tended to have a favorable view. As a result, whereas only a few (2 of 8) of the 1928 Generation leaders had positive first impressions of the Soviet Union, nearly half (10 of 24) of the 1945 Generation leaders interviewed did.

If America failed to live up to the high expectations of many Indonesians, the Soviets seem to have exceeded the expectations of most foreign policy elite members. Leaders who "had never given the Soviet Union much thought before" were surprised that it was the Russians, not the Americans, who supported Indonesia at the United Nations in 1946.

Nevertheless, most of the Indonesian leaders felt that Moscow had acted mainly in the hope of embarrassing the Western powers and persuading Indonesia to align itself with the USSR. Several leaders observed that the Soviets had raised the Indonesian issue in the UN in order to counter Britain's complaints about Soviet troops in Iran. Even so most Indonesians, and especially those who had regarded the Russians as genuinely anticolonialist and sympathetic to Indonesia's struggle, were shocked by the PKI rebellion in 1948. It was characterized as "a stab in the back" at a critical moment in the revolution, and most leaders felt the Soviets helped instigate it. By the end of the revolution, therefore, the Indonesian leaders had

32. Of 40 leaders, 30 said that the Soviets had helped, 8 felt that the Russians had failed to provide any significant support, 2 could not say. By generation: 5 of 9 leaders of the 1928 Generation thought the Soviets had helped the Republic, as did 22 of 26 leaders of the 1945 Generation, and all 3 in the 1966 Generation.

experienced a measure of disillusionment with both the United States and the Soviet Union.[33]

In contrast to the United States, Soviet policies toward Indonesia from 1950 to 1966 elicited very little criticism from the foreign policy elite members. There was virtual unanimity that the Russians had rendered important military and diplomatic support to Indonesia's campaign for West Irian and had given clear, if less significant, backing to Jakarta against the rebellions in 1958. The Soviets had even supported the confrontation with Malaysia, though Moscow had gently pressed the Indonesians to avoid a costly military endeavor.

A handful of leaders said that the substantial assistance which the Soviets had extended to Jakarta altered their initial negative impressions of the Soviet Union. In particular, several of the 1966 Generation leaders, like their elders unfavorably disposed toward the USSR because of their anti-Communism, found their feelings mellowing when Moscow backed Indonesia's West Irian claim.[34] Two young leaders, both devout Muslims, reached the conclusion that the Soviet Union was more sympathetic to nationalism in the third world than was the United States.[35]

The overwhelming majority, however, dismissed Soviet support as self-serving. It had enhanced the fortunes of the PKI by helping Jakarta crush an anti-Communist rebellion and by supporting Sukarno, who allowed the PKI reasonable scope to carry out its activities. The Soviets had also placed the United States in an awkward position by encouraging Indonesia to pursue a territorial claim that forced Washington to choose between Indonesia and the Netherlands, a NATO ally. Indeed, it was hard to imagine the Russians failing to back Jakarta on these issues.

Soviet aid disturbed many leaders in other ways as well. As political enemies of the PKI, they simply could not look with favor on

33. See also Kahin, "Indonesian Politics and Nationalism," pp. 170–71.

34. Of 7 leaders, 6 had completely negative first impressions, one had mixed impressions.

35. See also Hatta, "Indonesia between the Power Blocs," pp. 564–65.

that party's external supporter whatever Moscow's policies toward Indonesia might be. Welcome as it was, the roughly $1 billion in Soviet aid, mainly military equipment for the West Irian buildup, threatened to create a dependence on the USSR which would enable the Soviets to exert leverage on behalf of the PKI. Moscow's economic aid, which included "nonproductive projects" like a steel plant far from any iron supplies, was said to be intended merely "to obligate" the Indonesians.

If supportive Soviet policies toward Indonesia failed to change the foreign policy elite's essentially negative bias toward the USSR, the few who traveled to the Soviet Union returned, for the most part, with their negative prejudices confirmed.[36] Most frequently mentioned was the lack of freedom. PNI leaders asserted that "you could see in the faces of the people that they were living in a closed society," and characterized the Soviet Union as "a gloomy, slavic place." Restrictions on whom Indonesians were permitted to meet and attempts "to persuade" them were resented. Indonesians studying at Patrice Lumumba University in Moscow told a visiting technocrat of their irritation at the unceasing efforts of the Russians to make them into Communist cadres. Those who went to the Soviet Union in the middle 1950s also recalled their disappointment at the scarcity of consumer goods and the presence of slums, pickpockets, and prostitutes.

On the positive side, a few noted the USSR's technological and industrial progress, especially visitors in the 1960s. For example, a foreign ministry official who had made five trips to the USSR witnessed a constant increase in the quantity and quality of goods available. A navy admiral observed that when he was in the Soviet Union in 1963–1964 it had "already become a capitalist country—with decentralization and a limited incentive system." An economist who visited the USSR at roughly the same time was impressed not only by the quality of the Soviet educational system, but also by how "rational" the Soviets had become. Especially at the Academy

36. Of 14 who discussed this, 3 said their impressions had improved, 4 were less favorable, 7 claimed no change.

of Sciences, he recalled, the Russians "no longer felt under obligation to discuss everything in terms of ideology."

For most of the Indonesian leaders, however, the Soviet Union remained the "dangerous place" it had been from their school days.

The predominant image of the Soviet Union at the start of the 1970s was that of a totalitarian dictatorship. Asked for the term that best described the USSR, the Indonesian leaders mentioned dictatorship more than four times as often as any other term,[37] and the overwhelming majority (33 of 37) named characteristics that could be subsumed under dictatorship when they were discussing what they consider worst about the country. Two-thirds described the Soviet Union primarily in negative terms, while only a quarter were positive and the rest were neutral or mixed. None of the major groups viewed the Soviets with favor, though the PSI and army leaders were only slightly more negative than positive in their characterization of the USSR.

Despite the Indonesians' negative image of the Soviet Union and their belief that Moscow would, if given the opportunity, foster a revival of the PKI, the USSR was not generally viewed as a serious threat to Indonesia's independence.[38] There were three principal reasons: the lack of an effective PKI to support; the fact that the Soviet Union is, in any case, far away; and the fact that Indonesia is not presently dependent on the Russians for economic or military aid. Moreover, the Soviets' image has been improving slightly. Some 62 percent of the respondents believed that fundamental changes for the better have taken place in the Soviet Union in recent years.[39] They cited a modest expansion of human freedom and the loosening of constraints on individual economic initiative.

37. Of 41 respondents, 22 mentioned dictatorship; 5, interventionist; 5, Russian; 4, Godless Communist; 3, dedicated to social justice; 3, anticolonialist; 2, developed its economy rapidly; 1, racist; 1, hardworking; 1, "an economic power to be dealt with."

38. Only nine leaders, mainly Islamic and Catholic politicians, described the Soviet Union as a threat.

39. This view was held by 5 of 6 from the army, 4 of 5 foreign ministry officials, 2 of 3 each from the PSI and Catholic Party, 3 of 5 technocrats, 3 of 6 Muslim leaders, and 3 of 7 from the PNI.

The Indonesian leaders even found certain aspects of the Soviet system worthy of praise and emulation. Of 36 who responded when asked what they considered the USSR's best features, nearly half, including at least one representative of every major group, pointed to achievements in the area of social justice. Admiration was also expressed for the Soviet Union's success in reducing the gap between rich and poor and providing essential welfare services for the populace. Several individuals, including one representative of each group except the Islamic and Catholic politicians, suggested that those accomplishments could serve as a model for Indonesia.

Also singled out for praise was the USSR's rapid economic development along with the capacity of the Soviet people for hard work.[40] Even several Islamic party leaders who acknowledged that they were "a priori anti-Russia" had been impressed by the speed of the USSR's economic development and the efficacy of socialist techniques of economic mobilization and organization. Particular emphasis was placed on the Soviets' self-reliance and their ability to generate funds for development by cutting down on consumer goods. A few also made favorable allusions to Russian culture and patriotism and to the Soviet Union's anticolonialism and willingness to grant favorable terms of trade to underdeveloped countries.

All these words of praise for the Soviet Union, though, did not overcome the deep-rooted suspicions of most of the Indonesian leaders. Though the USSR's distance from Indonesia—in geographical, political, and economic terms—makes it possible for the foreign policy elite members to view the country with less concern than might otherwise be the case, the Russians clearly have made only minor progress in improving their longstanding negative image.

China

The 1928 Generation leaders initially viewed China with mixed emotions.[41] All of those who had sharply negative feelings did so

40. Social justice was mentioned by 44 percent, economic development by 33 percent, hard work by 25 percent. The total of the percentages exceeds 100 because some leaders cited more than one feature.

41. Of 6 leaders who could remember, 3 were clearly negative, the others were positive or mixed.

because of dislike of the local Chinese, not of China as a nation. Allusions were made to the economic aggressiveness of the Chinese in Indonesia and to the favored position they had enjoyed under the Dutch—for example, there were restaurants to which Dutch and Chinese were admitted, but not Indonesians. Favorable impressions of China in those early years were based mainly on admiration for the Chinese revolution of 1911.[42] One leader recalled that he became aware of the progressive character of the Chinese revolution when he observed that the Indonesian Chinese no longer wore their hair in braids. Others, through their studies in Europe or their study club discussions in Indonesia, came to admire the Kuomintang (KMT) as a possible model for Indonesia's revolutionary struggle.[43]

Only a handful of the 1945 Generation leaders had any clear impressions of China before the end of World War II. To the extent that they considered China at all, they thought of the country as "a loaf of bread sliced up by the imperialists," and of course as the homeland of the "exploitative" Chinese businessmen they encountered in Indonesia.

During the years of their revolution, the Indonesians did not have much time or inclination to think about China. There was strong resentment of the fact that a substantial number of Indonesian Chinese supported the Dutch, but most of the foreign policy elite members recall being only dimly aware of the progress of the Chinese civil war.[44] As we have already noted, a small number of leaders, mostly from the PSI, strongly sympathized with Mao.[45] An

42. Hatta felt that the Chinese revolution had been an important stimulus to Indonesian nationalism ("Objectives and Policy of the National Movement," p. 107).

43. The Indonesian delegation to the Brussels Congress against Imperialism and Colonial Oppression in 1927 declared its support for the Kuomintang's struggle (Hatta, "Brussels Congress against Imperialism," p. 162). In 1928, however, Hatta concluded that the death of Sun Yat-sen and the dissension in the nationalist army dropped a "dark curtain" on "the once so hopeful Chinese Revolution" ("Anti-Colonial Congress," pp. 194–95).

44. See Hatta's 1946 "Message to the Chinese Conference Group," in *Portrait of a Patriot,* pp. 497–99.

45. Kahin, in "Indonesian Politics and Nationalism," p. 172, observed sympathy for Mao during the immediate postrevolutionary period.

Islamic leader had heard of KMT generals fleeing China laden with gold, and he concluded that the KMT was so corrupt that the Communists deserved to win. Others, however, recalled that though they had disdained the KMT for its corruption, they appreciated the diplomatic support which the KMT consul in Jogjakarta gave the Republic. Both the Mao admirers and those who were grateful for the KMT consul's backing developed a more favorable orientation toward China, though they were not thinking of the same China.

The foreign policy elite's recollection of its feelings about the People's Republic of China (PRC) during the decade and a half after the revolution's end reflected a growing regard for the Peking government's achievements, accompanied, and in most cases outweighed, by a heightening concern about Chinese activities and ambitions in Indonesia. There were already signs of cordiality in the early 1950s. Jakarta supported Peking's admission to the UN from 1950 onward and abstained from voting on the American-sponsored resolution branding China an aggressor in Korea. In 1955 the Chinese made significant concessions to the Indonesian position in concluding a dual nationality treaty under which Peking abandoned its traditional claim that all overseas Chinese were citizens of China and agreed to let Chinese living in Indonesia choose to be citizens of either country.

Basically, however, relations with China remained cool until 1953, largely because of Indonesia's concern about the Chinese embassy's influence within the Indonesian Chinese community.[46] Even the PSI leaders who had been such avid admirers of Mao lost much of their enthusiasm after 1950. Of course, China's Communism contributed to the Indonesian leaders' distaste. A few leaders, mainly Moslems and Catholics, saw China simply as a Soviet

46. In the early 1950s, Radio Peking (like Radio Moscow) was sharply critical of Sukarno and Hatta (Kahin, "Indonesian Politics and Nationalism," p. 173). It was not until 1953 that Indonesia's diplomatic mission in Peking was headed by an ambassador.

satellite and a backer of the PKI. But for most, distrust of the Indonesian Chinese and of the other overseas Chinese living elsewhere in Southeast Asia continued to be the most important source of their concern about China. Members of the 1966 Generation, who obtained their largely negative first impressions of China during the early 1950s,[47] were motivated mainly by their dislike of the overseas Chinese: "When we thought about Communism, we thought about the Soviet Union."

Still, none of the foreign policy elite members recalled thinking of China as a serious threat in those days. China seemed too weak and too preoccupied with internal problems. In addition, Chou En-lai's conduct at the Asian-African Conference in Bandung in 1955 strongly impressed a number of the Indonesian leaders and did a great deal to foster an image of China as a reasonable nation. Even staunchly anti-Communist Islamic leaders admitted being "very favorably impressed" by Chou's performance at Bandung.

In the late 1950s and early 1960s, however, the Indonesian leaders increasingly became concerned about China. Though Peking fully backed Jakarta in its campaign for West Irian and its opposition to the rebellions, this was offset by resentment at Chinese interference in Indonesian affairs. The focal point of this was a 1959 Indonesian regulation that in effect prohibited resident Chinese from engaging in retail trade in rural areas. The Chinese embassy first protested the regulation and then encouraged the local Chinese to flaunt it. Though a rapprochement was effected in late 1960, China's action was viewed as an unacceptable intrusion into Indonesian domestic affairs.

In the early 1960s, several developments heightened the concern about an aggressive China. One was the increase in Chinese funds channeled to the PKI. Another was the increasing dependence on China for diplomatic backing after 1963, coupled with a growing isolation from alternative sources of support. Also cited was China's "invasion" of India in 1962, its encouragement of Communist

47. Of 5 leaders, 3 were negative, one neutral, and one positive.

rebellions in a number of Southeast Asian countries, and its alleged backing of the 30 September 1965 attempted coup in Indonesia.

Visits to China played an important role in making the Indonesian leaders aware of Chinese accomplishments. In contrast to those who visited the United States and the Soviet Union, Indonesian visitors to China, mainly technocrats, army generals, and PNI leaders, were generally favorably impressed by what they saw.[48] Most made one trip, either between 1955 and 1957 or between 1963 and 1965, though one leader had visited China four times and another three. The most enthusiastic praise came from those who visited during the latter period, and those who made several trips commented on how much conditions had improved from one visit to the next.

Especially admired was the success in providing the basic necessities of life for all people, and in virtually eliminating starvation, unemployment, corruption, and stealing. Many, including American-trained economists, found that China's progress far exceeded their expectations; they seemed overwhelmed by the industriousness and austerity of the Chinese. "That's really the way to carry out an austerity program," a technocrat observed somewhat ruefully. The Chinese were praised as a people who had real self-confidence and self-respect: "The Chinese wear the simplest clothes, and yet they don't feel inferior in their relationships with others." The principal negative impression was of regimentation and a lack of freedom. Some of those who were impressed with China's achievements added that they felt the human costs were too high, but as an economist recalled: "I knew about the costs before I went to China, but I did not know about the extent of their progress and austerity." And an army general who had made several visits noted a considerable increase in freedom and variety in dress.

China has been perceived since 1966 mainly as an aggressive force threatening Indonesia's independence. Of 59 leaders, 81 per-

48. Of 12 leaders, 8 had an improved image; 2, a worse one; 2, the same. In contrast to their comments on visits to the United States, their specific impressions confirmed this improved image, with 8 citing predominantly positive ones, 2 negative, and one mixed.

cent, including an overwhelming majority of every major group, expressed the view that China was aggressive. Two-thirds saw China as a serious threat to Indonesia[49] and more than half pointed to China as the principal threat.[50] Asked for the term that best described China, the foreign policy elite members responded overwhelmingly in negative terms; only three leaders, all from the PNI, spoke more positively than negatively.[51] Aggressiveness (with interventionism and arrogance subsumed under that category) was cited twice as often as the next most frequently used term—dictatorship.[52] Practically all of the Indonesian leaders singled out either aggressiveness or dictatorship as China's worst characteristic.

49. There were 54 respondents. China was perceived as a serious threat by all 6 PSI leaders, 7 of 8 Muslims, 3 of 4 Catholics, 7 of 9 foreign ministry officials, 5 of 7 from the army, 4 of 8 technocrats, and 4 of 9 PNI leaders.

50. With 63 leaders responding, China was named as the principal threat by 32—including 6 of 8 Muslim politicians, 2 of 4 Catholics, 4 of 6 PSI leaders, 5 of 8 technocrats, 5 of 9 foreign ministry officials, 5 of 10 generals, and 3 of 9 PNI leaders. Generational differences were not significant. Ten leaders—including 3 each from the PNI and the technocrats—cited Japan. Nine—including 3 from the army, 2 each from the foreign ministry and the PNI, and one PSI leader—pointed to China and Japan together as the yellow peril. International Communism was cited by 6—including 2 each from the Catholic and Islamic parties and one each from the PSI and the army. Four—including one each from the army and foreign ministry—said there was no external threat whatever, and 2—one each from the PNI and foreign ministry—saw the chief threat coming from "everywhere." The number in each category does not always equal the sum of those whose group affiliations are given because, as noted in Chapter 2, some leaders were not associated with any major group, while others belonged to more than one. Also, China (singly and subsumed under "yellow peril" and "international Communism") was named as the "principal" threat more often than as a "serious" threat; some did not believe that even the principal threat was really serious.

51. There were 30 who gave negative terms and 6 who were neutral or mixed.

52. Of 39 leaders, 18 mentioned terms that could be subsumed under aggressiveness; 9, dictatorship; 3, "Chinese, whether Communist or not"; 2, hardworking. Eight named other characteristics: "great masses of people," struggling for unity, experimenters, Communist, pleasant, smiling people, nonideological and undisciplined, people about whom nothing positive can be said, and orderly.

These Indonesians saw the Chinese threat mainly as one of subversion, either through a revived PKI or the local Chinese. They recalled that the Chinese embassy had repeatedly interfered in Indonesia's domestic affairs prior to the suspension of diplomatic relations in 1967. They were particularly concerned about Radio Peking's encouragement of the underground PKI. But many, including practically all the influential technocrats, viewed the problem of subversion more in economic than in military terms. "The only serious threat from China," said one cabinet minister, "is economic—China's policy of dumping goods on the Indonesian market in order to kill off Indonesia's domestic industries." Despite the suspension of relations, Chinese goods were channeled through Singapore and Hong Kong and continued to flood the Indonesian market. China's goal, the Indonesian leaders claimed, was to use Chinese exports and the economically influential Chinese population in Indonesia to gain a dominant position in the country's economy; economic influence would then be used for political ends. As one economist asserted, even the adoption of a more conciliatory posture by Peking would only exacerbate the danger of Chinese economic expansionism, because such a stance would assure the loyalty of the overseas Chinese. By 1975, with the emergence of China as an important exporter of crude oil to Japan, the Chinese economic threat had taken on an added dimension.

As to direct military action, most estimates were that China's domestic problems and technological deficiencies precluded this for the foreseeable future. But several leaders, all either navy officers or Islamic politicians, did emphasize Indonesia's vulnerability to such an attack. They spoke of invading forces launched from Hainan Island and of the ease with which the Indonesian island of Kalimantan (Borneo) could be reached by sea from a Communist-controlled Vietnam. China's lack of a modern navy was dismissed by an admiral: "The Chinese don't need naval power. They can just send their hordes, their human waves. They can swim. [Really?] Yes, they can swim and use junks. If they send 200 junks, our naval patrol craft would be able to stop only a fraction. There would be just too many of them. They have 800 million people. If they mobilize just 10 percent, that's 80 million. Fantastic. Genghis Khan with an atom bomb."

If most of the Indonesian leaders viewed China as a serious threat, they also respected its achievements. Though their descriptions of China were far more negative than positive, more than half of the leaders admired the self-reliance and capacity for hard work of the Chinese. More than a third praised China's success at economic development, while others were impressed by Mao's ability to unify China after centuries of disunity, and a few cited the way the Chinese have narrowed the gap between rich and poor.[53] There were even a number of leaders, including at least one from each important group except the Islamic politicians, who suggested that Jakarta would do well to emulate China's self-reliance, hard work, and mobilization of its people for economic development.[54]

The Chinese, then, are respected by many Indonesian leaders, but even more so they are feared. And as we shall see in Chapter 4, the dramatic change in Peking's international position since 1971 has by no means diminished the Indonesians leaders' perception of China as a serious threat.

Japan

The impressions of Japan which the 1928 Generation leaders remembered holding before 1942 were almost unanimously positive.[55] Several referred to Japan's victory over Russia in 1905 as an event in which all Asians could take pride.[56] The industriousness of

53. Of 34 leaders who said what they considered best about China, 18 (including 5 each from the technocrats and the PNI, 4 Islamic politicians, 3 army generals, and one PSI leader) mentioned hard work and self-reliance; 12, economic development; 6, Mao's unification of China; 2, reduction of the rich-poor gap; 1, strength of family ties. Six leaders said there was nothing good about China.

54. Of the 17 leaders asked about China as a potential model, 7 cited self-reliance and hard work; 4, economic development; 6, nothing.

55. Of 6 leaders, 5 recalled the Japanese favorably, and the sixth remembered them neither positively nor negatively but simply as barbers and shopkeepers.

56. See also Hatta, "Indonesia in the Middle of the Asian Revolution,"

the Japanese and their success at economic development were cited as added reasons for a favorable first impression, though mention was also made of the "poor quality" of Japanese products. Those 1945 Generation leaders who had any real perceptions of Japan before 1942 saw the country in largely the same favorable terms as their elders.[57]

There was some concern in the 1930s about Japanese imperialism. A PNI leader, for example, recalled having been persuaded by Dutch talk of the "yellow peril." But the foreign policy elite members, judging both from their own recollections and from contemporary sources, seemed more inclined to view Japan as their country's best hope for liberation, given their own inability to oust the Dutch.[58] According to Sjahrir's diary, Indonesians everywhere were convinced by 1937 of the impotence of the Dutch against Japanese power. That conviction was buttressed by popular belief in the Joyoboyo myth, which held that after the period of white domination there would be "a hundred days" of rule by yellow people from the north.[59] When the Dutch began harassing those regarded as pro-Japanese, even more sympathy was created for Japan.

Thus the Japanese were generally welcomed as liberators in 1942, and the ease with which the Japanese defeated the Dutch provided another big boost to the Indonesians' self-confidence. Typically, one leader recalled how deeply he had been affected by the sight of a long line of Europeans being marched off by two small Japanese.

Within months, though, there was considerable disillusion with

---

pp. 19–20; "National Claims," p. 313; "Colonial Resolution of the Second International," p. 362; and "Objectives and Policy of the National Movement," pp. 106–7.

57. Of the 8, 5 had positive impressions, one mixed, one neutral, one negative.

58. See especially Sjahrir, *Out of Exile,* pp. 112, 136, 186–88, 195: "Even Hatta" had for a time shown "unmistakable signs of Japanese sympathies." As early as 1928 Sukarno and other nationalist leaders hoped that Japan would aid Indonesia's struggle by administering a decisive blow to the West in Asia (Dahm, *Sukarno and the Struggle,* pp. 115–17).

59. Sjahrir, *Out of Exile,* pp. 186–87.

Japan. The Indonesian leaders repeatedly spoke of the cruelty of the Japanese occupation forces. A number of those interviewed had been arrested and, they claim, tortured by the Japanese; others had close relatives who were killed by the occupiers. In general, the Indonesians recall the years from 1942 to 1945 as a time when their country was brutally exploited as a source of rice and raw materials. Many felt that in its harshness and brutality, Japanese rule had been considerably more painful than that of the Dutch. The occupation left a profound suspicion of Japan and a bitter awareness that imperialism was by no means an exclusively western phenomenon.

The impact was not entirely negative, however. The Japanese gave positions of responsibility to nationalist leaders like Sukarno and Hatta who had previously been imprisoned by the Dutch, and this afforded the nationalist movement new scope for development. A number of Indonesian leaders formed personal relationships with individual Japanese who were sympathetic to the nationalist cause, and most of the Indonesian army leaders took their initial training under the Japanese.

The foreign policy elite's impressions of Japan during the 1945–1966 period are not entirely clear; in discussing their feelings about Japan most of the Indonesian leaders moved immediately from the occupation to the post-1966 era. This reflects the fact that only since then have Indonesia's relations with Japan been as important as those with the United States, the Soviet Union, and China.

The profound distrust of Japan sown by the years of occupation was the basis for the foreign policy elite's views of the Japanese in the 1950s and 1960s. The 1966 Generation's initial perceptions of Japan, acquired as children or through wartime stories were invariably negative. The restoration of contacts with Japan in the 1950s centered mainly on the issue of war reparations, which began in 1958. That, of course, revived bitter memories for many, but it also solidified some personal friendships with Japanese who had been in Indonesia during the war and who played a key role in the negotiations. In any case, few saw any basic conflict between Japan and Indonesia in those years, and Tokyo's political and economic relations with Jakarta were not perceived as a threat to Indonesia's independence.

In the early 1960s, however, foreign policy elite members returned from visits to Japan "impressed and worried." They recall that the economic strength of the country and the dynamism of its overcrowded population did stimulate concern about the potential for Japanese expansionism. This was intensified by the prevalent image of Japanese businessmen offering bribes and lavish entertainment in order to do business in Indonesia. That view was ultimately embodied in Sukarno's Japanese wife, a former bar hostess introduced to the President by Japanese businessmen for whom she was expected to serve as an intermediary. For the most part, however, during the two decades following the occupation the Japanese were distrusted without being feared.

Since 1966, however, Japan has been perceived as an expansionist nation posing a threat comparable to that of China. Though China was more frequently named as the principal threat, a response encouraged by the government's frequent portrayal of China as Indonesia's leading enemy, 84 percent of the foreign policy elite members described Japan as a serious threat, whereas only 67 percent considered the Chinese threat serious. A majority of every group viewed Japan as a serious threat, with only the Islamic politicians showing any hesitation.[60] Those who singled out Japan as the principal threat, or cited Japan and China as equal dangers, included members of all groups except the Islamic and Catholic politicians; technocrats and PNI leaders were especially emphatic in singling out Japan. Of the relatively small number asked for the term that best described Japan, most gave negative terms, with "expansionist" most frequently mentioned.[61]

60. With 55 respondents, Japan was seen as a serious threat by all 9 PNI leaders, all 6 PSI leaders, all 6 foreign ministry officials, 8 of 9 technocrats, 6 of 9 from the army, 2 of 3 Catholics, and 4 of 7 Islamic politicians. There were 7 of 10 leaders of the 1928 Generation, 32 of 37 from the 1945 Generation, and 7 of 8 from the 1966 Generation.

61. Of 17 leaders, 4 gave positive terms; 11, negative; 2, neutral or mixed.

Though Japanese expansionism possesses neither the ideological rationale nor the potential "fifth column" characteristic of the Chinese threat, some leaders saw Japan as more dangerous because of its greater strength and particular economic requirements. Japan, most agreed, wanted not only to control Southeast Asia economically but to become the hegemonic power of the region, much as the United States is in Latin America. Global powers, like the United States and the Soviet Union, already have their spheres of influence; though they seek influence in Indonesia, they were said to be too "settled" to seek complete control. China, on the other hand, might desire such control but was too economically underdeveloped and beset by internal weakness to achieve it. Japan, stronger than China but weaker than the superpowers, was ripe for expansionism.

Moreover, it was frequently asserted that "Japan needs a colony." To a degree unmatched by the other powers, Japan's prosperity depends on reliable trading relationships. "They have to have our raw materials," said an army general. "Without them, Japan is nothing." The easiest way to satisfy this need is to keep Indonesia and the other countries of Southeast Asia dependent on Japan, thus guaranteeing a supply of raw materials and at the same time assuring that Southeast Asian markets remain open to Japanese exports.

Tokyo would, of course, attempt to secure the needed raw materials and markets by peaceful means, but many Indonesians were convinced that should those efforts fail, the Japanese would not be reluctant to use military force. Japanese technology was believed to be capable of quickly developing a formidable military force. In a matter of weeks, the Japanese toy industry could be converted to the production of "war toys," commented a technocrat. Some 40 percent of the interviewees who discussed this issue, including a substantial majority of the foreign ministry and PNI leaders, expressed concern about Japan as a potential military threat. They were sure that where an economic stake has been developed, the political and

Expansionist was named by 10, economic development by four, industrious by three, and "negative in every way" by one.

the military cannot be far behind. In the words of an influential army general: "Japan is still under the control of expansionist elements whose goals remain basically the same as they were at the time of World War II, except that they are trying to achieve those goals through economic means now." Some voiced the fear that Japan might try to institute "a kind of Asian Monroe Doctrine," assuming responsibility for the "defense" of Southeast Asia and telling other powers to stay out.

In this connection, American suggestions that Japan take over a major portion of U.S. responsibilities for the maintentance of security in Asia drew an extremely hostile response from all of the Indonesian leaders who discussed the subject.[62] Foreign ministry officials noted with dismay that this would be helping Japan achieve the very things America went to war in 1941 to prevent. They wondered whether Washington fully understood the depth of concern about Japan felt by the inhabitants of the region.

This threat is all the more grave because Japan is an indispensable source of support for Indonesia's economic development effort. The assistant to one of the President's closest army advisers told the author in 1973 that Japan "can give us life or kill us." There was some suggestion from army sources that the Chinese threat really had been more severe before 1965, when Indonesia had close relations with Peking. Now that China had been "contained," it was Japan that was making a bid to dominate Indonesia. Only if Indonesia's economic development effort were to collapse completely would the subversive threat of China again become the principal danger, predicted a leading economist; otherwise, Japan would be the greater threat.

Most of the Indonesian leaders viewed Japanese expansionism

62. The 29 leaders expressing this view included 6 foreign ministry officials, 5 from the army, 4 Islamic leaders, 3 each from the PNI and technocrats, and 2 each from the PSI and Catholic Party. There were 5 leaders of the 1928 Generation, 20 in the 1945 Generation, and 4 in the 1966 Generation. A number of leaders, particularly army generals, stressed that their opposition was not so much against Japan specifically as against the whole concept of an outside power assuming responsibility for the defense of Southeast Asia.

not merely as a potential danger but as a process that was already well under way. "We are now experiencing what we call the second Japanese invasion," said an army leader. "Everything you see—on television, in Sarinah [Jakarta's leading department store], everywhere—is from Japan. . . . Japan wants to control us." The Japanese commercial onslaught worried many for cultural as well as economic reasons, and it moved one leading technocrat to prophesy that "we may wake up some day and find that everything we possess is Japanese except our wives."

There were repeated denunciations of the Japanese as crude, aggressive, and inscrutable. "You never know what they are thinking, what their real purposes are," said an army leader. Numerous complaints were voiced about Japanese negotiating tactics. What takes two days to negotiate with Westerners may take a week to resolve with the Japanese, according to an Islamic leader. "They raise direct issues and bring to bear pressures which others would be reluctant to mention." Japanese businessmen were characterized as totally unscrupulous. Indonesians, it was said, would rather deal with a Chinese businessman than a Japanese, because the Chinese are more trustworthy. Japanese aid and investment were dismissed as of little benefit to Indonesia, since all aspects of Japan's relations with Indonesia are calculated solely in terms of profit and loss to Japan.[63] Very few of the Indonesian leaders felt that Japan really wants to see Indonesia become a strong nation. Whereas 75 percent of the foreign policy elite had expressed confidence that the United States desires a strong Indonesia, only 23 percent were willing to make such a statement with respect to Japan.[64]

Particularly significant is the fact that suspicion of Japan ran very deep among technocrats, army generals, and foreign ministry officials who, as the people responsible for Indonesia's dealings with

63. For more on this point, see Chapter 7.

64. These included both Catholic respondents, 3 of 5 Islamic leaders, one of 6 from both the PNI and technocrats, one of 7 from the army, none of 3 PSI leaders, and none of 6 foreign ministry officials. By generations, there were 3 of 5 leaders of the 1928 Generation, 6 of 28 in the 1945 Generation, and none of 6 1966 Generation leaders.

Japan in recent years, have endured some bitter negotiating sessions with the Japanese. Almost without exception, the economists occupying key government positions aired their worries about Japan. A highly influential cabinet minister observed that the danger of Japan's gaining domination of Indonesia is "something we are strongly aware of all the time." Some army generals expressed in emotional terms a deep suspicion of Japan which they said represented the thinking of the army leadership as a whole, including the president himself. Even the one general who, both in public and in the interviews, had only kind words for the Japanese was said to have remarked to his associates that he would "kiss the feet of the Japanese as long as Indonesia needed them," but afterwards he would gladly see them tossed out.[65] In 1973 top foreign ministry and army leaders told the author that the Japanese threat was considerably more ominous than it seemed in 1970.[66]

Many Indonesian leaders, especially younger ones, stressed that their suspicions about Japan were based not primarily on the wartime occupation or on any conception of the Japanese as inherently aggressive, but on a pragmatic assessment of the facts of the situation. A realization of Japan's proximity, power, and economic re-

65. Another extremely influential general, with whom the author talked in 1973, acknowledged the lack of candor of top government officials on the subject, especially in public: "Indonesians, if they are outside the government, are afraid to speak up out of fear that they will differ with the government. Government officials, on the other hand, are reluctant to speak the truth for fear of upsetting our relations with Japan."

66. Continuing criticism of Japanese aid and investment, the need to develop relations with other centers of power in order to reduce dependence on Japan, and concern about a revival of Japanese militarism were all principal themes in the 1973 interviews. On these points see also, "Kecenderungan-kecenderungan Dibidang Internasional dan Pengaruhnya Terhadap Indonesia," Foreign Ministry document 001/STR, 28 November 1972 (mimeo.), p. 16; Malik's comments in *Research Landasan,* 6 (July-December 1971), 29; *Monthly Review* (May 1972), p. 4 (published by the Center for Strategic and International Studies in Jakarta) and *ibid.* (October-November 1972), p. 8; Ali Sastroamidjojo's remarks in *Politik Luar Negeri Indonesia Dewasa Ini* (Jakarta: Yayasan Indonesia, 1972), p. 31; Sayidiman, "Future of Southeast Asia," pp. 44, 47; and Soedjatmoko, "Japan: Architect of a Post-Nuclear World Order?" (unpublished paper, 14 December 1972), p. 10.

quirements was coupled with a sense that because of Indonesia's dependence on Japan their own bargaining power was limited. For most Indonesians remote from the policymaking process, memories of suffering during the occupation may be of central importance, but the foreign policy elite members, young and old alike, insisted that they were more influenced by their own recent encounters with the Japanese, or by stories they had heard of the difficulties experienced by Indonesians negotiators and businessmen.

The foreign policy elite's perceptions of Japan were not, of course, completely negative. Some who disliked the Japanese questioned whether they really are intent on dominating Indonesia. Several technocrats were hopeful that Japan's attitude was changing. They pointed out that there were farsighted Japanese who realized that a strong, economically developed Indonesia would be a better market for Japan's products. Trade, after all, is always greatest among economically advanced nations. These "reasonable" Japanese were said to be aware of their country's "ugly Japanese" image and trying to do something about it. They seemed to be growing in influence, the technocrats argued, and if this trend toward a "more mature attitude" were to continue, Indonesia's difficulties with Japan might be reduced.

Furthermore, Indonesian leaders representing every major group expressed admiration for Japan's success in carrying out economic modernization without sacrificing its national identity and oriental character. Some foreign policy elite members seemed awestruck by the capacity of the Japanese for hard work, though admiration was often mixed with contempt for the Japanese as "inhuman, like machines."

On balance, however, the foreign policy elite's hopes for a "more reasonable" Japan and its respect for Japan's accomplishments were heavily outweighed by the fear that Japan's resurgence as a power in Asia would create an increasingly dangerous threat in the coming years.

Many Roads to the Perception of a Hostile World

In the foreign policy elite's view of the world, there is a clear pattern of evolution from hope and trust to suspicion and concern.[67] Though initially inclined to see international politics as a process by which the strong exploit the weak, most Indonesian leaders began with strongly favorable impressions of the United States; with the passage of time and the accumulation of experience, America's image declined. The same may be said with respect to Japan, at least for the older leaders; the younger ones were negatively inclined toward Japan from the start. China was viewed initially with mixed emotions, but with time perceptions grew negative, though this was mitigated slightly when visitors to the People's Republic found that China had made impressive progress on a number of problems similar to those faced by Indonesia. Finally, the USSR was viewed negatively from the outset and never really improved its image. In general, then, the more the Indonesians have learned about the big powers, the less inclined they have been to trust any of them.

This perception is the product of experiences that span half a century. These leaders know a good deal about the outside world and have formed their views through extensive contact and experience with other countries. To estimate the extent of that exposure to the outside world, five key experiences have been identified, along with the percentage of the foreign policy elite that has undergone each one: an advanced Western education—either study abroad, university-level courses in Indonesia using Western political science texts, or an elite Dutch secondary education in Indonesia (79 percent); participation in a study club or a similar student association (72 percent); extensive travel abroad (82 percent); residence abroad for at least a year (62 percent); and personal involvement in negotiations or other diplomatic activities (61 percent).[68] Clearly,

67. For similar patterns among the French and Chinese elites, see Ole R. Holsti and John D. Sullivan, "National-International Linkages: France and China as Nonconforming Alliance Members," in Rosenau, ed., *Linkage Politics,* pp. 150–53.

68. These percentages are based on 66 leaders for each item except participation in a study club or similar student association. Information on this point was available for only 57 leaders. Also, those who had been abroad for only a few days or had never left Southeast Asia were not considered to have traveled extensively. It is noteworthy that 87 percent of the foreign policy elite members have visited the United States, even if only very briefly.

the Indonesian leaders have had a high degree of exposure to the outside world, with a substantial majority of the foreign policy elite having undergone each of the five experiences (see Table 3.1).

Within the foreign policy elite, however, there are significant differences among the generations and the major groups. The chief generational difference is, not surprisingly, between the youngest generation and the two older ones. As Table 3.1 makes clear, the two older generations have had roughly the same degree of exposure to the outside world. The 1966 Generation has had far less international experience, especially in diplomacy and residence abroad. It is possible, however, that the 1966 Generation's low score on the five key experiences may exaggerate somewhat its ignorance about international relations, since a number of the young leaders, though too junior to be directly involved in negotiations, are close to older leaders who have had such exposure.

As for the major political and occupational groups, the table demonstrates that the foreign ministry officials, technocrats, PSI, PNI, and army leaders have had a very high degree of exposure. Considerably lower in exposure are the Islamic and Catholic party leaders. Among the five high exposure groups, the foreign ministry officials are high (above 75 percent) on all variables, while the technocrats are equally high on all but diplomatic experience, and the PSI and PNI on all but residence abroad and diplomatic experience. The army leaders are high on the three "practical" experiences—travel abroad, foreign residence, and diplomatic experience—but lower on foreign education and study club participation. The Islamic party leaders are not high on any of the indices of exposure, and are especially low on diplomatic experience, while the Catholics have had more Western education and foreign travel, but are extremely low on residence abroad and diplomatic experience.

Each of the five key experiences has contributed directly to the foreign policy elite's perception of the world as dominated by powers seeking to subjugate Indonesia. Foreign education fostered an appreciation of the West and an acceptance of Western models and standards, but it also conveyed a deeper awareness of the exploitation to which Indonesia had been subjected and a con-

Table 3.1. Exposure to the outside world (in percentages)

	Advanced Western education	Participation in study club or equivalent	Travel abroad	Foreign residence	Diplomatic experience	Composite index
All respondents (n = 66)	79	72#	82	62	61	71
1928 Generation (n = 11)	91	82	73	55	64	73
1945 Generation (n = 46)	74	70*	89	74	72	76
1966 Generation (n = 9)	89	67	56	11	0	45
Foreign Ministry (n = 9)	78	83†	100	100	100	92
Technocrats (n = 9)	100	86‡	100	100	67	91
PSI (n = 6)	100	100	100	67	67	87
PNI (n = 9)	78	100§	78	67	67	78
Army (n = 12)	67	40‖	100	75	92	75
Islamic parties (n = 8)	63	63	50	50	25	50
Catholic Party (n = 4)	75	50	75	25	25	50

Note: Percentages have been used to facilitate comparison. Because of the small numbers of respondents, it would obviously be a mistake to attach importance to the precise percentages.

* n = 37.
† n = 6.
‡ n = 7.
§ n = 8.
‖ n = 10.
n = 57.

ceptual framework—be it Marxist, nationalist, or realist—within which imperialism could be seen as an integral part of the international system. From study clubs and other groups in which ideologies and the experiences of other countries were debated, the Indonesian leaders came to appreciate the revolutionary experiences and admire the ideals of other countries, but they focused most heavily on Marxist and nationalist interpretations of international relations, both of which emphasized the exploitation of the poor nations by the rich. Foreign travel and residence, mainly in the West, convinced many of the Indonesian leaders that they had friends and supporters abroad, but most of what they discovered made them less favorably inclined toward the countries they visited and more aware of the dangers of dependence on outsiders. Experience in negotiating with foreigners in many cases left the Indonesian leaders cynical about their foreign supporters and convinced them that there were basic conflicts of interest between Indonesia and her "friends."

The foreign policy elite's exposure to the outside world thus seems to have produced a progressively more suspicious view. This suggests the hypothesis that those with the highest degree of exposure are the ones most likely to see the world as hostile to Indonesia. The existence of a positive correlation between exposure and the perception of a threatening world is also indicated by the comments of some foreign policy elite members.

For example, several 1966 Generation spokesmen contended that there was a major difference between the attitudes of the top leaders of their generation and those of the middle level leaders and student masses below. As a result of their more extensive personal experience with the outside world, the top leaders were said to be much more sensitive to the dangers of dependence on outsiders and the unreliability of friends than were the student masses, who tended to see foreign relations simply as an extension of their own struggle with the PKI. In the words of one young leader: "The inclination of many Indonesian university students simply to ally with the West is entirely a product of their ignorance. They know they are anti-Communist, so they think this means that we should join the Western bloc. There is a process of evolution which takes place as the leaders, through reading, contacts with foreigners, and, in some cases, trips abroad, become more aware of the need for Indonesia to maintain a position in the middle of the road."

Many older leaders echoed these arguments: "Only after you have been a leader in a position of responsibility do you become fully aware of the pressures that endanger Indonesia's independence." The perception of danger was viewed as the result not of ignorance but of a deeper knowledge and understanding of the world.

Exposure to the outside world, of course, is not the only determinant of the Indonesian leaders' perceptions. Religion, as we have seen, sometimes plays a role.[69] Devout Muslims tend to be strongly anti-Communist, and this automatically predisposes them to trust the West and fear the Communist powers. But Islam also offers a strong basis for anti-Western feeling, inasmuch as the West is viewed as Christian, the source and sustenance of greatly-resented missionaries. Western support of Israel also disturbs devout Muslims. Moreover, close ties with the West invite an inflow of cultural influences that threaten to secularize Indonesian society, eroding respect for Islamic traditions. Catholics, on the other hand, tend to view the West with sympathy because of both their automatic anti-Communism and their sense of identification with fellow Catholics in western countries.

Economic and social class interests also influence perceptions of the outside world in a variety of ways. Foreign policy elite members in general are drawn from the top economic and social strata. Leaders of virtually all the political parties, whatever leftist pretensions they may have, are heavily involved in business and commercial activities. So are many of the military leaders, though they often work through Chinese whom they afford protection in ex-

69. The foreign policy elite included 57 Muslims, 5 Catholics, 3 Protestants, and one Hindu-Balinese. Among the Muslims, it was estimated that 30 were *abangan* (syncretist Javanese); 8 *santri* (devout Javanese Muslims); 16 non-Javanese Muslims, most of whom could be considered devout. The ethnic breakdown was: 42 Javanese/Sundanese, 24 from the other islands.

change. Economic interests certainly predispose the foreign policy elite to be anti-Communist; most would see close ties with the West as the best way to ensure the perpetuation of their economic and social advantages. Furthermore, foreign capital is often seen as helping to guarantee stability and preserve the status quo, as well as offering the possibility of financial gain for those involved in its distribution. On the other hand, Indonesian businessmen are very sensitive to the dangers of competition from foreign investment and from cheap imports under foreign credits.

At times, role considerations also impinge on the Indonesian leaders' view of the world. As previously noted, the armed forces are trained to think in terms of threats from the outside. To admit that there are no threats would bring into question the military establishment's raison d'etre. In addition, the armed forces conceive of themselves as the heroic strugglers for independence who drove out the Dutch and remain the jealous guardians of Indonesia's sovereignty. This factor is balanced, however, by the armed forces' continuing need for modern equipment and spare parts, which dictates a close relationship and a degree of dependence on at least one of the major powers. Similarly, technocrats are strongly predisposed to conceive of the world as a place that will support the kind of economic development plans they have been trained to produce. They simply cannot afford to assume that the risks of such plans and the resulting dependence on outsiders might outweigh their advantages.

Perceptions are also influenced by domestic politics. Many interviewees were incapable of considering the USSR on its merits, and perceived the country negatively simply because it backed the PKI, their domestic enemy. Similarly, the fact that a deterioration of relations with the Americans would strengthen the position of the PKI led PSI leaders to perceive the United States more favorably than they otherwise would. Furthermore, leaders out of power may be inclined to view outsiders as exploiters of Indonesia because this view confirms their judgment that those who hold power are incompetent. Incumbents, on the other hand, may see aid-giving countries as trustworthy since their judgment is at stake. We are speaking here not of the conscious manipulation of foreign policy for political ends, but of the more subtle ways a leader's political needs may affect his perception of the world.

The Indonesian leaders, then, have traveled many roads to the perception of an exploitative world. The anticolonial struggle, readings in Marxist literature, the immersion of many younger leaders in the doctrine of Morgenthauian realism, and a succession of disillusioning experiences with the great powers—these have been but a few of the major avenues leading to a view of the world as a place dominated by powers seeking to circumscribe Indonesia's independence.

4 | The Nature of World Politics in the 1970s

The foreign policy elite members were asked to analyze the significance for Indonesia of four contemporary international conflicts: the Cold War, the Middle East conflict, the Vietnam War, and the clash between what Sukarno referred to as the new emerging forces (NEFOS) and the old established forces (OLDEFOS). The Indonesians were sharply aware of the changing relationships among the big powers since the rise of detente and of how these changes had made the world safer for the less powerful states. But the easing of tensions among the powers did not cause them to view the international situation less ominously. On the contrary, they felt that the dangers for Indonesia might well have increased, because the threat was now more subtle.

The Cold War

Indonesia's leaders have traditionally viewed the Cold War as a source of both opportunity and danger. On the one hand, Cold War competition encouraged the great powers to pay attention to Indonesia and set in motion a substantial flow of material rewards. The greatest diplomatic triumph of the Sukarno years—the negotiations that forced the Dutch to yield West Irian in 1962—was facilitated by a military buildup made possible by Soviet aid. The United States responded to this by pressing the Dutch to make concessions; it feared a further rise in Soviet influence and the outbreak of an armed conflict which could threaten the stability of all Southeast Asia. The competitive international situation created by the Cold War thus made it possible for Indonesia to draw economic, military, and diplomatic assistance from both groups without becoming dependent on either.

On the other hand, there has always been the danger that the great powers would acquire too much influence. The Indonesians have been especially sensitive to that danger during periods when it has proved impossible for them to maintain a balance in their relations with the superpowers. A recurrent theme in the speeches of Indonesian leaders for many years has been the fear that their country would become so hotly contested by the Cold War protagonists that it might fall victim to a clash between them; that concern has been a principal rationale for nonalignment. Even when they acknowledge the material benefits which the Cold War has brought them, many Indonesian leaders are nagged by a disturbing feeling that the superpowers view Jakarta essentially as a pawn in their struggle for supremacy.

By the early 1970s the Cold War was seen in a new light. International developments since the early 1960s led some to conclude that the conflict was essentially over. Even among the great majority who felt otherwise, there were many who believed that the Cold War's importance as a factor in international relations was rapidly diminishing. This was attributed mainly to two developments: the declining role of ideology as a determinant of the behavior of nations, and the growing commonality of interests between Washington and Moscow.

Ideological conflict was named by a majority as the principal cause of the Cold War, while most of the rest felt that the conflict had begun essentially as a clash of national interests between the two big powers. For some, especially PNI and Islamic leaders, ideology was still the central factor in the Cold War, and the conflict would not significantly abate as long as ideological differences remained. Most, however, saw ideology as a diminishing force. More than 80 percent of the PSI, Catholic, army, and foreign ministry respondents considered ideology less important than it was previously (see Table 4.1).

In certain respects, those who perceived a decline in the importance of ideology found this trend reassuring. Quite a few saw

Table 4.1. The Cold War and ideology

	Is the Cold War over?		What was the chief cause of the Cold War?			Is ideology less important in international relations?	
	Yes	No	National interests	Ideology	Equal	Less important	Same as always
All respondents	9 (17%)	45 (83%)	15 (37%)	23 (58%)	2 (5%)	27 (58%)	19 (42%)
1928 Generation	1	9	3	5	0	4	4
1945 Generation	7	28	9	14	2	18	13
1966 Generation	1	8	3	4	0	2	5
PSI	3	2	3	0	2	5	0
Catholic Party	2	2	4	0	0	4	0
Technocrats	2	4	2	3	0	4	2
Army	2	5	3	2	0	6	1
Foreign Ministry	1	6	2	2	0	5	1
Islamic parties	1	6	1	4	1	2	4
PNI	0	9	0	6	0	0	7

ideology as a dangerous force and associated it with expansionism; every ideology, it was argued, seeks to dominate the world. These leaders saw the rise of a pragmatic younger generation in many countries as evidence that the sort of ideologically-based expansionism embodied in the Cold War was becoming obsolete. Typically, an army general noted that although ideological rigidities continued to drive the older generations of leaders in Japan and the United States toward expansionism, the younger generation in both countries "just wants to have a good life." Others saw the change taking place primarily on the Communist side, as manifested in Moscow's increasing "pragmatism." In any case, most of the foreign policy elite members would agree that the decrease in the ideological content of the Cold War had enhanced Indonesia's security in two ways: it had reduced the prospects of a cataclysmic clash between the superpowers, and it had led Washington and Moscow to ease their pressure on nonaligned countries to commit themselves.

But the decline of ideology also posed certain risks. The Cold War was generally seen as developing into a less sharply defined form of conflict—in effect, a competition among the great powers for spheres of influence. As long as the big powers were motivated by global ideological aspirations, the possibility of a de facto agreement on such spheres, not to mention active collusion, could safely be ruled out. Because of the decline of ideology, however, it was possible that Indonesia might face a more united front of big powers than would be conceivable were ideological conflict a more potent force.

If the reduced importance of ideology raised fears of collusion among the big powers, the growing perception of shared interests between Washington and Moscow provided even greater cause for concern. The foreign policy elite seemed more impressed by the interests and characteristics shared by the United States and the Soviet Union than by the points which separated them. They showed a strong inclination to lump the two superpowers together.

To begin with, despite the almost universally strong anti-Communism of the foreign policy elite, there was near unanimity that Washington was just as much to blame for starting and exacerbating the Cold War as Moscow. Only the Muslim politicians, several of whom suggested that the West was "merely reacting defensively" in the face of an "expansionist Marxist ideology," felt that the Communists were primarily responsible for the conflict.[1] Even among the Muslims there was some feeling that the West bore a share of responsibility for the conflict. In the words of a deeply anti-Communist NU leader: "It is accurate enough to say that it was the Communist side that was on the offensive while the West was trying to defend itself. That is natural because the Communists represent a new power while the old power resides in the West. The Communists asserted that they were morally right to replace the old power because of the injustice practiced by the imperialists. There is some truth in the Communist view. . . . The West cannot escape blame for the Cold War because it was its own refusal to admit mistakes that lent some truth to the Communist allegations."

The general view was that both superpowers aspired to control the rest of the world. There was remarkably little reticence even among some of the most committed anti-Communists to portray the United States in this manner. For example, a strongly anti-Communist army officer, asked whether he really meant to suggest that the United States wanted to dominate the world, replied: "Yes, of course it did." For many, John Foster Dulles symbolized the ideologically-based expansionism of the West; he was seen as the most aggressive Cold War protagonist on either side. But it was not a matter of personalities. "Big powers always aim toward world hegemony—the first and second world wars started that way, and that is how the Cold War began," asserted a former foreign minister. It was only after both sides realized that the costs were too high that they gave up the attempt to control the world, a current foreign ministry official noted.

1. Of 33 respondents, 28 felt both sides equally responsible. While 4 of 5 Muslim party leaders blamed the Communists, and one of 4 Catholic leaders did so, leaders of all the other groups unanimously asserted that both sides were equally responsible. Three of seven 1928 Generation leaders placed the blame on the Communists, while only one leader of the 1945 Generation and no 1966 Generation members did so.

A particularly striking manifestation of this view was the feeling of a sizable minority that the United States had more in common with the Soviet Union than with Indonesia, and as a consequence was better able to understand the Russians than to comprehend the Indonesians. Although the question was discussed with only twenty-four leaders, this view was advanced by a majority of the army, foreign ministry, PSI, and 1966 Generation leaders who mentioned it.

Many considered the economic interests shared by the United States and the Soviet Union as industrialized countries a key element in bringing the two superpowers closer together. One of President Soeharto's principal economic advisers declared: "We see the Soviet Union as another advanced nation, as an OLDEFO, if you want to use that terminology." As evidence of the superpowers' alignment on economic issues of importance to Indonesia, he pointed to the unwillingness of either Washington or Moscow to support the demands of the underdeveloped countries at the United Nations Conference on Trade and Development (UNCTAD). Indonesian leaders also found their impressions of the changed relationship between the superpowers confirmed by the encouragement American officials have given Jakarta to seek economic aid from the Soviet Union.[2]

The balance of power between the Russians and the Americans was said to facilitate an accommodation of mutual interests which a weaker state could never hope to achieve with a great power. Where Washington and Moscow could build a solid relationship, the Washington-Jakarta relationship was just too unequal to permit genuine cooperation. The holder of an American Ph.D. compared this problem to the awkwardness he feels when he returns to his village in Central Java. It is practically impossible, he noted, to communicate with former schoolmates who never went beyond secondary school. They simply don't possess the same frame of reference. The United States and the Soviet Union were also compared to two rich men who can easily work out a deal that will serve their mutual

2. Reports of such encouragement came from cabinet level officials and were confirmed by ranking American diplomats in Jakarta.

interests. "It is very hard," on the other hand, "for a rich man and a poor man to reach such an understanding. There is always suspicion and jealousy."

Some laid particular emphasis on cultural affinities between the two superpowers, in contrast to the cultural gap that impedes communication between Indonesia and the United States. The USSR, they stressed, is essentially a European country, both racially and culturally.[3]

The tendency of the Indonesian leaders to discuss the United States and the Soviet Union in similar terms undoubtedly reflects as well the fact that Jakarta's relationship with each focused on a number of common problems. In dealing with both superpowers, the Indonesians felt they had to find a way to draw material support without incurring excessive political risks. The same issues—debt repayments, terms of trade, conditions of aid, and the dangers of dependence—dominated Indonesia's relations with both Washington and Moscow.

Finally, there was some feeling among the foreign policy elite members that those differences which remained between the United States and the USSR were gradually disappearing. Of 32 respondents, 23 expressed the belief that the two countries were evolving in such a way that they would eventually possess essentially similar systems.[4]

In the years after the foreign policy elite members' first interviews, the danger of superpower collusion became a matter of even greater concern. A foreign ministry report issued at the end of 1972 warned that the rapidly progressing detente could "open broader opportunities for the big powers to divide the world into spheres of influence in accord with their own interests." The report also deplored

3. For an example of this argument see Roeslan Abdulgani's speech, reported in *Antara,* 29 April 1969.

4. Voicing this belief were 3 each from the technocrats and Catholics, 3 of 4 foreign ministry officials, 2 of 3 PNI leaders, 3 of 4 army officers, 3 of 5 Islamic politicians, and one of 3 PSI leaders. By age groups, there were 4 of 6 leaders of the 1928 Generation, 14 of 18 from the 1945 Generation, and 5 of 6 from the 1966 Generation.

the big powers' growing tendency to settle international disputes among themselves, without giving any role to the smaller countries of the region concerned.[5] Similarly, a top presidential adviser wrote in late 1972: "Latest developments show that small and developing countries *can never rely on the power of other countries.*"[6]

Detente, of course, involves not only the easing of tensions between the United States and the Soviet Union, but China's rapprochement with Washington and Tokyo as well. Although the rapprochement with China occurred after the first interviews had been completed in 1970, the comments of foreign policy elite members during the 1973 interviews, along with their earlier discussion of Chinese aggressiveness, permit some conclusions about its significance for Indonesia.

In the first place, China's aggressiveness was generally attributed more to the country's Chineseness than to its Communism. Of 51 leaders who explained why they considered China aggressive, only 29 percent cited Communism as the principal motivation, while 43 percent pointed to the "Chinese factor" and 27 percent accorded equal weight to Communism and Chineseness. Emphasis on the Chinese factor was especially strong among foreign ministry, army, and PNI leaders (see Table 4.2). Typical was this statement by an army leader: "It is not just the PRC, but China—the Chinese here, the Chinese in Taiwan, the Chinese anywhere. Don't think that because there is a Taiwan pavillion at the Jakarta Fair that we like Taiwan any more than the PRC. All Chinese are inherently aggressive."

Communism, it was argued, was merely an instrument for the Chinese. It was really "Chinese national chauvinism" that made them want to rule the world. Historical references reaching deep

5. "Kecenderungan-kecenderungan," pp. 13, 29. See also President Soeharto's concern about being "squeezed by the steamrollers of superpowers which are in competition with one another—both Communist and non-Communist—and which are now attempting to create a new sphere of influence in Southeast Asia" (*Pedoman,* 3 October 1973).

6. Major General Ali Moertopo, "Some Basic Considerations in 25-Year Development," *Indonesian Quarterly,* 1 (October 1972), 23. Italics in the original.

Table 4.2. The role of ideology in China's aggressiveness

	What is the chief motivation for Chinese expansionism?			Is China merely seeking in Southeast Asia what the United States has in Latin America?		Would a non-Communist China be a serious threat?	
	Chinese factor	Chinese factor and Communism equally important	Communism	Yes	No	Yes	No
All respondents	22 (43%)	14 (27%)	15 (29%)	23 (61%)	15 (39%)	29 (83%)	6 (17%)
1928 Generation	4	2	3	2	6	5	2
1945 Generation	14	11	9	16	8	19	3
1966 Generation	4	1	3	5	1	5	1
Army	6	2	1	4	0	6	0
Foreign Ministry	6	2	0	5	2	6	0
PNI	5	0	1	4	1	5	1
PSI	1	3	2	2	3	2	0
Islamic parties	1	4	3	1	6	5	1
Technocrats	1	3	3	2	0	4	1
Catholic Party	1	1	2	1	2	1	2

into China's past were frequently raised as proof: Genghis Khan, Attila the Hun, and in particular Kublai Khan, who in the thirteenth century dispatched an armada to attack Java, were all brought forth as aggressors whose spirit lives on in China. More recently, China's hostile attitude toward India and Burma, along with its alleged support of the 1965 PKI coup attempt in Indonesia, were said to demonstrate that the Chinese cannot refrain from attacking or subverting even relatively friendly states.

China was thought to be further impelled toward expansionism by the need to find space and food for its enormous population. One leader termed China "a hungry giant." The belligerent talk of China's leaders was also said to have been motivated by a hope that it would facilitate the awesome task of holding China together. And some—including technocrats, foreign ministry officials, army generals, PNI members, and leaders of the young generation—contended that Peking was "talking tough" mainly because of an underlying nervousness about the hostile forces around its periphery.

Some leaders emphasized that there was nothing peculiarly Chinese about the PRC's expansionism: "Like any other big power, China wants a sphere of influence." More than 60 percent of the respondents agreed that China's goal in Southeast Asia was to establish a degree of influence there comparable to that which the United States has in Latin America, though the Chinese have to be more belligerent about it because they are trying to effect a significant change in the status quo. Younger leaders were especially pronounced in this view, and only the 1928 Generation, Islamic, Catholic, and PSI leaders generally dissented from it (see Table 4.2).

It is hard to overemphasize the importance of the overseas Chinese in the foreign policy elite's perception of the Chinese threat. When asked what they thought about China, the foreign policy elite members frequently responded with comments on the Indonesian Chinese. Of 50 leaders, 30, including a majority of every major group except the Catholics and PSI leaders, brought the Indonesian Chinese into their discussion of China's aggressiveness.[7] An Islamic

7. Included were 6 of 7 PNI leaders, 5 of 6 technocrats, 5 of 7 from the

leader put it clearly: "We are not afraid of Mao's atom bomb; it is the overseas Chinese that worry us. The overseas Chinese are a trojan horse."

The Indonesian leaders vied with one another to demonstrate the depth of their hatred for the Chinese, and they usually did so by telling of their antipathy toward the Chinese in Indonesia, thus revealing the extent to which China and the local Chinese merged in their thinking. For example, one army general boasted: "We hate the Chinese . . . and I am well known as one of those in the army who most hates the Chinese. We have always hated the Chinese for their domination of the economy here, and now the more so for Mao's extremist ideology." A number of leaders pointed to Singapore and Hong Kong as forward outposts of the Chinese threat—forming an economic monolith in which China, Singapore, Hong Kong, and the Indonesian Chinese were indistinguishable from one another.

There was almost universal skepticism about the loyalty of the Indonesian Chinese to Jakarta. Most of the interviewees were convinced that an underlying loyalty to the Chinese fatherland could never really be eradicated. A foreign ministry official described the local Chinese as "a corps of agents" at the disposal of Peking any time it decides to launch a subversive action. "A Chinese is our enemy, that is to say, loyal to China, until proven otherwise," said an army leader.[8] Another general compared the local Chinese to "a cancer in our system" that will have to be either absorbed or expelled, but cannot continue to exist as a foreign element.

Though all of the Indonesian leaders would concede that China's Communist ideology heightens the danger to Indonesia, they overwhelmingly asserted that China would be a serious threat even if a non-Communist government were in power. Of 35 respondents, 83

---

army, 5 of 7 Islamic politicians, 5 of 9 foreign ministry officials, 2 of 5 PSI leaders, and none of 4 Catholics. By age groups, there were 5 of 10 leaders of the 1928 Generation, 20 of 32 from the 1945 Generation, and 5 of 8 from the 1966 Generation.

8. Some leaders claimed that there were local Chinese who had reversible pictures—with Mao on one side and Chiang on the other.

percent, including a heavy majority of every group except the Catholics, took that position (see Table 4.2). Furthermore, 60 percent—with clear majorities of the PNI and PSI leaders, army generals, and foreign ministry officials—claimed that a non-Communist China would be a threat of the same general magnitude as Mao's China.[9] As a 1966 Generation leader reasoned: "I have seen Chiang's maps—and all the areas he claims. It is a Chinese problem, not a Communist one." Another young leader spoke for most of the foreign policy elite when he concluded: "Any strong nation in Asia will constitute a threat to Indonesia."

Given this view, it is not surprising that the Indonesian leaders generally greeted China's moves toward "moderation" with a notable lack of enthusiasm. Of course, they were pleased that Radio Peking had softened its criticism of the Indonesian government.[10] And Chinese military aggression, never widely viewed as a serious danger, seemed even less likely at this time. In fact, top army and foreign ministry officials indicated to the author that diplomatic relations between Indonesia and China would be restored in the not-too-distant future. They tended to view such a development as a historical inevitability in light of general international trends, and in any case as something that might help to balance the rising power of Japan in Southeast Asia.[11] But whatever course China

9. With a total of 30 respondents, this view was expressed by all of 4 PNI members and 2 PSI leaders, 5 of 6 each from the army and foreign ministry, one of 4 technocrats, one of 5 Muslim leaders, and no Catholics (of one respondent). By generations, there were 3 of 5 leaders of the 1928 Generation, 14 of 21 from the 1945 Generation, and one of 4 from the 1966 Generation.

10. This was acknowledged by Foreign Minister Malik on 10 March 1972 (*Research Landasan,* vol. 7, pt. 1 [January-June 1972], (p. 24).

11. Ironically, strongly anti-Chinese Islamic politicians and businessmen interviewed in 1973 favored restoring relations with China. They hoped that indigenous Indonesian entrepreneurs could then import relatively inexpensive Chinese equipment and supplies that would strengthen their competitive position vis-à-vis the Japanese and the predominantly Chinese local partners of the Japanese. On this point see also Lie Tek Tjeng, "ASEAN and East Asia in the Seventies: Some Remarks," *Indonesian Quarterly,* 1 (January 1973), 13–17. Worth noting too is the suggestion of economist Thee Kian Wie

took, the Indonesian leaders believed that Peking's effort to subvert Southeast Asia through political and economic means would certainly continue.[12]

Thus the Indonesian government reacted very cautiously to the 1972 Nixon visit to China, making it clear that Jakarta would not be hurried into rapprochement with Peking.[13] There was no reason, as a technocrat put it, for Soeharto to pay homage to Mao, as Nixon and Tanaka had done. Despite the foreign policy elite's overwhelming support of China's admission to the UN, the Indonesian government, reportedly under heavy pressure from the Americans and Japanese, did not vote to admit Peking in the decisive UN vote of 1971.[14]

---

that Indonesia needed formal relations with China in order to regulate economic relations and prevent what could be a very damaging flood of Chinese goods entering Indonesia via Hong Kong and Singapore (*Politik Luar Negeri Indonesia Dewasa Ini,* p. 36).

12. See *Neutralization of South-East Asia* (Jakarta: Center for Strategic and International Studies, 1972), pp. 3–4, and Malik's statements in *Research Landasan,* 6 (July-December 1971), 23, 25, and *ibid.,* vol. 7, pt. 2, pp. 13, 22–23.

13. *Ibid.,* vol. 6, pp. 22–24, vol. 7, pt. 1, p. 40, and pt. 2, pp. 12–13, 22–23; and *Neutralization of South-East Asia,* p. 4. It was clear from the author's interviews that top army leaders preferred to wait as long as possible, and at least until mid-1975. See also *Pedoman,* 28 August 1973. According to *Sinar Harapan,* 23 July 1974, Malik asserted that Peking and Jakarta had agreed in principle to normalize relations, but that additional time was needed to prepare for such a step. A year later, with Malaysia having established diplomatic relations with Peking, the Philippines about to take that step, and Thailand expected to follow, it was stated that "everything has been readied" for Indonesia to do the same. But a May 1975 Radio Peking broadcast allegedly encouraging the PKI to continue armed struggle was said to necessitate a further delay. See Radio Jakarta, 14 May and 11 July 1975; *Kompas,* 28 May 1975; *Sinar Harapan,* 5 June 1975; and *Berita Buana,* 6, 12, and 16 June 1975. Malik told the author in September 1975 that diplomatic relations would be restored but "not this year."

14. Of 38 leaders questioned on the subject in 1969–1970, 34 supported China's admission to the UN, 4 dissented. Some of President Soeharto's closest army advisers argued strongly that Indonesia must continue to vote for China's membership in the UN. The dissenters were either Catholic or Islamic politicians. However, in the actual UN vote, Indonesia abstained on

The Indonesians interviewed in 1973 could find little that was reassuring in the prospect of a more moderate Chinese posture in international affairs. The rapprochement between China and the United States was viewed as the product of political calculations by those two powers. It reflected their own interests and not those of the Southeast Asian states, which played no role whatever in the process. In an April 1973 interview with the author, an army general very close to the president made it clear that he viewed the American rapprochement with China as evidence of a readiness to settle the fate of Asia without consulting other Asian states. Alleging that President Nixon went to China mainly to boost his 1972 re-election campaign, he asserted that the chief result has been a more active, less predictable, and therefore more dangerous China. It seemed to many of those interviewed in 1973 that respectability would probably make China more successful than before in broadening its influence in Asia. And a new worry, the possibility of cooperation between China and Japan concerning the "management" of Southeast Asia, was mentioned with alarm by several.[15]

In addition, Peking's new respectability and more active international role would strengthen China's claim on the loyalty of the overseas Chinese. A 1972 analysis by a research institute closely tied to one of the President's chief army advisers noted that overseas Chinese in Southeast Asia were increasingly siding with Peking. The report predicted that "Chinese industries outside China" would become a mere extension of China itself, just as American industries

---

the Albanian resolution to admit China and voted with Washington and Tokyo on the question of whether China's admission should be treated as an "important question." For the official position, see the Malik statements in *Research Landasan,* vol. 6, pp. 27–28; and vol. 7, pt. 1, p. 45, and *Analisa Previsionil Mengenai Asia Pada Umumnja, Asia Tenggara Pada Chususnja* (Jakarta: Center for Strategic and International Studies, 1972), p. 31.

15. See the remarks of Imron Rosjadi in *Politik Luar Negeri Indonesia Dewasa Ini,* p. 21; and Major General Sayidiman Suryohadiprojo, "Future of Southeast Asia," p. 44. See also *Kebudajaan Melaju dan Peranannja Sebagai Pendukung Konsepsi Ketahanan Regional* (Jakarta, 1972), p. 1, a limited circulation publication of the Center for Strategic and International Studies, a research agency with close ties to important army generals.

abroad are a projection of the United States.[16] Indeed, by 1973 hostility toward the Indonesian Chinese had for a variety of reasons increased sharply.[17] Normalizaton of relations with Peking, it was said, would only increase the capacity of China to exercise economic influence in Indonesia via the overseas Chinese.

Thus the Indonesians, once confronted by two Cold War blocs which they could balance off against one another, now face at least four potentially exploitative powers. Whatever benefits detente may have brought to the world, the dramatic improvement in relations among the Cold War adversaries appears to offer considerably expanded possibilities for collusion to divide up the spoils of Indonesia. The real danger is that the Cold War, now perceived as a competition among at least four powers for spheres of influence in places like Indonesia, will turn out not to be a competition at all.

The Middle East Conflict

Under Sukarno, Indonesia outspokenly supported the Arabs in their conflict with Israel. Indonesia even excluded Israel from the Asian Games held in Jakarta in 1962, thus precipitating an acrimonious conflict with the International Olympics Committee. For Sukarno, Israel was an outpost of Western imperialism in the Asian-African world.

After his removal from power, Indonesian support of the Arabs became considerably less pronounced. Jakarta continued to proclaim its undiminished sympathy for the Arab cause and to urge Israel's compliance with UN resolutions concerning the Middle East. But this mild verbal support was even further tempered by calls for "realism" and "moderation" on the part of the Arabs.[18] In mid-1972 Foreign Minister Malik journeyed to several Middle Eastern capitals to counter a "mistaken impression" among the

16. *Analisa Previsionil,* p. 6. See also Malik's comments on the prospects for a restoration of diplomatic relations in *Research Landasan,* vol. 7, pt. 2, p. 22, and in *Kompas,* 27 April 1973.

17. See *Indonesia Raya,* 9 August 1973.

18. See "Tjatatan Menlu Menghadapi Th. 1969," *Pewarta & Kronologi Bulanan,* 1 (1968), 32, and "Kecenderungan-kecenderungan," p. 46.

Arabs that Indonesia's support for them had flagged. While Malik agreed that Israel should withdraw from all occupied Arab territory and restore the "legitimate rights of the Palestinian people," he added that the Arabs had to be realistic enough to recognize "the existing situation." In late 1973 a newspaper reflecting the views of influential army leaders urged serious consideration of a settlement that would pay attention to the interests of both sides, acknowledging Israel's "right to live" and suggesting "a little change" in the pre-1967 borders.[19]

Judging from their interviews, few Indonesian leaders thought the Middle East conflict impinged directly on their country's national interests. Despite official sympathy for the Arabs, 23 of the 38 leaders who discussed the Middle East made it clear that they really feel little sympathy for the Arabs.

There were only two groups which identified strongly with the Arabs and favored a stronger pro-Arab posture. Those two groups, the Muslim party leaders and the PNI, are usually at odds with one another. Nonetheless, all of those who asserted that Indonesia's support for the Arabs was too weak were either PNI leaders, navy officers identified with the PNI viewpoint, or Islamic politicians. Although a few mentioned casually their hope that Indonesia would send volunteers to aid the Arabs, virtually no one took this idea seriously. The principal step urged was the granting of permission to Al Fatah to open a mission in Jakarta, similar to the representation previously accorded the national liberation fronts of Algeria and Vietnam.[20] Of the 15 leaders who argued that Al Fatah should

19. *Research Landasan,* vol. 7, pt. 2, pp. 31–34; and *Berita Buana,* 25 September 1973. See also *Sinar Harapan,* 6 June 1975.

20. For the government's reservations about the validity of Al Fatah's claim to represent the Palestinian people, see Malik's statement in *Abadi,* 1 May 1969. He did, however, indicate that Indonesia would not object to the opening of an office in Jakarta by the Palestinian Liberation Organization (PLO), which Malik described as the only official representative of the Palestinian people. But, he added, the PLO had not officially requested such representation (*Sinar Harapan,* 27 June 1974). A year later Malik said that Indonesia "basically" agreed to the idea of a PLO mission in Jakarta if it were set up in accordance with "established norms" (Radio Jakarta, 18 June 1975).

be permitted to open an office in Jakarta, all but 2 were identified with the PNI or the Muslim political parties.

Of course this coincidence of views between the Muslim politicians and the PNI rested on two essentially different perceptions of the conflict. The PNI saw anti-imperialism as the central issue, and the whole Middle East conflict as further evidence that imperialism still threatened the newly independent countries. Israel was regarded as a white, Western creation, an American outpost in the Middle East. PNI leaders also asserted that Indonesia's support of the Arabs had weakened because of the government's desire to maintain good relations with its Western creditors, especially the United States. In fact, the comments of several government officials, including a leading technocrat, suggested that the government did believe that Indonesia's "real interests"—meaning a secure supply of foreign aid for economic development—demanded "restraint" on the Middle East issue.[21]

Even a few leaders not associated with the PNI revealed a tendency to view the Middle East issue in terms of imperialism. A young leader with PSI associations declared that he saw the Middle East question "not as Arab or Muslim versus Jew but as a colonial issue. That is, immigrants from the United States and Western and Eastern Europe have come in and colonized the Arabs living there before." And Indonesians from practically all groups expressed concern about the plight of the Arab refugees.

On the other hand, the Muslim party leaders saw the Arab-Israeli dispute primarily as a situation requiring Islamic unity. Occasionally they even spoke of a holy war in the Middle East. Although their principal basis for identification with the Arabs was religion, the Muslim leaders did cite some additional considerations. They suggested that Indonesia was indebted to the Arabs for their support of the Republic during the revolution, when certain Arab states gave recognition to Indonesian diplomatic missions. The

21. One technocrat stressed as well the need for the Arabs to reach an accommodation with Israel in order to facilitate the reopening of the Suez Canal, thus expediting Indonesia's trade with Europe.

refugee problem was often mentioned, with one leader contending that a religious state which "just throws out residents because they have a different religion" is "archaic" and should not be permitted to exist.

Moreover, though they perceived the Middle East conflict mainly in terms of religious solidarity rather than anti-imperialism, many of the Islamic party leaders strongly resented both the Western role in the Middle East and the Western economic pressures which precluded Indonesia's giving stronger support to the Arabs. Like the PNI leaders, the Muslims viewed the Middle East conflict, to some extent, as an aspect of Indonesia's relations with the United States. If the activities of Christian missionaries in Indonesia made them uneasy about their country's economic dependence on the Judeo-Christian West, the Middle East conflict and Indonesia's muted support for the Arabs served as another reminder of that unpleasant dependence. Though some Muslim leaders were inclined to be favorably disposed toward the West because of a shared antipathy toward Communism, the Middle East conflict made them less so.

For most of the other members of the foreign policy elite, the Middle East dispute was simply a conflict among distant nations in which there was some sympathy for the Arabs because of Israel's alleged mistreatment of Palestinian refugees, but also a good deal of contempt for the Arabs' incompetence, and suspicion about their flirtation with the Russians. In foreign ministry, army, PSI, technocrat, and Catholic circles, there was a widespread feeling that a "rational" policy for Indonesia would be one which viewed the Middle East conflict not as a religious matter but as an issue between the Arab nations and Israel.

While almost no one criticized the post-Sukarno policy of "lip service support" for the Arabs, there was practically unanimous agreement that the Arabs were unrealistic to think of destroying Israel. Many pictured the Arabs as bumblers, alluding to their inability even to agree among themselves. One newspaper editor told of being approached by Arab embassies at the time of the Six Day War. The Arabs had asked him to report the war as a defeat for the

Israelis, but he refused and instead ridiculed the Arabs for their incompetence.

The Arabs' generally negative image was reinforced by animosities toward the economically influential Arab minority in Indonesia, and according to some by a belief that the Arab leaders were unreliable allies. Rebutting the contention that Jakarta owes the Arabs firm support because of their backing of Indonesia during the revolution, several leaders recalled that when Sukarno's exclusion of Israel from the Asian Games held in Jakarta drew the wrath of the International Olympics Committee, the Arabs refused to join Indonesia in withdrawing from the Olympics. Inasmuch as Jakarta's action was considered to be a move undertaken on behalf of the Arabs, their failure to share in the consequences was portrayed as proof of their untrustworthiness.

There was, in fact, a good deal of sympathy for Israel, though it was almost never expressed publicly. Especially among army officers, PSI leaders, and technocrats, there was admiration for what the Israelis have done by their own efforts. Several went so far as to mention Israel as the country which provides the best model for Indonesia. One army leader described the situation this way: "When we speak privately among ourselves, we cannot help admiring what the Israelis have done, though we feel bound to support the Arabs. We do feel it was wrong to establish Israel, but that question aside, they have provided an excellent example of what a nation can do by its own hard work. They have done a marvelous job of economic development. . . . True, a good deal of money is channeled to Israel from private citizens in the United States, but the Israelis have managed to defend themselves and develop their country largely by their own efforts—by self-reliance."

Concern about the Arabs' dependence on Communist aid is strongest in the army. "It is regrettable," said a general, "that Soviet, and even Chinese, influence has penetrated so deep among the Arabs that they are no longer independent. Look at Egypt. You cannot say they are independent. Look at Syria. It is sad that those nations have become victims of the Cold War." Al Fatah representation in Indonesia, army leaders argued, would be "very dangerous" because Communist influence in the guerrilla group is so great. Such a mission might provide a channel for the infiltration of Communist agents; certain Arab embassies were already serving that purpose, it was alleged. The generals were also worried that Al Fatah representation might cause trouble "with those embassies here that support Israel," perhaps trying to blow up the Swiss or U.S. embassy.

Even among Muslims who lamented Jakarta's tepid support of the Arabs, there was concern about Communist influence in the Middle East. An eminent Islamic leader contended that some Arab countries, like Syria, could not really be called Islamic; they were "secular, leftist." Although some Muslims sought to minimize this by pointing out that Communists have played a role in many national liberation movements, including Indonesia's, most were clearly uneasy about it.

To summarize, the Middle East conflict has not been a central concern for most Indonesian leaders, but their attitudes about it offer further evidence of the influence of the hostile world perspective. Practically all of the foreign policy elite members saw in the Middle East conflict the struggle of small nations trying to remain independent of the big powers.

The Vietnam War

The Vietnam conflict was never a matter of pressing national concern for most Indonesian leaders either, but it came to possess considerable symbolic importance. Although the government's attitude toward the war underwent changes in the late 1960s, reflecting the new leadership's anti-Communism and economic dependence on the West, there was a remarkably persistent inclination for leaders all along the political spectrum to see the war as proof of the big powers' willingness to pursue their national ambitions at the expense of weaker countries.

Since the early 1950s, there had been broad sympathy in Indonesia for the Viet Minh. Under Sukarno in the 1960s, Indonesia openly condemned the United States as the aggressor in Vietnam and expressed enthusiastic support for the "struggle for national independence" being waged by the North Vietnamese and the National Liberation Front (NLF). Characterized as certain to win, the NLF was hailed as an inspiration to Indonesia's own continuing revolution, while the Saigon government was widely pictured as an American puppet. In 1964 Indonesia raised its relations with Hanoi to ambassador level, which led Saigon to break diplomatic relations with Jakarta. The NLF subsequently established representation in Jakarta. In 1965 there was talk, but only talk, of sending Indonesian volunteers to fight alongside the NLF. Even after the attempted coup of 30 September 1965, army voices continued to speak of the possibility of sending "physical aid" to the Vietnamese; they pledged that determination to crush the PKI did not signify a diminution of Indonesia's sympathy for the patriotic struggle of the Vietnamese people against American "aggression."[22]

After Soeharto's accession to power in 1966, the government's stance shifted from clear-cut support of North Vietnam and the NLF to a consciously ambiguous policy of urging the settlement of the Vietnam problem by the Vietnamese people themselves without foreign intervention.[23] The New Order's early foreign policy pronouncements indicated that despite the many changes in policy, Indonesian support for the NLF and the North Vietnamese would continue. Foreign Minister Malik's first major exposition of the New Order's foreign policy noted improving relations with the United States but declared that Indonesia remained "steadfast in supporting the struggle of the Vietnamese people in opposition to United States military intervention;" Jakarta continued to believe that the United States should withdraw its forces from Vietnam, he added.[24] Even among the most stridently anti-Sukarno and anti-Communist ele-

22. See *Sinar Harapan,* 10 February 1965, and *Bintang Timur,* 2 and 23 April 1965; *Suluh Indonesia,* 3 and 22 April 1965; *Harian Rakjat,* 30 March 1965; and *Berita Yudha,* 27 November 1965.

23. In an interview with the author in Jakarta on 7 February 1970, Malik stated that Indonesia could avoid taking a clear public position because its own interests were not directly at stake.

24. *Politik Luar Negeri Indonesia Dipimpin Oleh Falsafah Pantja-Sila: Pidato Waperdam/Menlu Adam Malik Dimuka Sidang DPR-GR Pada Tanggal 5 Mei 1966* (Jakarta: Kementerian Penerangan, 1966), pp. 27–28.

ments, there was a tendency to exempt Vietnam from the litany of Old Order failings. For example, Sukarno's Independence Day address in August 1966 met with open hostility from 1966 Generation students, but when he urged America to "please get out of Vietnam," they applauded.

Though expressions of enthusiasm for the NLF and the North Vietnamese gradually cooled in the ensuing years, criticism of American intervention in Vietnam and respect for America's adversaries remained a prominent feature of Indonesian public commentary on the Vietnam problem. The American bombing of North Vietnam was very widely opposed in Indonesia.[25] Even relatively pro-American voices accused Washington of failing to understand Vietnamese nationalism,[26] while others continued to cite unjustified American intervention as the principal cause of the problem and to portray the Vietnamese people (significantly, the Vietnamese people as a whole, not the *South* Vietnamese) as fighting for independence from outside forces.[27]

25. *Angkatan Bersendjata,* 25 and 31 October 1966, 10 August 1967; *Harian Kami,* 11 July 1966, 27 November 1967; and Malik's statements reported in *Kabinet Ampera: Dokumen-dokumen Pokok tentang Kabinet Ampera Aktivitas-aktivitas dan Pelaksanaan Kebidjaksanaan* (Jakarta: Departemen Luar Negeri, 1968), p. 86; *Dasar-dasar Pegangan,* p. 81; and *Kompas,* 16 March 1967. On the 1972 Christmas bombing, see, for example, *Kompas,* 28 December 1972, and *Pedoman,* 30 December 1972. In response to the U.S. bombing of North Vietnam during the April 1972 Communist offensive, Malik did observe that the U.S. action was a result of the North Vietnamese "invasion," but he also noted that Hanoi had every right to defend itself against the American bombing (*Research Landasan,* vol. 7, pt. 2, p. 11).

26. The army newspaper *Berita Yudha,* 8 February 1968, pointed out that when American troops carried out humanitarian operations in Vietnam, the South Vietnamese were made to look like American puppets. A *Berita Yudha* editorial of 19 December 1969 asserted that the United States put too much faith in military measures and paid too little attention to Vietnamese national pride; moreover, the bombing of North Vietnam was said to have aroused the nationalist spirit of the Vietnamese.

27. For examples, see *Warta Bhakti,* 7 August 1967; *Duta Masjarakat,* 6 April 1968; *Suluh Marhaen,* 16 October 1970; and *Merdeka,* 5 November 1970 and 10 March 1971. Malik declared in October 1968 that peace would

Contempt for the Saigon government and respect for Hanoi and the NLF were clear even in the comments of those whose anti-Communism led them to hope that the Saigon government would succeed.[28] The death of Ho Chi Minh evoked an outpouring of praise for the North Vietnamese leader as a man who had struggled unceasingly for his country's independence and had lived up to ideals which the Indonesians set for themselves but seldom fulfilled.[29] And the incursions into Cambodia in 1970 and Laos in

---

be impossible so long as the "national interests of the Vietnamese people" were considered a "secondary matter." (*Dasar-dasar Pegangan,* p. 78). See also *Viet-Nam: Masalah Viet-Nam dan Pengaruhnja Terhadap Kedudukan Indonesia Dalam Rangka Politik Luar Negeri Republik Indonesia di Asia Pada Umumnja dan Asia Tenggara Pada Chususnja* (Jakarta: Departemen Luar Negeri, 1969), pp. 65–67; the lecture of the Foreign Ministry's Director-General for Political Affairs in *Kabinet Ampera,* p. 110; and Malik's June 1972 statement in *Research Landasan,* vol. 7, pt. 2, p. 10.

28. The generally scornful attitude toward the Saigon government is evident in *El Bahar,* 28 July 1967, 23 May 1969; *Angkatan Bersendjata,* 6 February 1968; *Berita Yudha,* 8 February 1968; *Kompas,* 12 February 1968; *Duta Masjarakat,* 27 February 1968; *Suluh Marhaen,* 4 November 1968; *Pedoman,* 9 June 1969; and *Merdeka,* 6 March 1971. The Indonesians were even more derisive in their comments on the Lon Nol regime in Cambodia, which was said to have failed because it made itself completely dependent on the United States ("Kecenderungan-kecenderungan," p. 49).

Admiration for the NLF and Hanoi can be seen in the statement of Lieutenant General Hidajat in *El Bahar,* 20 January 1967; *Sulah Marhaen,* 18 April 1967, 26 October 1967, 10 January 1968, 26 March 1971; *Kompas,* 14 June 1973; and the assertion of the strongly anti-Communist Islamic leader Mohammad Natsir, who in an interview reported in *Sinar Harapan,* 6 May 1971, pointed out that despite its advanced technology the United States had been unable to defeat "the power of a political idea which inspires the Vietnamese people."

29. President Soeharto cabled his "sincerest sympathy and profound condolences" on the DRV's "tragic loss." Soeharto and General Nasution both expressed admiration for Ho's dedication to the "fight for the liberation of colonized peoples all over the world" (*Antara,* 4 and 9 September 1969). *Angkatan Bersendjata,* 5 September 1969, praised Ho for his integrity, patriotism, and simplicity, and compared his stature to that of Gandhi and Nehru. The armed forces paper expressed sadness at seeing "an old hero forced to leave the battlefield where he had spent his life." *Indonesia Raya,* 10 September 1969, called Ho the only leader of the independence struggle besides Gandhi who continued to live simply amid the people and declared

1971 by Saigon drew a good deal of criticism in the Jakarta press.[30]

But if there were signs of reluctance to abandon support of the "independence struggle" in Vietnam, there was also uneasiness about supporting the expansion of Communist influence. The armed forces newspaper spoke of Indonesia's "split standpoint"—a reference to the conflict between a sense of obligation to support the independence struggle and a desire to keep the Communists as far as possible from Indonesia.[31] The latter side of the split standpoint was reflected in the ambiguity that sometimes clouded Indonesia's position on the bombing of North Vietnam.[32] Throughout the post-1966 period, there were occasional commentaries emphasizing the evils of Hanoi and the NLF and the virtues of Saigon as the bearer of the anti-Communist standard.[33] On one occasion, the influential

---

that his victory over the United States proved his greatness as a leader. See also *Pedoman,* 5 September 1969, and *Berita Yudha,* 5 September 1969. The North Vietnamese leaders were apparently moved by the warmth of Indonesia's condolences (Interview with Ambassador [to Hanoi] Nugroho, 25 September 1969, Jakarta).

30. For criticism of the Cambodian incursion, see Malik's disapproval in *Kompas,* 4 May 1970; *Harian Kami,* 2 May 1970; *Suluh Marhaen,* 4 May 1970; *El Bahar,* 5 May 1970; *Merdeka,* 5 and 8 May 1970; *Pedoman,* 6 May 1970; and the report of a student demonstration at the U.S. embassy in *Harian Kami,* 20 May 1970. Milder criticism is found in *Berita Yudha,* 5 May 1970. The Laotian invasion was seen by most as a failure. See, for example, *Berita Yudha,* 27 March 1971; *Suluh Marhaen,* 26 March 1971; and *Harian Kami,* 23 March 1971.

31. *Angkatan Bersendjata,* 14 July 1967.

32. For example, Soeharto's statements on Vietnam tended to be more equivocal than Malik's. See his *Pidato Kenegaraan Pd. Presiden Republik Indonesia Djenderal Soeharto Didepan Sidang DPR-GR 16 Agustus 1967* (Jakarta: Departemen Penerangan, 1967), pp. 37–38, and *Address by the President of the Republic of Indonesia before the Foreign Correspondents Club, Tokyo, 30th March 1968* (Jakarta: Department of Information, 1968), pp. 11–12. See also *Angkatan Bersendjata,* 18 January 1968.

33. See *Armed Forces Daily Mail,* 23 February 1967; *Berita Yudha,* 16 May 1969; Muslim politician Chalik Ali's remarks in *Antara,* 3 June 1969; Major General Sutopo Juwono's comments in *Nusantara,* 5 July 1969; *Suluh Marhaen,* 29 August 1969; General Panggabean's equivocal statements quoted in *Kompas,* 20 November 1969; and *Nusantara,* 4 September 1967, 11 and 30 November 1968. For a favorable response to the Cambodian and Laotian invasions, see *Nusantara,* 6 May 1970, 26 March 1971.

armed forces newspaper suggested a "reorientation" of Indonesia's Vietnam policy in light of Jakarta's interest in stopping the advance of Communism in Southeast Asia,[34] but those responsible for that editorial reportedly were chastized, and subsequent editorials returned to neutrality and the split standpoint. In the ensuing years, however, some newspapers associated with the army seemed to be edging toward a position in support of Saigon.[35]

Beginning in 1968 there was discussion of proposals, some of them emanating from the United States, that Indonesia send substantial armed forces to Vietnam as part of an American-sponsored "peacekeeping force" following the withdrawal of U.S. troops. Reportedly, the plan had some backing for a time among a small group of army officers who hoped that Indonesia might be rewarded for such a role by enormous economic and military aid.[36] The same officers proposed that Indonesia assume a role in Cambodia after the 1970 coup against Sihanouk.[37] But the Indonesian government ultimately decided that participation in a peacekeeping force would be possible only if such a force were formed under UN auspices or as a product of the Paris negotiations.[38] There was

34. *Angkatan Bersendjata,* 23 October 1967. The editorial asked: "What is the meaning of the policy of 'assisting in a peaceful settlement by the Vietnamese people themselves'? Does it mean we are pushing for a Vietnam settlement based on the victory of the Nasakom idea [coalition] . . . which certainly will not be beneficial to security and political stability in Southeast Asia? . . . Actually our national interests oblige us to try to drive the communist danger as far as possible from Indonesia's borders. . . ."

35. For the culmination of this trend, see *Angkatan Bersendjata,* 5 May 1972; *Berita Buana,* 16 July 1973; and *Suara Karya,* 23 August 1973.

36. *Duta Masjarakat,* 7 August 1968; *Sinar Harapan,* 9 and 31 October 1968; *Business News,* 18 October 1968; and *Angkatan Bersendjata,* 4 November 1968. For details, see Franklin B. Weinstein, "The Uses of Foreign Policy in Indonesia" (Ph.D. diss., Cornell University, 1972), pp. 224–25.

37. See Lau Teik Soon, *Indonesia and Regional Security: The Djakarta Conference on Cambodia* (Singapore: Institute of Southeast Asian Studies, Occasional Paper no. 14, 1972), pp. 5–7; Juwono Sudarsono's contribution to *Politik Luar Negeri Indonesia Dewasa Ini,* p. 15; and Weinstein, "Uses of Foreign Policy," pp. 639–640.

38. See Malik's statements in *Pelopor Baru,* 3 February 1969; *Sinar Harapan,* 8 February 1969; and *Dasar-dasar Pegangan,* pp. 83–85. There was

also some talk of restoring diplomatic relations with Saigon and evicting the NLF mission which continued to maintain an office in Jakarta,[39] but the government's decision was to do nothing along those lines until it had been determined who would govern Vietnam.[40]

The ambiguity of the Indonesian government's position and the contradictory nature of much of the public commentary on the war reflected an ambivalence which struck at the heart of the foreign policy elite members' perceptions of the outside world and of themselves. Many Indonesian leaders viewed the Vietnam problem with ambivalence because their anti-Communism ran counter to their belief that the war was an independence struggle and that they were men who supported such struggles. Their self-image as men dedicated to the liberation of all who have lived under colonial rule made it painful for them to support the United States, which they perceived as having obstructed Vietnam's independence; but their anti-Communism, as well as their desire to avoid needlessly antagonizing those on whom Indonesia is economically dependent, precluded their backing the NLF and Hanoi. This ambiguity should not, however, be permitted to obscure the fact that the Indonesian

---

virtually no criticism of Indonesia's participation in the peacekeeping force that resulted from the 1973 Paris settlement, though *Pedoman,* 27 June 1973, urged that Indonesia withdraw from its Vietnam role after it became clear that the force could not function effectively.

39. See *Antara,* 20 May 1969; *Djakarta Times,* 4 September 1969; *Berita Buana,* 16 July 1973; and *Nusantara,* 16 May 1969. But even some who generally supported Saigon felt that Indonesia could "be more useful to the West" as an intermediary or member of a peacekeeping force if it avoided antagonizing Hanoi. For details, see Weinstein, "Uses of Foreign Policy," pp. 226–27. Concern about the presence of the NLF representatives, who continued to be received at the Foreign Ministry, was expressed in *Operasi,* 31 March 1967; *Antara,* 14 May and 19 June 1969; and *Nusantara,* 6 September 1969.

40. *Antara,* 8 and 15 June 1969, and *Nusantara,* 5 November 1969. Indonesia did, however, walk out of the August 1972 Georgetown (Guyana) Conference of Nonaligned Foreign Ministers in protest against the meeting's decision to invite the Provisional Revolutionary Government of South Vietnam to take part. See *Monthly Review* (August-September 1972), pp. 6–9, and "Kecenderungan-kecenderungan," p. 28.

leaders saw Vietnam mainly as a tragic example of what can happen to a weak nation when the big powers are allowed to fight their battles on its soil.

The foreign policy elite's discussion of the causes of the Vietnam War left no doubt that the great majority viewed it primarily as the product of American intervention, and secondarily as the consequence of Saigon's own collaborationism, corruption, and repressiveness. The idea that the war resulted from Communist aggression was overwhelmingly rejected. Of 56 leaders who commented on the origins of the war, 80 percent held Washington and Saigon to blame; only 9 percent felt that the war resulted from Communist aggression, while 7 percent assigned responsibility equally to both sides. The majority view was most pronounced among PSI, foreign ministry, and PNI leaders, but it was also very strongly supported by technocrats and army generals. Even among the Catholic and Islamic politicians, the two groups most sympathetic to the Saigon government, a majority concurred in blaming the West. The young were only slightly less pronounced than their elders in rejecting Communist aggression as the explanation for the war (see Table 4.3).

A principal reason for this remarkable consensus was the similarity perceived between Vietnam's fight for independence and Indonesia's own struggle. Many Indonesian leaders found it hard to forget that Indonesia and Vietnam proclaimed independence within weeks of one another, that both negotiated agreements with the colonial powers promising plebiscites in the areas still under foreign control, and that both faced colonial authorities which violated their pledges and sought to reinstate their domination through the creation of collaborationist governments. Vietnam was said to have failed to match Indonesia's success in throwing off foreign domination only because the dominant role of Communists in Vietnam's independence struggle had led the United States to intervene on behalf of the government in Saigon after the Viet Minh reached the brink of victory.

From those early days, then, Ho Chi Minh's Democratic Republic of Vietnam was fixed in the minds of most Indonesian leaders as the legitimate embodiment of Vietnamese nationalism, the counter-

Table 4.3. Attitudes toward the Vietnam War

	Principal cause of the war				View of U.S. role		Sympathies		
	Communist aggression	U.S./Saigon actions*	Equal responsibility	Don't know	Approved (strongly)	Disapproved (strongly)	Saigon	NLF	Ambivalent
All respondents	5 [9%]	45 [80%]	4 [7%]	2 [4%]	7 (3) [13%] [5%]	48 (40) [87%] [73%]	12 [25%]	22 [46%]	14 [29%]
1928 Generation	1	7	1	0	2 (2)	9 (8)	2	2	3
1945 Generation	2	32	2	2	3 (1)	34 (27)	6	17	10
1966 Generation	2	6	1	0	2 (0)	5 (5)	4	3	1
Foreign Ministry	0	7	0	0	0 (0)	8 (5)	0	2	4
PSI	0	4	0	0	0 (0)	6 (5)	0	3	0
PNI	0	7	1	0	0 (0)	9 (7)	0	5	2
Technocrats	0	7	1	1	0 (0)	6 (4)	1	4	3
Army	2	7	0	0	2 (1)	7 (5)	3	2	5
Catholic Party	0	3	1	0	2 (1)	2 (2)	2	1	1
Islamic parties	2	5	0	1	2 (0)	3 (3)	4	0	1

* Combined in a single category because many of those who mentioned Washington's actions also blamed Saigon. Of the 45 leaders who blamed the U.S. and Saigon for the war, 33 specifically cited America's replacement of France as the chief obstruction to the achievement of Vietnamese independence.

part to Sukarno's Republican government. The Saigon government, on the other hand, was compared to the scorned puppet regime established by the Dutch. Staunchly anti-Communist Islamic politicians joined in asserting that the Communists in Vietnam were "fighting for their country" and possessed a base of popular support far broader than that commanded by Saigon. The notion that the North Vietnamese were guilty of aggression was widely ridiculed as a pretext intended to justify American intervention. As an economist who sits in the cabinet described it: "The North Vietnamese have no desire to seize South Vietnam. That's not how the war started. The Vietnamese just want to complete their struggle for independence—all they want is their independence."

North Vietnam's involvement in the south was widely viewed as justified because national unification was an integral part of Vietnam's independence struggle, as it had been for Indonesia. Thus a top foreign ministry official, noting that the north had "given full support to the southerners in their independence struggle," argued that this could not be considered aggression because Vietnam is one country. Citing the Geneva Agreements, a PNI leader spoke for many foreign policy elite members when he said: "The Vietnamese have every right to try to unify their country. To speak of aggression from the north is like accusing Indonesia of aggression in West Irian. If anyone is an aggressor in Vietnam, it is the United States. The whole world knows that." The division of Vietnam was "just like efforts to split Indonesia," observed an Islamic leader. "It cannot succeed."

While many Indonesians were reluctant, at least in talking to an American, to apply the label "aggressor" to the United States, close to 90 percent of the foreign policy elite voiced disapproval of America's involvement in Vietnam (see Table 4.3). Much of the criticism was extremely sharp. In the first place, American intervention was blamed for driving many Vietnamese nationalists into the arms of the Communists. The NLF's Communism was said to be the result of a common American error—that of branding as Communists all who oppose the repressive governments Washington supports. An army general recalled that Washington had "regarded us as

Communists when we were struggling for freedom because we were against the Dutch," and a leading cabinet member observed that had the United States unequivocally backed the Dutch during the revolution, "we might have been forced into working with the Communists, just as happened to the Vietnamese." American policies were also said to have forced Ho to move closer to Moscow and Peking. Army generals, Islamic leaders, and 1966 Generation figures joined others in arguing that Washington would have been wise to recognize Ho in 1945, when there would have been a reasonable chance of developing cordial relations between the United States and an independent Vietnam. The "present dangerous situation" was said to be Washington's own responsibility.

America's intervention in Vietnam was frequently cited as an example of Washington's disregard for the rights of weaker nations, including the right of self-determination. Army generals expressed their abhorrence at the idea of hundreds of thousands of American troops occupying an Asian country. One general tried to be gentle but could not avoid some harsh words: "Now I know that the motives of the United States were good—that is, to contain Communism—but it is hard to say that the United States has any business being in Vietnam. It is clearly an interventionist force—an aggressor." A former foreign minister known for his efforts to move Indonesia closer to the United States claimed that Washington had simply "decided to impose its system on Vietnam, because Dulles decided that a Communist system could not be tolerated there." Few were impressed by the argument that Saigon had invited the United States to intervene.[41]

Although most criticism of foreign intervention in Vietnam was directed at the United States, some condemned the Communist powers as well. Few considered the North Vietnamese to be "foreigners," but several leaders contended that Russian and Chinese

41. "You can always find someone to invite you in," asserted a young PNI leader. "If you looked hard enough, you could find among Indonesia's 110 million people somebody who would invite the United States to occupy Bali [in order] to defend Indonesia."

interference was as much to blame as America's. Both the United States and the Communist powers were said to be pursuing their own interests at the expense of the Vietnamese. Citing big power intervention as the cause of most international problems, a PNI leader typically claimed that the Vietnam conflict could be resolved if the big powers "would just stop interfering." In addition, several leaders accused both sides of using Vietnam as "a testing ground." A cabinet member voiced strong objection to what he described as the well-documented fact that America "uses the developing countries as a testing ground for new weapons, such as gas." The United States should "try out its new weapons in its own country," he said.

The few who did describe the war as a case of Communist aggression emphasized the inherent expansionism of Communist ideology. "All Communist countries want to seize their neighbors," contended a former Masjumi leader. The North Vietnamese were accused of having violated the Geneva Agreements from the very beginning, "which just proves again that you can never trust the Communists—they will never respect any agreement they make." An army general close to President Soeharto argued that the United States was not an aggressor in Vietnam because it was invited by the Saigon government to help repel the "ideological aggression" being carried out by both North and South Vietnamese Communists.

The prevalence of a belief that Hanoi and the NLF were fighting to free Vietnam from foreign domination did not, however, signify an overwhelming desire among the Indonesians for a Communist victory there. It simply meant that even Indonesians whose anti-Communism led them to hope for the defeat of the NLF and Hanoi conceded that they were not aggressors but rather were struggling for their nation's independence. There was, neverthless, reasonably strong support for the NLF among the Indonesian leaders. Nearly half of the foreign policy elite expressed the hope that the NLF would win, while 29 percent were ambivalent, and only 25 percent clearly backed Saigon (see Table 4.3).[42]

42. Except for the PNI leaders, most of those who were ambivalent probably leaned toward Saigon.

Many of those who hoped for an NLF victory were quite emphatic, even emotional, in asserting their views. Army generals said they felt a sense of identification with the NLF because its struggle reminded them of their own fight against the Dutch. Several generals spoke of widespread support for the NLF within the army based on the prestige of Ho and other Viet Minh leaders. Leading technocrats, some of whom left no doubt that they would prefer an NLF victory, claimed that sympathy for the NLF was very strong and broad-based throughout the Indonesian elite. These feelings, however, were seldom expressed publicly because, in the words of a 1966 Generation leader, the anti-Communist "political climate here does not permit it."

An important component of this sympathy was a belief that Communist success represented a heroic triumph of the weak over the strong and of man over technology. In Vietnam, argued a PSI leader, "we have demonstrated that power politics cannot win. The power of the United States has been defeated by a combination of idealism, nationalism, and also military power, but not primarily military power." A number of Indonesian leaders who are favorably disposed toward the United States have nevertheless gained satisfaction from seeing an underdeveloped, Southeast Asian nation withstand the military and technological might of the strongest nation in the world.[43]

The Saigon government was viewed almost universally with cynicism, if not derision. The epithet "American puppet" was frequently applied. "Real nationalists were forced to the other side by the dictatorial Diem regime," noted an Islamic politician. Corruption in South Vietnam was widely criticized as much worse than in Indonesia. Army generals, among others, were quite emphatic in their criticism of the South Vietnamese as incompetent, corrupt, and worst of all, collaborationist. The army's scorn for the Saigon

43. There has even been some suggestion that this triumph should serve as an inspiration to Indonesia to base its economic development on improvised techniques that do not require the technology which only a wealthy nation can supply. See Gunawan Muhammad, "In Search of a New Ethos," *Indonesian Quarterly,* 1 (October 1972), 75.

regime was evident in the remarks of a reputedly pro-American general, explaining to an intermediary his refusal to be interviewed by the author: "These Americans think that if they walk in, everyone must stop what he is doing to talk to them. I want this fellow to understand that I am not one of their Vietnamese generals."

Most of those who sympathized with Saigon did so not because they admired the South Vietnamese but because they feared the spread of Communism. For those leaders, the fact that Hanoi and the NLF represented Communist power simply outweighed all other considerations. Thus, an Islamic party leader acknowledged that Saigon was "just a puppet government," but he blamed the United States for this situation and declared that he supported South Vietnam because he was aware of the dangers of Communism. Some of those who backed Saigon stated that they had once favored the NLF but had changed their minds after the 1965 coup attempt in Indonesia. A student leader conceded that Sukarno's descriptions of the NLF's struggle had led him to sympathize with the NLF, but since 1965 he had come to realize that both Washington and Hanoi were aggressors, and the real issue was the need to stop Communism. A top-ranking army intelligence officer said he too had once felt an emotional bond with the NLF's struggle, but that bond had been dissolved by Hanoi's hostile attitude toward Indonesia since the coup.

Those leaders, nearly a third of the foreign policy elite, who exhibited an ambivalent attitude toward the war were men who found themselves caught between their desire to support the NLF's independence struggle and their fear of Communist expansion in Southeast Asia. An economist described the dilemma well: "We really don't think much about Vietnam. When we do think about it, there is great ambivalence in our feelings. For so many years we supported North Vietnam; that has been our traditional policy. Those feelings of sympathy for North Vietnam are still very widespread. You can't get rid of them just like that. . . . After all, we are all children of the revolution. . . . But there has recently been a change in our attitude too. Now we understand that we have certain common interests with the Saigon government." Some of these leaders chose to distinguish between "admiration for the NLF's struggle" and support of the NLF itself. They echoed the sentiments of the young PNI leader who said: "My sympathies lie with the NLF, but this does not mean that I want them to win." A number of leaders were quite open about admitting that they could support Saigon only by turning their backs on their own ideals. In the words of an army general: "There are two aspects to my thinking and to that of most Indonesians. On idealistic grounds, we have always supported the NLF and North Vietnam. . . . We see the war as one of liberation, in which the United States is the aggressor. . . . Ho Chi Minh was a great leader. But our reason tells us that it is to our advantage to have the United States in Vietnam and to have the progress of Communism slowed. In the precoup period, our ideals predominated; now our reason predominates."

If the Indonesian leaders' analysis of the nature of the Vietnam conflict revealed substantial admiration of Hanoi and the NLF, their discussion of the probable outcome and its impact on Indonesia reflected their confidence that the Vietnamese Communists would struggle just as hard to avoid domination by China. Fundamental to the Indonesians' assessment of Vietnam's impact on their own security was their belief that the real danger comes from the big powers, whether Communist or not, and that the decisive factor in determining the survival of smaller nations as independent entities is the strength of their nationalism and determination to stand on their own feet.

Though some hoped otherwise, few Indonesian leaders said they expected the Saigon government to survive. Of 57 leaders asked to predict the most likely outcome of the war, 70 percent, drawn almost equally from all groups, indicated their expectation that the United States and Saigon ultimately would be defeated and the NLF would come to power. Only 12 percent were optimistic about Saigon's chances of winning out, while 4 percent felt that Saigon could survive if needed reforms were implemented. The percentage of leaders who refused to predict the outcome was relatively high at 14 percent, consisting mainly of individuals who hoped for Saigon's success but were not so bold as to predict it (see Table 4.4).

Table 4.4. Most likely outcome of the Vietnam war

	Saigon government will survive	Saigon will survive if it reforms	NLF will come to power	Don't know
All respondents	7 (12%)	2 (4%)	40 (70%)	8 (14%)
1928 Generation	1	0	8	0
1945 Generation	6	1	26	6
1966 Generation	0	1	6	2
PSI	0	0	4	1
PNI	1	0	7	1
Foreign Ministry	1	0	5	1
Islamic parties	0	0	5	2
Catholic Party	1	0	2	1
Army	3	0	6	0
Technocrats	1	0	3	0

The fragmentary interviews carried out in early 1973 following conclusion of the cease-fire in Vietnam suggest that there may have been a slight increase in optimism about Saigon's chances of survival, but Saigon's leading backers in Jakarta rated its prospects no better than fifty-fifty.[44]

If most foreign policy elite members expected an NLF victory, few found this prospect alarming from the standpoint of Indonesia's security. Only 14 percent expressed fear that an NLF-ruled South Vietnam would pose a direct threat to Indonesia, while 18 percent felt there might be some indirect danger, and 68 percent said that it would have no impact at all on Indonesia. Concern that an NLF victory would prove a threat to Indonesia was found mainly among Islamic and Catholic party leaders (see Table 4.5).

The few who saw an NLF victory as a direct threat to Indonesia

44. On 21 April 1973, a columnist in *Nusantara,* the most strongly pro-Saigon newspaper in Jakarta, declared that Saigon's chances of survival had dropped to forty-sixty. Cambodia's chances were generally considered much worse, and it may be that the expectation that Cambodia would fall to the Communists prevented any real optimism about Saigon's prospects. A late 1972 foreign ministry assessment predicted that in any event Hanoi was sure to become the dominant power in Indochina ("Kecenderungan-kecenderungan," p. 51).

Table 4.5. Impact of an NLF victory on Indonesia

	Would it threaten Indonesia?			Would a unified Communist Vietnam make China a greater threat?			Is the domino theory valid?	
	Direct threat	Indirect threat	No impact	Yes	It will be a barrier to Chinese expansion	Cannot say	Has validity (much)	Not at all
All respondents	8 [14%]	10 [18%]	38 [68%]	8 [21%]	26 [67%]	5 [13%]	12 (4) [35%] [21%]	22 [65%]
1928 Generation	1	4	5	2	6	1	3 (1)	3
1945 Generation	5	4	28	3	16	3	4 (2)	17
1966 Generation	2	2	5	3	4	1	5 (1)	2
PSI	0	0	5	0	3	0	0 (0)	3
PNI	0	1	8	0	4	0	1 (0)	5
Foreign Ministry	0	1	6	0	3	0	1 (0)	5
Technocrats	1	1	6	0	2	2	0 (0)	4
Army	1	1	7	1	3	1	3 (2)	2
Catholic Party	2	0	2	1	2	0	0 (0)	4
Islamic parties	3	4	1	4	2	2	3 (1)	1

assumed that a Communist South Vietnam, because of its ideological commitment, would inevitably seek to subvert the rest of Southeast Asia. Their chief concern was that Vietnam would serve as a conduit for the infiltration of men and supplies to the underground PKI in Kalimantan. The indirect threat to which a number of leaders referred was the psychological boost that an NLF triumph might give the PKI.

By far the most common response to the prospect of an NLF victory was one of utter indifference. "If Vietnam falls, so what?" said an army officer. "It really does not make any difference to Indonesia whether the Saigon government lives or dies," declared a technocrat. "It just won't have any impact here." The notion that America's role in Vietnam had somehow helped to turn the tide in Indonesia in 1965 was widely ridiculed by members of the foreign policy elite. The lack of any connection was clearly articulated by an army general: "We know so little about Vietnam. It seems so far away to us. That is why it seemed so strange when the United States started saying that the American presence in Vietnam helped Indonesia crush the PKI. It never even occurred to us to think in those terms." Even a Catholic leader who strongly backed Saigon indicated that the prospect of an NLF victory did not worry him because "the generals I talk to tell me that a Communist South Vietnam will not pose any threat to Indonesia." Indeed, a top army intelligence general, speaking at a background briefing shortly before the 1973 cease-fire, reaffirmed this: "Our front line is not in Vietnam," he is reported to have declared.

Besides, many leaders emphasized, the Vietnamese were exhausted after a long war and unlikely to possess either the capacity or the desire to interfere in the affairs of others. According to a foreign ministry official, Vietnam would be aggressive only if it felt threatened by "those fanatic anti-Communists who insist on hitting at the Communists." Of course, a PSI leader noted, if the two Vietnams were to unite under Hanoi's aegis and then become a satellite of China, that would be a serious danger. "The real dividing line is between China and Communism elsewhere," he pointed out. "There is genuine, widespread fear of anything that will strengthen the ability of China to threaten Indonesia."

Most Indonesian leaders, however, believed that a unified Communist Vietnam would not necessarily strengthen China. On the contrary, 67 percent of the foreign policy elite expressed the view that a Vietnam united under Hanoi's leadership would constitute a more effective barrier against Chinese expansionism than a Vietnam divided and torn by war. Once again, only the Catholics and the Islamic party leaders dissented to any substantial degree (see Table 4.5).

The confidence of Indonesia's basically anti-Communist elite that a Vietnam united under Communist rule would be an effective buffer against Chinese expansion reflects a pervasive belief that nationalism is a stronger force than any other ideology. A 1966 Generation leader observed that a mainland Southeast Asia possessed of genuinely nationalist governments, even if they are also Communist, would constitute a better guarantee of Indonesia's security than the present anti-Communist regimes. A foreign ministry official went so far as to declare that Indonesia would welcome a unified Communist Vietnam "wholeheartedly," because a Vietnam that expressed the national aspirations of its people would fight as hard to avoid domination by China as it had fought to repel the Americans. Many leaders voiced confidence that the traditional anti-Chinese cast of Vietnamese nationalism would outweigh any ideological affinity between Peking and Hanoi.

Vietnamese Communism, an army general pointed out, contains an unusually strong nationalist component. Along with many other leaders, he predicted that Vietnam would become an Asian Yugoslavia, pursuing a course independent of the Communist powers. Some questioned whether a Vietnam deeply embittered toward the United States and without the leadership of Ho could create a Yugoslavia-like state, but there seemed to be wide agreement that Hanoi would be more likely to chart an independent course than it had been when forced to seek outside backing for its struggle against the United States. The top army general whose background briefing prior to the 1973 cease-fire was mentioned before is said to have reasserted his belief that a Communist Vietnam would be a nonaligned state, not a Chinese puppet.

The foreign policy elite's confidence that a Communist Vietnam would not threaten Indonesia's security was based not only on a belief that Vietnamese nationalism could be used to contain China, but also on a broad skepticism about the idea that the fate of Southeast Asia depends on the outcome in any single country. Nearly two-thirds asserted that the domino theory contained no truth at all, and only 12 percent felt that it had a great deal of validity; 23 percent believed that the domino theory was partially true, meaning that the fall of one state would endanger, but not necessarily doom, its neighbors. Those who saw at least some truth in the domino theory tended to be Islamic leaders and army generals, and members of either the youngest or the oldest generations (see Table 4.5).

Rejection of the domino theory was put in the strongest terms. "We are, all of us, definitely nondomino people," declared a technocrat holding a cabinet post. The suggestion that Indonesia or any other country would fall to Communism simply because Vietnam had done so was said to be "foolish." The predominant view was that the survival of each non-Communist state would depend much more on its ability to handle its own problems, especially economic development, than on the temporary encouragement that local Communists might derive from the NLF's triumph.

The Indonesian reaction to the 1975 denouement in Indochina tended to confirm the attitudes previously described. There was broad agreement that the collapse of America's allies in Indochina was due above all to their excessive dependence on outside aid, which prevented them from rallying their own populace.[45] Foreign

45. See Foreign Minister Malik's comments in *Kompas,* 2 April 1975; *Merdeka,* 2 April 1975; and *Tempo,* 17 May 1975. See also *Kompas,* 11, 12, and 23 April 1975; *Angkatan Bersenjata,* 2 May 1975; and *Sinar Harapan,* 8 and 23 April 1975 and especially 5 June 1975, which compares Lon Nol and Thieu to former PKI leader Aidit, all of whom were said to have been doomed by their dependence on outside support. Even the newspaper con-

Minister Malik asserted that Indonesia had always sympathized with the North Vietnamese. Acknowledging that there had been little public evidence of such support since the downfall of Sukarno, he claimed that "in principle we've continued to support them."[46] Though there were some expressions of concern about Communist expansionism and the encouragement that the PKI would gain from the events in Indochina, Malik denounced the domino theory as a device intended to intimidate Southeast Asians so that they would feel compelled to rely on the United States. He compared the Communist effort to control all of Indochina with Indonesia's own independence struggle and expressed confidence that the Indochinese Communists would not seek to expand beyond the borders of the former French colony. The Communist victory in Indochina, he concluded, posed no danger to Indonesia, and that was said to be the general view in Jakarta.[47]

To sum up, the Indonesian leaders generally perceived the Vietnam conflict as proof that the big powers would pursue their global ambitions even if it meant that weaker countries had to be deprived of their independence, or where necessary, destroyed.

The NEFOS-OLDEFOS Conflict

Cutting across this discussion of international conflicts was a tendency to emphasize the similarities rather than the differences among the big powers, and to lump together the rich, industrialized nations. It is by no means surprising that the concept of a conflict between NEFOS and OLDEFOS, despite its identification with

---

sistently most sympathetic to Saigon and the United States observed that events in Indochina had shown that Indonesia had to avoid dependence on the United States, which had proven itself untrustworthy. See *Berita Buana*, 18 April 1975.

46. *Tempo*, 17 May 1975.

47. See Malik's comments in *Pelita*, 16 April 1975; *Merdeka*, 17 April 1975; *Tempo*, 3 May 1975; and *Kompas*, 10 May 1975. See also *Kompas*, 27 March 1975 and *Merdeka*, 25 April 1975. For concern about Communist expansionism, see *Suara Karya*, 9 April 1975; *Pelita*, 16 April 1975; and the remarks of John Naro, deputy speaker of Parliament, in *Kompas*, 28 April 1975.

Sukarno, was still widely accepted by the Indonesian leaders as the most meaningful way to divide the world.

Sukarno defined the NEFOS as the "progressive revolutionary" forces of the world, and he explicitly included the Soviet Union and "revolutionary elements" within industrialized Western countries, though the Soviets' NEFOS credentials were increasingly in doubt during Sukarno's last years of power. Many of Indonesia's more recent leaders have recast the NEFOS-OLDEFOS conflict in more narrowly economic terms, preferring to speak less of ideology and more of a clash of interests between the rich nations and the poor nations of the world.

Whether they defined it in political or economic terms, though, nearly 80 percent of the foreign policy elite expressed agreement on the validity of the NEFOS-OLDEFOS formulation as a description of international realities. A similarly overwhelming majority, when asked which of the several conflicts discussed was most important from Indonesia's standpoint, chose the NEFOS-OLDEFOS conflict, though roughly half of those who did so disdained use of the Sukarno terminology.[48] Young and old, and all the major groups except the Islamic party leaders, showed broad agreement on the truth of the formulation, though some were restrained by their concern about its implications for Indonesia's aid-oriented foreign policy (see Table 4.6).

The tendency of the big powers to exclude the underdeveloped nations from international decision-making on key issues, remarked upon in the discussion of the Cold War, was one of the considerations that persuaded the Indonesian leaders of the validity of the NEFOS-OLDEFOS dichotomy. The Indonesians found evidence of this in the notion that international disputes, such as the 1962

48. Only 24 leaders, however, were asked this question. Of the 24, 79 percent named the NEFOS-OLDEFOS conflict, while 13 percent mentioned the Cold War, and 8 percent the Sino-Soviet dispute. See also *Pidato Presiden Soeharto didepan Foreign Correspondents Club* (Jakarta: Departemen Penerangan, 1968), p. 11; *Harian Kami,* 6 February 1968; Hatta's comments in *Portrait of a Patriot,* p. 586; and Soedjatmoko, "Japan: Architect of a Post-Nuclear World Order?", p. 9.

Table 4.6. Agreement with the NEFOS-OLDEFOS concept

	Agree (very strongly)	Basically disagree
All respondents	43 (23) [78% (42%)]	12 (22%)
1928 Generation	7 (5)	2
1945 Generation	28 (16)	9
1966 Generation	8 (2)	1
PNI	8 (7)	0
Catholic Party	4 (0)	0
Army	7 (3)	1
Foreign Ministry	6 (2)	1
PSI	5 (2)	1
Technocrats	5 (2)	2
Islamic parties	2 (2)	4

Cuban missile crisis and the Arab-Israeli wars, were to be resolved through negotiations among the major powers, which then would impose their solution on the parties to the dispute.

Several leaders claimed that the basic truth of the NEFOS-OLDEFOS idea was borne out by the institutionalization of great power domination in the United Nations, as manifested especially by their possession of veto rights in the Security Council. In the words of a cabinet minister: "The UN is run by the OLDEFOS, just as Sukarno said it was."[49] Sukarno's plan to organize a rival Conference of the New Emerging Forces (CONEFO) was, he added, a brilliant idea because it reflected the real world; it failed

49. Even Malik, on his return from service as President of the General Assembly, voiced criticism of the veto power in particular and domination of the UN by the superpowers generally. His statements, made in December 1971 and January 1972, are reported in *Research Landasan,* vol. 7, pt. 1, p. 42.

The Indonesians must have viewed the stalemated UN Conference on the Law of the Sea, held in Caracas in 1974, as further evidence of the confrontative relationship between the NEFOS and OLDEFOS. In the conference, which dealt with issues of considerable importance to Indonesia, as one of the nations bordering on the Straits of Malacca, the advanced countries—both Communist and non-Communist—generally opposed the views of the less developed states (*San Francisco Chronicle,* 30 August 1974).

to materialize because "the world simply was not ready for it yet." Resentment at big power arrangements which empowered them to make important decisions affecting the fate of all countries underlay the hesitant response of the Indonesian government to the treaty on the nonproliferation of nuclear weapons.[50] These Indonesians found it hard to avoid the conclusion that the big powers believed that only they were competent to solve international crises, and that this was motivated by feelings of racial superiority and the arrogance of established power.

Political and military pressures, however, were generally seen as less dangerous than economic ones. The most widespread basis for agreement with the NEFOS-OLDEFOS concept was the belief that the industrialized nations of the world did not genuinely desire the economic development of the less developed ones.[51]

Those directly involved at the highest levels in the formulation and implementation of Indonesia's aid-oriented policy certainly saw the relationship with the aid-giving countries as essentially confrontative. In negotiations concerning the terms of trade, aid, and investment, they repeatedly encountered what they regarded as evidence of the unwillingness of the industrialized countries to help the less developed. It was as a result of such disillusioning experiences that a key cabinet minister expressed doubt that the rich countries wanted the poor ones to advance at all. Other top officials voiced similar sentiments. The following statement, by one of Indonesia's most influential technocrats, was typical:

50. Several foreign ministry officials voiced such reservations. A particularly good statement is found in *Harian Kami,* 27 November 1969, which suggested that the treaty really amounted to the big powers declaring: "All right, you are small, stay small, there is no need to try to wear long pants." The 1966 Generation newspaper goes on to express understanding of the objections of China and France to such a treaty. See also *Antara,* 4 December 1968. The Indonesian government has, however, signed the treaty, though it had not ratified it as of mid-1975.

51. For a particularly good statement of this concern, see Rosihan Anwar's article in *Harian Kami,* 8 February 1968, which draws attention to the possible division of the world by the big powers into "vertical compartments," with Asia turned over to Japan.

> I think it is accurate to say that there is a basic conflict of interest between the advanced countries and the developing countries. It is not basically a cooperative relationship. For example, look at the UNCTAD sessions, in which it has proved impossible to reach agreement. Or look at the recommendation that the advanced countries give 1 percent of their GNP in aid—only a very few have met this standard. One more example—the recent decision by the United States to release its rubber stockpile is a severe blow to us. Whether it is for economic or political reasons, it is clear that there is . . . a real clash between the advanced countries and the developing countries. . . . It is definitely necessary for the developing countries to join together and struggle against the advanced ones to promote the common interests of the developing countries.

Even some of Sukarno's bitterest opponents, who scorned the NEFOS-OLDEFOS idea as sloganeering and dismissed it as Marxist cant, did not hesitate to assert that the relationship between the rich and the poor countries was a confrontative one.

Numerous arguments were made to substantiate the view that trade, aid, and investment were being used by the industrialized nations to subjugate the developing countries. A general long-term trend of rising prices for the industrial goods they bought and falling prices for the raw materials they sold gave many Indonesian leaders the feeling that they were being exploited.[52] (For some statistical data bearing on this point, see Appendix A.) Moreover, this trend was widely viewed as the result of a conscious exertion of power by the advanced countries. As a foreign ministry official said: "The rich countries are too heavily motivated by the short-term needs of their industrialists, which inevitably leads them to a position which is not beneficial to us."

A great many Indonesian leaders were also deeply impressed by the unwillingness of the industrialized countries to agree to an

52. See Agriculture Minister Thojib Hadiwidjaja's comments in *Angkatan Bersendjata*, 27 September 1969; *Merdeka*, 22 December 1969; and the comments of Deputy Prime Minister Sultan Hamengku Buwono IX in *Statement-statement Politik Waperdam Bidang Sospol/Menteri Luar Negeri dan Waperdam Bidang Ekubang* (Jakarta: Kementerian Penerangan, 1966), p. 11.

easing of trade terms within the framework of the UNCTAD discussions, which they, like the technocrat quoted previously, saw as a graphic demonstration of the reality of the NEFOS-OLDEFOS conflict. In the two UNCTAD meetings held in 1964 and 1968, the Western industrial powers stood against the bloc of seventy-seven less developed countries, with the Soviet Union adopting a neutral stance on certain key issues, which the Indonesian leaders tended to interpret as de facto opposition.

Further evidence that the NEFOS were being exploited in their trade with the OLDEFOS came from the tariff system maintained by the European Economic Community, which the Indonesians found very damaging. The Common Market countries were accused of establishing high tariff walls "to strike a blow" at the exports of the less developed countries. Their policy, according to a 1966 Generation spokesman, was to enrich themselves "by 'killing' the economy of the developing countries."[53] And when the United States dumped its stockpiled rubber and tin on the world market with serious consequences for the underdeveloped countries, leading technocrats did not hesitate to express their extreme dismay.[54] Even the armed forces newspaper reacted on one such occasion by observing that Indonesians felt they were "being toyed with, as if the U.S. gives with its left hand what it takes away with its right hand."[55]

By 1973 there was among the Indonesian leaders an even stronger

53. *Harian Kami,* 10 July 1970. The Indonesians were especially concerned about the 10 percent duty imposed by the Common Market on Indonesian pepper, and about their ability to export rubber, palm oil, coffee, mineral ores, and other products to Europe. See *ibid.* and *Harian Kami,* 13 July 1970; *Antara,* 9 September 1969; *Kabinet Ampera,* p. 90; and *Monthly Review* (October-November 1972), pp. 6–7.

54. One asserted that Indonesia's loss would exceed the amount of aid given by the United States. *Harian Kami* editorialized that the rich Western countries appeared to be more concerned with their own economic growth and prosperity than with helping the underdeveloped countries. The "morality of the rich countries," the newspaper concluded, is "give ½, get back ¾." See *Harian Kami,* 10 and 17 July 1970; *Ekspres,* 26 July 1970; and *Sinar Harapan,* 22 February 1971.

55. *Angkatan Bersendjata,* 19 February 1971.

sense that the interests of the advanced countries, as reflected in international trade, were not complementary with the interests of the less developed countries.[56] Following the frustrating experience of the underdeveloped nations at the 1972 UNCTAD meeting in Santiago, a foreign ministry report lamented the lack of support from the Communist nations. They seemed more interested in pursuing their own opportunities for trade and economic cooperation with the industrialized Western powers. Even China was criticized for the gap between its rhetoric in support of the less developed countries and its efforts to court the United States.[57] The UN Special General Assembly held in the spring of 1974 was said to be aimed at replacing the "present harsh competition which enlarges the gap between rich and poor" with a more equitable international economic system.[58]

The adverse effects of the underdeveloped countries' trade with the industrialized states were said to have been intensified by a number of recent developments: the rampant "stagflation" in the industrialized countries, the monetary crisis and dollar devaluation, and the arbitrary practices of shipping cartels that repeatedly raised freight rates.[59] Indonesia, of course, was a beneficiary of the 1973–1974 energy crisis, with the export price of Indonesian crude oil rising from $2.96 a barrel in January 1973 to $12.60 a barrel by July 1974. But the energy crisis convinced some observers of the inevitability of an eventual collision between the industrialized and the underdeveloped states over scarce natural resources, which the latter need for their own industrialization.[60] Furthermore, Foreign Minister Malik was among those who expressed doubt as to how long the inflated oil prices would last.

56. See "Kecenderungan-kecenderungan," pp. 14–17.

57. *Ibid.*, p. 22.

58. *Angkatan Bersenjata,* 10 April 1974.

59. See *Monthly Review* (April 1972), p. 5; Thee Kian Wie's remarks in *Politik Luar Negeri Indonesia Dewasa Ini,* p. 34; *Indonesia Raya,* 31 March 1973, which ridicules Professor Paul Samuelson's suggestion that the devaluation of the U.S. dollar would benefit the less developed countries; *Nusantara,* 13 June 1973; and *Kompas,* 24 July 1973.

60. Mochtar Lubis in *Indonesia Raya,* 17 July 1973.

Malik also noted that the energy crisis had had a number of negative effects on Indonesia, including a quadrupling of the prices of such vital imported commodities as cement and fertilizer. Moreover, since so much of Indonesia's crude oil is refined abroad, the Indonesians have had to pay highly inflated prices for imported petroleum products.[61] By mid-1975 it was estimated that the soaring cost of imports had reduced the real increment to per capita GNP resulting from the oil price rise from \$20 to \$6.[62] And because of declining demand in the industrialized economies, Indonesia's traditional exports, some of which are the product of relatively labor-intensive smallholder activity, fell in value by 41 percent from mid-1974 to early 1975.[63]

The recent efforts of third world nations to bring about a New International Economic Order, linking the question of oil prices with the prices of other raw materials and manufactured products, have presumably made the Indonesian leaders even more conscious of the confrontative relationship between rich and poor countries. A leading newsmagazine observed in 1975 that the NEFOS-OLDEFOS concept might have sounded "empty and arrogant" when Sukarno advanced it a decade earlier, but now it seemed to have been merely premature. The struggle of third world countries to change the structure of international trade, led since 1973 by the Organization of Petroleum Exporting Countries (OPEC), was cited as evidence that the NEFOS-OLDEFOS concept had become a reality.[64]

If there was wide agreement on the existence of a conflict between the NEFOS and the OLDEFOS, there was more limited acceptance of Sukarno's recommendation that the former unite in struggling to overcome the forces of exploitation. Slightly more than half, including some leading technocrats, agreed with Sukarno that the NEFOS must join in actively confronting the OLDEFOS, though

61. See the interview with Malik in *Far Eastern Economic Review,* 18 March 1974.

62. *Bulletin of Indonesian Economic Studies,* 11 (July 1975), 9–10.

63. *Ibid.,* 11 (March 1975), 2.

64. *Tempo,* 18 January 1975.

few would employ his uncompromisingly anti-imperialist rhetoric. As a PSI leader maintained: "It is a struggle—the poor countries must try to unite to force the rich ones to give them better terms. It is a mistake to expect, as we did in the UNCTAD meetings, that the rich will make concessions voluntarily." The NEFOS must, in the words of an army general, "pool what bargaining power they have as a result of their possession of raw materials and try to better their common lot." The spectacular success of OPEC has encouraged some of the Indonesian leaders to believe that united action can be effective, at least in certain sectors.[65]

Others, however, saw such a struggle as futile. In their view, the poor countries were too weak and disunited to think of imposing any demands on the industrialized nations: "To talk of the NEFOS mobilizing and crushing the OLDEFOS is unrealistic, nonsense." Conscious of the weakness of the NEFOS, most were pessimistic about their chances of bringing about any major changes in the nature of the international system, though they undoubtedly saw their bargaining position as having been strengthened by the natural resource shortages of 1973–1974. More than half indicated a belief that the gap between the rich and the poor nations was growing wider. As an army general asserted: "The rich get richer, and the poor have more children. The rich nations are moving ahead at 50 kilometers, we are moving at 20—how are we going to catch up? It's impossible." Even the economists responsible for Indonesia's development plan talked not of catching up but merely of trying to move ahead. In preparation for the September 1975 Special UN General Assembly on a New International Economic Order, the Indonesian Research Minister highlighted the widening gap between rich and poor nations, and some newspapers noted the continued reluctance of the industrialized nations, led by the United States, to permit any structural change to the advantage of the underdeveloped countries.[66]

For some members of the foreign policy elite, pessimism bordered on despair: "We are so weak that it is unrealistic to talk about a

65. For example, see *Angkatan Bersenjata,* 10 April 1974.

66. See *Kompas,* 21 August 1975; *Sinar Harapan,* 2 September 1975; and *Merdeka,* 3 September 1975.

conflict between the poor and rich. . . . There is a good chance that the industrialized countries will simply decide to ignore the poor countries, to let us stew in our own juices. Perhaps the prediction of Marx will come true—we will just wither away, cease to exist." Washington's mid-1970 announcement of plans to release rubber and tin from its stockpiles evoked a rare public expression of despair from a newspaper representing the anti-Sukarno 1966 Generation students: "It is truly dishonorable to rely on the pity of others. To form a bloc to challenge the strong countries is not quite realistic. . . . This helplessness is bitter indeed. It often stirs radical-revolutionary thinking in us, for what use is the slogan 'stability and security and peace in Southeast Asia' when we are being treated arbitrarily. . . . People are tired of begging."[67]

But many leaders, especially those with direct responsibility for the making and implementation of policies, felt that they simply could not afford to be pessimistic. To assume that no compromise was possible would be self-destructive, they felt. Though it was valid, as a Christian leader maintained, to say that the world must be changed before nations like Indonesia can develop, it was also necessary "to realize pragmatically that we are too weak—we will fail—and thus we must try to work with elements in the advanced countries that are sympathetic." The outlook was not promising, but the attempt had to be made, he contended. An economic official, noting the futility of talk about confronting the advanced countries, concluded: "The only thing for us to do is to try to work out compromises in a businesslike way with the advanced countries. For example, if the Common Market countries want to have high tariffs, then we say, all right, but then you should give us aid in such and such a form."

The few who completely rejected the NEFOS-OLDEFOS concept emphasized a number of other points, most of which also figured to some degree in the thinking of all the leaders. Several dismissed the whole idea as meaningless Sukarno propaganda, contrived by the former President because he needed some concept to

67. *Harian Kami,* 17 July 1970.

call his own. Others found the idea repugnant because they regarded it as a Marxist conception likely to lead Indonesia into an overly close association with the Communist powers. A movement on the part of the less developed countries to confront the industrialized nations would, they suggested, naturally lead to alignment with Peking as the leader of the NEFOS. Others dissented from what they saw as the Marxist perspective that economic differences necessarily mean conflict; they argued that it was possible to have parallel development.

The most widespread objection to the NEFOS-OLDEFOS idea was the belief that the advanced nations were in fact becoming increasingly aware that it is in their interests to foster development in countries like Indonesia. Army generals, technocrats, PSI leaders, and Islamic leaders cited the Pearson Report[68] and the increasingly prominent role of organizations like the World Bank as "encouraging signs." Some of the rich nations were coming to realize, it was said, that a developed, prosperous Indonesia would be a better market for their products than one in which buying power remained low. There might be some shortsighted people who refused to give the less developed countries fair terms because of their own short-term economic interests, a foreign ministry official noted, but that did not mean the relationship as a whole was unalterably confrontative.

These criticisms of the NEFOS-OLDEFOS concept, however, represented a minority viewpoint. Like the minority views on Vietnam and the Cold War, they remind us of the ambivalence and inconsistency found in the foreign policy elite's view of the world.

For the leaders as a whole, the NEFOS-OLDEFOS dichotomy remained an accurate description of international realities. Ambivalent though they were, most of the Indonesian leaders did see world politics in the 1970s as characterized by unremitting, if increasingly subtle, efforts by the powerful nations to subjugate and exploit the weak.

68. Lester B. Pearson, *Partners in Development: Report of the Commission on International Development* (New York: Praeger, 1969).

5 | The Meaning of an Independent Foreign Policy

Ever since the revolution, Indonesian governments have declared their intention to pursue an "independent and active" foreign policy. That formulation has become a basic referent in discussing the problem of relations with the big powers. In fact, it has come to be regarded as the unchallengeable doctrinal basis of Indonesian foreign policy.

This status has, however, been achieved largely at the expense of a clear understanding of its meaning. The independent-and-active policy has, in fact, survived because it has proved amenable to frequent redefinition. Nevertheless, all of the definitions have in some measure reflected the basic assumptions of a hostile world view. Though some definitions go much farther than others toward accepting a reliance on "friends," the independent-and-active policy, however it is defined, warns as much of the dangers of domination by potential allies as of the threat emanating from those seen as likely enemies.

Evolution of the Independent-and-Active Policy

The independent-and-active policy customarily is traced to the preamble of the 1945 constitution, which committed the new Indonesian republic to work for the abolition of colonialism and the creation of a new world order based on independence, peace, and social justice. As Cold War alignments developed in the ensuing years, this obligation was supplemented by an understanding that Indonesia would remain independent of the competing blocs. A government statement in September 1948 declared the country's determination to set its own course on international issues, rather than become an "object in the international political struggle."[1] Indonesia's disappointment with both the United States and the Soviet Union during the course of the revolution considerably strengthened this conviction.

Succeeding cabinets through the early 1950s developed and reiterated the following understanding of the independent-and-active policy: Jakarta would avoid tying itself to either Cold War bloc, but such a policy could not be considered "neutral" because Indonesia was working actively for world peace and the relaxation of international tensions.[2] Though its foreign relations were almost exclusively with the Western countries, Jakarta resisted pressures to back the United States in the Korean war, and the Indonesian parliament refused to approve the American-drafted Japanese Peace Treaty on the grounds that this might be interpreted as aligning Indonesia with the United States.

The sharpest definition of the policy in the early 1950s did not come from government declarations, though. It came from the violent public reaction in 1952 to American conditions for aid under the U.S. Mutual Security Act. When it became publicly known that Foreign Minister Subardjo had won an economic aid commitment by promising the American ambassador that Indonesia would make a contribution to the defense of the "free world," a storm of protest erupted, and the Sukiman cabinet fell. Henceforth, it was universally understood that the independent-and-active policy required that the government refrain from entering into any international agreements which would have the effect of committing Indonesia to one of the Cold War protagonists.

In the middle 1950s, during the tenure of the two cabinets of Ali

1. Quoted in J. M. Anton Soewarso, *Politik Bebas-Aktif: Mashab-Pemikiran Nasional Jang Historis dan Moral Filosofis* (Jakarta: Departemen Luar Negeri, 1969), p. 12.

2. For statements of the Natsir, Sukiman, and Wilopo cabinets, see *ibid.*, pp. 12–13. See also *Menudju Kemakmuran Rakjat lewat Keamanan: Keterangan Pemerintah atas Program Kabinet Soekiman* (Jakarta: Kementerian Penerangan, 1951), pp. 33–34, and Mohammad Hatta, "Indonesia's Foreign Policy," *Foreign Affairs,* 31 (April 1953), 441–52.

Sastroamidjojo, the original definition of the independent-and-active policy was broadened. Whereas the previous cabinets had followed an essentially pro-Western policy while avoiding actions that would constitute a formal commitment to the West, Ali proceeded on the assumption that an independent foreign policy involved not merely staying out of a pact but also creating a reasonable balance in Indonesia's relations with the two blocs. In December 1953 he negotiated Indonesia's first trade agreement with China, followed by a Dual Nationality Treaty in 1955. In 1954 he established diplomatic relations with the Soviet Union and several other Communist countries, describing those initiatives as proof that Indonesia's foreign policy was, at last, truly independent.[3]

If an independent policy was seen as requiring at least some effort toward balancing Indonesia's relations with the blocs, an active policy was understood as one marked by vigorous steps to oppose the remnants of colonialism, both in Indonesia and elsewhere. This required that the government "do everything to achieve as quickly as possible the same degree of emancipation as that of other States . . . [so that] the influence which controls the life of the people, especially in the social and economic fields, and is a remnant of the colonial period, will gradually be ended. . . ." Those in other countries who were struggling for their national independence were promised Indonesia's full support, and cooperation among the Asian and African countries was heralded as the appropriate way to work for the abolition of colonialism "in all its forms and manifestations."[4]

Ali's implementation of this more broadly defined independent-and-active policy was at times spectacular. The high point was the staging of an international conference of Asian and African heads of state at Bandung in April 1955. Ali's cabinet was the first to

3. See "Pertanjaan-Pertanjaan Seksi 'J' D.P.R. dan Djawaban-Djawaban Pemerintah (Kemlu)," *Pewarta Kemlu, 1* (June-July 1955), 140.

4. "Government Statement on the Programme of the Second Cabinet of Ali Sastroamidjojo to the House of Representatives at its Opening and Plenary Session on 9th April 1956, Read by Dr. Ali Sastroamidjojo, Prime Minister," *Pewarta Kemlu, 2* (January-April 1956), 31–32.

respond to nationalist feelings on the West Irian issue, and took a number of steps which at least conveyed the impression that something was being done. For the first time the Irian issue was raised in the UN, though even a relatively mild resolution was defeated, which the interviewees blamed on the United States.[5] Ali also associated himself with the mass demonstrations being held in Indonesia; he won the Bandung conference's endorsement of Indonesia's Irian claim; and he oversaw the first attempts at infiltrating troops into West Irian, though the government never admitted responsibility for this.[6] All in all, Ali's initiatives gave evidence that the government was working to reduce Indonesia's dependence on the West by cultivating relations with other power groups.

This increasingly bold approach was extended by Ali's successors. In 1956 the Indonesian government unilaterally abrogated all of the distasteful obligations undertaken in the transfer of sovereignty agreement with the Netherlands. In December 1957, following a third failure to gain UN support on the West Irian question, the Indonesians nationalized all Dutch businesses in the country and evicted all Dutch personnel except "experts." American and British assistance to separatist rebellions on Sumatra and Sulawesi in 1958 added new impetus to the movement toward a more balanced foreign policy. Western involvement in these rebellions was especially important in contributing to the growing feeling among army officers that Indonesia's closeness to the West had compromised the independent-and-active policy.[7]

Sukarno, who emerged after 1956 as Indonesia's principal for-

5. For the best discussion of the Irian problem, see Robert C. Bone, Jr., *The Dynamics of the Western New Guinea (Irian Barat) Problem* (Ithaca: Cornell Modern Indonesia Project, 1958).

6. Feith, *Decline of Constitutional Democracy,* p. 391.

7. See also interviews carried out by the Australian journalist Peter Polomka with what he describes as "a cross-section of army leaders involved in the events of the period." Polomka contends that this was the general view of those with authority; other officers may have pressed much more strongly in that direction, he adds ("The Indonesian Army and Confrontation: An Inquiry into the Functions of Foreign Policy under Guided Democracy" [M.A. thesis, University of Melbourne, 1969], pp. 34–36).

eign policy spokesman, made clear by mid-1960 his determination not to stake Indonesia's claim to West Irian on hopes for "a gift from the imperialists." He broke diplomatic relations with the Netherlands and undertook a substantial military buildup, based mainly on Soviet aid since the United States refused to sell Indonesia the needed equipment. His multifaceted strategy of confrontation also included mass rallies, calls for volunteers, and limited landings of Indonesian forces in West Irian. At the same time, however, diplomatic efforts continued: if the main emphasis of the Irian campaign was on Indonesia's willingness to mobilize its own resources to drive out the Dutch, another important component was the hope that the threat of armed conflict would spur American intervention on Indonesia's behalf.

That threat worked. The United States finally abandoned its "pro-Dutch neutrality" and in August 1962 pressed the Dutch to settle the dispute on terms advantageous to Indonesia. Though Washington gained considerable goodwill by its last minute assistance, the Irian victory was generally seen as a triumph for Sukarno's strategy of confrontation, not as a vindication of reliance on the West, nor for that matter on the Soviet Union.

By the start of the 1960s, the independent-and-active policy had been redefined still more broadly. In a 1958 article, Hatta had written that an independent foreign policy meant being "free from the influences of either the United States bloc or the Communist bloc, whether the influence be of capital or of ideology." While he asserted that Indonesia would develop relations with "the other nations of the East" because it was "fed up with the policies of the West," Hatta stressed that the policy forbid Indonesia from "drawing too close to one bloc at the expense of another."[8] In his 1960 Independence Day address, Sukarno clearly extended the idea of balance to economic relations: the independent-and-active policy had to be "step-by-step reflected in foreign *economic* relations, so that they do not lean to the West or to the East."[9]

8. "Indonesia between the Power Blocs," pp. 564, 568.
9. *"Laksana Malaekat Jang Menjerbu Dari Langit" Djalannja Revolusi*

Though economic relations with the Communist countries were intensified in the ensuing years, Indonesia's economy nevertheless continued to "lean" toward the West. (See the trade statistics in Appendix D.) By 1965, however, the definition of independence in foreign policy had gone beyond balance to a somewhat equivocal call for economic self-reliance, rejecting any "dependence on imperialism." Economic independence was said to be "the prerequisite for real independence in political and cultural affairs." The doctrine of self-reliance was characterized as the highest realization, the "summit," of an independent foreign policy.[10]

An active foreign policy now was understood to mean that Indonesia should take a leading role in bringing together the "progressive forces of the world in an international front for independence and peace in opposition to imperialism-colonialism."[11] Whereas in the 1950s foreign policy had been "independent and active, based on national interests and aimed at world peace," in the 1960s the customary formulation was "independent and active, anti-imperialism and colonialism . . . aimed at promoting the interrelated struggles to win full independence for Indonesia, national independence for all the peoples of the world, and world peace."[12]

Kita—The March of Our Revolution (Jakarta: Departemen Penerangan, 1960), p. 41. Italics in the original.

10. See Sukarno's 1965 Independence Day address, *Reach to the Stars! A Year of Self-Reliance* (Jakarta: Department of Information, 1965), p. 39; Sukarno, *After Ten Years, Still Onward, Never Retreat* (Jakarta: Department of Information, 1965), excerpted in Feith and Castles, eds., *Indonesian Political Thinking,* pp. 468–69; and *20 Tahun Indonesia Merdeka* (Jakarta: Departemen Penerangan, 1965), p. 8.

11. *Bahan-Bahan Pokok Indoktrinasi,* p. 653. On the leading role, see *Amanat Presiden Sukarno Pada Musjawarah Dinas Menteri Dalam Negeri dan Otonomi Daerah Dengan Para Gubernur Pada Tanggal 28 Djuni 1960* (Jakarta: Departemen Penerangan, 1960), p. 18, and *Amanat Presiden Sukarno Pada Konperensi Para Panglima Kodam Seluruh Indonesia* (Jakarta: Departemen Penerangan, 1964), p. 12. Sukarno spoke of this role as one of initiating ideas, but others went further. See, for example, the statement of the army commander, Lieutenant General Yani, that the "Indonesian armed forces feel they have the right to take responsibility for security . . . in Southeast Asia," reported in *Risalah Kronologi,* 5 (January 1965), 15.

12. For an example of the 1950s formulation, see then Foreign Minister

The advance to self-reliance and the leadership of an anti-imperialist international front was a logical outgrowth of Sukarno's post-1961 position that the key division in the world was not the Cold War but the conflict between NEFOS and OLDEFOS. According to Sukarno, imperialism still posed a serious threat to an Indonesia surrounded by hostile Western bases and exploitative economic interests. Independence in foreign policy, said Sukarno, did indeed mean not taking sides in the Cold War, but it also meant "firmly choosing the side of the progressive, anti-imperialist, anti-colonialist, anti-neocolonialist forces" in the more important NEFOS-OLDEFOS struggle.[13] One expression of this alignment, Sukarno declared in 1965, was an "anti-imperialist axis" of Jakarta, Phnom Penh, Hanoi, Peking, and Pyongyang, an axis "formed by the course of history itself."[14] Because the NEFOS were by definition opposed to exploitation, siding with them was seen not as a violation of the independent policy, but on the contrary as the only way to be truly independent. A policy that forced Indonesia to remain neutral in the struggle between NEFOS and OLDEFOS would mean acceptance of the exploitative status quo.

The most concrete expression of both the high priority attached to this alignment and the belief that it sometimes required militant action was the confrontation with Malaysia from 1963 to 1966. There had been virtually no public comment in Indonesia about the plan to unite the three British Borneo territories of Sarawak, Brunei, and North Borneo with Singapore and Malaya until an anti-Malaysia revolt broke out in Brunei in December 1962.[15] Given

---

H. Roeslan Abdulgani's "Perkembangan Politik Luar Negeri Indonesia Dalam Tahun 1956," *Pewarta Kemlu,* 2 (December 1956), 766. For the 1960s, see *Bahan-Bahan Pokok Indoktrinasi,* pp. 617–25.

13. *20 Tahun Indonesia Merdeka,* pp. 6–7. See also Sukarno's speech at the September 1961 nonaligned summit meeting, published as *From Non-Alignment to Coordinated Accumulation of Moral Force Toward Friendship, Peace, and Social Justice Among Nations* (Jakarta: Department of Information, 1961), and his *Conefo: Suatu Nasakom Internasional* (Jakarta: Departemen Penerangan, 1965), pp. 17–18.

14. *Reach to the Stars,* p. 16.

15. Apart from sporadic PKI criticism as early as December 1961, there had been only two rather vague public expressions of Indonesia's concern—

their talk of leading a worldwide anti-imperialist front, however, the Indonesian leaders could hardly fail to support what appeared to be an independence struggle taking place on their doorstep.

In the ensuing months, the Federation of Malaysia was said to pose a threat to Indonesia's own independence as well. Support for the struggle of the Borneo peoples against British colonialism escalated to a crusade against the Malaysia concept, which was now characterized as a scheme to perpetuate British domination, protect the "lifeline of imperialism," and ultimately prevent the normal extension of Indonesian influence in the region.[16] That British bases in Southeast Asia were a real threat to Indonesia's independence was clear enough to army generals who recalled the use of those bases to support the Sumatra and Sulawesi rebellions in 1958.[17] Army leaders also feared that the Chinese of Singapore and Malaya would eventually dominate the whole federation, thus leaving Indonesia even more vulnerable to subversion via its overseas Chinese population.[18]

Reports of American pressure on Jakarta to abandon the con-

---

the first by PNI General Chairman Ali Sastroamidjojo in September 1962 and the other by Foreign Minister Subandrio later the same month. Ali recalls that neither he nor Sukarno was really concerned about Malaysia before the Brunei revolt (interview with Ali Sastroamidjojo, Jakarta, 16 August 1969). That the rebels did, however, have extensive contacts with Indonesian army officers and foreign ministry officials even before the rebellions started was confirmed in a written interview with General Nasution (Jakarta, 11 March 1970) and in an interview with a top foreign ministry official of the confrontation period. For details, see Weinstein, "The Uses of Foreign Policy in Indonesia," p. 583. There is even some evidence that Indonesian army officers were training the rebels before December 1962. See Bunnell, "The Kennedy Initiatives in Indonesia," p. 230.

16. Typical were the comments of NU leader Djamaluddin Malik: "The British wanted to encircle and isolate Indonesia—to make us economically dependent on areas controlled by them" (interview, Jakarta, 10 September 1969).

17. Written interview with General Nasution, Jakarta, 11 March 1970. The same point was emphasized by an American army source close to a number of the Indonesian generals.

18. See Kahin, "Malaysia and Indonesia," p. 264, and Mohammad Hatta, "One Indonesian View of the Malaysia Issue," *Asian Survey,* 5 (March 1965).

frontation policy or face a loss of economic aid introduced the issue of independence in an even more direct way. It now became difficult to back away from confrontation without appearing to yield to foreign pressure. Nonetheless, an agreement in the summer of 1963 among all the parties concerned made the fate of Malaysia dependent on the results of a UN survey of popular desires in the British Borneo territories. The British and Malayans, however, subsequently announced that Malaysia would be formed on schedule regardless of the outcome of the UN survey. The Indonesians, already offended by the failure of the British to consult Jakarta before proceeding with the original plan, viewed this "premature announcement" as confirmation of Britain's contempt for the right of a truly independent Indonesia to be dealt with as a regional power.

Finally, the issue of independence surfaced in another form after the federation had come into being when Jakarta declared a trade embargo. This move considerably strengthened the independence appeal of the "Crush Malaysia" campaign, for dependence on Singapore as an entrepôt had long been bitterly resented. Not only did several generals recall that the army leadership had viewed the embargo as an essential step "to complete our independence." Even several technocrats whose primary concern had been with economic stabilization had supported the measure. As one summed it up:

> The cutting of trade relations with Singapore must be seen in longer historical perspective. Practically everyone was unhappy about the relationship with Singapore—even people like Sumitro. They were getting the profits from the labors of Indonesians, because they were sharper traders. There was virtually no opposition whatsoever to the cutting of trade relations. The traders were not especially happy, but even our economists, like Widjojo and Sadli, did not speak a word of opposition. I think they all favored the move. The same is true of other aspects of economic confrontation—such as making Sabang a free port. Economic confrontation as a whole was very widely supported—if people are honest, they will not deny this. When people say that confrontation was very damaging to the economy, they mean first the heavy military expenditures which caused inflation and second that it cut off the possibility of foreign aid. It may be that the short-run effects of cutting of

trade with Singapore were damaging, but I think it may well be in our own long-run interests to break the ties to Singapore and develop our own Singapore in Jakarta.

In any case, there ensued a full-scale Crush Malaysia campaign, consisting of an intensive domestic propaganda effort to "mobilize" the populace, a series of diplomatic and economic moves, a military buildup accompanied by sporadic raids across the border in Borneo, and after September 1964 occasional paratrooper drops on the Malay peninsula.[19] The culmination came after Malaysia was seated in the UN Security Council. In January 1965 Sukarno denounced the UN as imperialist-dominated and announced Indonesia's withdrawal from the organization.[20] He declared his intention to set up a rival Conference of the New Emerging Forces (CONEFO), with its headquarters in Jakarta.

Since the shift of power from Sukarno to Soeharto in March 1966, the definition of the independent-and-active policy has clearly changed, but public statements offer few reliable clues as to the policy's real meaning under the New Order. There has been a curious attempt to create a compromise version by combining formulations from all the previous periods in such a way as to justify the course which Soeharto has chosen to pursue. The ambiguity has been heightened by attaching new interpretations to old phrases, and by suggesting a need for flexibility and realism. The New Order has sought, through this redefinition, to demonstrate continuity with the past, while making clear the need to correct the Old Order's "deviations" from Indonesia's traditional policy.

The basic statement of the New Order's view of the independent-and-active policy is found in the foreign policy pronouncements of the MPRS (Provisional People's Consultative Congress) that met

19. General Nasution proposed moving even more strongly by "closing Singapore with modern weapons, in which case it could be hit at any time from our positions surrounding it" (written interview, Jakarta, 11 March 1970).

20. Sukarno's criticism of big-power domination of the UN antedated the Malaysia problem, however. His views were sharply expressed in his 1960 speech to the UN General Assembly.

in June and July 1966. Sometimes using language not markedly different from that of the Sukarno years, the MPRS strongly reaffirmed its vigorous opposition to imperialism and colonialism and pressed for continued efforts to foster Asian-African solidarity. Self-reliance was said to be "a good principle, in particular for longer-term national interests." Dependence on any state was ruled out, especially in economic relations, which must be conducted so as not to infringe on national sovereignty.[21]

Elsewhere, however, the MPRS offered a definition of the independent-and-active policy that seemed to return to the narrower "no pacts" interpretation of the early 1950s. Moreover, the MPRS asserted that the implementation of foreign policy should show "flexibility" so that it served the national interest, "especially giving priority to the People's economic interest." The early statements Adam Malik made as Foreign Minister also left the impression that the independent-and-active policy would not be permitted to interfere with the government's efforts to attract economic aid and investment capital from the West.[22]

The new "flexibility" soon found expression in foreign policy initiatives. By August 1966 the confrontation with Malaysia had been abandoned. In September Indonesia returned to the UN and the CONEFO project was dropped. The same month Indonesia's Western creditor nations met in Tokyo to discuss the rescheduling of Jakarta's debts and the establishment of new arrangements for channeling aid to Indonesia. Relations with the Soviet Union grew cool; by late 1967 diplomatic relations with China were suspended.

The understanding of foreign policy set forth in the MPRS decisions of 1966 has been further developed through speeches and

21. "Note No. 1/MPRS/1966," in *Indonesia's Foreign Policy as Based on the Pantja Sila Principles* (Jakarta: Department of Information, 1966), pp. 23–24, 26, 29–31.

22. *Ibid.,* pp. 24, 27; "Statement of Foreign Policy by the Minister of Foreign Affairs H. E. Adam Malik on April 4, 1966," in *ibid.,* pp. 3–5; and *Keterangan Wakil Perdana Menteri Bidang Sosial Politik/Menteri Luar Negeri Didepan Sidang DPR-GR* (Jakarta: Kementerian Penerangan, 1966), pp. 3–4.

statements in the years since then, but the essential ambiguity has remained. It is clear, though, that the New Order version has rejected several key features of Sukarno's foreign policy. A central theme has been that Sukarno had an exaggerated view of what it meant to be independent and active, with the result that Indonesia's national interests suffered. For example, Sukarno was said to have isolated Jakarta from all but the Chinese; bringing the country into an "axis" with Peking violated a central tenet of the independent policy and made Indonesia the instrument of an outside power.[23] His attempt to make Indonesia a "beacon" for other countries in the struggle against imperialism was sharply criticized as arrogant and unrealistic; he was accused of having squandered scarce resources in exchange for meaningless prestige.[24]

The Soeharto government has repeatedly asserted that the principal duty of foreign policy is to serve the country's economic needs, and policy pronouncements have continued to exalt realism, pragmatism, and flexibility.[25] Government spokesmen have tended to

23. See *Angkatan Bersendjata,* 29 July 1966, 13 April 1967; *Kompas,* 5 September 1966, 8 November 1966; and Soeharto's remarks in *Himpunan Uraian Ketua Presidium dan Para Menutama Kabinet Ampera* (Jakarta: Departemen Penerangan, 1966), p. 16, his *Pidato Kenegaraan* (Jakarta: P.N. Penerbit Pradnja Paramita, 1967), p. 41, and his *Briefing Pedjabat Presiden Republik Indonesia di Bali dan Nusa Tenggara* (Jakarta: Departemen Penerangan, 1968), p. 17.

24. Criticism was directed against such practices as paying transportation and lodging costs of foreign delegations to Jakarta-sponsored meetings. See, for example, *Business News,* 6 April 1966. For general criticism of the "beaconship" policy, and the counterargument that Indonesia should not seek a leading role in international affairs, see Soeharto's *Laporan Pemerintah Kepada Rakjat Bertepatan Dengan Berachirnja Tahun 1966 dan Tahap Penjelamatan* (Jakarta: Departemen Penerangan, 1967), p. 18, and his *Briefing Pedjabat Presiden,* p. 17; Soedjatmoko, "Sikap Nasional dan Hubungan Luar Negeri," *Pewarta & Kronologi Bulanan,* 1 (April 1968), 42–43; and Malik's statements in "Politik Luar Negeri Indonesia Tetap Bebas dan Aktif," *Risalah Kronologi dan Dokumentasi* (June 1969), p. 19; in *Dasar-dasar Pegangan,* pp. 28–29; and in *Djakarta Times,* 7 January 1970.

25. See *Business News,* 6 April 1966, 27 July 1966; the statements by Soeharto and Malik in *Himpunan Uraian,* pp. 16, 29, 38–39; Soeharto's 1967 *Pidato Kenegaraan,* pp. 33–34; his *Pidato Kenegaraan Presiden Republik Indonesia Djenderal Soeharto Didepan Sidang DPR-GR 16 Agustus*

hold to the narrow "no pacts" definition of independence.[26] Though there have been some moves toward a revitalization of Indonesia's relations with the Communist countries, progress has been modest.[27] In fact, dependence on the West has grown heavier with each year's commitment of aid and investment. While there has been no talk of military ties to the Western powers, the government has on several occasions raised suspicions that it might be moving toward acceptance of an anti-Communist pact limited to Southeast Asian

---

1968 (Jakarta: Departemen Penerangan, 1968), p. 54; and his reported advice to Indonesian ambassadors "to seek as much foreign aid as possible," in *Pedoman,* 28 August 1969. See also Soedjatmoko, "Sikap Nasional," especially pp. 40–43, and Malik's remarks in *Dasar-dasar Pegangan,* pp. 27–29; in *Djakarta Times,* 4 January 1969, 7 January 1970; in *Research Landasan,* 5 (January-June 1971), 6; and in "Indonesia's Foreign Policy," *Indonesian Quarterly,* 1 (October 1972), 28.

26. See Soeharto's 1967 *Pidato Kenegaraan,* p. 34, his *Briefing Pedjabat Presiden,* p. 17, and his February 1972 remarks in *Research Landasan,* vol. 7, pt. 1, p. 8; Malik's "Politik Luar Negeri Indonesia," p. 18; *Program Karya Pembangunan dalam D.P.R.G.R.* (Bandung: Pertj. "Bandung" P.T., 1969), pp. 15–17; *Kompas,* 11 June 1970; and *Berita Buana,* 8 May 1973, 6 July 1973.

27. According to high-ranking Indonesian and American sources, Jakarta's first move toward improved relations with the Soviets in 1969 came only after American officials encouraged it. In August 1970 a debt renegotiation agreement was signed with the USSR, and the next year the Indonesians held discussions with Moscow about the feasibility of resuming certain aid projects (*New York Times,* 25 August 1971). Key army and foreign ministry sources, however, indicated in 1973 that there had been little progress, owing mainly to Moscow's unwillingness to meet Jakarta's economic terms and to Soviet criticism of Indonesia's treatment of political prisoners. But by 1974 the non-Communist donor nations had toughened their own loan conditions in view of Indonesia's oil bonanza, so that the terms of Communist aid became acceptable (*Kompas,* 1 July 1974). Agreement was reached with the Soviets for aid to several projects, particularly in the fields of electricity and mining. Loans were sought from East European countries, and an agreement was concluded with Yugoslavia (*Indonesian Perspectives* [February 1975], p. 13; *Bulletin of Indonesian Economic Studies* [March 1975], p. 26). Also, by 1975 the Indonesians had agreed to purchase rice from North Korea, trade agreements had been signed with the Soviet Union and Poland, and Malik had made it clear that Indonesia was seeking to expand further its trade with the Communists (*Merdeka,* 12 July 1974; *Kompas,* 1 and 26 July 1974; *Indonesian Perspectives* [January 1975], p. 34).

nations.[28] Official spokesmen, though, have always been quick to distinguish between the kind of regional military cooperation they support and collaboration involving pacts or commitments.[29]

Like its version of independence, the Soeharto government's conception of an active foreign policy continues to have a good deal in common with the relatively narrow definition of the early 1950s. Where Sukarno sought to organize an anti-imperialist front, New Order spokesmen have suggested that fellow "moderates" join with Indonesia in reformulating nonalignment so as to de-emphasize "political" and confrontative or "anti" aspects of the movement, stressing instead the need for cooperation to secure peace and raise living standards.[30] In fact, Indonesia's status as a nonaligned country has come into question, particularly after the walkout of Ja-

28. The subject was raised initially by then deputy army commander Lieutenant General Panggabean, who reportedly said in December 1966 that a "joint defense organization" was needed to meet the threat of Chinese Communist expansionism (*Antara,* 25 December 1966). An Islamic party leader, a PNI parliamentary figure, and two army generals soon announced their agreement (*Antara,* 30 December 1966, 1 January 1967, 17 February 1967). See also *Angkatan Bersendjata,* 8 June 1967, 10 February 1968; *El Bahar,* 4 August 1967; *Duta Masjarakat,* 26 August 1967; *Harian Kami,* 19 February 1968; *Suluh Marhaen,* 10 February 1968; *Berita Yudha,* 4 March 1968, 20 November 1969; *Antara,* 25 April 1969; and *Kompas,* 28 January 1971. For additional discussion, see Weinstein, "Uses of Foreign Policy," pp. 333–34.

29. Acceptable forms of military cooperation included: training exercises; joint border operations, such as those along the Indonesian-Malaysian frontier in Kalimantan; cooperative efforts to combat smuggling; exchange of students and intelligence; and joint strategic planning without any commitments. See especially the interview with Panggabean in *Kompas,* 19 January 1967. Also consult *Angkatan Bersendjata,* 20 February 1967, 5 March 1968; *Berita Yudha,* 9 January 1967, 20 November 1969, 22 November 1969; *Sinar Harapan,* 19 January 1968; *Antara,* 7 February 1968; *Suluh Marhaen,* 27 February 1968; *Pewarta & Kronologi Bulanan,* 1 (February 1968), 24–26; *Kompas,* 7 and 18 March 1968; *Indonesian Observer,* 17 March 1969; Soeharto's *Pidato Kenegaraan* (Jakarta: Departemen Penerangan, 1969), p. 38; *Nusantara,* 24 June 1970; *Abadi,* 10 March 1971; *Research Landasan,* vol. 5, pp. 16–18; *Monthly Review* (April 1972), pp. 3–4; and *Berita Buana,* 25 April 1975. For elaboration, see Weinstein, "Uses of Foreign Policy," pp. 334–35.

30. See "Kecenderungan-kecenderungan," pp. 25–28; *Kompas,* 27 June 1973; and *Berita Buana,* 6 July 1973.

karta's delegation from the 1972 Conference of Nonaligned Foreign Ministers.[31] With its ardor for the nonaligned movement flagging, the government has sought to foster regional cooperation, primarily through the Association of Southeast Asian Nations (ASEAN) formed in 1967.

Though the New Order has seemed to break with Sukarno in its understanding of the independent-and-active policy, it has nevertheless retained some of the interpretations advanced in the late 1950s and early 1960s. There have been numerous indications that the broader "balanced relationships" definition still commands substantial support.[32] On occasion, not only balance but self-reliance has been held indispensable to a truly independent policy.[33] The key to the defense of Indonesia's independence, according to Soeharto, is the country's "national resilience," a concept he defined as the "ideological, socioeconomic, political, and military strength that together constitute a nation's real capacity . . . to resist" subversion or exploitation.[34]

31. See *Kompas,* 2 July 1973, and Juwono Sudarsono's remarks in *Politik Luar Negeri Indonesia Dewasa Ini,* p. 14. On the walkout, see *Monthly Review* (August-September 1972), pp. 6–9. Indonesia's coolness toward the nonaligned movement was also evident in Soeharto's failure to head the Indonesian delegation to the Nonaligned Summit Conference held in Algiers in September 1973.

32. Some Indonesians insisted that a genuinely independent policy required strengthening economic relations with the Communist countries so as to reduce dependence on the West. See *Harian Kami,* 28 September 1968, 2 September 1970; *Suluh Marhaen,* 27 January 1969; *Angkatan Bersendjata,* 7 February 1969, 28 June 1974; *Dwiwarna,* 23 February 1969; *Merdeka,* 23 February 1971, 24 May 1973, 5 and 26 July 1974; and *Kompas,* 26 July 1974. Others spoke of using China to counter Japan (*Merdeka,* 23 April 1971) and using relations with Western Europe to reduce dependence on the United States and Japan (*Kompas,* 8 September 1970, and Soeharto's comments reported in *Pedoman,* 3 October 1973). Malik himself did not deny the inconsistency between an independent policy and Indonesia's heavy reliance on Western economic aid; he simply argued that Indonesia had no choice (*Himpunan Uraian,* pp. 38–39, and *Antara,* 7 June 1969). See also *Pedoman,* 4 January 1969, and General Nasution's statements cited in *Angkatan Bersendjata,* 7 and 10 February 1969.

33. For example, Sayidiman, "Defence of Indonesia," p. 238.

34. Malik, "Indonesia's Foreign Policy," p. 29. For additional remarks by

In addition, the Indonesian leaders have periodically reaffirmed the need for continued opposition to imperialism, though these assertions have grown less frequent.[35] And while the meaning of imperialism has been altered somewhat by the occasional reminder that it comes not only from the West but from the Communist powers as well, Soeharto's definition of imperialism has perhaps been closer to Sukarno's than one might have expected. Soeharto described imperialism as "teachings or practices or intentions in any form on the part of one state . . . to dominate or exploit another state . . . merely for its own interests."[36] On the occasion of the twentieth anniversary of the Bandung conference in 1975, Soeharto restated what he saw as Bandung's essential truth—the need to create a world free from the interference of the big powers in the affairs of weaker nations. Even regional cooperation has sometimes been described as part of the struggle to ward off big power intervention in Southeast Asia.[37]

Soeharto and Malik, see *Research Landasan,* vol. 5, pp. 8–9, and vol. 7, pt. 2, p. 28.

35. See the statements by Soeharto in *Laporan Pemerintah Kepada Rakjat,* p. 18; *Konperensi Pers Pd. Presiden Republik Indonesia dengan Wartawan Dalam dan Luar Negeri* (Jakarta: Departemen Penerangan, 1967), p. 12; the 1967 *Pidato Kenegaraan,* pp. 32, 34, 42; *Briefing Pedjabat Presiden,* p. 17; and *Pedoman,* 12 February 1970. For Malik's statements, see *Himpunan Uraian,* pp. 30–32, and *Pewarta & Kronologi Bulanan,* 1 (April 1968), 78. See also *Angkatan Bersendjata,* 29 July 1966; *Berita Yudha,* 25 November 1966 and 3 May 1968; *Dasar-dasar Pegangan,* p. 27; *Merdeka,* 1 August 1970, 1 October 1970, 20 November 1970, 5 December 1970, 15 January 1971; Ali Sastroamidjojo's remarks in *Politik Luar Negeri Indonesia Dewasa Ini,* p. 26; and *Kompas,* 27 June 1973, which argued that anti-imperialism and efforts to raise living standards were just different aspects of the same struggle. The ambiguity of the New Order's commitment to anti-imperialism was evident in the 1973 MPR (People's Consultative Congress) decree on foreign policy (*Indonesian Daily News* [Surabaya], 23 March 1973).

36. *Konperensi Pers,* p. 12. See also *Briefing Pedjabat Presiden,* p. 17. For reminders of Communist imperialism, see *Harian Kami,* 10 August 1966; *Kompas,* 27 September 1966; *Berita Yudha,* 6 March 1968; and *Angkatan Bersendjata,* 13 April 1967, 13 June 1969.

37. See *Himpunan Uraian,* pp. 19, 37; *Kompas,* 9 August 1967, in which Malik asserted that the Southeast Asian nations must "unite to develop [economically] and . . . get rid of negative influences" from outside the re-

Despite warnings against a revival of the "beaconship" policy, there have been frequent expressions of the view that Indonesia should play a leading role in Southeast Asia and among the non-aligned nations in general.[38] Foreign Minister Malik made it clear in 1975 that the independent-and-active policy required efforts by Indonesia to help win economic justice for the third world from the industrialized countries and national independence for the remaining colonial territories in Africa.[39] The passivity of the New Order's foreign policy has in fact been that policy's most common public criticism, perhaps because it is more obvious and less politically sensitive than an alleged lack of independence. As a forum where Indonesia can demonstrate that it has an active foreign policy, ASEAN has proved disappointing. Far from leading the way, the Indonesians were cool, at least initially, toward the chief political initiative to emerge from ASEAN, Malaysia's 1971 proposal for neutralization of the region.[40]

---

gion; and Malik's comments in *Antara,* 25 April 1969. Soeharto's remarks on the meaning of Bandung are reported in *Tempo,* 3 May 1975.

38. See Malik's remarks in *Himpunan Uraian,* pp. 32–34, 38–39; General Panggabean's assertion that Indonesia must be prepared to "maintain peace and stability" in Southeast Asia (*Antara,* 27 February 1967) and a similar argument in *Gotong Rojong,* 24 and 25 May 1967; *Duta Masjarakat,* 23 March 1967, 3 and 13 July 1967, 20 April 1968; *El Bahar,* 4 July 1967; *Harian Kami,* 28 December 1967, 27 June 1973; *Sinar Harapan,* 2 February 1968; *Kompas,* 15 February 1968, 13 July 1970; *Operasi,* 3 January 1969; *Dwiwarna,* 23 February 1969; *Suluh Marhaen,* 8 September 1970; *Research Landasan,* vol. 5, pp. 6–7; and *Indonesia in Regional and International Cooperation: Principles of Implementation and Construction* (Jakarta: Center for Strategic and International Studies, 1973), pp. 9, 11.

39. *Kompas,* 20 June 1975.

40. For Indonesia's initial lack of enthusiasm for the neutralization proposal, see *Neutralization of South-East Asia,* p. 5, and Malik's statement in *Research Landasan,* vol. 6, p. 32. The principal objections were the lack of agreement on the meaning of neutralization and a belief that the weakness of the Southeast Asian states made it premature. Indonesian leaders did, however, urge the big powers to refrain from intervention in the region and affirmed their opposition to foreign military bases, though the countries directly involved were supposed to determine whether existing bases should be abolished (*Kompas,* 19 January 1967, 12 August 1967; *Sinar Harapan,* 11 August 1967; *Antara,* 17 June 1969; and Sayidiman, "Future of Southeast

Elite Views of the Independent-and-Active Policy

If the public discussion of the independent-and-active policy has been marked by inconsistency and ambiguity, the interviews with the foreign policy elite also reflected a good deal of ambivalence. When asked what was the most important foreign policy problem facing Indonesia, the foreign policy elite divided almost evenly between those who felt that foreign aid deserved highest priority and those who considered it more important to preserve a truly independent-and-active foreign policy. Moreover, those closest to power were the most ambivalent. The Islamic and Catholic politicians unanimously agreed on giving priority to aid-seeking efforts, while the PNI and PSI occupied the opposite pole; foreign ministry officials, technocrats, and army leaders were fairly evenly split (see Table 5.1).

But this ambivalence was not matched by any real uncertainty about the basic definition and requirements of a genuinely independent-and-active policy. If pragmatism and realism led the government publicly to lean toward a narrow interpretation of the policy, the leaders interviewed clearly felt closer to the broader and more activist conceptions enunciated in the late 1950s and early 1960s.

An Independent Foreign Policy

Two-thirds of the foreign policy elite, including an overwhelming majority of each of the major groups except the Islamic and Catholic politicians, asserted that the independent-and-active policy

---

Asia," p. 46). Indonesia's attitude toward the neutralization proposal changed after the end of the Indochina war. Malik told the author in September 1975 that Jakarta now supported the proposal and expected an ASEAN summit meeting to give serious consideration to a more detailed version then being drafted. Malik had also indicated that the time had come for Thailand and the Philippines to take over the foreign bases in their countries (*Tempo,* 3 May 1975). Disappointment with ASEAN was evident in *Kebudajaan Melaju dan Peranannja Sebagai Pendukung Konsepsi Ketahanan Regional,* p. 1, and "Indonesia's Foreign Policy," p. 30, where Malik acknowledged that ASEAN's progress was mostly "intangible."

Table 5.1. The most important foreign policy problem

	To get foreign aid	To preserve the independent-and-active policy	Equal emphasis on aid and the independent-and-active policy	Other
All respondents	23 (39%)	22 (37%)	9 (15%)	5 (8%)
1928 Generation	5	2	1	1
1945 Generation	14	17	7	4
1966 Generation	4	3	1	0
PNI	2	7	0	0
PSI	1	3	1	0
Foreign Ministry	2	2	1	3
Army	3	2	3	1
Technocrats	4	2	2	0
Catholic Party	4	0	0	0
Islamic parties	7	0	0	0

required maximum efforts to maintain a balance in Indonesia's relations with the contending power blocs. The remainder were almost evenly divided between those who felt that balanced relationships were desirable but not really important, and those who accepted the narrow "no pacts" definition (see Table 5.2). Most believed that even if Indonesia did not enter a military pact, its independence would be seriously diminished if it moved so close to one of the big powers as to enter its orbit. Indonesia must, in the words of one of Soeharto's army advisers, stay "truly in the middle."

Critics of the government's foreign policy contended that Indonesia had already lost a substantial portion of its sovereignty by leaning too far toward the West. Though some of them acknowledged that Indonesia had little choice because of its need for foreign aid, they were nevertheless deeply disturbed by policies they felt were compromising their country's independence. PSI and PNI leaders were particularly vocal in expressing such feelings. Many were clearly embarrassed when they found that Communist and

Table 5.2. Definition of an independent policy

	Maximum effort to maintain balance in relations with power blocs	Balanced relations desirable but not essential	Just no pacts
All respondents	42 (67%)	11 (17%)	10 (16%)
1928 Generation	4	2	4
1945 Generation	34	7	3
1966 Generation	4	2	3
Technocrats	8	1	0
PNI	8	1	0
Foreign Ministry	7	1	0
PSI	5	1	0
Army	9	2	1
Catholic Party	2	1	1
Islamic parties	1	2	5

nonaligned countries treated Indonesia as a nation that had already entered the Western orbit.[41]

Among army leaders, technocrats, and foreign ministry officials directly responsible for these policies, many admitted being troubled by the imbalance in Indonesia's relations with the major powers. According to a technocrat close to a number of the army leaders, some influential generals privately admitted that Indonesia had gone too far toward the West. The same view was reflected in comments made to the author by army officers, several of whom complained bitterly that Indonesian policymakers felt compelled to consider any prospective policy position in the light of its potential effect on relations with the principal aid-giving countries. An economist recalled a meeting of Indonesian businessmen where one of them sought to dismiss these fears. Though it was "a closed meeting with no need for propaganda sound-offs," virtually every other participant joined in voicing dismay at the prospect of Indonesia's "selling itself to the West."

41. For example, the Indonesian ambassador to North Korea reportedly found himself treated as the representative of a capitalist country and his movement restricted, where once he had been able to move freely.

Moreover, though foreign policy must indeed reflect economic interests, "those are not the only interests we have," asserted a leading economic planner. Several American-trained economists stressed that balanced relations were necessary not merely to avoid excessive foreign influence in policymaking but also to safeguard the country's self-respect, sense of national identity, and international image. Some technocrats even argued that a restoration of relations with the Communist states would probably improve Indonesia's bargaining position with the West, since Jakarta could play the two sides off against one another.

To conceive of an independent and active policy as simply requiring that Indonesia stay out of a pact was to indulge in outmoded thinking, it was argued. Participation in a pact, many leaders observed, was not necessarily an accurate measure of a nation's independence. Pakistan, whose relations with the powers were, at the time of the interviews, more nearly balanced than those of almost any other nation, was repeatedly cited as the best example of a country with an independent foreign policy, despite its membership in a pact.[42] France and Rumania were also mentioned in that category. An economically dependent nation was more surely bound than one which had entered a pact but remained independent economically, argued an eminent Islamic leader.

It was clear, then, that balancing relationships meant improving relations, especially economic ones, with the Communist powers. While few expected that it would be possible to get enough aid from the Communist countries to balance that which came from the West, most considered it important to get as much as possible. Of 56 leaders who discussed the question, 66 percent said it was very important to get such aid, 18 percent considered it desirable but not important, 12 percent said they could "take it or leave it," and 4 percent preferred not to have it at all. Technocrats, PSI leaders, and foreign ministry officials were especially emphatic on

42. This evaluation of Pakistan was also made in a foreign ministry report ("Sekitar Masalah Penjegaran Kembali Kedudukan Non-Alignment," *Research Reconnaissance,* no. 1 [April 1969], p. 16).

the need for aid from the Communists in order to avoid what one technocrat called the "dangerous situation" of total reliance on the West (see Table 5.3).

Table 5.3. Economic aid from Communist countries

	Very important	Desirable	Take it or leave it	Undesirable
All respondents	37 (66%)	10 (18%)	7 (12%)	2 (4%)
1928 Generation	4	2	3	0
1945 Generation	28	7	2	1
1966 Generation	5	1	2	1
PSI	6	0	0	0
Foreign Ministry	7	0	0	0
Technocrats	5	1	0	0
PNI	6	2	0	0
Army	5	2	1	1
Catholic Party	2	0	2	0
Islamic parties	2	2	1	1

The achievement of balanced relationships, however, hinged substantially on a degree of reciprocity from powers over whom Indonesia had little influence. The Indonesians leaned toward the West, a number of leaders contended, not by choice but because the Communists, displeased by Jakarta's domestic politics, were unwilling to have friendly relations with them. "It is not our fault if we are unable to maintain balanced relations," said several leaders, using roughly the same language. "We have opened the door but the Communists have not come in." The important thing, they emphasized, was Indonesia's attitude, which demonstrated its readiness for friendly relations. Most felt that sooner or later the Communist countries would be more approachable because, as one general said, "they don't want Indonesia to move too far to the right." The most that could be done at present was to keep the door open, while trying to avoid excessive dependence on any one or two Western powers by encouraging as many as possible to become active in Indonesia. But for the time being, it was generally agreed, Indonesia would find it hard to create the balance necessary for a truly independent foreign policy. Using a popular, if perplexing, formulation, a number of leaders conceded that for some time Indonesian foreign policy would remain "independent in principle but not in practice."

Those who considered balanced relationships desirable but not essential emphasized a variety of points. An army general asserted that although relations with the Communist powers would be helpful, there was little cause for concern so long as relations with the West were distributed among a number of countries. A Catholic party leader contended that there was no need to try to rectify the existing imbalance, because it would be corrected anyway through the natural course of events. Some found the idea of conscious efforts at balancing relationships repugnant. A PSI member suggested that although aid from the Communist countries was important, the "Sukarno idea of balancing the [American-constructed] Jakarta Bypass with the [Soviet-built] Senayan sports complex reflects a lack of self-confidence." Playing both sides against each other to get more aid was denounced by two 1966 Generation leaders as "immoral, a kind of prostitution," and "a cynical Sukarno device." A foreign ministry official worried that insisting on balanced relationships might mean refusing American aid if it were not matched by assistance from the Communists. In any case, argued a technocrat, the amount and terms of aid were more important than its source.

The few who employed the narrow "no pacts" definition were overridingly anti-Communist and relatively confident that the West had no desire to exploit Indonesia. Several Catholic and Islamic leaders asserted that so long as Indonesia stayed out of a military pact, they did not worry about being totally reliant on the West, because their emotions led them to "feel comfortable" with that bloc. Balanced relationships would be undesirable, it was argued, since closer ties to the Communist powers would only enhance their capacity to bring about a revival of the PKI.

The foreign policy elite unanimously rejected Indonesian participation in a pact with the West, and the reasons are instructive. Of the 54 leaders who gave a reason, 69 percent, including at least 60 percent of every major group except the Islamic politicians and the technocrats, said that a pact would invite domination by the stronger allies. Significantly, of eight 1966 Generation leaders, all but one expressed concern that a pact would impair Indonesia's independence. Besides the fear of losing independence, there was an overwhelming belief that pacts were ineffective as a means of defense and might actually invite hostility from the enemies of one's allies. This view was expressed by 74 percent; 13 percent stated that a pact was unacceptable because of the domestic political repercussions it would have (see Table 5.4).[43]

Table 5.4. Why refrain from joining a pact?

	It would endanger Indonesia's independence	Pacts are ineffective	Domestic political repercussions
All respondents (n = 54)*	37 (69%)	40 (74%)	7 (13%)
1928 Generation (n = 10)	4	6	1
1945 Generation (n = 36)	26	28	3
1966 Generation (n = 8)	7	6	3
PNI (n = 9)	8	5	1
Catholic Party (n = 4)	3	2	2
Army (n = 10)	7	8	1
Foreign Ministry (n = 8)	5	6	0
PSI (n = 5)	3	4	0
Technocrats (n = 5)	2	5	0
Islamic parties (n = 6)	2	6	1

* Some cited more than one reason.

The fear of domination by an alliance's more powerful members reflects both a sense of Indonesia's weakness and an estimate of the

43. The reasons given by those who accepted the narrow definition did not differ substantially from those of the foreign policy elite as a whole: Of 17, 68 percent rejected a pact because of the danger to independence, 82 percent because it would be ineffective, and 18 percent because of the domestic political consequences.

exploitative motivations of its potential allies. While a fundamental goal of an alliance is to assure the weak of the backing of stronger powers against a common enemy, Indonesia's leaders felt that it was precisely their country's weakness which made it too dangerous for them to enter a pact. "An alliance between the weak and the strong is nonsense," an Islamic leader maintained.[44] Once Indonesia became economically, militarily, and politically strong, it might be possible to consider alliances, but at present Indonesia would be "too easily dominated." If a weak nation enters a pact, it was argued, it automatically assumes an "inferior position" and becomes a "second class nation." France and Pakistan could join pacts without sacrificing their independence because they were stronger than Indonesia. Though allied with the United States, France could still criticize Washington because it shares the same Western culture, noted an army leader, and even the French have had to maneuver to avoid American domination. As for Pakistan, several argued that Indonesia's strategic location and natural resources made it a more attractive object for domination, while economic weakness and lack of national unity made it more vulnerable. Besides, the country's colonial experience and hard-fought struggle for independence made Indonesia more sensitive to threatened domination than either France or Pakistan.

Whatever the motivations of the big powers in forming an alliance, it was said to be inevitable that they would use it to manipulate the weaker partners for their own purposes. Catholic, Islamic, PSI, and army leaders emphasized that pacts are always run by the more powerful members. Many pictured a pact as merely a convenient device employed by the big powers in their relentless drive to subjugate the weak. In the words of an Islamic leader: "Why do the big powers form alliances anyway, if not to dominate the weaker members?"

For a good many leaders, the mere act of subscribing to a pact would be an intolerable abridgement of freedom: a nation automatically surrenders some of its independence when it joins a pact

44. Imron Rosjadi in *Politik Luar Negeri Indonesia Dewasa Ini,* p. 54.

because it has to fulfill certain obligations. Said a PNI spokesman: "To enter a pact is to commit oneself. To speak of being in a pact and having freedom at the same time is a contradiction. As a political scientist, you should be able to see that." As an example of how Indonesia's freedom of action would be narrowed by a pact, a 1966 Generation leader questioned whether defending Malaysia would be in Indonesia's interests. An Islamic representative in parliament suggested that if Indonesia entered a pact, "we would be obliged to send our best troops to places like Vietnam, as the South Koreans have had to do." Membership in a pact would involve Indonesia in conflicts that are not its business, argued an army leader, and at the same time reduce its bargaining power on matters of real concern.

More subtle, perhaps, but no less compelling was the fear that participation in a military alliance would impair Indonesia's image as an independent nation, both in the eyes of others and in the eyes of the Indonesians themselves. Even where it was not linked to specific fears of domination or constricted freedom of action, joining a pact would clearly impose on many Indonesians a heavy psychological burden—a feeling of being bound. Army officers regarded as close to the West indicated that a pact was completely unthinkable because "pact is a dirty word." The general view was that joining a pact would be regarded as something dishonorable, not distinguishable from selling the country's independence. A leading newspaper editor maintained: "We just couldn't do it."

Frequently mentioned was the belief that a nation inevitably loses something of its identity when it enters a pact. Joining an alliance would make Indonesia just one among a number of members, rather than a nation with a unique international position. "If you have entered a pact," stated a 1966 Generation leader, "other people already have a very clear picture of your policy, of where you stand. We don't want that." While some suggested that it was Indonesia's lack of self-confidence that precluded the country's entry into a pact, many leaders stressed that Indonesia's national identity was a highly self-confident and nationalistic one. Indonesia, declared an Islamic leader, was "a fighting nation." Aligning with the West would completely undermine this: "If we were to enter a bloc, we would run the real risk of ending up like the Philippines, a country which has no real identity of its own. I have visited there, and it is very depressing. It is more like the West than Asia, but too Asian to be Western. It is nothing. There is no sense of national pride. Thailand also suffers from the same malady. Malaysia too is too much under foreign influence. . . . Our sense of national pride is our greatest capital. I disagree with Sukarno's foreign policy on many things, but I must admit that he did give us a sense of national pride."

Whether or not they feared that a pact would imperil Indonesia's independence, most agreed that military alliances were futile as a means of defense. In the first place, it was repeatedly emphasized, pacts were irrelevant to the threat of subversion, which the Indonesians felt they faced. Army generals were among the many who insisted that the only way to guarantee security in Southeast Asia was for each nation to strengthen itself internally, which essentially meant improving economic conditions. Moreover, each nation must bear the responsibility for its own defense. Bringing in foreign troops only helps the enemy: the Vietnamese experience was frequently cited as evidence.

In the unlikely event of an attack by the Russians or the Chinese, the Indonesian leaders were generally confident that the United States would come to their assistance, even in the absence of a pact. "It wouldn't take more than an hour to arrange it," suggested a 1966 Generation leader. Besides, contended an army general, pacts only convey a false sense of security: they are "just scraps of paper." It was generally agreed that SEATO's failure had proved that pacts are worthless relics of an obsolete strategy. Worse still, participation in a pact may be an "invitation for subversion" by those against whom the alliance is directed. "To join a pact is to say that certain countries are your enemies," asserted another general, and it only heightens international tensions by encouraging one's potential enemies to act like enemies. As a 1966 Generation member put it: "If we were to join the Western bloc, the Chinese would feel free to interfere in certain areas that are hard to defend."

The leaders who opposed joining a pact because of domestic political repercussions predicted that such a move would generate dangerous political tensions which enemies of the government could easily exploit. A Catholic leader and a young Islamic leader both declared that the domestic turmoil that was sure to ensue would be a windfall for the underground PKI. Although only a few leaders mentioned this danger, most would agree that such a departure from Indonesia's traditional policy could not be made without generating an internal crisis.

The prohibition against participation in a military pact was generally considered applicable to purely Southeast Asian endeavors as well, as evidenced by the fact that the foreign policy elite rejected a military alliance among the ASEAN nations almost as resoundingly as one with the Western powers. Of 42 who discussed the question, only 3 voiced no objection to such a pact, though several others indicated it might be considered at some future date, assuming the existence of a clear external threat and a willingness on the part of the other prospective members to sever their ties to the Western powers. Army generals and foreign ministry officials in particular went to great lengths to stress that there was no leader of any consequence in the government who favored any form of military cooperation involving a commitment to send Indonesian troops to fight in other countries.[45]

The reasoning behind the rejection of an ASEAN pact reflected many of the same concerns as the discussion of a pact with the Western powers. The emphasis, however, was less on the danger than on the utter uselessness of such an alliance. Quite a few simply dismissed a pact among weak nations as pointless. "The idea is ridiculous. What could it possibly accomplish?" asked one general.

45. Specifically rejected in the strongest terms was the concept of a joint counterinsurgency force proposed by one American political scientist (Bernard K. Gordon, *Toward Disengagement in Asia: A Strategy for American Foreign Policy* [Englewood Cliffs: Prentice-Hall, 1969], pp. 150–165.) Of 27 who were asked about this possibility, not a single one expressed any sympathy for the idea. The 27 included 8 representatives of the army, 7 from the foreign ministry, 7 technocrats, 2 each from the Catholic, Islamic, and PSI groups, and one PNI leader. For their discussion of this proposal, see Weinstein, "Uses of Foreign Policy," pp. 365–66.

The independent-and-active policy was even held to rule out participation in a nonmilitary organization if this appeared to be clearly pro-Western and anti-Communist. Of 39 leaders, only one, an Islamic politician, supported Indonesia's entering the Asian and Pacific Council (ASPAC). Participation in this was overwhelmingly felt to be the equivalent of a commitment to the West.[46] In addition, more than a few leaders expressed concern about Japanese domination of ASPAC. Participation, they said, would only subject Indonesia to the unpleasantness of being in a Japanese-dominated organization, while offering no tangible benefits: "If we were to enter an organization with Japan now we would be consumed."

An Active Foreign Policy

In the view of most Indonesian leaders, an active foreign policy was integrally related to independence. In fact, the mere existence of an active, assertive foreign policy was taken as a mark of independence. For many of those who emphasized this, the chief consideration was not so much an expectation of achieving the avowed goals, but more a feeling that passivity connotes acquiescence to circumscribed independence. Partly, this was a matter of demonstrating their independence to themselves. The Indonesian leaders often spoke of an active policy as essential to the preservation of their self-respect, national identity, and image. Like membership in a pact, a passive international role would convey a feeling of being taken for granted, of being less than fully independent. An assertive foreign policy would also contribute concretely by forcing others to woo their country through appropriate concessions.

There is more to independence than merely fending off big power intervention, though. It is not enough for Indonesia to be "left

46. Membership in ASPAC was publicly rejected by the government, though there was some hedging. See Malik's statements in *Kompas,* 4 April 1967, and *Research Landasan,* vol. 7, pt. 1, p. 18, and Soeharto's in *Indonesian Observer,* 17 March 1969. For more ambivalent statements, see Malik's comments in *Operasi,* 12 August 1967, *Pedoman,* 4 June 1969, and *Pewarta & Kronologi Bulanan,* 1 (August 1968), 13, 20.

alone." The great majority of the Indonesian leaders saw their country as an important nation capable of playing a significant role in world politics and a leading role in Southeast Asia. Indonesia could be considered fully independent, they believed, only when it had "resumed" an international position befitting a nation of its size, population, and other assets.

A World Role

An active policy meant not merely "contributing to world peace," but also acting as a leader of the third world. Sixty-one percent of the Indonesian leaders felt that it was essential for Indonesia to play an important role in world politics, while 9 percent thought it advisable to concentrate on Southeast Asia for the time being, and 30 percent asserted that Indonesia should "turn inward" to devote all its energy to economic development. Only the Islamic and Catholic politicians gave predominant support to the passive alternative. There was, however, some hesitation among the oldest and youngest leaders and among technocrats about the importance of playing a major world role. A number of them indicated that Indonesia was simply too weak to carry out such a role. Better, they argued, to make Indonesia strong by developing economically, so that there would be a solid foundation on which to base such international leadership in the future (see Table 5.5).

The step most frequently urged was Jakarta's taking the initiative in organizing the third world, mainly through conferences among the nonaligned and the Asian-African nations. Some 63 percent, including a majority of the respondents in each of the major groups except the Muslim politicians and the technocrats, considered it important for Indonesia to play a leading role in nonaligned conferences, while the remainder agreed that Indonesia should at least take part. The Asian-African forum was seen as somewhat less worthwhile, but 45 percent nevertheless felt that Indonesia should work to arrange such meetings, 48 percent favored participation but not leadership, and 6 percent thought participation pointless. The PNI and the army showed the greatest enthusiasm for Asian-African conferences, while the Catholics and technocrats showed

Table 5.5. **Should Indonesia seek a major role in world politics?**

	Important to do so	Better to concentrate on Southeast Asia for the time being	Turn inward
All respondents	33 (61%)	5 (9%)	16 (30%)
1928 Generation	4	0	5
1945 Generation	25	4	7
1966 Generation	4	1	4
PNI	9	0	0
PSI	5	1	0
Foreign Ministry	4	1	0
Army	6	0	2
Technocrats	3	2	2
Catholic Party	0	1	3
Islamic parties	1	0	6

the least. The youngest and the oldest generations were cool toward both forums (see Table 5.6).

Even those who thought a leading role in such meetings important anticipated only modest concrete results. Army generals claimed that nonaligned and Asian-African conferences were useful for exchanging ideas and mobilizing public opinion. Although detente and the new multipolarity had rendered superfluous a mediating role between the superpowers, some leaders suggested that the meetings could still serve to "remind the superpowers of the rich-poor gap, that they have to pay attention to the needs of the underdeveloped countries or else trouble will break out." And several leaders asserted that a nonaligned conference would be useful because it would strengthen the position of Marshal Tito, whom they saw as Indonesia's link to the socialist countries: "If we can establish good relations with Yugoslavia, then we can more easily take the next step to the socialist countries."

Rather than stressing concrete benefits, however, most argued that an active role in these conferences had mainly symbolic significance. It was good for Indonesia's image to promote such meetings because they presented "an unobstructed forum" in which Jakarta could play a more important world role. Cultivating this

Table 5.6. Indonesia and international conferences

	Indonesia should take a leading role	Indonesia should merely participate	Indonesia should not participate
Of the nonaligned nations			
All respondents	25 (63%)	15 (37%)	0
1928 Generation	3	5	0
1945 Generation	22	5	0
1966 Generation	0	5	0
PNI	6	0	0
Foreign Ministry	4	1	0
PSI	3	1	0
Army	5	2	0
Catholic Party	2	1	0
Technocrats	2	2	0
Islamic parties	2	4	0
Of the Asian-African nations			
All respondents	15 (45%)	16 (48%)	2 (6%)
1928 Generation	3	5	0
1945 Generation	12	8	0
1966 Generation	0	3	2
PNI	5	0	0
Army	4	2	0
Islamic parties	2	3	1
PSI	1	3	0
Foreign Ministry	1	3	0
Technocrats	0	1	0
Catholic Party	0	2	0

image as a leader of the nonaligned countries would bring credit to Jakarta because the nonaligned movement had contributed significantly to flexibility and multipolarity in international relations. Even those who had no enthusiasm at all for such meetings acknowledged the symbolic value of participation, if not leadership. Though they termed the meetings "a waste of time," they agreed with the Islamic leader who said: "We cannot afford not to take part."

Besides these conferences, it was suggested that Indonesia could play a world role through several other channels. Some, especially PNI leaders, stressed the importance of backing independence movements, such as those in southern Africa, in the UN. Others called on Indonesia to lead the less developed countries in the battle against the rich nations at the UNCTAD conferences. If the Indonesians failed to seek an important role in international forums like UNCTAD, they would find themselves "influenced without being able to do anything at all," observed a leading economic policy-maker.

A number of leaders emphasized the importance of Indonesia's contributing to world peace by serving, if needed, as an intermediary between the blocs and by continuing to condemn "power politics." Though some, especially among the younger leaders, considered it wiser to accept power politics as an inevitable fact of international life, a roughly equal number contended that vigorously opposing those methods was not futile.[47] Vietnam and Czechoslovakia were cited as places where the superpowers had been defeated in their attempts to achieve their goals by power politics. Several army generals and foreign ministry officials noted that it was unthinkable to accept the inevitability of such tactics, because it would mean acquiescing in domination by the big powers. "If we ever come to the conclusion that power politics is inevitable," declared a PSI leader, "then there will be no point in living."

Some who acknowledged that Indonesia could not do much on a global scale at present insisted that turning inward would hamper Indonesia's ability to assume international leadership in the years to come. An army general obviously resented the suggestion that Indonesia remain passive: "Why can't we influence world politics?

47. Of 23 respondents, 12 felt that Indonesia should continue to vigorously condemn power politics, while 11 thought it should be accepted as an unavoidable reality. All 5 of the 1928 Generation leaders favored continued opposition, the 14 leaders of the 1945 Generation split evenly, and all 4 from the 1966 Generation argued for acceptance. The PNI, army, and Islamic leaders were the most concerned, while the technocrats and Catholics were least, with the others split evenly. Those who urged acceptance of power politics observed that even underdeveloped countries engaged in such tactics when in a position to do so.

As recently as the beginning of this century, nobody was talking about America. They talked about France, the United Kingdom, Turkey —but not America. Times change. If you look at the potential of Indonesia, who is to say that at some point in the future we will not have a significant influence on world politics."

Others emphasized that Indonesia was simply too important to remain silent concerning world affairs, the country's present weakness notwithstanding. Whether they liked it or not, they felt compelled by "objective factors" to seek a global role. In the words of a former foreign minister: "[A major role] is dictated by our history, all the way back to Sriwijaya. . . . When the Romans were sailing around the Mediterranean, we were going all the way to Christmas Island, as one of my teachers in Holland pointed out. Our role is dictated by our location and our resources. We are not any less intelligent than the Japanese or any other people. We have a different kind of reasoning. It is intuitive. We start with the answer and then work back, rather than working step by step toward the answer."

Finally, there was a widespread belief among the foreign policy elite members that playing an important world role was essential to the maintenance of national identity and self-respect. "Every nation must have a role in world politics, must make some contribution, or else it is nothing," asserted a foreign ministry official. The more so for Indonesia, he added, because it had previously had such a role and had won the respect of other nations for it. International leadership had become part of Indonesia's national identity.

The ambiguity and passivity of Indonesia's foreign policy since 1966 were sharply criticized as indicative of the extent to which the national identity had been betrayed and independence compromised. A technocrat complained that Indonesian foreign policy seemed to be "active only in begging" for aid, making the country look like a "camp follower of the United States." Some lamented the fact that nations which once looked to Indonesia for leadership now regarded Jakarta with derision. A 1966 Generation leader commented sadly that he could "really feel the difference" in Indonesia's status when he traveled abroad. The foreign policy elite members seemed very sensitive to the sarcastic remark sometimes heard in diplomatic circles: "Does Indonesia *have* a foreign policy?" One of the most militantly anti-Sukarno leaders of the 1966 Generation agreed that most Indonesians he knew still had a "longing to be known in the world."

Leadership in Southeast Asia

Like a world role, Indonesian leadership in Southeast Asia was seen as an essential expression of an active foreign policy, as well as of national independence. Of 53 respondents, almost 90 percent asserted that Indonesia should be the leader of the region, and most felt it should bid for such a role now. PSI and foreign ministry leaders were the most eager, while the PNI and army leaders, who had been strongest for a world role, expressed the least interest.[48] Young people, who saw themselves as realists, also showed more interest in leading Southeast Asia than in a world role (see Table 5.7). Many of those who did not favor a world role did consider a Southeast Asian role important. If all who favored a world role and

Table 5.7. **Should Indonesia take a leading role in Southeast Asia?**

	Yes, now	Yes, eventually	Leading role unimportant
All respondents	28 (53%)	19 (36%)	6 (11%)
1928 Generation	3	4	2
1945 Generation	21	12	2
1966 Generation	4	3	2
PSI	6	0	0
Foreign Ministry	4	3	0
Islamic parties	4	4	0
Catholic Party	2	2	0
Technocrats	3	2	2
Army	3	5	0
PNI	2	4	2

48. Some of them viewed talk of a Southeast Asian role as an indirect way of saying that Indonesia should not seek a role beyond the region. Others felt that it would be unbecoming of Indonesia to seek such a role; it would have to come at the request of the other countries.

a Southeast Asian role are combined, then the belief in the importance of Indonesia's assuming some form of international leadership appears to be quite strong.

This is especially impressive in light of the Indonesians' obvious concern that they might appear to be espousing "expansionist" views. Some warned that even talking about regional leadership could give rise to "misunderstandings." A foreign ministry official who thought it "appropriate" for Indonesia to have a leading role in Southeast Asia, added that he would "never put it that way, because nations like Malaysia and Singapore are very worried about Indonesia in light of the recent past."

Most Indonesian leaders felt that their country's physical attributes alone made it natural that Jakarta assume a leading role in Southeast Asia. A number of leaders, including army generals, technocrats, and foreign ministry officials, spoke of the four "big powers" of Asia: Japan, China, India, and Indonesia. A foreign ministry official predicted that in the future there would be three "spheres of influence" in Asia: Japan's in the north, India's in the south, and Indonesia's in Southeast Asia. Indonesia, he pointed out, occupies the focal position between the northern and southern spheres and thus in a sense holds the key to Asia. It is the "heart of the Malay world, and that is quite a big world," noted an army general. Given its strategic position, the highest officials said confidentially, "Indonesia cannot avoid its responsibilities as a great power in Asia." Even those who were cool toward this role felt that once the country had grown stronger, a leading role would be "natural."

Most foreign policy elite members would agree with the 1966 Generation leader who asserted that Indonesians expected to have a leading role in Southeast Asia because basically they felt superior to their neighbors. Whether they admitted it or not, a PSI leader observed, most Indonesians saw themselves as "elder brothers" to the rest of Southeast Asia.

At the heart of that feeling of superiority was a belief that Indonesia's more highly developed sense of national identity made the country more politically advanced, and in effect more genuinely independent, than its neighbors. The Indonesians saw themselves as possessing a high degree of political consciousness, a strong tradition of anticolonial activism, a vigorous and autonomous cultural life through which the unique qualities of the Indonesian people could find expression, and an intellectual tradition capable of synthesizing these political and cultural dimensions to form a coherent Indonesian identity. Thus Indonesia's claim to leadership in Southeast Asia rested not only on the country's size and strategic location but on a belief that the country had attained a deeper sense of its national being and a fuller measure of independence than its neighbors. In contrast, most of the other Southeast Asian states were found by the Indonesians to be notably deficient in precisely those attributes which bear on the strength of their national identity and the authenticity of their independence.

The Indonesian leaders could find little worthy of praise in any of these neighbors, but by far the most negatively perceived was the Philippines. More than 80 percent, including a majority of the respondents in every major group, felt not only that the Philippines lacked genuine independence but that it was an undesirable place to live.[49] They found the Philippines "frightening" and Filipinos a people without depth. The most frequently voiced criticism was that the country was still a colony of the United States, but almost as common were comments on violence and the absence of a national identity.[50] Reflecting the prevailing scorn for the Philippines, one leader recalled his difficulties when he was mistaken for a Filipino during his travels abroad. In Hong Kong, he claimed, Filipinos were required to pay their hotel bills in advance because they could not be trusted; Indonesians were treated with more respect. When asked whether there was anything at all in the Philippines worthy

49. The group breakdown was as follows: the 2 PSI leaders, one Catholic, and 2 foreign ministry officials took that position, as did 4 of 5 from the army, 4 of 5 PNI leaders, 2 of 3 technocrats, and 3 of 5 Muslim politicians.

50. Excessive American influence was named by 13, violence and the lack of national identity by 9 each, corruption and lack of regard for the Filipinos as a people by 3 each, and unjust land regulations, great extremes of wealth and poverty, and excessive individualism by one each.

of emulation by Indonesia, over 80 percent could find nothing.[51] There is some evidence, however, that the Philippines' image has begun to improve as a result of its more independent foreign policy in 1975.[52]

Perceptions of Thailand were not as negative, but they were hardly positive. Of 34 who discussed it, only 2 saw anything suitable as a model for Indonesia.[53] Most described Thailand in distinctly unfavorable terms, either as a feudal military regime unconcerned about the opinions of its people, as a SEATO member and therefore an American satellite, or as a place that is "even more corrupt than Indonesia." The Thai, according to an army general, lack the strong sense of national identity which Indonesians possess: "They don't care if Thailand becomes dependent on the United States, they just don't care who does what." Indonesians, he added, would never stand for the kind of subordination which the Thais willingly accept. In early 1973, at a time when Japanese economic domination and American military bases were drawing the wrath of Thai students, the foreign policy elite members interviewed by the author viewed Thailand as a sad example of a nation that had failed to safeguard its independence.

As for Malaysia, there was more to admire, but there were still grave doubts about the authenticity of its independence. Of 35 leaders, 25 felt that Malaysia was not yet genuinely independent because of excessive British influence or, according to a few, domination by the economically powerful overseas Chinese.[54] In fact, with

51. Those who could find something named the following: democratic system, miracle rice, good leadership, direct election of the president, and a free press. Each of these received one mention; 22 leaders saw nothing worthy of emulation.

52. See, for example, *Merdeka,* 13 June 1975.

53. One leader praised the Thai ability to make effective use of foreign aid to further economic development, while another, apparently being sincere, mentioned their ability to make corruption serve the needs of development. Among those in the negative were 7 Muslim leaders, 5 each from the army and the PNI, 3 each from the PSI and the technocrats, 2 foreign ministry officials, and one Catholic.

54. The generational differences were striking. While 6 of 9 leaders of the 1928 Generation and 14 of 19 from the 1945 Generation felt that Malaysia

44 leaders expressing their views, 27 asserted that Sukarno's objections to the formation of Malaysia were valid, though roughly two-thirds of them added that those objections did not justify his policy of confrontation.[55] And of 26 who discussed Malaysia as a potential model for Indonesia, 18 could find nothing worthy of praise.[56] The Malaysians, it was said, were lacking in ideas, imagination, and political consciousness, and were "too timid in facing foreigners."

Most regarded Malaysia as quite clearly within Indonesia's sphere of influence. The foreign policy elite members often talked of Malaysia's looking to Indonesia for inspiration. In fact, according to an army general, Indonesia was in a position to give Malaysia aid in the form of "political and spiritual experience." Some contended that Malaysia could also take a lesson from Indonesia in solving one of its most pressing problems—how to "handle" its Chinese minority.[57] One leader, an eminent Islamic figure, even went so far as to say: "Actually, we feel that Malaysia is a part of Indonesia."

Singapore, which withdrew from the Federation of Malaysia in

---

was not fully independent, 5 of 7 from the 1966 Generation asserted that Malaysia's independence was complete. The close identification of the Malaysia question with Sukarno may help to explain this divergency. The only major groups to take the position that Malaysia was fully free were the Muslim politicians (5 of 8) and the army (3 of 5). Disagreeing were both PSI leaders and all 3 technocrats, 5 of 6 PNI leaders, 2 of 3 Catholics, and one of 2 foreign ministry officials.

55. Again the 1966 Generation dissented from the majority view. While 6 of 10 leaders of the 1928 Generation and 18 of 26 from the 1945 Generation thought Sukarno's objections valid, only 3 of 8 from the 1966 Generation agreed. Among the major groups, all 7 PNI leaders, all 4 foreign ministry officials, 5 of 7 from the army, and 2 of 3 Catholics agreed, but only 2 of 6 Muslims, one of 2 PSI leaders, and 2 of 4 technocrats did so.

56. Three praised the way the Malaysians had used foreign capital; two mentioned the rural community development program; the "rule of law," managerial abilities, competent civil service, and successful development techniques each received one mention.

57. Several leaders claimed that Malaysia's former Prime Minister, Tunku Abdul Rahman, had suggested that Jakarta encourage Indonesians to emigrate to Malaysia in order to increase the numerical superiority of the non-Chinese.

1965, is of course a case apart from the other Southeast Asian nations. In discussing Singapore, the Indonesians exhibited respect mixed with contempt. There was grudging admiration for Singapore's economic prowess, but few saw Singapore as being really Southeast Asian. Rather, it was Chinese. Roughly half of those who discussed Singapore characterized its relationship with Indonesia as one of fundamental conflict.[58] There was a broad feeling that Singapore was exploiting Indonesia economically. Many talked of a need to curtail Indonesia's dependence on Singapore's entrepôt facilities, though most acknowledged that Indonesia would suffer serious short-run damage from an abrupt break in the relationship. Some foreign policy elite members saw the conflict as essentially a product of disparity in levels of economic development, but the depth of hostility suggests that anti-Chinese feelings were equally important. The widespread contempt for Singapore was manifest in the remarks of a PSI leader: "The problem is that they are so arrogant. They think they are better than everyone else." But Singapore could never hope to lead Southeast Asia, he added. "They may be fat, happy, and stinking now, but they are just too small to be a leader."

What did the Indonesians mean when they spoke of their country as the leader of Southeast Asia? The leadership which they envisaged had relatively little concrete content. They did not conceive of a leading role in terms of defined responsibilities, institutional arrangements, and specific benefits. Rather, they expected that other Southeast Asian nations would defer to Indonesia and look to it for inspiration and advice. Leadership meant recognition that Indonesia, by virtue of both its physical attributes and its more authentic independence, stands first among the nations of Southeast Asia.

It would be quite misleading to conclude from the talk of leadership that the Indonesians expected to gain genuine material rewards by taking a prominent role in ASEAN. Though there were a few

58. Of 21 leaders, 11 felt the relationship was one of conflict, including one technocrat, 3 of 4 PNI leaders, 2 of 4 from the army, one of 2 from the PSI and the Catholics each. Also dissenting were 4 of 5 Muslims and one foreign ministry official.

who spoke glowingly of Indonesia leading ASEAN toward significant achievements in the field of economic cooperation, the majority considered this unlikely. Only 38 percent held out hope that ASEAN could accomplish anything significant within the next decade.[59] Technocrats, army generals, and PNI leaders, along with members of the two younger generations, were especially skeptical (see Table 5.8). Contending by 1973 that the organization had

Table 5.8. **Can ASEAN accomplish anything significant within the next decade?**

	Yes	No
All respondents	19 (38%)	31 (62%)
1928 Generation	6	4
1945 Generation	10	23
1966 Generation	3	4
Foreign Ministry	4	2
Islamic parties	5	3
PSI	3	2
Catholic Party	2	2
PNI	3	5
Army	3	6
Technocrats	0	6

already proved to be a "waste of time," several 1966 Generation leaders urged the author to disregard the public claims of accomplishment because "everyone knows" that the organization can achieve nothing of consequence. Significantly, the government official who in 1970 had been most enthusiastic about ASEAN was quite pessimistic about its prospects in 1973.

59. Economic cooperation was mentioned by 14 leaders. Specifically cited was the possibility of shared production techniques, common pricing and marketing arrangements, and coordinated efforts in such fields as communications, transportation, shipping, and tourism. A few voiced hopes for a Southeast Asian common market which could withstand "the economic threat of the giants, especially Japan." Cultural cooperation (that is, getting to know one another) was mentioned by 13, security cooperation by 4, and helping to settle disputes by 3.

Effective economic cooperation was said to be ruled out by the fact that the economies of the member countries were essentially competitive, with all trying to sell the same commodities. An Islamic leader observed that because the Southeast Asians "all live from hand to mouth, with a very narrow margin of survival," it was "hard to imagine that Malaysia, for example, would observe a price agreement with Indonesia if it had the opportunity to sell its rubber below the agreed price." Regional cooperation even in a relatively innocuous field like tourism posed problems, because "a Chinese tourist from Kuala Lumpur might turn out to be a spy for Peking." In any case, ASEAN was widely regarded as doomed to insignificance by a lack of political consensus among its members and by the exclusion of Burma and the Indochinese states. Some went so far as to condemn the organization as a pro-Western front.[60] A pre-eminent leader of the 1928 Generation vigorously denounced ASEAN as not only useless but "a bind, a violation of the independent and active policy . . . [which] has already been labeled a tool of the United States by North Vietnam."

Most leaders, however, were inclined to accept Indonesian participation in the organization as harmless, perhaps even somewhat useful as a symbol of a good neighbor policy and a gesture to Washington, which was known to be keen on regionalism. Above all, the leaders saw ASEAN as a forum for Jakarta's largely symbolic leadership.

Asked to define what a leading role meant, the foreign policy elite members mentioned most frequently Indonesia's being consulted on developments of significance in the region. Also named, in order of frequency, were: taking initiatives, serving as an example or older brother, helping to settle disputes, having a sphere of influence, and possibly undertaking (at some indeterminate date) military responsibility for the region.[61] Almost all of the above,

60. Three leaders pointed out that the name ASEAN first appeared in a book by an American political scientist, suggesting to them that the organization was a tool of American policy. The book is Russell H. Fifield, *Southeast Asia in United States Policy* (New York: Praeger, 1963), pp. 426–29.

61. Being consulted was named by 12, taking initiatives by 7, serving as an

however, were really different ways of saying that Indonesia ought to be deferred to and asked to participate in the solution of the region's problems. For example, when the Australians and the Malaysians met to discuss security arrangements following Britain's withdrawal from the area, Indonesia expected to be (and was) consulted. A case in which this "right" to be consulted had been ignored was Britian's decision to form the Malaysian federation without first discussing the matter with Indonesia. Sukarno, it was agreed, had been right to protest. "We want to have to be taken into account in Southeast Asia," declared a technocrat. If the American president "says he has talked to the leaders of Southeast Asia," said a young Catholic leader, "he must have talked to Soeharto. He can leave out Singapore, but not Indonesia."

Several leaders talked of "giving direction" and "setting the tone" in Southeast Asia by taking initiatives, but virtually no specific initiatives were proposed. It was up to Indonesia to serve as an "inspiration" to the other countries of the region, and as a 1966 Generation leader described it, to take a "more spectacular" role. A few pointed to the dispute between Malaysia and the Philippines over Sabah as one in which an Indonesian initiative to bring about a settlement would have been appropriate. Many asserted that Indonesia should take the lead in opposing foreign bases in Southeast Asia, in order to prove to nations like Thailand and the Philippines that it was possible to survive independent of the big powers.[62]

In sum, Indonesian aspirations to lead Southeast Asia were inseparable from the need to reaffirm the nation's identity as an inde-

---

older brother or example by 7, helping to settle disputes by 7, having a sphere of influence by 3, and undertaking military responsibilities by 2.

62. Of 49 leaders, 40 felt that all foreign bases in Southeast Asia should be abolished, while 7 said it was up to the country in which the base was located to decide, and 2, both from the Islamic groups, said that bases served a useful purpose. Favoring the abolition of such bases were all 6 PSI leaders and all 5 technocrats, 7 of 8 from both the PNI and the army, 4 of 5 foreign ministry officials, 3 of 4 Catholics, and 4 of 8 Muslim politicians. Foreign bases, it was generally agreed, only invited Communist attacks, allowed the Chinese to say they were threatened, corrupted the spirit of the people, and reflected a lack of confidence.

pendent state and a pioneer in the struggle against big power domination. Deference to Indonesian leadership would be tantamount to recognition that Indonesia's independence was authentic. Conversely, as a newspaper editor put it: "If Indonesia does not have an important role in Asia, then independence has no meaning."

Conclusion

The foreign policy elite's understanding of an independent-and-active policy made Indonesia's position awkward. By the Indonesian leaders' definition of the term, one could question the degree of their country's independence. They found themselves in the curious position of denouncing dependence as their country became ever more dependent, and aspiring to lead others in the struggle for greater independence even as Indonesia discovered that its own capacity to act as an independent nation was in jeopardy.

The Indonesian leaders' self-respect, definition of national identity, and claim to international leadership all rested in some measure on the assumption that Indonesia was genuinely independent. It was precisely because the Indonesian leaders saw a link between their independence and recognition of Jakarta as a regional leader that they were, as a technocrat acknowledged, especially sensitive to insults or the feeling that they were being treated as a "second class nation." They were caught between an awareness of their weakness and their self-perception as a leader. Seeing their independence threatened by the big powers, they sought to reassure themselves that they were really independent by assuming a role of leadership over other underdeveloped nations, and this made them extraordinarily concerned about how others perceived them. That is why a 1966 Generation leader could get as upset as he did about the Asian Development Bank's failure to name Indonesia to its board of directors; he took it as a sign that the big powers considered Indonesia an unimportant country with which they could trifle at will. Convinced of his country's superiority to its neighbors, and at the same time dismayed to find it treated without dignity by the big powers, he was left to lament Indonesia's "isolation in the world . . . without any clearly defined place in the family of nations."

The independent-and-active policy was interpreted by the foreign policy elite in a manner closer to Sukarno's broader, more activist definition than indicated by official statements of the New Order's foreign policy. There were, of course, substantial differences. Being resentful at the failure of the Asian Development Bank to elect Indonesia to its board of directors was far indeed from Sukarno's anti-imperialist crusade. But the continuities are important: an independent-and-active policy was still viewed as a necessity imposed by the need to survive in a hostile world. Independence still meant balancing off the forces that sought to subjugate Indonesia. Being active still meant working to reduce the power of those exploitative forces and, at the same time, reaffirming Indonesia's independence by assuming a role of international leadership appropriate to the nation's physical attributes and true to its self-image as a pioneer in the struggle against big power domination.

6 | Evolving Views of Foreign Aid

The belief that their country can develop economically only with foreign assistance has persisted among Indonesia's leaders. Aid is justified by its proponents on the ground that it will contribute as well to the achievement of genuine independence in the long run by providing the capital and technology that can enable an underdeveloped country to transform its economy structurally from an appendage of some industrialized nation's economy to a viable, essentially self-sustaining economic unit.

But the need for aid creates the basis for dependence: the more Indonesia's leaders have felt they could not do without aid, the more they have worried about losing their independence. Obviously, a country which allows control of its industrial life to pass into the hands of foreigners has already sacrificed an important part of its independence. Aid, then, can be either a path to development and ultimately a higher level of independence, or a bridge to domination and perpetual dependence.

1945–1954: First Thoughts about Aid

Even during the revolutionary years there was a growing realization of the need for economic aid to support reconstruction and development. But the overwhelming preoccupation of Indonesia's leaders prior to 1950 was winning Dutch recognition of Indonesian sovereignty, and there was little opportunity for serious thought about reconstruction, much less development. Moreover, much of the talk about the future role of foreign aid and investment in Indonesia was a tactic to reassure the Dutch and the Americans that their economic interests would be safe in an independent Indonesia, and that they therefore should support its demands for sovereignty.[1]

Whatever the motivation, as early as November 1945 the Indonesian government talked of "a great plan for prosperity" requiring large credits from abroad; hopefully the United States would contribute substantially. According to Hatta, the Indonesian leaders were "fully aware" that they would need foreign aid "for many years to come" in order to "[build] up our country." The Ten Year Plan for Reconstruction and Development, announced in 1947, was to be financed partly by foreign loans and partly by foreign investment capital. Throughout the revolutionary years, Hatta led the way in emphasizing Indonesia's receptivity to foreign capital and credits. Other top leaders expressed similar sentiments.[2]

The transfer of sovereignty was rapidly followed by efforts to mobilize the resources of the Western powers for Indonesia's economic reconstruction and development. The Republic's Trade Commissioner in the United States immediately indicated his intention to seek American capital investment.[3] In a February 1950 speech, Sukarno dwelt at length on the need for foreign loans to cover the balance of payments deficit, to finance development projects, and to facilitate the purchase of such necessities as rice,

1. For an excellent example of this, see Hatta's opening speech at the Round Table Conference in August 1949 (*Portrait of a Patriot,* pp. 511–13).

2. See the foreign policy manifesto in Osman Raliby, ed., *Documenta Historica* (Jakarta: Penerbit Bulan Bintang, 1953), vol. 1, pp. 526–27; *Portrait of a Patriot,* p. 511; *Merdeka,* 8 and 9 April 1947; John O. Sutter, *Indonesianisasi: Politics in a Changing Economy, 1940–1955* (Ithaca: Cornell Southeast Asia Program, 1959), vol. 2, pp. 532, 655; Charles Wolf, Jr., *The Indonesian Story: The Birth, Growth, and Structure of the Indonesian Republic* (New York: John Day, 1948), pp. 83–84; Sukarno's 20 September 1945 interview with Australian war correspondents in Sutter, *Indonesianisasi,* vol. 2, p. 310, and his speech reported in *Merdeka,* 12 July 1947; Sjahrir's *Our Struggle,* trans. Benedict R. O'G. Anderson (Ithaca: Cornell Modern Indonesia Project, 1968), pp. 22, 31, and his statement in *Merdeka,* 2 December 1946; and the statement of Masjumi leader Jusuf Wibisono in *Merdeka,* 2 July 1947.

3. Sumitro Djojohadikusumo's statement in a Reuters dispatch, 28 December 1949, as cited in Sutter, *Indonesianisasi,* p. 655.

medicine, and cheap textiles. Foreign investment was also badly needed, said Sukarno, and he stressed the importance of maintaining security and order as an inducement for this.[4]

The need for foreign credits and investment was asserted by leaders in each of the cabinets that held office through the middle 1950s.[5] While there was considerable debate concerning the conditions under which foreign capital should be permitted to operate, with Masjumi leaders like Sjafruddin Prawiranegara and Jusuf Wibisono urging that restrictions be minimized, even the PKI did not categorically reject the idea of allowing alien capital a role in Indonesia's development. Wibisono had noted two ways for a nation to develop its economy—the "autarkic approach" (self-sufficiency) and the "supported approach"—and he contended that the former entailed totalitarian techniques which had to be rejected on moral and humanitarian grounds. For all the disagreement among the Indonesian leaders on the issues of nationalization and the terms of foreign investment, there seemed a consensus on the need for a "supported approach" to development.[6]

Thus the official development plan of the period, the Economic Urgency Plan of 1951, was drawn up with the expectation of foreign assistance. Support had already been promised by the United States in 1950 with the announcement of a $100 million loan from

4. *Merdeka Berarti Berdjuang* (Jakarta: Kementerian Penerangan, 1950), pp. 46–49.

5. See Sutter, *Indonesianisasi,* pp. 778, 1128, 1141, 1144, 1207, 1213, 1217. On the Sukiman cabinet, see also *Menudju Kemakmuran lewat Keamanan: Keterangan Pemerintah atas Program Kabinet Soekiman* (Jakarta: Kementerian Penerangan, 1951), p. 16.

6. Sjafruddin, for example, suggested that there was no need for Indonesians to control a majority of the stock in joint enterprises. Indonesia required as much foreign capital as possible, he claimed, adding that risk-bearing capital was preferable to foreign loans. For his views, see Sutter, *Indonesianisasi,* pp. 780–81, 1144, 1210, and his speech of 11 May 1957 published in *Peranan Agama dan Moral Dalam Pembangunan Masjarakat dan Ekonomi Indonesia* (Jakarta: P. T. Bulan Bintang, 1966), pp. 15–16. On Wibisono, see Sutter, pp. 1204, 1219, 1222. PKI leaders stated in 1953 that they did not object to foreign capital as long as it fulfilled a number of conditions as to field of operations, transfer of profits, etc. (Sutter, pp. 1209–10).

the Export-Import Bank. The importance of foreign investment was made clear in the guidelines set by the Industrialization Commission appointed after the announcement of the Economic Urgency Plan. While it was stipulated that Indonesians should control 51 percent of the stock in basic or key industries, the only areas closed to foreign investment were a few vital industries, such as public utilities and defense-related manufacturing, and small-scale industries traditionally operated by Indonesians. Some spokesmen suggested that foreign investors should be given an even freer hand.[7]

On the other hand, as the need for loans and investment capital became evident, there was a corresponding rise in awareness of the risks of dependence on aid. Concern that continued domination of Indonesia's economy by foreign capital might make a mockery of independence had been expressed as early as 1945.[8] Tan Malaka, for example, argued that only by seizing all foreign property would Indonesia be able to establish the heavy industries essential for the country's development. In fact, even leaders like Hatta and those who devised the Ten Year Plan were sensitive to the need for industrialization in order to break out of the pattern of serving as a supplier of raw materials for the advanced countries; only an industrialized Indonesia, they believed, could raise the living standards of its people and achieve a reasonable degree of self-sufficiency. Hatta, however, claimed that foreign capital would help to accelerate the industrialization process. In his defense of the Round Table Conference agreements of 1949, which defined the terms of the transfer of sovereignty and guaranteed the rights of foreign capital, he argued that reliance on foreign aid and investment need not signify a continuation of the exploitative economic relationships

7. See Sutter, *Indonesiaisasi,* pp. 772, 774–82, and Douglas S. Paauw, "From Colonial to Guided Economy," in Ruth T. McVey, ed., *Indonesia* (New Haven: HRAF Press, 1963), pp. 215–18.

8. At its very first meeting, the KNIP (Central Indonesian National Committee), a body appointed by Sukarno as advisers to the executive but subsequently transformed into a legislative council, passed a resolution noting that in Latin America and China no real freedom existed because of the dominating role of foreign capital.

of the past. On the contrary, the government's power to supervise foreign capital would assure that foreign influence remained limited. But critics of the Round Table Conference agreements denounced them as a leap back to 1940, signifying a restoration of Dutch economic influence and an expansion of that of the United States.[9]

The Indonesians' apprehension increased most dramatically when the political strings associated with the 1952 Subardjo aid agreement were revealed. But the limitations on Indonesia's freedom were evident on other occasions. In 1950 the U.S. State Department put strong pressure on Indonesia to recognize the Bao Dai government in Vietnam, and the leaders became convinced that American financial assistance, specifically implementation of the promised Export-Import Bank loan, was being delayed pending Jakarta's acquiescence.[10] The American request for a UN embargo on shipment of strategic raw materials to China aroused considerable suspicion that the United States was just trying to monopolize the purchase of such commodities as rubber, thereby enabling it to force prices down.[11] The Indonesians went along with the embargo, however. It was a similar fear of losing American aid that led Jakarta in 1951 and 1952 to reject Soviet offers to buy Indonesian rubber at 10 percent above the world market price.[12] Furthermore, the Indonesians were dissatisfied with American trade terms and dismayed at the post-Korea decline in rubber prices, which they attributed at least in part to Washington's actions.

9. Sutter, *Indonesianisasi,* pp. 281, 332–33, 335, 497–98, 666, 665. See also the comments of socialist party leaders Subadio Sastrosatomo and Djohan Sjahruzah in *Politik dan Diplomasi* (Jakarta: Sekretariat Dewan Partai, Partai Sosialis Indonesia, 1956), pp. 53–54, 60.

10. Kahin, "Indonesian Politics and Nationalism," p. 174.

11. *Ibid.,* p. 177.

12. Usha Mahajani, *Soviet and American Aid to Indonesia, 1949–1968* (Athens, Ohio: Ohio University Center for International Studies, 1970), p. 6. Though they rejected the Soviet offer, Indonesian government officials indicated that they were still studying it, which led the United States eventually to counter the Soviet proposal by agreeing to purchase Indonesian tin for three years at relatively high prices.

By 1953 only modest foreign credits and relatively little new investment had come to Indonesia. Economic Urgency Plan projects were foundering for lack of capital, and foreign exchange earnings were falling because of a decline in international market prices for Indonesia's exports.[13] Consequently, discontent about the economic situation was on the rise. On the one hand, the need for external economic support was clearer than ever; but at the same time, there was growing doubt about the willingness of the advanced nations to provide it with relatively few strings attached.

This concern found expression in several forms. One was a call for accelerated nationalization of the foreign capital already active in Indonesia. In 1950 Sukarno had suggested that domestic and foreign capital would complement one another until the former had become substantial. But the cabinets that held office in 1953 and thereafter, though still committed to seeking foreign investment, did so with markedly less enthusiasm, especially as they became inclined to blame Indonesia's economic difficulties on foreign control of the economy. Another expression of concern was Sukarno's argument in a 1952 speech that self-sufficiency in rice production was an essential ingredient of independence. Talk of an "independent policy" would be meaningless, he claimed, if Indonesia had to depend on others for its food supply. He called for a "development revolution" and urged his countrymen to become "heroes of development," making their country strong and "free in the real meaning of freedom." Furthermore, in 1950 Sukarno had contended that efforts to raise production would fail to achieve their targets unless the government could halt inflation, and the way to stop inflation, he asserted, was by obtaining a foreign loan to cover the budgetary deficit. By 1953 he was arguing that intensified efforts to raise pro-

13. *Ibid.,* p. 7, and Sutter, *Indonesianisasi,* p. 777, 1203. In mid-1952, Prime Minister Wilopo had to announce an extension of the time allotted to completion of the short-term projects. By 1954 the only short-term project completed under the Economic Urgency Plan was the construction of several printing presses. Paauw places considerable emphasis on the lack of capital with which to import raw materials and capital goods ("From Colonial to Guided Economy," pp. 180, 186).

duction were more important than monetary and fiscal measures, and that the key to development lay not in foreign loans but in Indonesia's own efforts.[14]

1954–1965: Aid under Attack

As the pursuit of independence increasingly came to mean balanced relationships, anti-imperialism, and finally self-reliance, there was also an escalation of rhetoric about the dangers of foreign economic involvement. But there was a good deal of equivocation too, and new formulations were devised to keep foreign capital flowing to Indonesia.

Foreign Investment

Amid rising criticism of foreign capital, the Ali cabinets of the mid-1950s substantially accelerated the pace of the economy's Indonesianization by providing credits, licenses, and a protected position for large numbers of new Indonesian firms. With the abrogation in 1956 of the obligations undertaken in the transfer of sovereignty agreement, and the take-over of Dutch enterprises at the end of 1957, the attack on foreign capital grew considerably more intense. While the confiscation of Dutch capital was part of an effort to induce the Dutch to relinquish West Irian, it also coincided with a deepening conviction that foreign capital would lead not to industrialization and economic self-sufficiency but rather to a perpetuation of the "drainage policy," whereby profits derived from Indonesia's natural resources flowed out of the country.

Several Sukarno speeches in 1958 and 1959 summarized the increasingly predominant line of thinking on foreign investment.[15] At

14. See Sukarno's *Merdeka Berarti Berdjuang,* pp. 47–49; Sutter, *Indonesianisasi,* p. 1228; and Sukarno's *Soal Hidup atau Mati* (Jakarta: Kementerian Penerangan, 1958), pp. 25–26, and *Sesudah Satu Windu* (Jakarta: Kementerian Penerangan, 1953), p. 17.

15. *Saving, One Way to Accumulate Our Own Capital* (Jakarta: Ministry of Information, 1958), pp. 5–10; *Penemuan Kembali Revolusi Kita* (Jakarta: Kementerian Penerangan, 1959), pp. 4–7, 36–38; *Amanat Presiden Soekarno Pada Sidang Pleno Pertama Dewan Perantjang Nasional Pada Tanggal 28 Agustus 1959* (Jakarta: Kementerian Penerangan, 1959), pp. 11–12; and

the time of the revolution, Sukarno observed, the Indonesian leaders had intended to sever all economic ties with colonialism, but they had found it necessary to compromise in order to "buy recognition of our sovereignty." Unfortunately, some people failed to realize that the guarantees given to foreign investors had only been a tactic. It was time to face the fact that Indonesia's economic structure remained colonial, a condition Sukarno defined as having three elements: serving as a market for the goods of the industrialized countries, as a source of their raw materials, and as a place for the investment of their capital. So long as "economic and political imperialism" continued "sucking [Indonesia's] blood," there was no hope of using the country's natural resources for its economic development. According to Sukarno, Indonesia's failure to develop economically during the 1950s was mainly due to foreign economic and political intervention on the one hand, and the instability resulting from Indonesia's eight-year experiment with liberal democracy on the other hand.

Now, said Sukarno, Indonesia had entered a new period of socio-economic revolution that would produce a just and prosperous society and make a reality of the slogan "transform a colonial economy into a national economy." The take-over of Dutch enterprises had been a major step in that direction, placing the economy "70 percent in our hands." But, he noted in mid-1959, there were still Dutch companies to be taken over. Later the same year, Indonesia's first foreign investment law, promulgated only a year earlier, was repealed.[16]

Despite the sharp criticism of foreign capital, however, the Indonesian policymakers were clearly unwilling to do without it. The Ali cabinets had undertaken no large-scale nationalization of for-

---

"Lampiran Keputusan Dewan Pertimbangan Agung Tentang Perintjian Amanat Pembangunan Presiden Tanggal 28 Agustus 1959 (Jang Diutjapkan dan Jang Tertulis)," in *Amanat Pembangunan Presiden* (Jakarta: Jajasan Prapantja, 1963), pp. 17–25. See also his 1961 speech, *Untuk Kemerdekaan dan Keadilan* (Jakarta: Departemen Penerangan, 1961), p. 23.

16. Originally drafted in 1953, it had been approved by the cabinet in June 1956, and passed by the parliament two years later. See Hong Lan Oei, "Implications of Indonesia's New Foreign Investment Policy for Economic Development," *Indonesia*, no. 7 (April 1969), p. 36.

eign business. The Five Year Plan announced in 1956 actually accorded a central role to foreign investment. Even in the speeches cited previously, Sukarno insisted that he was not completely opposed to foreign investment as a last resort, after domestic capital and foreign loans had been exhausted. And the Eight Year Plan of 1960, like its predecessor, relied heavily on anticipated foreign investment to finance Indonesia's economic development. As Sukarno ruefully acknowledged in 1965, ambiguous references to a "mobilization of Indonesia's national resources" as the chief source of funds for the Eight Year Plan had in fact masked a decision to base Indonesia's development on foreign investment.[17]

Moreover, the government's rejection of "conventional investment" in the early 1960s was accompanied by a serious effort to devise less objectionable arrangements. A 1960 law vested all rights to mineral exploration in the state and declared that foreign companies henceforth could operate only as contractors, not as concession-holders. In 1963 the three Western oil companies agreed to relinquish their concession rights and serve as contractors to the state oil company. In exchange for long-term contracts, the companies were required to pay cash bonuses, to agree to surrender their distribution, marketing, and refining facilities to the state company in a prescribed period at agreed prices, and to divide profits with the government at a ratio of 60-40 in favor of the government. But the major conceptual innovation was production-sharing, which defined contracts with foreign companies as credits to carry out specific projects, to be repaid within a stipulated period of time with an agreed percentage of the product of the enterprise. Ownership and management of the project remained in Indonesian hands.[18]

17. *Ibid.;* Paauw, "From Colonial to Guided Economy," pp. 228–31; and *Berdiri Diatas Kaki Sendiri* (*Berdikari*) (Jakarta: MPRS dan Departemen Penerangan, 1965), pp. 21, 37–38.

18. See Alex Hunter, "The Oil Industry: The 1963 Agreements and After," *Bulletin of Indonesian Economic Studies* (hereafter abbreviated *BIES*), no. 2 (September 1965), pp. 16–18, and Joyce Gibson, "Production-

Even these new formulations soon drew criticism as simply a subtler way of perpetuating foreign economic domination. Both the PKI's chairman and an army general compared production-sharing to the practice of sharecropping.[19] Sukarno saw the basic problem in these terms: "At every move we make for economic reconstruction and up-building, we find that they [the imperialists] exploit their technological superiority to manipulate conditions in order that our nations can be kept eternally subservient to their selfish interests."[20] By 1965 Sukarno appeared to have lost enthusiasm for production-sharing. He assailed the series of projects which were to have financed the Eight Year Plan, contending that they kept Indonesia dependent on foreign capital: "The principle of building an economy without foreign monopoly capital has become a principle which, for us, is no longer subject to amendment."[21]

Indeed, the foreign capital remaining in Indonesia was increasingly in jeopardy. In 1963 British property was expropriated in connection with the Malaysia confrontation, and in 1965 some American interests were taken over. In May 1965 the current law guaranteeing foreign investments was repealed. And pressures for a take-over of the foreign oil companies were building. At the end of the year, despite the suppression of the PKI, which had led in demanding expropriation of the oil companies, the Indonesian gov-

Sharing," *ibid.*, nos. 3, 4 (February, June 1966), pp. 52–75, 75–100, and especially pp. 52–57.

19. Gibson concluded that production-sharing did perpetuate Indonesian dependence on foreign capital. She argued that the high price of the capital and the reliance on the foreign party for marketing even beyond the repayment period resulted in the de facto creation of an irredeemable equity, rather than a redeemable credit, as the government contended (Gibson, "Production-Sharing," p. 97). See also D. N. Aidit, *Sosialisme Indonesia dan Sjarat-Sjarat Pelaksanaannja* (Jakarta: "Aliarcham," 1962), pp. 97–98, cited in Oei, "Implications of Indonesia's New Foreign Investment Policy," p. 37, and the comments of Major General Aziz Saleh, minister of people's industry (Gibson, "Production-Sharing," p. 97).

20. Quoted in J. D. Legge, *Sukarno: A Political Biography* (New York: Praeger, 1972), p. 344.

21. *Berdiri Diatas Kaki Sendiri,* pp. 21, 37–38, and *Reach to the Stars,* p. 35.

ernment bought out one of the three companies and indicated that active negotiations were underway with the other two.[22]

Still, even as the attacks on foreign capital reached new heights, signs of Sukarno's reluctance to make a complete break were evident. As late as October 1964, he had issued a call for stepped-up production-sharing credits. In response to that appeal, the Presidium released a report in January 1965 proposing that restrictions on the foreign party in production-sharing projects be eased substantially. Of course the proposal was never implemented, but the fact that it could be considered at all indicates a residual ambivalence about renouncing foreign investment.[23] Finally, it is worth noting that the foreign oil companies, important earners of foreign exchange, were not taken over even in the most violent days of anti-Americanism, though there was movement in that direction at the end of 1965.

Foreign Credits

Although foreign credits gradually came to be seen as preferable to private investment, even aid in that form grew more suspect. Back in 1956, Foreign Minister Abdulgani had argued that Indonesia's economic development did not have to depend essentially on foreign aid. He stressed that the $100 million in foreign loans required for the Five Year Plan would constitute a very small percentage of its overall financing. Implicitly acknowledging that the plan was rather modest compared to expectations of the early 1950s, he noted that it would be possible to speed up development by getting more foreign aid, but that this might restrict Indonesia's foreign policy and would burden future generations with a heavy debt. Similarly, the chairman of the National Planning Board was said to have opposed financing the Eight Year Plan with extensive foreign loans on the grounds that the burden of debt repayment would be too heavy.[24]

22. Alex Hunter, "The Oil Companies: Diverging Interests?" *BIES,* no. 3 (February 1966), p. 77.

23. Gibson, "Production-Sharing," pp. 56–57.

24. H. Roeslan Abdulgani, "Uraian Tentang Perkembangan Politik Luar

By 1962 Sukarno was warning of the dangers of thinking only of foreign credits and underestimating Indonesia's own capital. There were nations in Asia, he observed, that lived on aid, but Indonesia would never become such a nation; Indonesia would never beg. Though he made it clear that he had no objection to accepting aid, Sukarno urged his countrymen not to forget that only a nation that is self-reliant can become great.[25]

Despite the growing sensitivity to the dangers of dependence on foreign aid, it was only after 1956 that Indonesia began to receive truly substantial aid. Hoping to increase the amount of aid while reducing dependence on the West, the government sought and received considerable aid from the Soviet Union and East European countries, as well as from the West. The aid was mainly in the form of long-term loans, but it also included trade credits from Japan and several West European countries, American agricultural products at greatly reduced prices, Japanese war reparations, and technical assistance from the United Nations and under Colombo Plan auspices. In November 1964 an aid agreement with China was concluded. By the end of 1965 Indonesia had accumulated a foreign debt, including both economic and military aid, of $2.4 billion, of which $1.4 billion was owed to Communist countries. (For details see Appendix B.) But it is important to remember that assistance received from the Communists was predominantly military aid related to the West Irian campaign, not economic aid.

Moreover, both the Five Year Plan of 1956 and the Eight Year Plan announced in 1960 acknowledged the need for foreign credits.[26]

Negeri Selama Tahun 1956," *Pewarta Kemlu,* 2 (December 1956), 767–68, and Oei, "Implications of Indonesia's New Foreign Investment Policy," p. 36.

25. *Segala Aktivitet Kita Adalah Untuk Menjelematkan Revolusi Kita* (Jakarta: Departemen Penerangan, 1962), p. 12, and *Mari Kita Berdjalan Terus Menggalang Segala Kekuatan Nasional Untuk Memasukkan Irian Barat Kedalam Wilajah Kekuasaan R.I. Tahun Ini Djuga* (Jakarta: Departemen Penerangan, 1962), pp. 10–11.

26. *Penjelenggaraan Pembangunan Semesta Dalam Rangka Mendjalankan Undang-Undang Dasar Pasal 33* (Jakarta: Departemen Penerangan, 1960),

Respected leaders like Hatta and Prime Minister Djuanda strongly emphasized the indispensability of foreign aid, and even Sukarno as late as 1959 could speak of his preference for credits over foreign investment without dwelling at all on the risks of dependence.[27] In fact, in the 1961 speech that introduced the NEFOS-OLDEFOS concept, Sukarno talked of a convergence of interests between the aid-givers and Indonesia. Economic development in countries like Indonesia, he suggested, would make them even better markets for the products of the advanced countries.[28]

Following the successful completion in 1962 of the West Irian campaign, which Sukarno acknowledged had slowed the country's economic development, he declared that Indonesia now could move full speed ahead on the economy. Of course he was careful to stress that this did not mean "stuffing aid down our throats." On the contrary, he asserted, "prosperity which is the result of begging is meaningless."[29] But in fact, at the very moment in early 1963 when Sukarno made that statement, the Indonesian government was engaged in a serious effort to get major economic aid from the West, though Western insistence on linking aid to an unpopular stabilization program only created new objections to the aid relationship.

By 1964, when it had become clear that Western aid was tied to

---

pp. 19–21; "Lampiran Keputusan Dewan Pertimbangan Agung," pp. 34–35, 44; and Paauw, "From Colonial to Guided Economy," pp. 228–31.

27. Hatta, *Ekonomi Terpimpin* (Jakarta [?]: Penerbit Djembatan, 1959), pp. 57–59; the 1959 report of the Djuanda cabinet, *Mendjelang Dua Tahun Kabinet Karya* (Jakarta: Kementerian Penerangan, 1959), p. 14; Djuanda's speech of 18 June 1963 (*Keterangan-Keterangan Pemerintah Mengenai Soal-Soal Pelaksanaan Deklarasi Ekonomi* [Jakarta: Departemen Penerangan, 1963], p. 23); and Sukarno, *Penemuan Kembali Revolusi Kita,* p. 38.

28. *From Non-Alignment to Coordinated Accumulation of Moral Force,* pp. 13–14. See also *Speech by President Sukarno Before Colombo Plan Conference at Jogjakarta* (Jakarta: Department of Information, 1959), pp. 4–5. Economic aid, said Sukarno, was not charity but "enlightened self-interest" based on a "recognition that the sickness of one man is contagious for all."

29. He claimed that the West Irian campaign and efforts to restore security together had consumed 80 percent of the budget (*Djalankan Pantja Program, Ganjang Semua Tantangan* [Jakarta: Pengurus Besar Front Nasional, 1963], p. 26).

a termination of Indonesia's confrontation with Malaysia, many Indonesian spokesmen began to dwell on the use of foreign aid to influence Indonesia's political stance.[30] They were now more skeptical than ever that Western aid could be obtained at a politically acceptable cost. Sukarno claimed that the imperialists were trying "to defeat the Indonesian revolution by scaring us, if Indonesia continues to crush Malaysia, for example, if Indonesia continues to pursue socialism, we will withdraw our economic aid. Economic aid, economic aid, economic aid, economic aid, always economic aid is made a threat, a weapon, so that we will follow their desires. And if we do not follow their desires, they say economic aid will be withdrawn. . . . If they want to withdraw aid, we say OK, you may withdraw your economic aid to Indonesia. We are not going to retreat a step, because we have lots of resources." He also warned against "selling our souls for a plate of beans or even for a lot of aid, however much," and declared: "If some nation says to us, you can have aid, but you have to end confrontation, then I say 'go to hell with your aid.' "[31]

While he stressed that self-reliance did not rule out cooperation based on equal standing and mutual advantage, Sukarno increasingly denigrated the value of aid and claimed that Indonesia could develop without it. If nations poor in natural resources could develop, surely Indonesia could: "We feel free. . . . Now we are really self-reliant. This is the great advantage of teaching ourselves to become a free people, no longer one that always asks 'aid, aid

30. *Suluh Indonesia,* 21 March 1964, 8 April 1964; *Bintang Timur,* 26 March 1964; *Merdeka,* 7 May 1964. *Trisakti,* 3 September 1965, notes other American conditions such as the requirement that American property be protected from demonstrators or that aid recipients refrain from carrying goods to North Vietnam.

31. *Pengusaha Nasional Swasta, Djadilah Penjumbang Konstruktif untuk Penjelesaian Revolusi!* (Jakarta: Departemen Penerangan, 1964), pp. 8–9; speech of 26 March 1964, published as *Dewan Produksi Nasional untuk Meningkatkan Produksi* (Jakarta: Departemen Penerangan, 1964), p. 10; speech of 9 April 1964, entitled *Agungkanlah Ibu Pratiwi dan Bapak Angkasa!* (Jakarta: Departemen Penerangan, 1964), pp. 8–9.

please.' Give us aid, please, give us aid. Some time ago I said go to hell with your aid. We don't need it."[32]

In view of Sukarno's increasingly sharp condemnation of dependence on foreign aid, it is easy to forget that he continued through 1965 to speak of the need for additional aid, and that discussions of a proposed Three Year Plan to run from 1966 to 1968 acknowledged this need.[33] Indeed, aid figures for 1965 suggest that as much as $470 million in new foreign credits were secured during 1965, though many of those credits were never realized.[34] Even PKI chairman Aidit, who in 1964 had stressed self-reliance, indicated in 1965 that foreign credits might be necessary.[35]

Although Aidit, Sukarno, and others had for some time talked of shifting the emphasis in both aid and trade from the imperialists to the socialist countries and the NEFOS,[36] aid and trade relations in 1965 still focused on the West. Indonesia had received considerable aid, mainly military, from the Communist countries, but this did

32. See *Indonesia Keluar dari PBB* (Jakarta: Tjendekia, 1965), pp. 9-10, in which Sukarno also contended that FAO and UNICEF technical experts did not understand Indonesian style agriculture. In *Reach to the Stars,* p. 39–40, he declared: "I always start from the stand that it is imperialism that needs us, not we who need the imperialists. That is why having been told to go to hell with their aid, the imperialists are now trying to approach us again and trying to offer us 'aid' again." See also *Pentjangkulan Pertama Musim Penanaman Padi 1961* (Jakarta: Departemen Penerangan, 1961), pp. 8–9; *Genta Suara Revolusi Indonesia* (Jakarta: Departemen Penerangan, 1963), pp. 30–31; and *Dewan Produksi Nasional,* p. 9.

33. See *Deklarasi Ekonomi,* (Jakarta: Departemen Penerangan, 1963), p. 19; *Berdiri Diatas Kaki Sendiri,* p. 25; and *Kesimpulan-Kesimpulan dan Kertas-Kerdja2 Rapat Paripurna Ke III MUPPENAS* (Jakarta: Sekretariat MUPPENAS, 1965), p. 49.

34. *BIES,* no. 2 (September 1965), p. 5, and no. 3 (February 1966), pp. 15–16.

35. See Aidit's *Djadilah Komunis Jang Baik dan Lebih Baik Lagi* (Jakarta: Jajasan Pembaruan, 1964), pp. 58–59, and his speech in *Kesimpulan-Kesimpulan,* pp. 275–76, which stipulated that foreign credits not exceed 20 percent of the volume of financing for all development.

36. *Amanat Pembangunan Presiden,* pp. 35, 101. On Aidit, see *Kesimpulan-Kesimpulan,* p. 276. See also the paper of Sutikno Slamet, a former assistant to Djuanda, in *ibid,* p. 49, and Mohammad Yamin's remarks in *Penjelenggaraan Pembangunan Semesta,* pp. 19–21.

not basically alter the country's economic dependence on the West, and it certainly did not make Indonesia economically dependent on the Communists. Of the $470 million in foreign credits believed to have been secured in 1965, 74 percent came from non-Communist countries, with Japan the largest single contributor. The three main markets for Indonesian exports in 1965 were Japan, the United States, and West Germany. In fact, Indonesia purchased 15 percent more from the United Kingdom in 1965 than in 1964, despite Jakarta's policy of confrontation.[37] And Aidit indicated to an American interviewer in early 1965 his awareness that Indonesia would have to continue selling its raw materials to the West for some time.[38]

Development Strategies

If the years from 1954 to 1965 were generally characterized by a heightening consciousness of the risks involved in foreign aid and investment, they also brought a deepening of the conviction that independence could be assured only through a development strategy that met two conditions: an emphasis on industrialization, as well as agricultural self-sufficiency, and overcoming inflation through an increase in production, not primarily through monetary measures.

Government statements asserted that only industrialization, especially the development of heavy industry, could free Indonesia from dependence on foreign imports: "In the absence of heavy industry, self-supporting will merely be a slogan which can never be realized, because ultimately the basic questions of production and transportation will depend on foreign sources."[39] The Eight Year Plan was thus aimed at building an economy that would not be dependent on fluctuations of the world market and at establishing basic and heavy

37. *BIES*, no. 2 (September 1965), p. 6, and no. 3 (February 1966), pp. 15–16. See also *Komando Presiden-Pemimpin Besar Revolusi Kepada Angkatan 45* (Jakarta: Departemen Penerangan, 1963), pp. 36–37.

38. I am indebted to Ruth McVey for this information from her interview with Aidit.

39. *Explanatory Statement by H. E. President Sukarno: Planned National Overall Development* (Jakarta: Department of Information, 1960), p. 6.

industry.[40] The inauguration in 1962 of the Tjilegon iron and steel factory project, to be constructed with Soviet aid, was hailed as a major step away from the colonial economic orientation by which Indonesia produced mainly raw materials for export.[41]

Combating inflation by increasing the supply of goods, rather than by drastically reducing the flow of currency, was appealing because it could be seen as leading toward industrialization and self-sufficiency. Monetary measures, on the other hand, not only meant austerity and considerable short-term hardship. They involved a de-emphasis of those expenditures that would increase production, thus delaying the process of creating jobs, raising purchasing power, and developing the industries that would reduce Indonesia's dependence on the world market for its exports. The production approach also fit well with Sukarno's contention that the way to solve Indonesia's economic problems was not through conventional economic measures but through revolutionary means—that is, through a mobilization of human and natural resources, which required putting the unemployed to work, demanding sacrifices, and arousing the fighting spirit of the Indonesian people.[42] Efforts to carry out land reform, to improve the tax system, and to purge Indonesia of the remnants of feudalism and imperialism all were justified, at least in part, by the contribution they would make to raising production.[43]

40. *Buku Ringkasan Pembangunan Semesta* (Jakarta: Departemen Penerangan, 1961), p. 11. For an expression of First Minister Djuanda's concern about dependence on world markets, see *Keterangan Pemerintah Mengenai Situasi Negara* (Jakarta: Departemen Penerangan, 1962), pp. 11–13.

41. Speech of Foreign Minister Subandrio on 21 May 1962, published in *Komando Pelaksanaan Pembangunan Pabrik Besi-Badja di Tjilegon* (Jakarta: Departemen Penerangan, 1962), p. 14.

42. See *Buku Ringkasan Pembangunan Semesta,* p. 16; *Tahun Kemenangan* (Jakarta: Departemen Penerangen, 1962), p. 39; *Deklarasi Ekonomi,* especially pp. 3–5, 11–12; *Genta Suara Revolusi Indonesia,* pp. 30–33; *Komando Presiden-Pemimpin Besar Revolusi Kepada Angkatan 45,* p. 35; and *Laksanakan Serempak Pantja Program Front Nasional dan Tri Program Pemerintah* (Jakarta: Pengurus Besar Front Nasional, 1964), p. 16.

43. On land reform, see *Laksanakan Serempak Pantja Program Front Nasional,* p. 22; on taxes, see *Deklarasi Ekonomi,* pp. 17–18.

In the year following the end of the West Irian campaign in mid-1962, when considerable attention was directed toward plans for overcoming Indonesia's economic difficulties, the need to raise production in order to create economic self-sufficiency and overcome inflation continued to be stressed. The major document of this period, the Economic Declaration issued in March 1963, viewed increased production as the key to rescuing the economy.[44]

There remained, however, a certain inconsistency in the government's attitude. The same statements that talked of industrializing immediately also spoke of providing adequate food and clothing as a "basis" for industrialization, which was to be deferred to the second stage of development. Though monetary measures were always unpopular, Sukarno did acknowledge that increased production accompanied by uncontrolled inflation would be self-defeating.[45] Statements calling for increased production to overcome inflation criticized reliance on monetary measures alone, but did not always rule them out completely. The strongest testimony to the persistent influence of the monetary approach was the government's economic stabilization plan of 1963.

The 1963 regulations had their origin in late 1962, when Washington made it clear that Indonesia's request for aid would be considered only if the government were to carry out a stabilization program acceptable to the IMF. Though the original plan had been formulated chiefly by Sutikno Slamet, an Indonesian who had served in Washington as the IMF executive director for Indonesia, the government was forced to modify that version on key points in order to win IMF approval.[46] In May 1963 the government issued

44. See *Tahun Kemenangan* (Jakarta: Departemen Penerangan, 1962), p. 39; *Deklarasi Ekonomi,* pp. 11–12, 17–19, 22–23; *Laksanakan Serempak Pantja Program Front Nasional,* p. 16; *Djalankan Pantja-Program Front Nasional,* p. 11; and *Genta Suara Revolusi Indonesia,* pp. 30–33.

45. *Amanat Pendjelasan Presiden Republik Indonesia Tentang Tindakan-Tindakan Pemerintah Dibidang Keuangan dan Ekonomi* (Jakarta: Kementerian Penerangan, 1959), pp. 6–8. See also *Explanatory Statement,* pp. 9–10; "Lampiran Keputusan Dewan Pertimbangan Agung," pp. 42, 47–48; *Deklarasi Ekonomi,* pp. 17–19; and *Kesimpulan-Kesimpulan,* p. 29.

46. An IMF team which had visited Jakarta in December listed the fol-

a series of regulations reflecting the monetary approach as part of an overall economic stabilization program.[47] But the regulations met with violent and widespread opposition on the grounds that they not only increased the suffering of the people but were inconsistent with the production approach spelled out in the Economic Declaration. They were also denounced as a clear demonstration of the dangers of reliance on foreign aid and as further evidence of the OLDEFOS' determination to sustain the existing exploitative system.[48] Sukarno declared that he viewed such criticism as a welcome manifestation of "economic patriotism."[49]

---

lowing ingredients of an acceptable stabilization program: a balanced budget, reduction of military expenditures, tight credit policy, devaluation of the rupiah and institution of a multiple exchange rate system, price decontrol on all commodities and elimination of government subsidies, and the postponement of debt repayments. The Indonesian plan, as relayed to Washington and the IMF in February 1963, called for cutting expenditures as part of a gradual move toward a balanced budget, price decontrol only with respect to rice, and the establishment of differential exchange rates without a general devaluation. The IMF yielded on the question of exchange rates and to some extent on the balanced budget, accepting an Indonesian proposal that would lead to a balanced budget in roughly two years. But the Indonesians gave in on price decontrol, and it was on this aspect of the regulations that criticism subsequently centered.

47. This included austerity in government expenditures and a tight money policy for the banking system; a 400–600 percent increase in certain public utility and service costs which had become extraordinarily cheap; the introduction of a new set of foreign exchange regulations which amounted to a de facto currency devaluation; the release of foreign exchange for a "crash program" of imports, particularly of spare parts and raw materials for industry (which government spokesmen could cite as evidence that the regulations did in fact aim at increasing production); and an increase in the salaries and allowances of civil servants (J. A. C. Mackie, *Problems of the Indonesian Inflation* [Ithaca: Cornell Modern Indonesia Project, 1967], pp. 39–40).

48. See *Harian Rakjat,* 29 and 30 May 1963, 10 June 1963, 17 July 1963; *Bintang Timur,* 18 June 1963, for both the editorial and the analysis by the Marxist economist Carmel Budiardjo, and 26 June 1963, 1 July 1963, 26 March 1964; *Suluh Indonesia,* 28 May 1963, 1 April 1964; *Duta Masjarakat,* 25 June 1963; and *Komando Presiden-Pemimpin Besar Revolusi Kepada Angkatan 45,* pp. 23, 35, 41.

49. *Genta Suara Revolusi Indonesia,* p. 34. The above discussion of the stabilization plan is based on internal Indonesian government documents made available to the author and on interviews with Indonesian officials, in-

With the monetary approach thus discredited by its association with the IMF-sponsored stabilization plan, emphasis on the production approach grew even heavier after 1963. And in the 1965 planning for the Three Year Plan, there was a clear commitment to increased production as the way to stem inflation gradually.[50]

1966–1975: Putting Aid First

Setting the New Course

Following the attempted coup of 30 September 1965, the Indonesian leaders' thinking about the role of foreign capital in economic development appeared to undergo a complete reversal. By the end of 1966, the New Order leadership had fixed a set of economic policies which emphasized stringent monetary measures aimed at stabilization, heavy reliance on foreign loans, and an eager welcome to foreign investment.

The first clear challenge to the economic approach of the Guided Democracy years came in late November 1965, with the publication of a series of essays by leading University of Indonesia economists. They vigorously attacked the notion that the production approach alone could solve Indonesia's economic problems, and that monetary measures were to be rejected as conventional, antipeople, and unpatriotic. According to the economists, the adherents of the production approach, who argued that credits for investment would be noninflationary so long as they were tied to increases in production, were making the unwarranted assumption that production increases could keep pace with the growth of the money supply. However successful the attempt to raise production, they countered, its fruits would be drowned in the flood of monetary expansion unless measures were employed to decrease the money supply. Also, given the

---

cluding one who played a prominent role in the formulation of the plan and in the subsequent negotiations with Washington and the IMF. For an excellent discussion, drawing on a wide range of Indonesian and American sources, see Bunnell, "The Kennedy Initiatives in Indonesia," pp. 308–441.

50. *Kesimpulan-Kesimpulan,* p. 45. See also *Komando Presiden-Pemimpin Besar Revolusi Kepada Angkatan 45,* p. 35; *Dewan Produksi Nasional,* p. 10; and *Berdiri Diatas Kaki Sendiri,* pp. 24–25.

inducements to speculation afforded by the existing inflationary situation, it was by no means certain that the extension of credits would lead to an increase in production. Only after the government had restored economic stability through basic monetary measures found in any economics textbook could efforts to increase production profitably be undertaken.[51]

The first sign of changing attitudes toward foreign aid came in January 1966 when one of the economists publicly acknowledged that "the only way out" of Indonesia's worsening economic dilemma was through an effort to obtain new foreign credits. With a rescheduling of Indonesia's debts and $300 million in new multipurpose credits, argued Professor Mohammad Sadli, the government could repair the economy without giving rise to dangerous social disruption. Sadli noted that criticizing his recommendation as a violation of the doctrine of self-reliance was easy. But, he pointed out, even though the Sukarno government claimed that its policies had been drawn up without any expectation of new foreign aid, that government was busily, if unsuccessfully, searching for such credits. Sadli added that Indonesia had been receiving foreign credits for years and thus had never really been self-reliant. Foreign credits wisely used would give Indonesia a basis for hoping to eventually achieve self-reliance, he concluded.[52]

After the transfer of authority to Soeharto in March, the government quickly made known its intention to seek foreign aid and to take steps to stabilize the economy. On 4 April, Foreign Minister Malik announced that Indonesia would seek an expansion of economic cooperation with both Western and socialist countries. On

51. See Mohammad Sadli, "Masalah2 Ekonomi Jang Timbul (Atau Ada) Sekitar Coup G-30-S," and Ali Wardhana, "Masalah Inflasi di Indonesia," in *Masalah2 Ekonomi dan Faktor2 Ipolsos* (*Ideologi, Politik, Sosial*) [Jakarta: Lembaga Ekonomi dan Kemasjarakatan Nasional, 1965], pp. 29, 37, 39, 42–51. See also the introduction by Widjojo Nitisastro, "Persoalan2 Ekonomis-Tehnis dan Ekonomis-Politis Dalam Menanggulangi Masalah2 Ekonomi," p. 7.

52. "Masalah2 Ekonomi-Moneter Kita Jang Strukturil," in *The Leader, the Man, and the Gun* (Jakarta: P. T. Matoa, 1966), pp. 92–93. Sadli's paper was read at an economic seminar sponsored by the Indonesian University Students Action Front (KAMI).

the same day Sultan Hamengku Buwono IX, deputy prime minister for economic affairs, indicated that while Indonesia was still aiming for self-reliance, the government would welcome all foreign economic aid without political strings and would seek rescheduling of its debt repayments. In his statement that day and in a subsequent one on 12 April, the Sultan emphasized Indonesia's intention to embark on an austerity program and to take other measures to achieve economic stabilization, though there was some evidence in his earlier statement that he was thinking in terms of the production approach.[53] In early May, Malik told the parliament that the government intended to improve its economic relations with the United States, and the Sultan announced plans to send a technical mission to Japan and several eastern and western European countries to discuss debt rescheduling and to clarify the possibility of obtaining new credits.[54]

The new course became official state doctrine in July with the establishment of new economic guidelines by the MPRS. Drafted by the economists, the MPRS decision affirmed the need for foreign credits, called for the immediate preparation of a law setting up procedures for foreign investment, and stressed the urgency of a drastic austerity program. For the short-term, all efforts were to be directed toward stabilization and rehabilitation, specifically controlling inflation, providing an adequate supply of food and clothing, repairing the infrastructure, and increasing exports. Development, as distinguished from stabilization and rehabilitation, was deferred to the

53. *Statement-statement Politik Waperdam Bidang Sospol/Menteri Luar Negeri dan Waperdam Bidang Ekubang,* pp. 5, 8–10, 16–18, 24–26.

54. *Keterangan Wakil Perdana Menteri Bidang Sosial Politik/Menteri Luar Negeri Didepan Sidang DPR-GR* (Jakarta: Kementerian Penerangan, 1966), p. 13; *Keterangan Wakil Perdana Menteri Bidang Ekonomi, Keuangan dan Pembangunan Didepan Sidang DPR-GR* (Jakarta: Kementerian Penerangan, 1966), pp. 8–9; and *Djawaban Wakil Perdana Menteri Bidang Ekonomi, Keuangan dan Pembangunan Atas Pemandangan Umum DPR-GR* (Jakarta: Kementerian Penerangan, 1966), p. 4. The magnitude of the problem was clear from the figures for 1966: estimated foreign exchange earnings were $360–400 million, while debt repayments due totaled $530 million. See *Sumbangan Fikiran TNI-AD Kepada Kabinet Ampera* (Bandung [?]: Seskoad [?], 1966), p. 90.

long-run, with priority given to (1) agriculture, (2) infrastructure, and (3) industry, mining, and oil. While warning against dependence on outsiders, the MPRS stated that the principle of self-reliance should not preclude use of outside capital, technology and expertise.[55]

In September, Indonesia's Western creditors met in Tokyo to hear Jakarta's plans for repairing the economy and to learn the IMF's evaluation of those plans. The group agreed in principle to reschedule Indonesia's debt repayments, while the IMF and several of the participating countries expressed a readiness to support, again in principle, the extension of new assistance. The non-Communist creditor nations, under the rubric of the Inter-Governmental Group on Indonesia (IGGI), later pledged $200 million in new aid for 1967. Meeting every six months to hear Indonesian reports on economic performance, requests for new aid, and the evaluation of the IMF resident team, the IGGI nations subsequently agreed to supply aid in increasing sums—from $360 million for 1968 to $920 million for the 1975/76 fiscal year. (For details, including a breakdown by countries, see Appendix B.) In 1970, agreement was reached on the long-term rescheduling of Indonesia's debts to both its Western and Soviet creditors. American military aid resumed in 1971 at a level of about $20 million a year; in 1975 the Indonesians requested more than double that amount, and the initial response from Washington was encouraging.[56] By 1975 the Indonesians had also won modest aid commitments from the Communist nations and from the Middle Eastern oil exporting countries.[57]

55. *Ketetapan-Ketetapan dan Keputusan-Keputusan Sidang Umum Ke-IV MPRS* (Jakarta: Departemen Penerangan, 1966), pp. 57–59, 62–63.

56. The State Department recommended that Congress vote $42.5 million in military aid to Indonesia for fiscal 1976 (*Palo Alto Times,* 21 October 1975).

57. Discussion of new Soviet aid began in 1971 with the visit of a Soviet technical team. Though nothing resulted for several years, by 1975 the Soviets had agreed to aid projects in electricity, mining, and other industries. Yugoslavia had agreed to lend $80 million for a steam-generated electric power center and another $40 million for the expansion of facilities for producing heavy equipment. In addition, Saudia Arabia had pledged $100 million and

With respect to foreign investment, in December 1966 the Indonesian parliament passed a new law which was considerably more liberal than the 1958 law.[58] Steps were also taken to bring about the return of foreign companies, mainly British and American, that had been taken over during the Guided Democracy period. After a slow start, investment applications began to flow in rapidly, and by the end of 1974 nearly $4 billion had been approved for investment (excluding oil and banking), though only a small percentage of that sum had actually been invested.[59] Nearly $2 billion was approved for investment in oil under production-sharing contracts between 1966 and the end of 1974. This does not include investments made by some of the largest companies, such as Caltex and Stanvac, under the work contract system, for which no figures are issued. Thus it is impossible to estimate the total investment in oil. (For a breakdown on foreign investment by countries and fields of activity, see Appendix C.)

Indonesia's plans for improving the economy were embodied in the regulations of 3 October 1966. Among the key points were: a balanced budget, a tight money policy (which the government's spokesmen preferred to call a selective credit policy), an end to government subsidies and an increase in the prices of most public utilities, decontrol and greater scope for competition and market forces, simplification of export regulations, and increased tax collec-

---

Iran had offered $200 million for construction of a fertilizer plant (*Indonesian Perspectives* [February 1975], p. 13; *Kompas,* 7 June 1975; and Radio Jakarta, 8 July 1975).

58. Oei, "Implications of Indonesia's New Foreign Investment Policy," p. 39. For a comparison of the two laws, see Ismail Suny and Rudioro Rochmat, *Tindjauan dan Pembahasan Undang-Undang Penanaman Modal Asing dan Kredit Luar Negeri* (Jakarta: Penerbit Pradnja Paramita, 1968), pp. 11–13. For the investment law and supplementary material on investment procedures and results, see *Investment: Policies, Procedures, Fields of Investment, and Progress Report,* 2d ed. (Jakarta: Japenpa, 1969).

59. Initially, most investment was in extractive industries. In 1974 there was a major shift from forestry and mining toward manufacturing (and real estate) and from the United States to Japan (*BIES,* vol. 11, no. 2 [July 1975], pp. 24–25).

tion.[60] As the Sultan had indicated in early September, the government was "clearly beginning by trying the monetary approach," and would seek to increase production and improve infrastructure after monetary measures had succeeded in overcoming inflation.[61] The tight money policy, which initially set annual interest rates at 72–108 percent, depending on the category of the loan, was gradually eased, but even in early 1973 interest remained at 12–36 percent a year and many businessmen still regarded credit as tight.[62]

In 1969 the government inaugurated a Five Year Development Plan with the central goal of achieving self-sufficiency in rice; other goals included rehabilitating the infrastructure, raising production in export-oriented mining industries through foreign investment, and increasing production in industries related to agriculture and secondarily in other specified industries.[63] Approximately 73 percent of the total financing for the Five Year Plan was to come from

60. *The New Regulations on Economic and Financial Policies* (Jakarta: Department of Information, 1966), and *BIES,* no. 5 (October 1966), pp. 3–11.

61. *Himpunan Uraian,* pp. 55–56.

62. By May 1969, shortly after the start of the Five Year Development Plan, interest rates had been lowered to 30–72 percent. For data on the tight money policy, see *Keterangan Pemerintah Mengenai Langkah-Langkah Baru Meletakkan Dasar-Dasar Stabilisasi Ekonnomi dan Rehabilitasi Untuk Tahun 1967* (Jakarta: Departemen Penerangan, 1967), pp. 11, 13; *Pidato/Briefing Pedjabat Presiden Republik Indonesia Ketua Presidium Kabinet Ampera pada Musjawarah Kerdja Antara Pemerintah Pusat dan Pedjabat-Pedjabat Daerah* (Jakarta: Departemen Penerangan, 1967), p. 28; *BIES,* no. 9 (February 1968), pp. 2–3; David Cole, "New Directions for the Banking System," *BIES,* vol. 5, no. 2 (July 1969), p. 62; and *Monthly Review* (May 1972), pp. 4–6. When the inflation rate soared to 47 percent for the twelve month period ending in March 1974, interest rates were raised again (*Kompas,* 10 April 1974, 19 June 1974).

63. See "The Five Year Plan," *BIES,* vol. 5, no. 2 (July 1969), p. 71, and *Indonesia Develops: Five Year Development Plan April 1969–April 1974* (Jakarta: Department of Information, 1969). The specified industries were "fertilizer, cement and chemical industries, the textile industry, the pulp and paper industries, printing industries, pharmaceutical and light industries, and people's industries, metal industry, machines, equipment and infrastructural industries." Planned expenditures on industrial development amounted to 17.7 percent of the total Five Year Plan expenditures.

foreign sources, including private investment, and close to 80 percent of the government's development budget for the period of the plan was to be met by foreign aid.[64]

The Price of Aid

From the earliest days of the New Order, it was evident that in order to attract foreign aid Indonesia would have to adjust its policies to the desires of the creditor nations. The obvious first step was to end the policy of confrontation, for the cessation of aid from the IMF and the United States had been unmistakably linked to Indonesia's campaign to crush Malaysia. Though the Indonesians probably would have moved to end confrontation even if they had not urgently needed Western economic aid, they were well aware that the termination of the costly conflict with Malaysia was an implicit, and occasionally explicit, precondition for the re-establishment of economic cooperation with the West.[65]

Nor was there any doubt in the Indonesians' minds that they

64. See Bank Indonesia, *Indonesian Financial Statistics: Monthly Bulletin* (February 1973), p. 196; and *BIES,* vol. 5, no. 2 (July 1969), p. 73. The anticipated annual contribution of foreign aid to the government's development budget was as follows: 1969/70—80%; 1970/71—78%; 1971/72—81%; 1972/73—79%; 1973/74—76%. Figures on actual expenditures for the first three fiscal years show that the contribution of foreign aid was slightly lower than planned (*Indonesian Quarterly,* 1 [January 1973], 85, and *BIES,* vol. 7, no. 1 [March 1971], p. 29). The absolute amount of the Indonesian contribution to the development budget has risen significantly, but the percentage has not, because total expenditures for development have also grown substantially.

65. See the newspaper editorials and statements attributed to Foreign Minister Malik and cited in Weinstein, *Indonesia Abandons Confrontation,* pp. 74–75. See also Malik's *Kita Mengabdikan Politik Luar Negeri Indonesia Kepada Kepentingan Nasional* (Jakarta: Departemen Penerangan, 1966), pp. 17, 20–21. A top official of the Central Bank told the author that when he visited his counterparts in the United States, Japan, and other Western creditor countries in February 1966 to discuss postponement of Indonesia's debt repayments, virtually all of those contacted emphasized the need to end confrontation immediately and to avoid "such costly adventures" in the future. And David Bell, head of AID, made it clear that Washington would consider giving aid to Indonesia only if the government were "interested in peace in the area" (*Antara,* 15 July 1966).

could count on substantial Western aid only if Indonesia were to undertake economic policies acceptable to the Western creditors. A central bank official who visited most of Indonesia's non-Communist creditors in February 1966 was advised that Indonesia needed to make basic changes in its economic policies. Besides urging a balanced budget and a tight money policy, the officials with whom he talked suggested that Indonesia should adopt a more receptive attitude toward foreign capital. They pointed to certain other countries and asked: "Why can't you be like that?" In May, according to a leading technocrat, the first official effort to arrange debt rescheduling and get new aid "ran into difficulties" because the creditor countries were "hesitant to make commitments so long as Indonesia's new economic policies remained unclear." In August, when the Indonesians informed the IMF of their desire to postpone repayment of the debt, the answer was: "First tell us your plans for improving the economic situation in Indonesia."[66] Actually, the Indonesian leaders knew what the IMF wanted to hear, for the IMF's conception of an acceptable stabilization program had been fully spelled out in 1963. With the assistance of an IMF team, the Indonesians in August and September drafted a comprehensive economic stabilization and rehabilitation plan that they hoped would meet the expectations of their Western creditors.

To be sure, Indonesia's long-frustrated economists needed little prodding from the IMF to formulate either the sweeping stabilization plan adopted in October 1966 or the foreign investment law enacted in December. Perhaps reflecting their American education and their longstanding friendship with the head of IMF's Asia section, Tun Thin, who had once taught economics at the University of Indonesia, the economists found the IMF's desires quite compatible with their own inclinations. In the words of one of them: "We think the same way IMF people think." Having drafted the MPRS statement on economic affairs in June and discussed proposed poli-

66. Interview with Frans Seda, Jakarta, 20 December 1969. Seda, as minister of finance, was the official directly responsible for dealings with the IMF.

cies in some depth at a seminar at the army staff and command school in Bandung during late August, the economists were already well advanced in their own planning by the time the IMF team arrived in Indonesia.

Nevertheless, though their recommendations met with general IMF approval, certain of the economists' proposals were rejected as unrealistic.[67] In September, when the Indonesians set forth their plans before a meeting of their non-Communist creditors in Tokyo, the conference deferred any specific decisions until a December meeting, by which time the participants hoped to have a "more concrete picture" of Indonesia's economic policies.[68] Following the Tokyo session, Indonesia's stabilization plan crystallized into a set of regulations rather more drastic than some had anticipated.[69] That the Indonesian leaders did indeed feel strong pressure to conform to the IMF's desires, both at the time of the Tokyo meeting and subsequently, was confirmed by Malik: "There is no question that the advice of the IMF was an important factor in the decisions having to do with the tight money policy. I don't know whether or not you can say this influence was determining, but it was certainly important. There was the feeling that failure to follow the IMF's advice might lead to a loss of aid."[70]

In the years after the basic course of the New Order was set,

67. For example, a recommendation to increase revenues through augmented taxes was rejected by the IMF as too ambitious. Also, on certain technicalities where the Indonesians felt they lacked a basis for comparison, the IMF was able to help (interviews with the economists involved).

68. *Antara,* 21 September 1966.

69. That the regulations did not "crystallize" until after the Tokyo meeting was reported by a top official of the Central Bank. One of those who found the regulations more drastic than expected was Sarbini Sumawinata. He was involved in some of the deliberations and fully supported the general thrust of them at the time, but he said he was astonished to discover, when the regulations were announced on the radio, that the tight money policy was so tight (interview, Jakarta, 27 February 1970).

70. Interview, Jakarta, 7 February 1970. According to Sarbini (interview, 27 February 1970), an IMF official told him that Indonesia would indeed have to follow the tight monetary policies recommended, if it hoped to have the backing of the IMF in its efforts to get new credits.

the Indonesian leaders were subject to a variety of external pressures as a consequence of their country's dependence on Western economic support. Sometimes they succeeded in deflecting those pressures, usually by enlisting the support of some of the powers in opposition to the demands of others; on other occasions they had to submit, and in some cases it is hard to say whether they yielded or not. In the latter part of 1966, proposals for the establishment of a "tight" aid-Indonesia consortium were successfully resisted by the Indonesians, who feared that such an institutional arrangement, involving a permanent secretariat in which considerable influence might be concentrated, would constitute an unacceptable infringement of Indonesia's sovereignty.[71] Within the framework of the "loose" IGGI, the Indonesians have fought stubbornly to maximize their influence over the form and terms of aid and investment. A major victory, achieved after initial opposition from all but the Dutch, was the extension of the BE (bonus export) system to foreign aid, enabling Indonesians to determine which commodities would be purchased with the credits extended to them.[72]

Aid agreements with a number of the IGGI countries were signed only after extended haggling over terms,[73] but nowhere was

71. According to several technocrats, proposals for a "tight" consortium (meaning decisions would be binding on its members) emanated mainly from the United States, which hoped that such an arrangement would facilitate a "sharing of the burden." Indonesia's resistance was substantially assisted by the unwillingness of a number of the creditor countries to accept such an arrangement. In any case, the idea apparently never received very serious consideration.

72. According to *Antara,* 22 March 1967, Japan agreed to accept the extension of the BE system "at the request of the IMF." Under the BE system, certificates entitling importers to purchase commodities on the "BE list" were sold on the open market. Thus it was the level of demand among importers for particular items, rather than decisions on the part of either Jakarta or the creditor governments, that ultimately determined how the credits were to be used. In most cases, however, aid was "tied" to the commodities of the particular creditor country. For additional discussion, see *BIES,* no. 7 (June 1967), pp. 18–25.

73. For example, serious difficulties had to be overcome in reaching agreement with West Germany on the amount of aid and with France on interest rates (interview with Rachmat Saleh, Jakarta, 10 February 1970).

the struggle to preserve a semblance of independence more apparent than in relations with Japan. From the commencement of aid negotiations in early 1967, the Indonesians claim they sought to demonstrate to Tokyo that they could not be pressured into accepting exploitative economic conditions. The conflict reached a peak in 1968 when Jakarta tried unsuccessfully to force Tokyo's hand by sending Soeharto himself to the Japanese capital in order to seek the desired commitment of aid. When this failed, the Indonesians, angered by the "insult" to their chief of state, made a symbolic gesture of independence by refusing to issue a joint communique.

Though a compromise was finally reached for 1968, the next year, according to several of the economists, Japan proved to be such a "troublemaker" that the IGGI almost collapsed. The Indonesians were unsuccessful in their 1969 demands concerning the interest rate for Japanese aid, but with important backing from Washington they were able to win their arguments with Tokyo on three other key points. These arguments illustrate well the nature of the pressures to which an aid recipient is subject. The Japanese had proposed that investment be included in IGGI aid, an arrangement which would have enabled the Japanese government to lend money to Japanese firms to invest in Indonesia and call it aid to Indonesia. The Japanese also wanted to establish joint ventures in which the Indonesian partner would receive a Japanese loan, thereby giving the Japanese side complete control. Finally, the Japanese wanted all their infrastructure project loans to be determined entirely by Tokyo, which of course would have enabled them to coordinate their project aid with the needs of Japanese investors. The Indonesians, on the other hand, insisted on and won the right to set their own investment priorities by presenting potential investors with a list of projects from which they might choose.[74]

Of course pressures stemming from Indonesia's dependence on Western aid were felt in many areas other than economic affairs.

74. For details, see Weinstein, "Uses of Foreign Policy," pp. 633–39, which draws on interviews with Indonesian and Japanese officials.

According to foreign ministry sources, up to 1968 there was a good deal of pressure from the United States for a change in Indonesia's position on the Vietnam issue. Though it is hard to say which were the decisive motivations for Jakarta's failure to support Peking's admission to the UN in 1971, a variety of reliable Indonesian sources confirmed that there was heavy pressure from both Washington and Tokyo. The Americans were also said to have "sabotaged" Indonesia's planned establishment of ambassadorial relations with the People's Republic of South Yemen.[75] Jakarta was successful in resisting Japan's repeated entreaties to join ASPAC, even though the Japanese allegedly stated that entering the organization would make it easier for Indonesia to get aid on favorable terms. But when some Japanese explicitly tied negotiations over fishing rights to Indonesia's chances of obtaining the desired economic aid, the Indonesians felt compelled to submit.[76]

Finally, the Indonesians were called upon in 1968 to prove their commitment to a "responsible" foreign policy when the Singapore government, ignoring Soeharto's personal appeal for clemency, executed two Indonesian marines convicted of sabotage activities during the days of confrontation. This flaunting of Indonesian sensitivities revived concern about the country's dependence on Singapore as an entrepôt and stirred intense pressures for some kind of retaliatory action. But the Jakarta government, according to several top leaders, was mindful of the need to protect Indonesia's "real interests" (generally translated as "foreign aid"); the Indonesians thus ignored the popular outcry and refrained from any significant retaliatory steps.

Indonesia's dependence on foreign aid stimulated occasional ex-

75. The Americans discovered an article critical of Soeharto in the South Yemeni press and made this known to certain army generals who opposed the plan. The furor that resulted prevented the diplomatic move. Reports of the American role came from both foreign journalists and Indonesian foreign ministry sources.

76. Interviews with army and foreign ministry spokesmen. Japanese diplomatic sources, conceding that "unofficial" spokesmen might have linked the fishing rights question to aid, denied that it was the government's intention to do so.

pressions of public concern. Most of the discussion focused on the wisdom of the government's development strategy, particularly the emphasis on a monetary approach to economic stabilization and the heavy reliance on foreign capital to develop the economy. The impact of these policies on the development of indigenous Indonesian business capacities was, and remains, a matter of particular concern.

In the early years of the New Order, critics attacked the government's policies of maintaining extremely tight credit, importing consumer goods under foreign credits to drive prices down, and refusing to embark on an expansionary public works program by 1967 or 1968. These were blamed for killing off domestic industries, aggravating unemployment, and reducing effective demand. It was argued that permitting domestic industries to wither would hinder any efforts to establish a structural basis for development without uncontrolled inflation, and would leave the country dependent on a continuing supply of foreign aid. Only through an expansionary policy aimed at increasing production and raising buying power, along with tax reforms that would provide new domestic savings for development, could Indonesia hope to solve its inflation problem in a manner conducive to development and self-sufficiency.[77]

By mid-1967, as domestic economic activity stagnated amid complaints of a liquidity crisis, the critics were strengthened in their conviction that the drastic measures adopted were dangerously excessive, and that insufficient attention was being given to the expansion of production. Though government spokesmen insisted that too rapid an expansion of credit or government spending might endanger efforts to bring inflation under control, they did on occasion concede that their policies were having a stifling effect on domestic

77. Among the leading critics have been former Masjumi leaders, like Sjafruddin Prawiranegara, and PSI leaders, like the economist Sarbini Sumawinata. On Sjafruddin's ideas, see *Kompas,* 27 May 1969, and his *Membangun Kembali Ekonomi Indonesia* (Jakarta: Bulan Bintang, 1966), especially pp. 15, 17, 33–34, 38, 41, 60–63. Sarbini's views are elaborated in *BIES,* no. 8 (October 1967), pp. 12–13, and his "Indonesia," a paper presented to the Experts Meeting on the Current Economic Situation and Economic Policies, ECAFE, Bangkok, January 29–31, 1970. See also *Pedoman,* 29 January 1970.

enterprises.[78] To be sure, spectacular success was achieved in bringing down the rate of inflation, though prices began rising sharply after rice crop failures in 1972 and continued to do so until mid-1974; moreover, considerable increases in output were recorded in those mining and manufacturing fields where foreign capital was active. But up through 1975 the complaint could still be heard that the government's tight money policies were causing economic stagnation, except for the sectors of the economy dominated by foreign or overseas Chinese capital.[79]

Especially after 1970, concern began to focus on the growing strength of the overseas Chinese businessmen, who had their own sources of credit, as compared to the languishing indigenous businessmen.[80] During 1973 and 1974 the government responded to

78. Soeharto, *Pidato/Briefing . . . pada Musjawarah Kerdja,* p. 28; *Pidato Penutupan Pedjabat Presiden R.I./Ketua Presidium Kabinet Ampera pada Musjawarah Kerdja Antara Pemerintah Pusat dan Pedjabat-Pedjabat Daerah* (Jakarta: Departemen Penerangan, 1967), pp. 19–20; and *Laporan dan Pendjelasan Pedjabat Presiden pada Pembukaan Sidang Umum Ke-V MPRS* (Jakarta: Departemen Penerangan, 1968), p. 24. See also *Keterangan Pemerintah Mengenai Langkah-Langkah Baru,* p. 6; *Pokok-Pokok Kebidjaksanaan Kabinet Ampera Selandjutnja Setelah Sidang Istimewa MPRS/1967 dan Rentjana Pembangunan Selandjutnja* (Jakarta: Departemen Penerangan, 1967), p. 23, in which Soeharto acknowledged that the monetary policies appeared to have brought on a recession; and *Government Report to the Gotong-Royong House of Representatives on the Implementation of the Programme for Economic Rehabilitation and Stabilization on 10th July 1967* (Jakarta: Department of Information, 1967), pp. 12, 21–22.

79. For example, see *Monthly Review* (May 1972), pp. 4–6; *Pedoman,* 13 April 1973; *Nusantara,* 13 April 1973; *Suara Karya,* 7 August 1974; and *Merdeka,* 12 April 1975. See also *BIES,* vol. 11, no. 2 (July 1975), p. 18.

80. *Indonesia Raya* (25 May 1973), a newspaper edited by Mochtar Lubis, who was an archfoe of Sukarno and spent the Guided Democracy years in jail, claimed: "In independent Indonesia, indigenous entrepreneurs were expected to get ample opportunities, but because of lack of capital and lack of government guidance, they have been eliminated one by one. The Old Order/Soekarno era still offered a chance to bona fide private entrepreneurs to advance but the New Order era is marked by diminishing numbers of indigenous businessmen and industrialists." See also *Indonesia Raya,* 29 August 1973, 21 June 1973; *Nusantara,* 13 April 1973; and *Ringkasan Peristiwa,* 16–30 November 1972, p. 5.

that concern, but there was skepticism about the effectiveness of the measures proposed. In 1974 it was reported that Chinese and other nonindigenous Indonesians accounted for 75 percent of all capital invested under the domestic investment law and for 91–94 percent of the capital invested by Indonesian citizens in association with foreign investors under the foreign investment law.[81] In 1975 Trade Minister Radius Prawiro acknowledged the failure of efforts to strengthen indigenous businesses.[82]

Criticism was aimed not merely at the substance of the government's economic policies but at the fact that they had been imposed by the IMF as a precondition for economic aid.[83] Few questioned the sincere commitment of the economists to the policies they advocated, but many, even including some Americans who knew them well, felt that they were overly sensitive to the wishes of the IMF. Though they shared the government's eagerness for foreign aid, the critics complained that if the government persisted in its present development strategy, Indonesia would for years be excessively dependent on aid and ultimately controlled by foreigners. Some also expressed reluctance to impose so heavy a debt on their children. On a few occasions the criticism became even sharper, as in the case of an editorial entitled "How to Sell a Nation/People" which appeared in late 1970.[84] When the American Senate temporarily cut

81. *Tempo,* 9 March 1974. Skepticism about the 1973 measures was expressed in *Harian Kami,* 13 April 1973, 10 August 1973; *Nusantara,* 13 April 1973; and *Indonesia Raya,* 24 August 1973. The major step was the declaration of a government policy that henceforth 65 percent of new domestic investment credits would be channeled to indigenous Indonesians. On the 1974 measures and the difficulty of implementing them, see *BIES,* vol. 10, no. 2 (July 1974), pp. 18–20.

82. *Suara Karya,* 5 April 1975, 28 May 1975.

83. See Sarbini's criticism in *BIES,* no. 8 (October 1967), pp. 12–13; Sjafruddin's interview with *Kompas,* 27 May 1969; and Jusuf Wibisono, "Rehabilitasi Politik Anggaran Belandja Negara," in *Masalah Ekonomi Beserta Pemetjahannja* (Jakarta: Senat Mahasiswa Fakultas Ekonomi, Universitas Indonesia, 1968), p. 38.

84. *Merdeka,* 7 December 1970. Though Sjafruddin, for example, had urged gratitude toward the aid-givers and dismissed the notion that they had any aspirations to dominate Indonesia (*Membangun Kembali Ekonomi

off all foreign aid in late 1971, consciousness of the dangers of dependence was elevated. By 1973 there was growing evidence of disillusionment with the results produced by aid compared to the costs involved.[85] In November 1973, the arrival in Jakarta of the IGGI chairman stimulated a demonstration by students who identified themselves as the "Movement of Indonesian Students for Indonesia" and assailed their country's dependence on foreign aid. One of their placards read: "Millions of Dollars Foreign Aid, Millions New Unemployment."[86]

The swiftly rising wave of protest reached its peak in January 1974, when Japanese Prime Minister Kakuei Tanaka encountered violent anti-Japanese demonstrations on his arrival in Jakarta for a visit. But even in the much more tightly controlled political atmosphere that prevailed after the 1974 demonstrations, critics of Indonesia's dependence on IGGI aid and advice could still be heard.[87]

Similarly, foreign investment began, especially after 1970, to draw more pointed criticism. The entry of foreign capital, it was alleged, was leading toward a revival of the colonial policy by which Indonesia was "drained" of its resources.[88] Worse still, the policy of offering an incentive-strewn welcome to foreign investors,

---

Indonesia, pp. 61–63), see his interview in *Kompas,* 27 May 1969. See also *Dwiwarna,* 15 August 1969; *Merdeka,* 20 October 1969, 2 December 1969; *Pedoman,* 7 January 1970; and Thee Kian Wie's comments in *Politik Luar Negeri Indonesia Dewasa Ini,* p. 34.

85. Of particular interest is Mochtar Lubis' lengthy critique in *Indonesia Raya,* 19, 22, and 24 September 1973. See also *Abadi,* 12 October 1973; *Pedoman,* 3 October 1973, in which Soeharto is reported to have accused several big powers of using aid to create spheres of influence; *Indonesia Raya,* 14 and 25 July 1973, and 12 June 1973, in which foreign advisers at the National Planning Board are said to be superfluous; *Kompas,* 24 July 1973; *Merdeka,* 2 August 1972; and "Kecenderungan-kecenderungan," pp. 16–17.

86. *Sinar Harapan,* 12 November 1973.

87. See *Merdeka,* 16 and 28 March 1974, and *Topik,* 6 March 1974.

88. For example, see *Merdeka,* 10 July 1970, 19 November 1970, 5 December 1970, 29 January 1971, 1 July 1972; *Harian Kami,* 3 March 1971, 22 April 1971, 23 August 1971, 10 April 1973, 28 June 1973; *Nusantara,* 21 April 1972, 19 March 1973, 14 August 1973; *Indonesia Raya,* 21 June 1973, 29 August 1973; and *Abadi,* 23 July 1973. For an example of the government's response to this criticism, see *Angkatan Bersendjata,* 10 April 1973.

whose efficiency and access to capital already made them highly competitive, was said to have contributed a great deal to the difficulties faced by indigenous businessmen, many of whom were being forced out of business. Meanwhile, it was said, unemployment was increasing, and the economy was gradually sliding ever more into the hands of foreigners and overseas Chinese, who in turn paid off the ruling generals. It was this situation which stimulated student demonstrators in November 1973 to exhibit a placard declaring: "Foreign Capital Assists Internal Colonialism."[89] While no one publicly called for the ouster of foreign capital, there were voices urging that more emphasis be placed on intermediate technology, which would not only reduce dependence on foreign capital and expertise but would, by virtue of its labor intensive character, help to alleviate unemployment.[90]

Some critics called into question the entire strategy of basing economic development mainly on foreign credits and investment. If the government's policies were carried out, warned one newspaper, indigenous businessmen would end up as "mere grocers . . . in the same position they held under Dutch colonial rule. Was the struggle for Independent Indonesia confined to achieving only a political goal and is the economy to be left to foreigners and Chinese middlemen?"[91] Notwithstanding these expressions of concern, however, public criticism of foreign aid and investment was generally quite restrained. Private criticism, we shall see, was not so restrained.

89. *Sinar Harapan,* 12 November 1973. The paradox of increasing production accompanied by rising unemployment is discussed in *BIES,* vol. 9, no. 3 (November 1973), pp. 13–14.

90. See, for example, Sarbini Sumawinata, "Some Perspective for a Long-Term Planning for Indonesia's Development," *Warta Ekonomi Maritim Review,* 5 (October 1972), 14–15, 38–40, and Soedjatmoko, "Technology, Development, and Culture" (paper presented at colloquium, Santa Barbara, April 10–12, 1972). For more recent examples, see Thee Kian Wie's comments in *Tempo,* 29 March 1975; the remarks of the general chairman of the Indonesian Chamber of Commerce (KADIN) in *Merdeka,* 15 May 1975; and *Kompas,* 5 June 1975. The government view on unemployment is set forth in *Suara Karya,* 12 March 1973.

91. *Indonesia Raya,* 29 August 1973.

7 | The Need for Aid and the Fear of Dependence

That the public criticism of the government's aid-oriented foreign policy did not reflect the depth or breadth of concern was clearly demonstrated by the interviews with the foreign policy elite. Despite the official welcome to foreign aid, the ambivalence about aid which had existed since the earliest days of Indonesia's life as an independent nation had by no means diminished. On the contrary, with the size of foreign credits growing, the flow of investment accelerating, and the government's development strategy emphasizing monetary stabilization and a relatively free hand to foreign investors, the foreign policy elite members were increasingly fearful for their country's independence. Still, they believed, Indonesia desperately needed aid.

The Indispensability of Aid

Foreign aid was viewed by 81 percent of the interviewees as indispensable to Indonesia's economic development. There were minor variations among the groups, with the 1966 generation leaders slightly stronger in agreement and the Islamic party leaders somewhat less pronounced, but in general all segments of the foreign policy elite concurred on the need for foreign economic aid (see Table 7.1).

The suggestion that Indonesia could develop without foreign aid was widely ridiculed as "nonsense," "dreaming," "totally unrealistic," and "empty talk." While a few blamed Sukarno for making such a mess of the economy as to necessitate foreign aid, most

Table 7.1. Is foreign aid indispensable to economic development?

	Yes	No
All respondents	42 (81%)	10 (19%)
1928 Generation	7	2
1945 Generation	28	7
1966 Generation	7	1
Army	9	0
Technocrats	7	0
PSI	5	0
Catholic Party	4	0
Foreign Ministry	5	2
PNI	5	2
Islamic parties	4	3

pointed to more fundamental considerations—the insufficiency of domestic capital; the predominantly low level of education and technical skills; and the ineffectiveness of Indonesia's bureaucracy, which limits severely its capacity to mobilize domestic resources for development. Many alluded to the importance of holding to self-reliance as a long-term principle, but for the forseeable future, they argued, it was incompatible with development. It was frequently asserted that foreign aid would be needed for many years. In the words of an army general: "We would like to be able to say we can develop without aid. . . . Maybe after fifty years, we will be able to say we don't need aid."

It was also made clear that the amount of aid required was considerable. While it was acknowledged that Indonesia's previous attempts at development had suffered from many deficiencies, there was a tendency, especially on the part of some foreign ministry officials, to attribute past failures primarily to the lack of adequate funding—that is, to insufficient foreign credits and investment. In fact, there were those, especially among the PSI and Islamic party leaders, who considered the amount of aid received since 1966 seriously inadequate. A PSI leader's research convinced him that none of the nations that had successfully carried out economic development in recent years did so with less than $10 per capita in annual aid. By his calculations, Indonesia therefore needed at least $1.3 billion a year.

Indonesia's failure to gain such massive aid, PSI and 1966 Generation leaders claimed, was leading to the growth of resentment toward the West, especially the United States. Some members of virtually every group criticized Washington's "stinginess." Most Indonesians were said to be incredulous when told that the United States was unable, not just unwilling, to give more. As for the idea that America's resources needed to be channeled toward the solution of domestic problems, a technocrat contended that "on any objective scale, the needs of developing countries are far greater than those of the poor in the United States."

The few who did not consider aid indispensable, and many of those who did, argued that Indonesia was capable of a much greater mobilization of domestic resources than had yet taken place. The most frequently mentioned proposal was a revamping of the tax system, coupled with strenuous efforts to combat corruption. PSI leaders in particular claimed that if the substantial amount of money paid to corrupt officials were channeled into the coffers of the government, Indonesia would not be so dependent on foreign aid. Other leaders, especially those from the Islamic parties and the 1966 Generation, stressed that "rationalization" of the bureaucracy, meaning a sharp reduction in its size, would simultaneously save money and increase its efficiency. Strong measures against smuggling were also urged as a means of enlarging tax revenues.

The majority, however, rejected the idea that a mobilization of domestic resources could significantly reduce the need for foreign aid. On the one hand, expansion of the tax base, curtailment of corruption and smuggling, and rationalization of the bureaucracy were said to be not alternatives to aid but measures that needed to be carried out anyway, if aid was to be used effectively. On the other hand, many leaders cautioned against unrealistic expectations that such measures could be implemented.

With respect to taxation, technocrats and generals emphasized the need for patience while a well thought-out tax structure was devised and civil servants were trained for tax and customs work.

With the corporate tax setup in disarray and only a few hundred thousand out of 130 million people paying any income taxes, tax reform was not a problem that could be "solved one, two, three, just like that." While government officials noted that tax receipts had in fact increased considerably in recent years, they ruled out any dramatic broadening of the tax base on the grounds that people were already suffering enough from taxes.[1] Drastically raising taxes would be a severe psychological blow, it was said. Islamic party leaders, among others, claimed that present taxes on business enterprises were excessive, given the other financial difficulties which most businessmen face. An army general told of his own "hardship" when he imported a dog valued at $1000 and found he was supposed to pay a tax exceeding that amount. An economist questioned the seriousness of those who called for increased tax collection, pointing out that many of them did not even pay their own taxes. "Everyone wants the tax system improved," he noted, "but no one wants to be asked to pay himself." In any case, it was observed, even increasing tax revenues would not necessarily reduce the percentage of aid in the development budget, because the budget's overall size was constantly growing.

As for the possibility of increasing government revenues by curbing corruption and smuggling, many officials pointed out that stringent measures to eliminate the ubiquitous petty corruption would cause grave social problems, since local officials needed this money to survive. Any serious effort to root out the widespread corruption at higher levels would raise unacceptable political risks. "If you went after all the corrupt people high in the government," one technocrat claimed, "the whole apparatus would collapse. It is not just the army that is corrupt but the parties too." Even one of the PSI leaders who urged harsh measures against those who exact

1. In the years since the interviews, tax revenues have continued to increase, but revenues from personal income taxes and import duties have consistently fallen below expectations. The IMF and the World Bank, in reports to the May 1975 IGGI meeting, both stressed the need for dramatic improvement in Indonesia's tax system (*BIES,* vol. 11, no. 2 [July 1975], pp. 10, 17).

illegal taxes acknowledged that he was asking the government to take action against its own people, something it was unlikely to do. The most flagrant corruption was said to be that of certain key army generals, against whom the government could not move without undermining its own legitimacy and jeopardizing the army's unity.

Because the government was not strong enough to fight corruption vigorously, the only alternative, several leaders pointed out, was to hope that an improving economic situation would lessen some of the pressures that drive so many to corruption. "Once we raise living standards," an army general predicted, "corruption will disappear." In the interim, some leaders expressed the hope that moves against a few conspicuous offenders might make others slightly more reticent about committing flagrant acts of corruption. It was also proposed that simplifying administrative procedures—for example, requiring five signatures for a permit rather than twenty-two—might reduce the opportunities for corruption. Though such measures were not seen as likely to effect a dramatic change in the situation, most of the foreign policy elite members holding high government positions did not seem overly concerned. They believed that, excluding the petty corruption of people struggling to survive, the sum of money drained off through corruption simply was not large enough to have any significant effect on the need for foreign aid.

Like efforts to curtail corruption, rationalization of the bureaucracy was seen as posing enormous political and social problems. Several leaders expressed the fear that the large-scale firing of civil servants would create a bloc that could easily be exploited by opponents of the government. The demobilization of any sizeable portion of the army, widely conceded to be vastly larger than needed to cope with existing or potential security threats, promised to be even more hazardous politically.

If there seemed little chance of dramatically increasing domestic funds through these reforms, many Indonesian leaders did acknowledge the existence, at least in theory, of one serious alternative to a high level of dependence on aid. Indonesia could develop with little or no aid if it were to attempt what was often referred to as "the Chinese Communist way." The Chinese model connotes a reliance on intermediate technology and labor intensive techniques, a relatively even distribution of wealth, and the use of "ruthless coercive measures" to mobilize domestic resources for the development effort. In the 1973 interviews, the Chinese model seemed to be growing more attractive to PSI and 1966 Generation leaders disillusioned with the results achieved by Indonesia's aid-oriented policy, but they, like virtually all the other members of the foreign policy elite, were repelled by the coercive aspects of the Chinese approach. "The PKI wanted that," commented a foreign ministry official, "but we just couldn't do it. The Indonesian people have suffered enough, and I don't see how we can squeeze any more out of them."[2]

Army generals and foreign ministry officials noted that for all of the major industrial powers, both capitalist and Communist, the road to economic development had been strewn with "victims." Indonesia was seeking "a different road, one which does not require so many sacrifices," said an army officer. "We do not want to have to tighten our belts any more than necessary. Of course, it is foreign aid that makes the new road possible." In any case, there was a general belief that Indonesia did not possess the political or administrative apparatus to carry out successfully a Chinese Communist style mobilization for development.

The Indonesian leaders thus found themselves confronted with what they perceived as a choice between pursuing development with as much foreign aid as they could get, or abandoning any hope of making significant economic progress in the near future and developing slowly with their own resources. The latter alternative too was regarded as dangerous, for if Indonesia lost its race to boost income at a rate faster than the rapid growth of population, the result would be a land crowded with hungry people susceptible to

2. From time to time, the "Chinese Communist way" has been mentioned in newspaper discussions of foreign aid. For example, *Angkatan Bersendjata*, 15 December 1970, in discussing the need for foreign credits, states that Indonesia does not "have the heart to apply forced labor to enable us like People's China to build a giant dam in six months."

the appeal of Communism. Moreover, the New Order government had clearly staked its claim to legitimacy on its ability to bring about economic development. Army generals and technocrats argued that if development did not advance fast enough, Indonesia would descend into chaos. Only with substantial foreign aid was there any chance of winning that race.

The concern with which the Indonesian leaders viewed a future without foreign aid emerged clearly in their response to a query about the probable consequences of a drastic cut in aid. Of 48 respondents, 67 percent predicted that a substantial cut in foreign aid would produce a political crisis, while the others suggested that it would merely slow the rate of development. Slightly more than a quarter of those who foresaw a crisis expected the government to survive by the expanded use of coercion, while the rest were uncertain. The youngest generation was especially strong in its belief that the loss of aid would lead to severe political difficulties, and among the major groups only the PNI showed a pronounced inclination to minimize the effects of an aid cut, while the foreign ministry, army, and Islamic leaders were fairly evenly divided (see Table 7.2).

Those who foresaw no political crisis emphasized Indonesia's resilience. "We will go on," said a PNI leader. "According to Western scientific predictions, all of our civil servants should have been dead long ago. But we survive." Some stressed that if left with no choice, Indonesia could develop on the basis of self-reliance. One Islamic leader even suggested that the country could carry out a Chinese Communist style mobilization, though he asserted that to do so the present army leadership would have to be replaced by officers who were "younger, more patriotic, more idealistic than those now in power." A few leaders claimed that they would welcome the curtailment of aid. A newspaper editor, for example, declared that an aid cut would oblige Indonesia to stand on its own feet, rather than timidly depending on others.

Predictions that a major aid cut would generate a political crisis mainly reflected concern about the psychological impact of such a move. While some PSI and Islamic leaders thought the exchange

Table 7.2. Probable consequences of a drastic cut in aid

	Political crisis—government may fall	Political crisis—government will survive by becoming more coercive	Just slower development
All respondents	23 (48%)	9 (19%)	16 (33%)
1928 Generation	4	2	2
1945 Generation	16	3	14
1966 Generation	3	4	0
Technocrats	5	2	0
PSI	6	0	0
Catholic Party	2	2	1
Islamic parties	2	2	3
Army	4	0	4
Foreign Ministry	3	0	4
PNI	1	0	4

rate would run out of control and inflation would return in full force, most leaders believed there would be no immediate economic collapse, though development would slow down. "We are suffering now. We would just suffer a little more," said a technocrat. But politically, he conceded, the government would be in trouble.

Among the foreign policy elite, in fact, the assumption was widespread that whatever the cause of the curtailment of aid, it would be interpreted by Indonesians as a lack of confidence in their government and could easily be exploited by critics, who would attack from all sides. According to a former foreign minister, the result would be chaos and catastrophe, with the rise of "social revolution from the left, right, everywhere." Several leaders mentioned the possibility of a coup from within the army. While some talked of a PKI comeback, a more common prediction was the reinvigoration of the radical left, though not necessarily the Communists. Many leaders anticipated that anti-Western feeling would rise sharply, for emboldened left-wing critics would have new evidence that the West was not to be trusted.

To survive, argued PSI, Islamic, and 1966 Generation leaders in particular, the government would probably make a drastic shift leftward, partly in an effort to get aid from the Communist countries and partly as a manifestation of its sense of betrayal by the West. Several predicted that Indonesian foreign policy would return to the "adventurous, stridently anti-Western" posture of Sukarno's Guided Democracy years. Members of the same three groups emphasized that the anti-Communist army leadership was fully capable of a radical swing to an extreme anti-Western position. The generals had been perfectly at home under Guided Democracy, it was argued, and there was no reason to think that they could not adjust to such a foreign policy orientation again. A prominent Islamic leader even went so far as to question the anti-Communism of the army leaders, branding them "opportunists," while a young leader observed, more charitably, that the generals "may be anti-Communists but they are nationalists first . . . and would react strongly to a cut in Western aid."

The possibility of such a sharp switch in orientation was in fact acknowledged by a spokesman for the most pro-American faction of the army. Noting that the Western powers were growing reluctant to give foreign aid, he asserted: "It is possible that tomorrow they will not be our friends." Soeharto might well align himself with army elements that were not enthusiastic about Indonesia's present aid-oriented foreign policy, it was suggested. A technocrat predicted that Indonesia might gravitate toward a position similar to that of Cairo. Such shifts, combined with coercive measures against domestic critics, might well enable the present leadership to survive an aid cut, the foreign policy elite felt, but the situation would be difficult.

Whether the bonanza created by the quadrupling of oil prices in 1973–1974 will soon lead a majority of the Indonesian leaders to view foreign aid as dispensable cannot be stated with certainty, but it seems unlikely. When the 1973 interviews were held, Indonesia's need for foreign aid was generally viewed as undiminished. Toward the end of 1973 there was a brief "debate" on whether Indonesia might in the next few years use its rapidly growing oil revenues to reduce the country's dependence on foreign aid, but the debate ended, at least for the time being, when government officials declared that substantial IGGI aid would be needed for many years to come.[3] There is no doubt that they continued to hold this view up through 1975.[4] Those foreign policy elite members who might have argued that foreign aid could be sharply reduced were, for the most part, silenced politically after the January 1974 anti-Japanese demonstrations.

The Indonesian leaders' continued belief in the importance of aid was reflected in the government's declaration that, because of the expanded development budget, the country needed $2 billion in aid for fiscal year 1975/76, more than double the previous year's assistance. The World Bank and the IMF reported to the May 1975 IGGI meeting that the oil revenues had not lessened Indonesia's need for aid. The donor nations pledged a record $920 million, besides giving support to Jakarta's planned efforts to seek an additional $1 billion outside the IGGI framework. Wide editorial support was given to efforts to win aid from the Middle Eastern oil exporting nations and from the Communist countries. Looking to the future, the World Bank estimated that assuming maintenance of the present nominal price of oil, Indonesia would face a foreign exchange gap over the 1975–1980 period of $14 billion at current prices. Private foreign investment was expected to supply about $5 billion, with the remaining gap of $9 billion to be closed by commercial borrowing or aid on concessional terms. Allowing for the lag of disbursements behind commitments, this meant a program of loans and aid rising from $2 billion in 1975 to about $4 billion in 1980.[5]

Moreover, Pertamina, the state oil company, itself generated a new need for foreign aid. In the euphoria of the oil bonanza, the company overextended itself, accumulating a short-term debt (due within 12 months) of $1.5 billion, and in early 1975 it was unable

3. See, for example, *Pedoman,* 21 November 1973, and *Indonesia Raya,* 23 November 1973.

4. *Kompas,* 12 May and 7 June 1975, and *BIES,* vol. 11, no. 2 (July 1975), pp. 8–15.

5. *BIES,* vol. 11, no. 2 (July 1975), p. 10.

to meet obligations to foreign banks amounting to $100 million. The government had to step in, with the Central Bank paying the overdue loans and guaranteeing all of Pertamina's overseas debt. The government subsequently raised $575 million from foreign banks to strengthen Indonesia's foreign exchange reserves, in effect funding a major portion of Pertamina's short-term debt, and indicated its intention to borrow more later in the year. Because of Pertamina's financial distress, the projected surplus in the government's budget failed to materialize.[6]

If the oil windfall seemed unlikely to diminish Indonesia's need for foreign aid, neither could it be assumed that the oil money would be spent in ways that would maximize its impact on development. A principal use of the oil revenues in 1974 and 1975 was to facilitate the stockpiling of rice and fertilizer in order to assure domestic price stability, but there was considerable concern about the danger of large losses through deterioration and pilferage. The enormity and complexity of Indonesia's developmental task was such that even though the quadrupling of oil prices had more than doubled government revenues, it added only $20 to per capita income in nominal terms. The impact of the windfall was further diminished by declining demand for Indonesia's traditional non-oil exports (the value of which dropped 41 percent from mid-1974 to early 1975) and by the sharp concurrent rise in the price of many commodities which Indonesia imports. As already noted in Chapter 4, the price of such key items as cement and fertilizer quadrupled in 1973–1974, and Indonesia was obliged to pay highly inflated prices for imported petroleum products since Indonesia exports most of its crude oil for refining abroad. If the soaring cost of imports is taken into account, the increase in per capital income drops from $20 to $6 at fiscal 1972/73 prices.

Indonesia was subject not only to the effects of the prevailing worldwide inflation; the oil bonanza itself threatened to exacerbate domestic inflationary pressures by creating a demand that far outdistanced Indonesia's capacity to produce. The Indonesian economy's

6. *Ibid.*, pp. 1–7, 11, 13.

capacity to effectively absorb additional capital was in any case limited by deficiencies in infrastructure and administrative capabilities. Furthermore, there was doubt, expressed by Foreign Minister Malik among others, as to how long the inflated oil prices would last; the danger of a glut of oil on the world market could not be dismissed. By mid-1975 the Indonesians were growing quite concerned about the threat to the Japanese market posed by China's rising exports of oil comparable in quality to Indonesia's but priced 50 cents a barrel lower.

Finally, some experienced diplomatic observers of the Indonesian scene privately predicted that a major effect of the oil windfall would be to heighten the conspicuously extravagant lifestyle of the wealthy few and thus to exacerbate tensions stemming from the widening gap between rich and poor. Ironically, the oil bonanza generated new expectations of economic progress which, given the difficulty of translating the oil money into visible evidence of development, could not easily be fulfilled. The result was to make foreign aid seem as essential as ever, so that there might be a chance of meeting at least some of the added expectations.[7]

The Dangers of Dependence

The firm conviction that Indonesia needs foreign aid was balanced, however, by a profound concern about the dangers of dependence. Of 64 members of the foreign policy elite with whom the subject was discussed, 63 percent expressed their concern about dependence on aid, and most of them were seriously worried. This apprehension was reflected to roughly the same degree in the thinking of all three generations. Concern about dependence on aid was voiced by at least half of every major group except the Catholics, though the PSI and PNI were markedly more intense in expressing such feelings than were the others (see Table 7.3).

Moreover, these findings may be understated. Many leaders were clearly uneasy about expressing sentiments that might jeopardize

7. Concerning the impact of the oil bonanza on development, see *ibid.*, pp. 9–10, 14–15; vol. 10, no. 2 (July 1974), pp. 1–7, 31–34; and vol. 11, no. 1 (March 1975), p. 3.

Table 7.3. Concern about dependence on aid

	Worried (very worried)	Not really worried
All respondents	40 (33) [63% (52%)]	24 (38%)
1928 Generation	7 (5)	3
1945 Generation	28 (23)	17
1966 Generation	5 (5)	4
PSI	6 (4)	0
PNI	7 (7)	2
Foreign Ministry	6 (4)	3
Army	7 (5)	5
Technocrats	5 (3)	4
Islamic parties	4 (2)	4
Catholic Party	0 (0)	4

their country's chances of getting the aid they believed it needed. A number of those interviewed volunteered the information that other leaders (who expressed no such concern to the author) were quite worried about Indonesia's dependence on aid, even though they might be reluctant to speak of their feelings to those whom they did not know well. For example, technocrats noted the depth of concern among politicians of all groups, while other leaders reported that certain leading technocrats had confided their own fears to them. Several alluded to the existence of substantial concern within the army, especially among certain elements of it. And there were stories, which could not be verified, that Soeharto himself was worried about being remembered as the man who sold Indonesia to the West.

Those who dissented from this view acknowledged that theirs was very much a minority view. One economist ridiculed the allegation that he had once argued in government councils for a tight money policy in order to obtain aid: "We would have to be crazy to try that argument. We realize that people here are very wary about foreign aid, not happy at all about it. When we got the [recent aid commitment], the papers were not glad. They only talked about new debts being piled up. People here see aid as a necessary evil; they tend to view it as begging. So we always take a low posture on aid domestically. For us to try to justify something in terms of the need for aid—that would kill us." Several technocrats, and some party leaders as well, claimed that there was no point in worrying about Indonesia's dependence because there simply was no alternative to the present course. Weak nations are always dependent on more powerful ones, observed a young Catholic leader. Other leaders stressed that they could accept Indonesia's dependence on aid because it was only temporary and not as severe as that of such countries as Taiwan and South Korea.

A primary source of the distress associated with dependence on foreign aid was psychological. Dependence on outsiders does considerable damage to the Indonesian leaders' self-esteem and to their image of Indonesia as an independent nation. Representatives of every major group except the Catholics complained, often with considerable embarrassment and self-derision, that Indonesia's aid-oriented foreign policy amounted to "begging." One senior army general, for example, contrasted the Soeharto government's policy of "begging for credits" with Sukarno's foreign policy, which he said was "at least based on the principle of anti-imperialism/colonialism." Others described Indonesia's dependence on aid as "sinful" and a "spiritual sell-out." An Islamic leader who for years had been one of the most outspoken advocates of heavy foreign aid observed: "Aid can be corrupting. It is so easy for us to fall into the posture of begging. This has very damaging effects on our inner being, our spirit. It is very dangerous to rely completely on foreign aid, as this government is doing. All right, it may be necessary for one or two years, but then we must guarantee that foreign aid becomes merely supplementary, not central."

Indonesia's position was repeatedly decried as undignified. One of the most militant leaders of the action fronts that led the anti-Sukarno movement in 1966 complained of feeling "subordinated." He observed: "If we don't fulfull the requirements, we don't get the aid we need. There has been too much begging. We have already lost too much pride." As for the economic progress which the New Order's aid policy had facilitated, an army general said: "It's not their [the technocrats'] achievement. It was accomplished because of aid from the West. And at what a cost! Our own pride, our self-respect. Everything we do has to be approved by the IMF. And in international relations we have become so passive. It used to be that when Indonesia made a speech in the UN or elsewhere, people paid attention to us. Now nobody cares what we say. This is partly the result of a lack of imagination on Malik's part, but it is also the result of a fear of doing something wrong, that is, doing something that will jeopardize aid. This is humiliating." How could Indonesia hope to influence the course of world politics when "we are just beggars," asked a former foreign minister, extending his palm and smiling weakly. Indonesia, asserted a PNI leader, "should have an image as something other than a country that is always asking for aid, always with its hand out."

A continuing emotional attachment to the idea of self-reliance was manifest, despite the absence of a willingness to accept its consequences. Thus a technocrat declared that Indonesia could not develop without substantial aid, but asserted that "we need to have the feeling that we can succeed on our own." Aid should not be given in such a way as to remind Indonesia of its dependence, he declared. For example, AID's handshake of cooperation displayed on the sides of American-supplied school buses was an unpleasant reminder that "we must rely on others for these things"; such aid, he predicted, might have a "boomerang effect." Almost in a single breath, a navy officer vigorously urged expanded American aid to Indonesia and then branded Indonesia's current dependence on aid "a betrayal of everything we have strived for" since the beginning of the struggle for independence.

A particularly embarrassing manifestation of Indonesia's dependence was the requirement that Jakarta report to the IGGI every six months on its economic performance and projected aid needs. Top level officials who acknowledged being "bothered by the feeling of dependence" pointed to the "insulting" practice by which Indonesian representatives at IGGI meetings were "tested," even interrogated, as one of the chief irritants: "When we have to report every six months to the IGGI and tell them how hard we've tried and how well we've done, we feel like small children."

Leaders from practically all of the major groups voiced the hope that aid could be put on a long-term basis and the IGGI meetings, reminders of Indonesia's dependence, held to a minimum.[8] As it was, they complained, Jakarta was kept in a constant state of uncertainty, never knowing for sure whether the needed aid would be forthcoming. Several proposed a five-year aid commitment for each Five Year Plan. A few felt that dispensing with the IGGI format altogether and dealing with the creditor nations entirely on an individual basis would make it easier to play them off against one another. PSI and Islamic leaders, among others, contended that the Indonesian government was exacerbating the problem by giving so much public attention to each successful IGGI meeting. New aid commitments and favorable IMF reports had come to be presented as evidence of Indonesia's success, even if the average Indonesian could not feel any progress. Drawing attention to those meetings could easily backfire, noted a leading academic figure, if visible economic progress was not forthcoming soon and people were left with the impression that dependence had yielded nothing more than empty words of praise from Indonesia's creditors. Similarly, it was observed, should meetings in the future produce more criticism than praise, Indonesia's leaders are likely to regret having attached so much importance to them in the past.

Several technocrats, however, defended the IGGI arrangement. One claimed that he enjoyed the meetings which others found so embarrassing: "Frankly, I am proud to have the opportunity to report before these meetings the progress we have made. When you can go to meetings like these and say you have reduced the inflation rate from 650 percent to under 10 percent in a matter of three years, such meetings are not something to worry about." These technocrats contended that the IGGI system worked to Indonesia's advantage, since the other members would object if any one were to try to impose outrageously exploitative conditions.

8. The meetings are now held only once a year.

If the majority of the Indonesian leaders were embarrassed by their country's conspicuous dependence on outsiders, they also believed that their national sovereignty had already been challenged, and to some extent compromised, as a consequence of their need for aid. Of 38 leaders with whom it was possible to discuss this sensitive question, 66 percent made clear their belief that Indonesia's policymakers had capitulated to foreign pressures. All three generations concurred in this view, though the young somewhat less so. Only the Catholics clearly dissented from that judgment, though of course it may be assumed that foreign ministry officials, technocrats, and army generals, who were underrepresented in the group of 38, would also have found such an evaluation difficult to accept.[9]

A less delicate matter, and one on which there was even stronger agreement, was the desire of the creditor nations to exploit Indonesia's dependence on aid as a means of influencing Jakarta's policies. More than 75 percent felt that Indonesia had been or was likely to be subjected to such pressures. Older leaders were especially pronounced in this view, as were technocrats and leaders of the PSI and PNI (see Table 7.4).

Most outspoken in condemning the sacrifice of Indonesia's sovereignty were PNI and PSI leaders. "We have no more freedom," said a PNI leader. "If we decide that our foreign policy requires a course which is not agreeable to our creditors, we run the risk of having aid stopped." Indonesia had "sold basic control over its own policies," it was alleged. Much criticism was directed at the technocrats, but some leaders contended that a willingness to capitulate to foreign pressures could be traced all the way to the

9. This issue was too delicate to raise with most of the foreign ministry officials, technocrats, and army generals directly responsible for policy making; many would have taken offense at such a line of questioning. In any case, it would have been illusory to hope for frankness on a subject that so directly involved their personal competence and patriotism. Of the 38, foreign influence was said to be excessive by 7 of 8 PNI leaders, 3 of 4 each from the PSI and the army, 5 of 8 Islamic politicians, one of 2 technocrats, and none of the 3 Catholics and one foreign ministry official who responded. By generations, excessive foreign influence was seen by 8 of 9 leaders of the 1928 Generation, 12 of 20 from the 1945 Generation, and 5 of 9 from the 1966 Generation.

Table 7.4. Have aid-givers tried to influence policy?

	Yes	No, but likely in the future	No/Yes, but it does not worry me
All respondents	32 (68%)	4 (8%)	11 (23%)
1928 Generation	7	0	1
1945 Generation	23	2	6
1966 Generation	2	2	4
Technocrats	6	0	0
PNI	5	0	0
PSI	5	1	0
Foreign Ministry	3	1	2
Islamic parties	5	0	3
Army	4	0	3
Catholic Party	2	0	2

top. "No one knows what Soeharto thinks on any subject, except for one thing," said a PSI leader. "The central consideration in Soeharto's political world is foreign aid. He will not do anything to jeopardize foreign aid. . . . But it is impossible for us to base a foreign policy on trying to please other people." These sentiments were in some measure echoed by Islamic leaders, generals, and 1966 Generation figures. As a militantly anti-Sukarno Islamic leader explained: "I'm pro-U.S. It's no secret. But I must say that as a nationalist it bothers me to see foreigners deciding our foreign policy for us."

Many leaders pointed to the deference accorded foreign advisers as a sure sign that outsiders were excessively influential in the policymaking process. There was a widely held belief that Indonesia's decision-makers valued foreign advice more highly than that of their countrymen. The shortest route to Soeharto, it was said, was via a foreign country. He might ignore what domestic critics said, but if foreigners said the same thing, he would listen. A senior army general criticized the inordinate influence of the IMF and World Bank, asserting that he had heard "from a high officeholder of a department that originally the foreigners were advisers to our officials, but now apparently it is the reverse." Shock at the cavalier manner in which the technocrats were treated by their foreign advisers led a PSI leader to declare: "You should see the way they talk to, or rather listen to, foreigners, You should see some of the reports the Harvard Advisory Group writes to Widjojo. What have you done about this? What about that? All these demands. I have been shown these reports by certain people. There is no point in my making it public, but I make a note of these things." Alluding to the "incredible sensitivity" of Indonesians to foreign opinion, a newspaper editor wryly observed that the best way to fight corruption probably would be to publish six stories of foreign investors who were frightened away by corruption.

The economists in high government positions were, according to a technocrat, "fully conscious of the influence of foreigners in our decision-making," but they were "equally aware that we just don't have enough weight to tell anybody what to do." One of the most influential economists did, in fact, suggest the same conclusion when he complained: "People don't realize how weak our bargaining position really is." Others, however, argued that the top decision-makers submitted to foreign pressures because they were "pervaded by an inferiority complex" and lacked the self-confidence they needed to avoid being taken advantage of in negotiations. The economists were said to be still tied to their American textbooks and still aiming to please their American professors. Islamic leaders and army generals accused them of seeking the plaudits of the IMF and the IGGI much as a student tries to satisfy his teachers.

As evidence of the restrictions imposed by Indonesia's dependence on foreign aid, some leaders pointed out that on a number of issues "Indonesia is not really free to say what it believes." In the words of an army general: "If I look at Malik's statements, I have the feeling that everything is said with the United States and the Netherlands in mind. There is the constant feeling of dependence. It is quite apparent that on Vietnam Indonesia has attuned its policy to the United States." Another army spokesman asserted that when "we arrest Japanese fishermen for fishing in our territorial waters, the central government frees them because it is afraid of offending the Japanese and jeopardizing aid." Others argued that

Indonesia had been afraid to declare its wholehearted support for a new nonaligned conference or to seek aid from Communist countries until the United States gave its approval. And there was widespread distress at the U.S. AID director's reported suggestion in late 1969 that Washington might have to reconsider its aid commitment because Indonesia was maintaining ambassadorial relations with Hanoi and Pyongyang but not with America's friends in Saigon, Seoul, and Taipei. Moreover, a key economist argued that aid negotiations were "always a bargaining process in which many other factors are involved." Trade and investment could not be separated from aid, he asserted. "They are three cards held in one hand. Questions of investment concessions and trade terms often come up in aid negotiations."

But the sharpest criticism of foreign intervention in Indonesia's decision-making process was directed at the IMF and Japan. Of the foreign policy elite members who discussed the IMF, 64 percent felt that it had excessive, if not decisive, influence in the determination of Indonesia's economic policies. PNI, Islamic, and PSI leaders overwhelmingly condemned the IMF's role, and there were some strong army and foreign ministry critics as well (see Table 7.5). Only the technocrats, whose policymaking position made it hard for them to criticize the IMF without criticizing themselves, and the Catholics

Table 7.5. The IMF's influence on economic policies

	Excessive	Appropriate
All respondents	28 (64%)	16 (36%)
1928 Generation	8	1
1945 Generation	17	12
1966 Generation	3	3
PNI	6	0
Islamic parties	5	1
PSI	4	1
Army	4	4
Foreign Ministry	2	3
Technocrats	1	6
Catholic Party	0	2

expressed little resentment of the IMF's influence. The IMF's defenders contended that it certainly had Indonesia's interests at heart because of its own stake in the country: "If Indonesia fails economically, it will be the failure of the IMF too, and it will be very embarrassing for them."

Even stronger were feelings about Japan. Of 54 leaders, 91 percent, representing an overwhelming majority of every group, said they were worried about the Japanese using aid to subjugate Indonesia (see Table 7.6).

Table 7.6. Concern that Japan is using aid to exploit Indonesia

	Worried	Not worried
All respondents	49 (91%)	5 (9%)
1928 Generation	8	1
1945 Generation	33	4
1966 Generation	8	0
PSI	6	0
PNI	5	0
Catholic Party	4	0
Technocrats	8	1
Islamic parties	7	1
Foreign Ministry	6	1
Army	6	2

Noting that aid negotiations with Japan had often proved bitter and protracted, many leaders complained that the Japanese were unwilling to give aid without demanding concessions and making counterproposals. The Japanese were also said to be "extraordinarily crude" in their bargaining techniques. As for specific instances in which the Japanese had attempted to use their aid to extract concessions on unrelated issues, two cases were most frequently mentioned. First, it was widely believed that the Japanese on several occasions clearly indicated that aid negotiations would go more smoothly if Indonesia would agree to join ASPAC. Second, most of the foreign policy elite members were convinced that the Japanese had threatened to withhold aid if Indonesia did not consent to an agreement on fishing rights which the overwhelming majority of the Indonesian leaders considered injurious to their country's interests.[10] Moreover, considerable resentment was expressed at Jakarta's lenient treatment of unauthorized Japanese fishermen following a reported warning by Japanese diplomats that a failure to release them might negatively influence the Diet's disposition to extend aid.

Those who were unworried by the political and economic demands of aid-givers either denied the existence of such pressures or dismissed them as a fact of international life which need not be a cause for concern. Despite all the talk of aid "without strings," a foreign ministry official noted, "all countries that give aid expect certain policies in return. This is never stated explicitly. If it were, we would have to reject it, but we know what is expected." Several foreign ministry officials and army generals conceded that "if you lend me some money, I will be more disposed to try to make you happy. . . . It is only natural that we will think more seriously about the suggestions the aid-givers make." But if the creditor nations could "try to persuade us, using aid as a bargaining point," the Indonesians were "still free to decide for ourselves." There was "no problem so long as Indonesia's attitude remains firm" in the face of such pressures.

Moreover, the foreign ministry officials and army generals cited above suggested that the problem of external pressures was largely academic, because Indonesia's desires generally coincided with those of the principal creditor nations. They thus had no reason to pressure Indonesia, and reported cases were brushed off by these leaders as "misconceptions" fostered by the press. Besides, no threat to cut off aid would be credible, it was said, because Washington and Tokyo realized that if they withheld aid and Indonesia's development effort failed, there would be "chaos," which was not in their interests. A leading economist dismissed talk of excessive foreign influence on policymaking as the reflection of an inferiority com-

10. According to *Kompas,* 25 July 1973, Indonesia had lost millions of dollars each year because of the vagueness of the fishing agreement with Japan.

plex. If there was a relationship with foreign groups, it was assumed that the foreigners were "running things," he contended.

The foreign policy elite's concern about dependence on foreign aid was rooted in a profound suspicion of the motivations of those who gave aid. Some 80 percent were convinced that the industrialized countries assisted Indonesia only to serve their own interests. This belief was strongest among the youngest generation, but it was shared by a substantial majority of all the major groups (see Table 7.7). As for the few who dissented from this view, none suggested

Table 7.7. Why nations give aid

	To achieve their own economic and political goals	To help the poor nations develop
All respondents	37 (80%)	9 (20%)
1928 Generation	3	2
1945 Generation	27	6
1966 Generation	7	1
PNI	5	0
Technocrats	5	1
PSI	4	1
Army	6	2
Catholic Party	3	1
Foreign Ministry	4	2
Islamic parties	4	2

charity as a motivation for giving aid, but several talked of a "growing recognition of the need for cooperation" and of the likelihood that an industrialized Indonesia would be a better trading partner for the West and would provide a surer guarantee against a PKI resurgence.

Despite its obvious affinity to the Leninist interpretation of imperialism, the argument that the industrialized countries gave aid mainly to guarantee markets for goods they could not sell at home was advanced by leaders of diverse political orientations. Even Catholics and Muslims who detest Marxism and admire the West subscribed to this argument with enthusiasm. As in the case of concern about external pressures stemming from Indonesia's dependence on aid, the Japanese were a prime target of criticism. A PNI leader aptly stated the prevailing view: "The Japanese have decided that they need countries like Indonesia to absorb their surplus. They are aware that buying power is very low here. So they give us credits to buy their products and call it aid." (For an indication of Japan's success in establishing the desired commercial relationships, see the data on trade in Appendix D, which reveal that Japan in 1973 accounted for 53 percent of Indonesia's exports and 29 percent of its imports, as compared with 7 and 18 percent respectively in 1961.)

But this complaint was by no means confined to Japan. "Japan is no worse than the others," said a PSI leader. "They are all thinking only of economic expansion. There is no such thing as 'aid.' The United States gives 'aid' to protect the capitalist system and to create new markets for itself. That is perfectly obvious." Islamic leaders referred to American aid as a mere export-promoting device and asked: "Where else would they get rid of their products?" According to an army general, a principal reason for Washington's emphasis on the use of fertilizer was a desire to promote the fertilizer industry in the United States. Another general, along with a highly influential foreign ministry official, complained that "foreign aid is now being used to keep Indonesia in a subordinate position" because it has the effect of creating markets without increasing domestic productive capacities.

Intimately related to this conviction was the fear that the aid-givers really had little desire to see Indonesia develop industries of its own. Of the 30 respondents on this particular point, nearly two-thirds expressed the belief that the advanced countries would give little or no support when a serious effort was made to industrialize Indonesia. These views were especially pronounced among PNI, army, and foreign ministry representatives.[11]

11. Indonesia could expect little or no aid, according to 2 PNI respondents, 4 of 5 from the army, 3 of 4 from the foreign ministry, 3 of 6 from the Islamic parties, 2 of 4 technocrats, 1 of 2 Catholics, and none of the 2 leaders of the PSI. This view was voiced by 3 of 5 from the 1928 Generation, 13 of 21 leaders of the 1945 Generation, and 3 of 4 from the 1966 Generation.

The principal argument to support this conviction was the contention that an increased productive capacity in the hands of Indonesians would only provide unwanted competition for the goods the creditor nations were now selling. It was simply "illogical" for the advanced countries to foster industrialization in Indonesia, thus hindering their own efforts to get rid of their surplus production. A foreign ministry official asserted that anyone who denied the obvious truth of that statement was just not being honest. A cabinet minister recalled that from the early 1960s Indonesia had been frustrated in its efforts to gain aid for industrialization from the West. He claimed that Prime Minister Djuanda had once complained to him of this unwillingness and of the West's insistence that Indonesia emphasize agriculture to the virtual exclusion of industrial development.

While there was a good deal of criticism of America's unwillingness to support industrialization, by far the harshest words were again reserved for Japan. Most leaders, from all groups, agreed that Japan had no interest at all in seeing Indonesia industrialize. They cited Japan's proximity and the structure of the Japanese economy as factors; a semideveloped agrarian Indonesia with its market controlled by Japan was what the Japanese desired. Of course, some leaders, especially technocrats, contended that an industrialized Indonesia would be a better trading partner for the advanced countries, including Japan. Indeed, the Japanese were said to have told several Indonesians that their strategy was to support industrialization in Indonesia in order to raise buying power so that they could sell their more sophisticated products there, while the cheaper goods now being disposed of in Indonesia would be sold in Africa.

There was considerable skepticism, however, as to whether most Japanese were actually motivated by such a farsighted perspective. Foreign policy elite members typically dismissed such claims with the observation that the Japanese were more likely to think in terms of current profits and market control than to foster industrialization, which would mean foregoing present export sales in the hope of selling more expensive products in the future. Even a key technocrat who suggested that such farsighted Japanese were becoming more influential argued that the Japanese government was still very heavily influenced by "ruthless" businessmen who took a "short-term profit-loss approach to relations with Indonesia."

If their need for markets was believed to discourage the advanced countries from fostering industrialization in Indonesia, an equally important reason for keeping Indonesia underdeveloped was the desire to guarantee a continuing supply of certain raw materials. Using Indonesia's oil for domestic industrial development would reduce the amount available for export. Once again, Japan took the brunt of the criticism. The belief that Japan wanted to sustain the colonial pattern by which an underdeveloped country serves as a source of raw materials for the industries of advanced countries proved especially strong among cabinet ministers, technocrats, and foreign ministry officials who had dealt with the Japanese on aid matters. While the Indonesian leaders hoped that they would be able to earn enough foreign exchange from their exports of raw materials to finance industrialization in the absence of adequate aid for that purpose, there were fears that the reliance on raw material exports might perpetuate the colonial pattern of economic dependence, with the result that Indonesia would be drained of its natural wealth without ever industrializing and achieving economic self-sufficiency.

The desire to engage in economic exploitation was not, of course, the only reason for giving aid, according to the Indonesian leaders. While Japan's aid was generally seen as economically motivated, for the United States political interests were said to be at least as important as economic ones. From an economic standpoint, Indonesia was not nearly as important to the United States as to Japan. America's primary concern, the foreign policy elite members felt, was the maintenance of an anti-Communist Indonesia. Since the foreign policy elite members themselves were committed to preventing a revival of the PKI, there was no basic conflict here, though problems did arise, as we have seen, on issues such as China's entry into the UN. It was, however, clearly economic exploitation that the Indonesians feared most.

An additional source of the Indonesian leaders' concern about their country's dependence on foreign aid was their perception of some of the negative effects of the aid itself. Some suggested that aid, as presently implemented, was actually an obstacle to development, because it enabled the government to defer indefinitely the difficult but necessary reforms discussed earlier. Even Islamic and PSI leaders who called for vastly increased aid contended that the present use of aid was impeding development. South Vietnam, and less frequently South Korea, were cited as examples of countries where the availability of aid had kept the government from undertaking measures to mobilize its own resources. It was also argued that too much aid sapped the spirit of hard work and sacrifice. According to PNI and Islamic leaders, among others, the cultural invasion that had accompanied Indonesia's reliance on foreign aid was threatening the country's national identity, and in so doing was weakening its moral fiber.

Many leaders felt that the aid Indonesia was receiving not only served as a disincentive to work hard and undertake needed reforms, but that it exacerbated some basic problems. Foreign aid, argued Islamic, PSI, and 1966 Generation leaders, was inviting corruption on a larger scale than ever before. "The corruption you see," said an Islamic leader, "really is made possible by foreign aid. That is what creates the opportunities." A PSI leader, among others, argued that aid benefited "only the military establishment involved in its implementation," because officers received a "cut" of most transactions in which they were involved. Aid would not change the situation in any way "except to fill the pockets of a few." An Islamic leader known as an economic authority claimed that under the "BE system," by which the government sold foreign credits to Indonesian importers, the only beneficiary was the government, which "sucks up all the money and spends it in unproductive ways." Besides, he asserted, the government was "more concerned about stability than real development." The only people making money were "generals and Chinese." Other leaders, young and old, warned against the kind of "development" that only benefited "the present ruling elite" and provided merely "the illusion of development."

PNI, PSI, Islamic, and a few army leaders argued further that foreign aid was composed of an excessively high percentage of credits for the import of consumer goods, many of which could be produced in Indonesia. As a result, the impact of aid was to stifle rather than stimulate Indonesia's economic development. Even key government officials joined in complaining that although the credits were extended at low interest rates, the items imported under those credits were often priced above world market prices. The credits which comprised the bulk of foreign aid actually profited the creditor nations more than they benefited Indonesia, argued a PNI leader, because they were "simply taking products they could not otherwise sell and forcing us to buy them at higher than normal prices."

What Indonesia needed, many leaders maintained, was more credit to import basic materials that would increase the productivity of Indonesia's industries; more project aid to finance infrastructure, including such massive projects as a canal from Palembang to Riau, an idea the IGGI was said to have rejected as too ambitious; short-term loans, said to have been prohibited by the IMF, for the development of small scale industries and the clearing of new rice fields that would create jobs and yield a rapid payoff; and unrestricted credits to be spent as the Indonesians felt necessary. While many attributed their country's failure to get such aid to the aid-givers' lack of any real interest in Indonesia's development, the top decision-makers in Jakarta were also criticized. An Islamic leader claimed that the government did not really want aid for infrastructure, but preferred instead BE aid because it could make a profit on the sale of those credits. A PSI leader blamed both the aid-givers and his own government: "The National Planning Board and the United States embassy don't worry about the fact that foreign aid, especially in the form of BE credits on certain commodities, is having a damaging effect on domestic industries. The textile industry has been very badly hurt, for example. . . . They are prepared to accept stagnation. [A very high official of the Ministry of Industry] recently said that industry only accounted for 10 percent of the national income anyway, so why worry about its present difficulties. With a man like that, what can you expect?"

Finally, there was concern about the size of the debts which the government was incurring as a result of foreign aid. To the pre-1966 debts of $2.4 billion have been added new aid commitments which by mid-1975 totaled more than $5.6 billion. When the newly committed aid has been disbursed, therefore, Indonesia's aid debts will have gone beyond $8 billion, and given the increasing annual commitments, the debt has been rising at an accelerating rate. PNI, Islamic, and 1966 Generation leaders, in particular, gave expression to their worries about Indonesia's growing indebtedness. So did an important foreign ministry official, who observed that despite the fact that much of the aid received either was employed inefficiently or vanished through corruption, all the credits would have to be repaid.

Naturally, those who occupied key policymaking positions tended to deny that aid was impeding development. They argued that the level of dependence was not so high as to produce such negative effects. Furthermore, they noted that the proportion of project aid was rising, while credits for consumer goods were declining. And as an army general put it when confronted with the allegation that aid was damaging Indonesia's industries and inhibiting reforms: "My answer is a short one. We are not that stupid."

Development Strategies and the Perpetuation of Dependence

If foreign aid was perceived by a substantial majority of the foreign policy elite as a serious threat to Indonesia's independence, so was the whole strategy of economic development which the New Order government had adopted. The attempt to achieve and maintain economic stability through very strong measures of monetary restraint, and to base development mainly on foreign loans and investment, was widely assailed on the grounds that it had been imposed by Indonesia's creditors and better served the interests of foreign investors than those of Indonesia's own troubled businessmen and impoverished masses.

Virtually all agreed that some degree of monetary restraint had been necessary to curb the runaway inflation of 1966, but a clear majority considered the government's economic strategy inconsistent with the demands of both economic and political independence. Of 55 leaders who discussed economic strategies, 62 percent favored greater reliance on efforts to raise indigenous production, rather than monetary restraint, as the best way to slow inflation while laying the groundwork for development. Criticism of the government's adherence to the monetary approach was especially strong among PNI, Islamic, and PSI leaders, while Catholics and technocrats were equally firm in defending the monetary approach, and the army and foreign ministry were in between. The oldest generation was much more wholeheartedly in accord with the production approach than the younger leaders (see Table 7.8).

Table 7.8. Attitudes concerning development strategies

	Do more to raise production and worry less about inflation	Stabilization/ Monetary approach is correct
All respondents	34 (62%)	21 (38%)
1928 Generation	8	1
1945 Generation	21	16
1966 Generation	5	4
PNI	7	1
Islamic parties	7	1
PSI	5	1
Army	4	5
Foreign Ministry	2	4
Technocrats	1	7
Catholic Party	0	4

Most of the foreign policy elite members were especially disturbed by two elements of the government's approach to stabilization: the tight money policy and the importing of substantial quantities of consumer goods under foreign credits in order to keep prices in check. Unable to find money with which to finance business operations and forced to compete with imported goods that were of higher quality and lower cost, domestic manufacturing concerns were said to have suffered a disastrous setback. The government's policies were widely blamed for having "paralyzed" Indonesian industry in general and "killed off" a great many businesses. While many of the victims were acknowledged to have been basically unsound, engaged more in speculation than in production, many well-established firms were also said to have succumbed. Though no one claimed that Indonesian industries had been thriving before the October 1966 regulations, many asserted that there had been a reasonable amount of productive activity, and much of it had ceased as a result of the government's economic policies. Textiles, chemicals, medicines, matches, ceramics, and soap were among the industries most frequently cited as casualties of the tight money and cheap imports combination.

The majority felt that even if some tightening of credit and limited importing of consumer goods was necessary in October 1966, there was no justification for the "excessiveness" of those policies, or for their maintenance in such an extreme form beyond the first few critical months. Indonesian industries were said to have been hit so hard by the stabilization measures that when the government slowly began to loosen the tight money policy, it was too late to help them. By 1970 government spokesmen were contending that the real problem was not the tightness of credit, since interest rates had dropped a good deal, but finding sound firms that would accept credits which the government was eager to extend. But critics attributed the government's inability to find acceptable recipients to the fact that so many potential borrowers had already been financially destroyed. Numerous leaders, including some army generals, went so far as to blame these excessively "liberal" economic policies for the "destruction" of Indonesia's indigenous middle class, on which both economic and political development were said to depend.

In addition, argued many of the interviewees, the government's efforts were not only too late but too little. Credit was still too tight. Qualifying for a loan often required feasibility studies that few could afford to carry out. Under-the-table payments to expedite credits also were said to drive up the cost of a loan. Furthermore, at a time when government banks were paying extremely high interest rates on deposits (6 percent a month at the peak in 1969), there was little incentive to invest. A key cabinet minister complained that a proposal to channel the money attracted by the high interest paid on deposits into infrastructure investments had been rejected because of the fear of reviving inflation: as a result, the money remained idle. "What has been achieved," said a PSI leader, "is stability on the basis of stagnation."

Moreover, a clear majority of the foreign policy elite members felt that the government's stabilization policy had caused considerable suffering in the name of economic accomplishments that were much more meaningful to Indonesia's foreign creditors than to Indonesians. With unemployment up, buying power down, and prices stabilized at a very high level, the government's achievement in drastically reducing inflation was characterized as "meaningless." At least the construction projects of the Sukarno years, however inefficient a utilization of resources, had created jobs for Indonesians and stimulated demand for Indonesian products, said a PNI leader. Even one technocrat acknowledged that only a small segment at the top of Indonesian society had benefited from the improvements in the economic situation. Muslim and PNI politicians talked of paralysis, stagnation, and suffering in Central Java. As an army general said: "The progress achieved so far has not meant anything for the people. Life is harder than before. Before, rice was 200 rupiahs, but 200 rupiahs was easy to get. Now [September 1969] it is 30 rupiahs, but money is so scarce that people are starving. It is really pathetic to see conditions in East Java. . . . Only a very small group of people in Jakarta have benefited from the economic stabilization that has been achieved." Though rice production was on the rise, even that achievement was criticized by Islamic party leaders as beneficial mainly to urban dwellers, because the increased supply had lowered the price, leaving the heavily indebted peasant growers worse off.

In 1972 and 1973, serious shortfalls in rice production sent inflation up sharply again, and in the 1973 interviews complaints about unemployment, tight money, and stagnation in indigenous enterprises were louder than ever. Foreign policy elite members perceived a rapidly widening gap between rich and poor, city and countryside, with most Indonesians more impoverished than before.

In this deteriorating situation, criticism of the government's development strategy was even harsher than it had been three years earlier.

Perhaps the sharpest and most widespread criticism of the New Order's monetary policies, especially in 1973, was that the chief beneficiaries were foreigners and domestic Chinese. When government officials spoke of rising exports, and by 1973 of increased production of manufactured goods, they really were talking almost exclusively about sectors of the economy dominated by foreigners and local Chinese, many leaders pointed out. The government's preoccupation with "stability at any cost" allegedly reflected not Indonesian interests but those of the IMF, which, as a "banker's institution," was "naturally more concerned about ensuring a favorable climate for foreign investment than about stimulating economic activity among Indonesians."

The widespread belief that the stabilization policy was essentially a foreign product was reflected in criticism aimed at the conceptual basis of the policy. Numerous leaders argued vigorously that the policy was a doctrinaire application of theories drawn from Western textbooks, applicable perhaps in industrialized states but wholly inappropriate in an underdeveloped country. In an industrialized country a tightening of credit and restriction of government expenditures may stem inflation without strangling productive activity, but in an underdeveloped country, where inflation is rooted in a basic lack of productive capacity, such policies are likely to yield stagnation and thus to inhibit economic development. Too strong an attack on inflation would inevitably have disastrous results because a certain amount of inflation is necessary for development. A foreign ministry official asserted that a cabinet member's proud announcement in early 1970 that inflation had fallen to zero actually meant that no development was taking place. Leaders of several groups criticized the formulators of the Five Year Plan for setting overly modest goals because of their preoccupation with holding down inflation.

Moreover, the New Order's triumph over inflation was said to be artificial and therefore illusory. Indonesia's economy was still "structurally in an inflationary stage." Only an improvement in productive capacity could provide a long-term basis for closing the gap between the flow of goods and the circulation of money, but according to the government's critics, the method chosen to combat inflation was actually diminishing productive capacity rather than raising it. As one Islamic leader explained: "We haven't really licked inflation at all. We're only keeping it down through the use of foreign aid, through standby funds. . . . If aid were cut, inflation would take off again."

The production approach, on the other hand, was viewed by most Indonesian leaders as "more consonant with the requirements of national independence." By energetically encouraging investment in indigenous productive capacity, even at the cost of increased inflation, it would be possible to make meaningful progress toward development without neglecting the demands of independence, argued the government's critics. Indonesia also needed a development plan that emphasized the mobilization of domestic resources to undertake public works projects and the like, with people at all levels brought into the development effort. The Five Year Plan was generally viewed as "a policy of the government, not as something in which everyone should participate," observed a foreign ministry official. The government, he suggested, should have had political party cadres, down to the lowest echelons, getting people out and involved in development activities. Instead, the parties had found their role curbed by the government. Advocates of the production approach also urged that imports of items that Indonesia could produce be curtailed, or at least that adequate tariff protection be afforded to Indonesia's industries.

The government's monetary approach did have its defenders among a minority of the foreign policy elite members, mainly Catholics and the technocrats directly responsible for the policy. They stressed that it was impossible to increase production before overcoming inflation and removing the distortions that years of inflation had left in the Indonesian economy. The technocrats insisted that their policies had been adopted not because of any pressures from the IMF but because of a set of compelling conditions, which both they and the IMF were able to see clearly. An extremely tight money policy was needed to administer a decisive blow to inflation and to the inflationary psychology of the Indonesian people. Indonesians had to be shown that if they worked hard and saved their money, they would be able to buy something with it. They also had to be shown that the government was capable of setting an economic goal and then achieving it, so that people would say: "If we could lick inflation, we can lick development." Only after inflation had been brought under control could the government afford to spend money on projects to stimulate development without giving rise to runaway inflation, but even then extreme caution was required, for the "patient" was "not yet entirely recovered."

Stabilization, the technocrats acknowledged, was necessarily a painful process, and there had to be sacrifices. That a tight money policy would slow the rate of growth was "elementary economics," they agreed:

> Much as we wanted to help domestic industries hurt by the stabilization policy, we would not allow it to interfere with our efforts to control the inflation. Those who are outside the government say that we could have played it more cleverly and done both—controlled inflation and also given aid to domestic industries. But we are only as clever as we are, and we did not feel confident that we could play it both ways. . . . We kept to the tight money policy . . . because we were afraid that inflation would rise again. We had to play it safe. If domestic industries were hurt, that is the price that had to be paid.

Some claimed that the great majority of those businesses that had been hurt were basically unsound to begin with. One cabinet minister compared the inflation to a river that had flooded over wide portions of the land. Many wild fish (speculators) were stranded and lost in the effort to channel the waters back into their proper path. The tight money policy initiated a "purification process, . . . survival of the fittest." A young Catholic leader declared that businessmen who were hurt by the tight money policy had only their own inefficiency to blame: "It was better to let them die, and then to start over on a sounder basis."

To the suggestion that the production approach would have

sufficiently stemmed inflation while fostering development, the technocrats replied mainly with scorn. "What were they going to produce?" asked one economist sarcastically. It was "nonsense" to say that Indonesia could have stopped inflation without the sort of tight money policy that had been implemented. So long as inflation persisted, it was illusory to hope for production increases. In previous years, licenses to establish factories had been doled out to friends without regard to economic conditions, and they had survived on subsidies and speculation. In the inflationary situation that prevailed, one could make more money trading his government allotment of cotton and thread than using it to produce textiles. Only by first creating stable prices could the government make it more profitable to produce than to speculate. Besides, given the limited resources available and the need to use most of the available foreign aid in the early years of the New Order for stabilization, there was little money left to bring about major improvements in productive capacity. It is "incredibly difficult" to raise production, and even harder to do it without feeding inflation, asserted the economists. Moreover, they noted, the governmental apparatus for spending money was so inadequate, especially in those early years, that much of the money simply would not have been spent in the manner intended.

Besides criticism of the government's emphasis on monetary measures to achieve and maintain economic stability, there was considerable unhappiness with policies concerning industrialization and the role of foreign investment. Some, mainly PNI and Islamic party leaders, sharply criticized the first Five Year Plan for giving priority to agricultural development at the expense of broad-based industrialization. A former foreign minister contended that the New Order government was willing to keep Indonesia an agrarian country for a long time. While all agreed on the importance of achieving the plan's goal of agricultural self-sufficiency, a pre-eminent leader of the 1928 Generation, among others, argued that agricultural development and industrialization had to proceed simultaneously, receiving equal attention. A major effort to industrialize should not be postponed to future five-year plans, as was the government's avowed intention. Only by undertaking industrialization on a scale far greater than that contemplated in the Five Year Plan could Indonesia alleviate unemployment and break out of the colonial pattern of exporting raw materials and importing manufactured products.

The contention that the solution to the unemployment problem lay in expanding industrial investment rapidly was rejected by the government's defenders. They argued that it was necessary first to increase demand by raising the buying power of the peasants, who could increase their income, despite falling rice prices, by expanding production. The way to reduce unemployment was not through industrial expansion but public works projects, and that was the government's policy. As for the suggestion that the government should do more to mobilize human resources for development, an economist pointed out that there were two approaches: the government could, through stirring speeches, "fire up the spirit of the peasant as he attacks his rice field," or it could rely on economic incentives, like public works contracts, to mobilize people. The government had decided to do the latter.

Supporters of the government's policy considered it unrealistic to place as much emphasis on industrialization as on agriculture. Indonesia simply lacked the capacity to do both. "India," a foreign ministry official noted, "tried to develop heavy industry, failed, and had to beg the United States and the Soviet Union for food. So there is your independence." Given the substantial amount of foreign exchange expended on rice imports, agricultural self-sufficiency would save Indonesia more foreign exchange than even the best industrial investment could be expected to yield in a short time. The economists took the position that they were as strongly committed to eventual industrialization as anyone else, but that the development process had to be viewed in terms of three five-year plans—the first agricultural in emphasis, the second bringing agricultural and industrial development into balance, and the third, assuming the success of the first two, an all-out push to industrialization.

The majority of the foreign policy elite members were concerned that the industrial development anticipated by the government in the first and second Five Year Plans would be dominated by foreign investment. Though virtually no one disagreed that foreign investment in some form was indispensable to economic development, there was considerable apprehension that foreign capital was gaining so strong a position that it jeopardized the country's independence. More than two-thirds of the leaders who discussed foreign investment in 1969 and 1970 expressed concern about domination by it, and half of those who voiced such fears indicated that they were seriously worried. The older generations were more intense in their concern, but a majority of the 1966 Generation leaders showed at least moderate concern. Among the major groups, the PNI and PSI leaders were most deeply worried, but at least half of each group except the Catholics and Muslim politicians expressed concern (see Table 7.9). These percentages almost certainly understate the degree of uneasiness felt by the Indonesian leaders in subsequent years. One of the sharpest changes between the 1970 and 1973 interviews was the further elevation of concern about foreign investment, reflecting the large increase in the amount of foreign capital active in the country.

A major reason for the widespread apprehension about the role of foreign investment in Indonesia's industrial development was the

Table 7.9. Concern about foreign investment

	Expressed concern (strong concern)	No real concern
All respondents	30 (15) [68% (34%)]	14 (32%)
1928 Generation	4 (4)	3
1945 Generation	22 (11)	8
1966 Generation	4 (0)	3
PNI	6 (6)	1
PSI	3 (2)	1
Technocrats	3 (0)	1
Army	4 (1)	3
Foreign Ministry	3 (1)	3
Islamic parties	2 (1)	3
Catholic Party	1 (0)	2

belief that foreign investors were perpetuating economic patterns by which Indonesia had since colonial times been kept dependent on outsiders. Many of the Indonesian leaders strongly suspected that foreign investors generally had little interest in Indonesia's development toward self-sufficiency. They saw confirmation of this in the principal features of the foreign investment entering their country.

First, they were dismayed at the reluctance of foreign investors to build the processing facilities that would enable Indonesia to break the colonial pattern of serving merely as a supplier of raw materials. Foreign ministry officials, technocrats, and 1966 Generation leaders were among the many who voiced such concern. The initial concentration of foreign investment in capital-intensive extractive industries, such as mining, forestry, and fishing, was also discouraging to some Indonesian leaders because those industries were not considered likely to lead the country toward self-sufficiency. There was too much investment in the extraction of raw materials for export and not enough in the production of those materials needed for Indonesia's own industries. A 1966 Generation leader called for more investment in "areas that fit our own interests—such as the growing of cotton in East Indonesia, so that our textile industry could reduce its dependence on imported cotton." Indonesia needed more small-scale investments to establish factories that would provide jobs, raise buying power, and inject life into the economy. Also of importance were investments in basic industries that would facilitate the development of smaller industries.

Considerable criticism was aimed at the inclination of some investors to make exorbitant demands and engage in exploitative practices. Such allegations of unfairness came from technocrats and generals, as well as from political party leaders. One economist expressed his dismay at the demands of American businessmen for monopoly rights throughout Indonesia. "I told some of them," he recalled, "that I had studied economics in the United States, and everything I learned about monopolies was bad. How could they come here and ask for monopoly rights?" Another economist complained of businessmen who made outlandish demands, such as a twelve-year tax holiday, and then, when their demands were rejected, went off and told stories about the "terrible corruption in Indonesia." There was particularly sharp criticism, even from those who otherwise had only kind words for foreign investors, of their alleged reluctance to hire Indonesians.[12]

By and large, Japanese businessmen were the most bitterly criticized. According to an army general, they were "cheating us blind in everything they do—fisheries, forestry, joint ventures, in every field." Many denounced the fishing agreement with Japan as "a clear case of exploitation." An Islamic party leader noted that in 1968 Indonesia "gave Japan fishing concessions worth $50 million, which damaged our own fishermen, and Soeharto did it to get a $60 million additional credit, which was hardly more than the loss to Indonesia by the concession." Furthermore, some Japanese were accused of dishonesty in their implementation of the fishing agreement. Another army general told of their practice of maintaining two fleets of fishing vessels, each with identical markings, sending one out to fish while the other was in port, and paying for fishing rights for only one fleet. Other leaders brought forth additional cases of alleged Japanese trickery; for example, they had promised to build processing facilities as part of an investment agreement, and then simply failed to do so. On one occasion they were said to have interpreted a commitment to build a hospital as meaning they would provide the beds and equipment, but not construct the building. The image of Japanese investors as exploiters gained added currency from their reported practice of stripping Indonesia's forests without replanting. The Japanese, however, were by no means the only ones criticized. A PSI leader, for example, characterized both Japanese and American investors as "vultures."

Many leaders felt that foreign investment had already acquired a dangerously influential position in Indonesia's economic life. Foreign credits at least kept control in the hands of Indonesians, but investment gave the foreigners direct managerial authority. One

12. At the end of June 1974 there were 19,452 foreigners working in Indonesia, of whom 7,851 were in forestry; 4,092 in oil and natural gas; and the rest in other fields, especially textiles. Most came from Japan, the Philippines, and Malaysia (*Merdeka,* 20 August 1974).

leader of the 1928 Generation claimed that the government was encouraging what amounted to a restoration of the colonial system wherein all industrial and export-oriented enterprises were in the hands of foreigners. Several, including an army general, expressed regret that Indonesia had returned some of the foreign enterprises taken over during the Sukarno years to their former owners.

Even joint ventures, generally the preferred form of investment, were portrayed by some leaders as potential channels for the extension of foreign domination. "Joint enterprises are not really joint because we have no capital," observed an eminent Islamic leader. "We need joint enterprises that really share control and make use of Indonesians." But under even the most auspicious circumstances, a former foreign minister stated, it was nearly impossible to work out effective joint enterprises, because the Indonesian partner would always feel overwhelmed by the superior knowledge of the foreigner. And it was damaging to the Indonesians' pride, he contended, when they were revealed before their countrymen as lacking in authority compared to foreigners.

Though some, as already noted, had called for more foreign investment in manufacturing industries, there was considerable apprehension, even among those who urged such investments, about the competition this would provide to Indonesian firms. Many foreign policy elite members argued that the incentives offered foreign investors had placed Indonesia's fledgling manufacturing enterprises at an unfair disadvantage. The foreign investment law of 1967 was sharply attacked for making excessive concessions to foreign investors. Said one army general: "The foreign investment law is absolutely crazy, devised by people with no practical experience. There is no other country in the world that gives the kind of concessions we are giving." PNI and Muslim party leaders, among others, bitterly lamented that the foreign investment law gave foreigners a longer tax holiday than that afforded to Indonesian businessmen under the domestic investment law enacted in 1968; and before the passage of the latter law, Indonesian investors had no tax holiday at all. At the very time when Indonesian enterprises were said to be encountering enormous difficulties due to high taxes, tight money, and the curtailment of government subsidies, foreign capital was being invited in with attractive terms and was being helped to establish a strong position quickly.

There was fairly broad agreement among the Indonesian leaders that the government had experienced considerable difficulty negotiating investment agreements beneficial to Indonesia and had found it even harder to hold investors to their commitments. In 1973 an army general, and one of Soeharto's very closest advisers, acknowledged that in its eagerness to attract foreign capital the government had concluded many investment agreements that were not to Indonesia's advantage—especially in the forestry and mining fields.[13] He claimed that Indonesia was now becoming more selective, however. The inability to compel investors to fulfill their obligations was admitted by a top government official charged with implementation of the foreign investment law: "We cannot force businessmen to carry out the provisions of the foreign investment law as we would like them to do. At this stage . . . we feel it is best to let the investors begin functioning here, and once they have a stake here, then we can press our demands that they build processing plants and so forth. But it seems unwise to press it now. . . . We need the investment, and at this stage we must do what is necessary to get it. There may be weaknesses in the law, but the foreign businessmen also want greater incentives."

As a result of the government's policy of offering incentives to foreign investors and failing to enforce the restrictions imposed on them, domestic firms were said to have suffered badly in various fields. Most frequently cited was the textile industry, in which Japanese capital had gained a dominant position. In 1970 an Islamic party leader observed that foreign capital in Indonesia was "so far ahead we cannot possibly catch up." By 1973, when quite

13. In 1974 Mining Minister Mohammad Sadli, former head of the Foreign Investment Committee, declared publicly that some of the early contracts had been injurious to Indonesia. He also asserted that multinational corporations had distorted and harmed the economic development of the less developed countries (*Sinar Harapan,* 13 April 1974, and *Kompas,* 13 April 1974).

substantial foreign investment had begun flowing into manufacturing industries, there was truly intense concern that this was destroying or subordinating indigenous economic capabilities and, because of its capital-intensive nature, exacerbating the unemployment problem. Many of the "manufacturing" industries established by foreign investors were criticized as in fact assembly or packaging industries which involved little transfer of technology; they were intended to circumvent tariff barriers and ensure access to the Indonesian market by making essentially foreign products appear to be "made in Indonesia." In any case, PSI and 1966 Generation leaders strongly advocated that Indonesia forego the modern factories established by foreign investors and seek to make greater use of intermediate technology, which would provide more jobs, reduce social inequities, and lessen dependence on outside capital and technology. Those interviewed in 1973 also stressed that foreign investment was stimulating patterns of extravagant elite consumption inappropriate to a country as poor and underdeveloped as Indonesia.

As with aid, increased corruption was said to be another damaging consequence of foreign investment. The real problem here, it was argued, was that the enormous opportunities for personal enrichment presented by foreign investment discouraged officials from paying attention to the needs of domestic businessmen. As one Islamic leader maintained: "Some of the generals close to Soeharto are making a great deal of money through kickbacks on foreign investment. That's why they really don't care so much about domestic industrial development. From the standpoint of their own personal interests, there is more for them in foreign investment here." PSI leaders talked of the "comprador relationship between the generals around Soeharto and foreign capitalists," and added that the CIA "backs its friends" primarily by encouraging investment deals in which the generals play the role of middleman and receive substantial commissions. The Japanese were characterized as "incredibly crude" in their flagrant efforts to bribe cabinet ministers, presidential assistants, and businessmen. "They got used to doing that sort of thing during the Sukarno period, and they think they can still do things that way," observed a 1966 Generation leader.

Even the technocrats and generals most directly responsible for Indonesia's foreign investment policies displayed some concern that they might have "sold the country to foreigners." An army general, noting the rising tide of criticism directed at foreign investment, suggested that the "present open attitude toward the outside world" may be only "a temporary thing—a reaction against the Sukarno period." A key economist acknowledged his fear that foreign capital might gain too much influence in Indonesia, and unlike most of his associates voiced more concern about the United States than about Japan:

> Actually, what worries us is having so much of the foreign investment coming from one country—that is, from the United States. . . . The United States virtually controls all of our oil industry. The same is true of mining in general. Even in lumber the United States has at least half. The Japanese just don't have the experience in these matters. When the Japanese get an oil concession, they subcontract it out to an American firm. The Philippines is concerned about American influence, not Japanese. . . . If you look at the facts, then, there is really more reason to worry about American economic domination than Japanese. What we want to see is a distribution of investment—a kind of balance.

There was even a report of a meeting in which a highly respected ambassador to an aid-giving country was said to have confided to Soeharto his nervousness about standing at the gateway ushering in foreign capital. Soeharto reportedly answered: "I'm worried too." But as the economist quoted above observed, the Indonesian leaders, however worried they might be, could see no alternative. "There will be dangers whatever we do," he stated. "It is all right to say I am worried about domination—but there is nothing we can do about it."

The minority who expressed no significant concern about foreign investment denied that foreigners were gaining excessive influence and expressed their confidence that eventually all foreign enterprises would voluntarily be turned over to Indonesians. In the meantime, foreign investment was said to be creating jobs, boosting exports, and introducing new technology; when the tax holidays had expired, there would also be tax benefits for Indonesia.

Even the much-criticized fishing agreement with Japan was characterized by several leaders as quite fair to Indonesia. A general pointed out that given Indonesia's technological limitations, the fish would simply go uncaught without an agreement allowing the Japanese to fish. Moreover, he explained, there was a special variety of tuna which the Indonesians lacked the technical expertise to catch, and part of the agreement stipulated that the Japanese train Indonesians to catch those tuna. Besides, a technocrat pointed out, the Japanese had been fishing illegally in Indonesian waters for years. Even though he conceded that the agreement was too favorable to Japan, he insisted that the situation was at least better than before.

Complaints that special treatment of foreign investors had damaged Indonesian business interests were brushed aside by some leaders. Foreign capital had to be offered special incentives not available to domestic businessmen because it was necessary to attract the foreigners from abroad, while local capital was already present. A well-placed technocrat pointed out that foreigners often got more favorable terms than domestic businessmen because theirs were much larger and higher-risk enterprises; taking size and risk into account, Indonesian investors actually received better terms. Besides, if foreign capital posed a threat, asserted a cabinet minister, it was not a matter of dollars or tax advantages but a more effective way of doing things. Only by inviting the foreigners in could Indonesians learn from them.

The foregoing analysis clearly reveals the ambivalence the Indonesian leaders feel in their relations with their presumed benefactors. Heavy reliance on foreign loans, an economic strategy consisting of stabilization measures that stifle domestic enterprises, a development plan that defers major efforts at indigenous industrialization, and an open door to foreign investment—all are accepted, in some degree, as necessary to facilitate economic progress. On the other hand, all are seen as obstructing any real advance toward economic self-sufficiency, which all the leaders view as an essential component of both economic development and independence. The central question is whether the "short-term" acceptance of dependence on aid and a development strategy that postpones any massive push to industrial self-sufficiency will facilitate the ultimate achievement of economic and political autonomy, or will in fact preclude it.

The majority of the foreign policy elite perceived the risks of dependence as dangerously high. Judging from the trend of public commentary and from the 1973 interviews, the Indonesian leaders' pessimism about the likely outcome of their country's aid-oriented policies is even greater in the mid-1970s than it was at the time the bulk of the interviews took place. It is increasingly apparent that with respect to aid, as in the case of the independent-and-active policy, the foreign policy elite members perceive the problem in essentially the same terms as Sukarno did. Though the inclination to trust the aid-givers is by no means wholly absent, the dominant theme among the Indonesian leaders is the belief that those who aid their country do not, for the most part, desire either its independence or its development. To be sure, there are obvious differences with Sukarno: most critics of foreign aid hasten to assert that they, unlike Sukarno, do not reject aid in principle, but merely object to the terms on which aid is given and to its apparent effects on economic development and national independence.[14]

That disclaimer notwithstanding, the similarities between the Indonesian leaders' perception of foreign aid and Sukarno's have been increasingly obscuring the differences. And much of the strongest criticism of aid comes from PSI and Islamic leaders who were among Sukarno's bitterest enemies. Suspicion of the aid-givers and concern about the dangers of dependence has transcended ideological and political boundaries, reaching in moderate degree even the officials most directly responsible for the New Order's aid-oriented policy. We can hardly escape the conclusion that the sharp reversal of Indonesia's foreign policy in 1966 was accompanied by much less change than might have been expected in the elite's underlying perceptions of the world and attitudes toward aid and independence.

14. In point of fact, neither did Sukarno object to aid in principle.

8 | Perceptions, Politics, and Foreign Policy

If the Indonesian foreign policy elite's view of the world and of the dilemma of dependence has changed so little from the perspectives identified with Sukarno, then we must confront some perplexing questions: Why has Soeharto given clear priority to the search for foreign aid, where Sukarno put independence first? What difference has it made that the Indonesian leaders have viewed the world as a hostile place? How have their perceptions affected the resolution of the aid-independence dilemma?

Clearly, the elite's view of the world does not by itself determine the course of foreign policy. If the hostile world view has provided a substantial impetus toward a foreign policy that gives priority to full independence, the basic weakness of Indonesia's economic and political institutions has generated strong countervailing pressures to seek foreign aid and to accept a considerable degree of dependence. Booming or declining economic conditions, eager or reluctant aid-givers, and increasing or diminishing national unity are among the many factors that help to determine the outcome.

In the last analysis, foreign policy is the product of a continuous interaction between perceptions and politics. To understand the differing responses of Sukarno and Soeharto to the dilemma of dependence, we must focus on how political incentives and risks in the Indonesian system are shaped by the elite's view of the world and made stronger or weaker by changes in the intensity of political competition. The political incentives and risks which in varying degrees faced both presidents had begun to take shape in the days of the revolution.

The Early Years

During the revolution the aid most desperately needed by the Indonesians was not economic but diplomatic. While it would obviously be misleading to equate attempts to win diplomatic backing against the Dutch with subsequent efforts to gain economic aid, the two were by no means wholly unrelated in their domestic political implications.

Within a week of the proclamation of independence, Vice President Hatta had issued an "appeal to the world powers, who are now determining the future world structure, to approve of Indonesia's independence." Hatta voiced "absolute confidence" that Indonesia's case would be dealt with "justly and fairly."[1] Although Sjahrir, the Republic's first prime minister, admitted a suspicion that the existing imperialist and capitalist international power structure would permit Indonesia nothing more than "independence in name only," he believed that Indonesia's weakness left it no choice but to hope that the United States, the new hegemonic power of the Pacific, would live up to its anticolonial rhetoric and press the Dutch to agree to the transfer of sovereignty. In the hope of winning American support, Sjahrir urged his countrymen to refrain from antiforeign actions.[2] At the same time, he sought to strengthen his negotiating position with the Dutch by demonstrating the military capability to make the struggle costly.

But Sjahrir's policy of attempting to win independence by combining military struggle with a search for foreign diplomatic support encountered sharp criticism, especially from Tan Malaka and his followers, who called for an all-out armed struggle to gain "100% independence." Tan Malaka demanded the confiscation of all foreign factories and agricultural estates in order to inspire the masses to "fight as lions."[3] The Dutch would not leave until forced to do so,

1. Hatta, "Indonesian Aims and Ideals," in *Portrait of a Patriot,* p. 503.

2. Feith and Castles, eds., *Indonesian Political Thinking,* pp. 443–44. For a fuller exposition of Sjahrir's views, see *Our Struggle.*

3. See Kahin, *Nationalism and Revolution in Indonesia,* pp. 173–74. See also Tan Malaka, "Fighting Diplomacy," in Feith and Castles, eds., *Indonesian Political Thinking,* pp. 444–48. An excellent discussion of the struggle-

and those who believed that foreign powers would pressure the Dutch into giving up Indonesia were deluding themselves, he warned. He exhorted his countrymen to rely on their own efforts and to reject negotiations as long as Dutch troops remained on Indonesian soil. Thus, although the choice was certainly never a matter of "either-or," a central issue for the revolutionary leaders was the extent to which Indonesia should rely on hoped-for foreign support in order to achieve recognition of its independence.

In any case, when Sjahrir finally succeeded in negotiating an agreement with the Dutch in March 1947, nearly universal opposition to the concessions he had made in the agreement and in subsequent talks on its interpretation led to his resignation as prime minister. In July the Dutch launched a major attack against the Republic. The Indonesian government appealed to the United Nations, but the Security Council, following Washington's lead, refused to back Indonesia's call for arbitration and a Dutch withdrawal from territory taken in the attack.[4] Though Indonesians of all political persuasions were bitter, Prime Minister Amir Sjarifuddin yielded to "perceptible American pressure" and in January 1948 accepted Indonesia's second negotiated agreement.[5] In exchange for substantial territorial concessions, the Indonesians were promised a plebiscite in the areas overrun by the Dutch, with the understanding that the United States would ensure its fairness. But like Sjahrir before him, Sjarifuddin encountered an avalanche of critics, who charged him with having compromised the country's independence, and he was soon replaced as prime minister by Hatta. The Hatta government immediately began carrying out the Republic's part of the new agreement, but when an impasse developed with respect to the plebiscite, Washington failed to provide the promised backing in the UN. In December the Dutch unleashed a second offensive.

---

diplomacy conflict is contained in Benedict R. O'G. Anderson, *Java in a Time of Revolution: Occupation and Resistance, 1944–1946* (Ithaca: Cornell University Press, 1972).

4. Kahin, *Nationalism and Revolution in Indonesia,* p. 220.

5. See the comments of a member of the Indonesian delegation, Dr. Johannes Leimena, quoted in Alastair M. Taylor, *Indonesian Independence and the United Nations* (London: Stevens and Sons, 1960), p. 311.

In late 1949 the Dutch finally agreed to the transfer of sovereignty for several reasons: the Republic's resistance to their military initiative had proved strong enough to convince them that they could occupy Indonesia only at great cost; they had failed to find any credible political allies among the Indonesians; and Washington at last had begun to exert pressure on them to compromise.[6] But American pressure also led the Indonesians to accept some extremely onerous provisions in the agreement, the most significant of which were: the Indonesian government's assumption of the debt of the previous Dutch administration, which meant that it would be paying for the operations that had been carried out against the Republic; the retention by the Dutch of West New Guinea (West Irian) pending the outcome of further negotiations to be concluded within one year; and safeguards for Dutch economic interests in Indonesia.[7]

There were two political lessons relevant to the dependence dilemma to be drawn from the experience of the revolutionary period. First, the Indonesian leaders' disillusioning experience with the United States, and to a lesser extent with the Soviet Union, made them aware of the constraints on decision-making imposed by the expectations, demands, and, ultimately, unreliability of foreign powers.[8] Second, the fate of both Sjahrir and Amir Sjarifuddin made it clear that a policy of negotiating concessions which appeared to compromise the nation's independence carried dangerously high political risks.

6. Washington, hitherto concerned that any anti-Dutch action on its part might affect European security, realized that a prolonged Dutch campaign in Indonesia would be equally disastrous. Also, a Senate effort to cut off Marshall Plan aid to the Netherlands was gaining support. And the State Department feared that the Sukarno-Hatta leadership, having proved itself anti-Communist by its suppression of the 1948 PKI rebellion, might be totally discredited because of the failure of its cooperationist policy, with the result that leadership of the revolution would fall into the hands of pro-Communist elements (Kahin, *Nationalism and Revolution in Indonesia,* p. 417).

7. Leslie H. Palmier, *Indonesia and the Dutch* (London: Oxford University Press, 1962), p. 68. The United States promised economic aid to the Indonesians if they were successful in reaching agreement with the Dutch.

8. The Communist rebellion of 1948 was taken as evidence that the USSR was untrustworthy, despite continuous Soviet backing of the Republic in the UN.

During the early and middle 1950s, the political dangers of trading a portion of Indonesia's independence for anticipated foreign aid found reaffirmation on several occasions. The most striking example was the downfall of the Sukiman cabinet in 1952, already noted, as a consequence of the commitment Foreign Minister Subardjo had made in order to win American aid. In fact, all the first four cabinets during this period of parliamentary democracy were weakened politically by their willingness to tolerate political and economic vestiges of colonial rule. While it would be misleading to suggest that only their desire for Western economic aid kept them from pursuing a foreign policy aimed at removing the limitations on Indonesia's independence, all of them were eager to project an image of reasonableness that would inspire Western confidence in Indonesia and win support for economic reconstruction and development. The independence issue took various forms—including the questions of rights guaranteed to foreign capital, the continued presence of Dutch troops in Indonesia, and the retention of Dutch nationals in government positions—but the most clear-cut choice concerned West Irian.[9]

When the year's deadline set by the transfer of sovereignty agreement for resolution of West Irian's status had passed with the disputed territory still in Dutch hands and no prospect of a settlement, President Sukarno urged abrogation of the agreement and exertion of pressures on Dutch businesses in Indonesia. But Prime Minister Mohammad Natsir sought to avoid arousing domestic emotions, holding to the view that the best way to facilitate negotiations was to demonstrate that Indonesia would honor its commitments and safeguard the rights of foreigners. To the extent that he was genuinely concerned about the fate of West Irian, he hoped that either Dutch

9. Under the terms of the transfer of sovereignty agreement, the Netherlands was to "attempt" to withdraw its 80,000 Royal Army troops from Indonesia within six months. The last troops did not leave Indonesia until June 1951, however. The agreement also provided for a Netherlands Military Mission of 600 men to be stationed in Indonesia to help train the Indonesian army (Feith, *Decline of Constitutional Democracy*, pp. 15, 89).

reasonableness or American pressure on the Dutch would somehow enable Indonesia to realize its claim. The conflict with Sukarno on this (and other) issues contributed to the downfall of the Natsir cabinet several months later, as Sukarno, fearful of becoming a figurehead president, effectively used the West Irian issue to strengthen his own political position.

Another noteworthy illustration of the political risks inherent in policies that paid insufficient attention to independence was the case of the Burhanuddin Harahap cabinet, which held power in 1955–1956 during the interval between the two cabinets of Ali Sastroamidjojo. Where the first Ali cabinet had laid more stress on independence-oriented policies than had its predecessors, the Burhanuddin cabinet represented a return to the approach of the early 1950s, emphasizing economic stabilization, the search for foreign capital, and the restoration of close cooperation with the West. Partly in the hope that the Dutch would see the wisdom of making concessions that would strengthen the political position of their "friends" in Indonesia, the Burhanuddin cabinet launched an "offensive of reasonableness." It refrained from raising the Irian issue at the 1955 session of the UN and moved to revive direct negotiations with the Dutch.

But this return to the path of negotiations and reasonableness evoked great hostility in Indonesia, and the government was accused of "begging" from the West. Nor did the Dutch respond as their Indonesian "friends" had hoped they would. With the cabinet caught between domestic political opposition and the Dutch unwillingness to make concessions, the talks broke down. Then, in a sudden reversal, the Burhanuddin cabinet broke the impasse by announcing the unilateral abrogation of the Netherlands-Indonesian Union, which when subsequently enacted by parliament was declared to include all of the other onerous obligations undertaken in the transfer of sovereignty agreement.[10] The abrogation, taken in

10. The formal parliamentary action did not take place until after the second Ali cabinet had assumed office. For details, see Palmier, *Indonesia and the Dutch,* pp. 95–96.

the name of independence and self-reliance, was so enormously popular that it enabled the Burhanuddin cabinet to avert the imminent danger of falling before the date already set for its replacement by a cabinet based on the recently held national elections.

By the latter 1950s, then, there was not only an awareness that reasonableness in the pursuit of independence was likely to prove futile. There was also a growing abundance of evidence concerning the serious political hazards attached to policies which could be interpreted as compromising the nation's independence, and concerning the political capital to be gained from taking a militant stand on issues related to independence, even at the risk of offending potential aid-givers.

Sukarno's Guided Democracy

The Elite's View of the World

A central characteristic of the political environment during the middle 1950s was the political elite's deepening disillusion with the fruits of Indonesia's successful struggle for freedom from Dutch colonial rule. After a brief boom stemming from the favorable impact of the Korean War on Indonesia's exports, economic conditions deteriorated and it became evident that prosperity and rapid economic development were not imminent. At the same time, the succession of short-lived cabinets in the early 1950s suggested that Indonesia was on a political treadmill. After Indonesia's first nationwide elections in 1955, the sense of malaise spread as it became clear that the elections, which some had viewed as a panacea, really had changed very little.

From the standpoint of foreign policy, the most important consideration was the fact that the economic and political ambience in which this frustration arose was Western-dominated. In its trade and aid relations with the outside world, Indonesia looked almost entirely to the West; at home, Western capital still played a very important role in the country's economic life. The Dutch still occupied West Irian, a constant reminder that even the struggle for formal sovereignty remained incomplete. And the political framework was that of parliamentary democracy—that is, an ideology imported from the West. If the fruits of independence were unsatisfying, it was easy to draw the conclusion that this was because Indonesia still depended too much on the West. It was not merely a matter of finding it convenient to blame the West for Indonesia's troubles, though that motivation was undoubtedly present. Because the system which had proved so unsatisfying was in fact a product of Western economic domination and ideological influence, a protest against that system was, by logical extension, a protest against the West. And the easiest way to demonstrate independence from the West was by cultivating friendly relations with its adversaries.

If the growing dissatisfaction with economic and political conditions had inherently anti-Western implications, it also fostered changes in the balance of political power which reinforced this tendency. By 1957 Sukarno was articulating and to some extent manipulating the growing conviction that the political parties and the parliamentary democracy system as a whole had failed. He urged that the old system be replaced by one with a stronger executive—by Guided Democracy. Ready to join with Sukarno in blaming the parties and the parliamentary system for Indonesia's troubles was the leadership of the Indonesian army, which had hitherto intervened only sporadically in political affairs.

In 1957 a major crisis—the rapid deterioration of relations between Jakarta and the outer islands—opened the way for Sukarno and the army leadership to enlarge dramatically their role in national politics. The declaration of martial law in March 1957 provided a rationale for Sukarno's personal intervention to form an emergency, extraparliamentary business cabinet as the second Ali cabinet's successor, thus reducing the cabinet's independent decision-making role. At the same time, martial law provided a justification for army involvement in a broad range of political matters. Also in the ascendancy, but still in a precarious position, was the PKI. From a party whose leaders were in danger of arbitrary arrest as late as 1951, the PKI had grown to become the fourth strongest party in the 1955 elections; the PKI emerged as the strongest party in elections held in 1957 on Indonesia's most populous island, Java.

Having prospered under parliamentary democracy, however, the PKI faced an uncertain future under Guided Democracy. Finally, when anti-Communist rebellions broke out on the islands of Sumatra and Sulawesi in early 1958, the inclusion among the rebel leaders of some of the principal leaders of the early parliamentary democracy cabinets resulted in the effective elimination of their parties from the political arena.[11]

The rise of Guided Democracy brought to center stage a leader who, as we have already seen, had been from the early 1950s one of the foremost advocates of putting independence first. Sukarno's anti-imperialist ideology clearly predisposed him toward policies emphasizing independence. His inclination to move Indonesia away from the West was probably further strengthened by his 1956 trip to China and the Soviet Union, where he reportedly was impressed by what he saw, and to the United States, where he was treated coolly by President Eisenhower. Moreover, Sukarno's personality, political style, and perhaps psychological needs all pointed toward a foreign policy marked by militance in the pursuit of national independence. Possessed of great oratorical skills and charisma, he was convinced that strong leadership meant flamboyance, boldness, and unpredictability. Besides, he was utterly fascinated by the idea of revolution and bored by economics. Possibly he felt as well some inner need to endlessly recast and refight the anti-colonial battle which had given his life meaning; maybe there was an underlying insecurity, bred by the experience of living under colonial rule, which pushed him to demonstrate again and again that Sukarno's Indonesia was not to be trifled with. Whatever his underlying psychological needs, Sukarno's personality would have made it difficult for him to tailor his policies, and his style of leadership, to the prescriptions of Western aid-givers.

While Sukarno's main concern was with the dangers of Indonesia's being dominated by the Western powers, the Communist

11. For comprehensive accounts of these developments, see Feith, *Decline of Constitutional Democracy,* and Daniel S. Lev, *The Transition to Guided Democracy: Indonesian Politics, 1957–1959* (Ithaca: Cornell Modern Indonesia Project, 1966).

nations were by no means free from suspicion. The Moscow-Washington detente that developed in the early 1960s cast doubt on the Soviet Union's anti-imperialism, and the Soviet leaders' prescriptions for Indonesia sometimes sounded uncomfortably similar to those of the Western powers. Sukarno chafed at Soviet advice, however gentle, to ease the confrontation with Malaysia and pay more attention to economic needs.[12] As Indonesia drew closer to China in 1964 and 1965, the Soviets grew cooler. In late 1964 the foreign minister, who usually reflected Sukarno's views, was said to have argued that the Soviet Union could "no longer be relied on as an 'umbrella' in the struggle against Nekolim (neo-colonialism, colonialism, imperialism)."[13]

Even China, which by 1965 had become Jakarta's principal foreign diplomatic backer, was viewed with some hesitation. For example, when General Yani, the army commander, declared in 1965 that the main threat to Indonesia was from the north, mean-

12. According to a very reliable source, when General Nasution went to Moscow in November 1963 to ask for new military equipment Khrushchev told him: "I consider myself to be Sukarno's chargé d'affaires, and I will do whatever he asks. . . . But you might just give a little thought to the idea that it would be better to pay a little more attention to Indonesia's economic needs, and not place so much emphasis on a confrontation that will have a damaging effect on the economy." On other occasions, the Russians were apparently less gentle. Russian military officers were said to have ridiculed Sukarno's "war of speeches." High foreign ministry sources reported that on a number of occasions, including Deputy Prime Minister Mikoyan's June 1964 visit to Jakarta, Soviet diplomats made clear their skepticism about confrontation and their reluctance to give aid that would be used for confrontation. And Peter Polomka, citing his June 1969 interview with General Nasution, reported that Sukarno, on a visit to Moscow in September-October 1964, was harangued at length by Khrushchev, who complained about a number of recent Indonesian actions and statements ("The Indonesian Army and Confrontation: An Inquiry into the Functions of Foreign Policy under Guided Democracy" [M.A. thesis, University of Melbourne, 1969], p. 121).

13. *Ibid.*, pp. 115–16. Subandrio reportedly put this view forward during the October 1964 Conference of Nonaligned Nations in Cairo and again during talks in Peking in January 1965. Polomka's source was *G-30-S Dihadapan Mahmillub 3—Perkara Dr. Subandrio* (Jakarta: P.T. Pembimbing Masa, 1967), vol. 1, pp. 195–203.

ing China, Sukarno countered that the threat came from all sides. He seems to have made no effort, at least in private, to deny that China was a threat.[14] A variety of foreign policy elite members, some of whom had known Sukarno well, told the author in 1969 and 1970 of their conviction that Sukarno had merely been "using" the Chinese, whom he never really trusted. Though China's revolutionary élan obviously appealed to Sukarno, there were by 1965 reasons to believe that the Chinese would prove no more reliable as supporters than others had. The Chinese leaders made it known to Jakarta that they could not continue to back Indonesia's demand that Malaysia be excluded from the proposed second Asian-African conference. Despite its consistent public support for the NEFOS, Peking was also said to have informed Foreign Minister Subandrio privately in January 1965 of its reservations concerning Sukarno's bipolar division of the world; the Chinese asserted that they retained instead a Marxist-Leninist view of world politics.[15] Nor did they respond with much enthusiasm to Sukarno's talk of a Jakarta-Peking axis. According to two of his closest associates, Subandrio had stated with reference to China: "Any big power is a potential imperialist nation." That was claimed to represent Sukarno's view as well.[16]

Of course, these reported suspicions about Moscow and Peking hardly constitute solid evidence. Such concerns were almost never expressed in public. They probably were not very deeply felt, for Indonesia never became dependent on aid from the Communist powers, and such dependence never seemed imminent. Still, for Sukarno there was no big power that could safely be trusted to aid

14. The Yani-Sukarno exchange was described by army officers interviewed by the author in Bandung in October 1969, as well as by an Army source in Jakarta. Polomka reports, however, that Sukarno did say at the April 1965 army seminar that the West had an enemy in the north, but that Indonesia did not. Indonesia's enemy was "not in the north . . . but . . . from Nekolim" (*ibid.*, p. 215).

15. The source is a senior member of the Indonesian delegation that accompanied Subandrio to Peking in January 1965, cited by Polomka, "Indonesian Army and Confrontation," p. 248.

16. On this apprehension about China, see also Kahin, "Indonesia and Malaysia," p. 264.

Indonesia and respect the country's independence. Thus, Sukarno's view of the world, as well as his personality, strongly predisposed him to emphasize the need to safeguard Indonesia's independence.

It would be a mistake, however, if the foreign policy of the Guided Democracy years were to be seen simply as an expression of Sukarno's personal predispositions. Though we obviously cannot obtain data for an earlier period comparable to that which was acquired by interviewing the foreign policy elite in 1969–1970, there are strong reasons to believe that Sukarno's view of the world as a hostile place coincided with the perceptions of most foreign policy elite members of the Guided Democracy years. In the first place, if the interviewees, many of whom had been members of the Guided Democracy foreign policy elite as well, expressed substantial distrust of the West, it is hard to imagine that such views would have been any less widespread at a time when public criticism of imperialism was so sharp. The foreign policy elite's favorable assessment of Sukarno's foreign policy, noted in Chapter 2, suggests the same conclusion.

The army leadership and the PKI clearly shared Sukarno's essential perception of the Western powers as avaricious neocolonialists. No one is likely to question the PKI's desire to sever Indonesia's dependence on the West. In the case of the army leaders, a distinction needs to be drawn between their natural affinity for the West as a logical backer in the domestic struggle for power with the PKI (about which more will be said later) and their increasingly suspicious view of the Western powers' intentions vis-à-vis Indonesia. Much as they preferred to deal with the anti-Communist West for both ideological and technological reasons, the army leaders were increasingly drawn in the late 1950s to the conclusion that the West did not want Indonesia to become strong. American and British involvement in the 1958 rebellions, along with Washington's unwillingness to provide military assistance for the West Irian campaign, significantly strengthened this apprehension.[17] Not only did the pub-

17. See Polomka, "Indonesian Army and Confrontation," pp. 34–36. Polomka concludes from his interviews with a "cross-section of army leaders involved in the events of the period" that these were "the general views of

lic statements of top army leaders gradually come to employ the anti-imperialist rhetoric of Sukarno; it was in fact General Yani who coined the acronym "Nekolim," which became Sukarno's favorite pejorative appellation for the Western powers.[18] Moreover, the views and recollections described by army leaders interviewed in 1969 and 1970 suggest that army suspicions of the West were indeed deep-rooted.

The army leadership and the PKI also seem to have shared, albeit in vastly differing degrees, Sukarno's doubts about the reliability of the Communist powers. Though Indonesian generals like Nasution came to have relatively cordial relations with Moscow, their anti-Communism made them inherently suspicious of the Soviet Union's intentions. Their anti-Chinese sentiments were well-known and found clear expression not only in army support of moves against the Indonesian Chinese in 1959 and 1963 but also in the army commander's 1965 assertion that the danger to Indonesia came from the north.

The PKI, as it moved closer to Peking's position on issues related to the Sino-Soviet dispute, found its relations with Moscow strained. Initially annoyed at Khrushchev's failure to consult with other Communist parties prior to his 1956 attack on Stalin, the PKI leaders grew genuinely suspicious of Moscow's commitment to the anti-imperialist struggle. At a time when it was politically essential for the PKI to have Sukarno pursue a policy of militant agitational nationalism, Moscow was urging moderation and peaceful coexistence. Moreover, by 1963 the Soviets had made it clear that they had no intention of competing with the United States in providing large-scale economic aid to Indonesia. This too upset the PKI leaders, for the availability of Soviet aid significantly strengthened the party domestically. Thus by 1964, the PKI leaders had ceased to advocate

---

those with authority." Other officers, he adds, may have been even more inclined to share Sukarno's skepticism. This conclusion is also supported by the author's interviews with army members of the foreign policy elite, as reported in Chapter 3 above.

18. General Nasution recalled this with evident pride in a 1970 written interview with the author.

Soviet aid as an alternative to American, as deepening suspicions of the Soviets led to the extension of PKI strictures against foreign capital to include the Communist powers as well. The rudeness encountered by PKI chairman Aidit on a 1963 visit to Moscow and the Soviet flirtation in 1964 with some of the PKI's bitterest rivals added to the party leaders' disillusion with the Soviet Union.[19]

The PKI had far fewer problems with China, whose anti-imperialist propaganda and willingness to allow allied parties to deviate from its theses on armed struggle and Communist hegemony met the Indonesian Communists' needs.[20] Nevertheless, though there certainly is no clear evidence, there may even have been some tensions developing in the relationship between the PKI and China, as suggested by the fact that Peking sent a surprisingly low level delegation to the PKI's 45th anniversary celebration in 1965.[21] In any case, China did not have the capacity to give aid on a scale comparable to the United States or the Soviet Union. In addition, the widespread resentment of the overseas Chinese in Indonesia made it likely that too close a relationship with Peking would significantly heighten domestic tensions and could well provoke violent manifestations of anti-Chinese sentiment.

Of course, Indonesia never became significantly dependent on the Communist powers, so concern about their domination could hardly become a pressing issue, even for the anti-Communists. From the fragmentary evidence available, however, it is reasonable to surmise that latent doubts about Moscow and Peking would have become considerably sharper had such a relationship developed.

19. Moscow's 1960 excommunication of Albania, with its negative implications for the independence and identity of national Communist parties, and the Soviet handling of the 1962 Cuban missile crisis, in which a settlement negotiated by the two superpowers was imposed on Cuba, particularly worried the PKI leaders (Rex Alfred Mortimer, "The Ideology of the P.K.I. under Guided Democracy" [Ph.D. diss., Monash University, 1970], ch. 8, pp. 9, 17, 22, 26). See also ch. 5, p. 47, ch. 6, pp. 51–52, ch. 8, pp. 25–28, 31, 41–42. Ruth McVey has characterized Moscow's contacts with the Murba party as part of a broader Soviet policy of relying on the army, not the PKI, to advance its interests in Indonesia (cited in *ibid.*, ch. 8, p. 42).

20. *Ibid.*, ch. 8, p. 29.

21. I am indebted to Ruth McVey for this observation.

Thus, although there were unquestionably substantial differences in the intensity with which Sukarno, the army leadership, and the PKI harbored suspicions of the major powers, it may be said that all three of the political forces in the ascendancy as Guided Democracy took root were seriously distrustful of the West. And we also have some basis for assuming that doubts about the Communist powers would grow in intensity if Indonesia were to become dependent on them.

The predominance of a view of the world as a hostile place created an environment which encouraged Sukarno to indulge his personal predilection to take an increasingly sharp anti-imperialist line. Because Sukarno's perceptions and personal inclinations in general coincided with those of the foreign policy elite of the Guided Democracy years, he was relatively free to "be himself." Of course, the relationship between Sukarno's thinking and the foreign policy elite's view of the world was reciprocal: his personal impact on the foreign policy elite's views was substantial, and it is fair to say that Sukarno, given a basically sympathetic elite, was generally able to mold the elite's perceptions so as to make them conform even more closely to his own views.

The Structure of Political Competition

If the mutually reinforcing relationship between Sukarno's personal predispositions and the elite's view of the world helped to produce a foreign policy that emphasized independence, the same might be said of the interaction between elite perceptions and the pressures generated by the competition for political power. The pattern of political competition, as it evolved during the Guided Democracy period, was a complex one, with Sukarno, the army leadership, and for most of the period a much weaker PKI maneuvering for political advantage. Of course, many others—including individual party and nonparty politicians, bureaucrats, technocrats, and naval and air force officers—continued to exert some influence on policy decisions and to affect marginally the balance among the three principals. But the essential shape of political competition during the Guided Democracy years was triangular, and it was the increasingly tense struggle between the army leadership and the PKI, with Sukarno attempting both to sustain and to limit that rivalry in order to enhance his own position, that came to dominate the politics of the period.

Sukarno, who had no organizational base of his own, needed a political force with which to balance the army's power if he was to avoid becoming dependent on the army leadership. The PKI had appeal for Sukarno not only as a "progressive revolutionary" party with which he could to some extent identify ideologically, but as a group with a truly effective organization and capacity to mobilize people down to the village level. Thus Sukarno fostered the development of the PKI as a counterweight to the rising power of the anti-Communist army. He made himself the indispensable unifying element in the political system and distributed political rewards in such a way as to prevent either of the two bitter rivals from rising too high or falling too low.

The PKI, for its part, needed Sukarno's protection from army leaders who clearly would have preferred the destruction of the party. The "pivot" of the PKI leadership's strategy was avoiding political isolation, which could leave the party defenseless against its enemies.[22] As the PKI's position grew stronger after 1963, its leaders presumably hoped that their increasingly close identification with Sukarno would provide a shield that would ultimately make it possible to purge the army of its anti-Communist leadership and remake it as a progressive revolutionary force.[23] The army leaders, on the other hand, looked to Sukarno not for protection but for the legitimacy which he could bestow upon the army's growing role in political and economic affairs. During the Guided Democracy years, the army leadership sought not to topple Sukarno but to persuade him to limit the power of the PKI.

By the latter part of the Guided Democracy period, it was evident that the army leadership and the PKI were locked in a struggle to the death. Indonesian politics grew highly polarized, as the less influ-

22. Mortimer, "Ideology of the PKI," ch. 5, p. 30.

23. On Aidit's hopes that the army could be neutralized, see *ibid.*, ch. 9, pp. 10–11.

ential political groups, or factions within them, chose sides with either the PKI or the army leaders. The Islamic and Catholic party leaders, along with the young Western-trained technocrats and leaders associated with the banned socialist party, tended to align with the anti-Communist army generals; the PNI, navy, and air force leaderships were dominated by anti-Communists, but toward the end of the period important elements in those groups drew closer to the PKI. After 1963 Sukarno seemed increasingly to favor the PKI, though it was by no means clear that he was prepared to foster a conclusive PKI triumph over the anti-Communist generals.[24] For, as already noted, Sukarno's own independent position as the paramount leader depended to a substantial degree on the perpetuation of competition between these forces. His increasingly strident anti-imperialism notwithstanding, it is likely that Sukarno's overriding commitment was to the national revolution, not to a social revolution that promised to rupture the unity of the nation.[25]

The intense competition of those years was to some extent masked by the authoritarian character of the Guided Democracy system, in particular the glorification of Sukarno's leadership and the absence of any formal opposition. Actually, the exaltation of Sukarno was itself a reflection of the increasing intensity of competition, for obeisance to the president was a legitimizing umbrella under which attacks against one's adversaries could be pressed with some degree

24. On Sukarno's move to the left, see Herbert Feith, "President Soekarno, the Army, and the Communists: The Triangle Changes Shape," *Asian Survey,* 4 (August 1964), 969–80. For an attempt to show that Sukarno had in fact chosen the PKI, see Peter Christian Hauswedell, "Sukarno: Radical or Conservative? Indonesian Politics 1964–5," *Indonesia,* no. 15 (April 1973), pp. 109–43. This argument, however, fails to distinguish between the proposition that Sukarno wished to be succeeded by leaders he regarded as progressive, for which there is strong evidence, and the much slimmer possibility that he was prepared to see a PKI accession during his lifetime, with the resultant diminution of his power.

25. On the underlying conservatism of Sukarno's approach, see Legge, *Sukarno,* p. 383. Of course, it is true that Sukarno's anti-imperialist foreign policy and his radical rhetoric posed a potential threat to the essentially conservative elite of politicians and bureaucrats on whom he depended at least partially for support. On this contradictory aspect of Sukarno's character, see Mortimer, "Ideology of the PKI," ch. 6, pp. 59–60.

of safety.[26] Sukarno, for his part, sought to solidify his own role and to prevent an open clash between the army leaders and the PKI by coopting the competitors into the government. Thus, in the day-to-day handling of foreign policy and the formulation of the accompanying ideology, Sukarno was given considerable latitude, but in setting the general direction of policy and in taking the key decisions he had always to consider the effect of foreign policy on the political balance among the three forces. As a result, though Sukarno clearly dominated the making of Guided Democracy foreign policy, his real freedom was much less than it seemed.

Naturally, all of the major political actors hoped to use foreign policy to maximize their political assets and minimize their weaknesses. Sukarno clearly stood to derive certain political benefits from a policy of putting independence first. Such a policy would create a demand for the particular kind of leadership he was eminently qualified to give. His impressive oratorical and solidarity-making skills were as well-suited to a crusading confrontation with foreign enemies as they were irrelevant to a policy of "pragmatically" accepting a high degree of dependence on foreign aid and adopting the economic and political policies desired by the Western aid-givers. Second, given the intensifying struggle between the PKI and the army leadership, a policy stressing defense of the nation's independence in the face of serious external threats would lend urgency to Sukarno's call for national unity under his leadership. Similarly, directing the nation's attention to the struggle with imperialism would also convey the impression that revolutionary momentum was being sustained, while avoiding truly revolutionary social change. Perpetual crisis and revolutionary struggle with imperialism might be politically beneficial to Sukarno, but a real domestic revolution would have destroyed the balance that made Sukarno politically indispensable and therefore relatively independent.

On the other hand, given the fact that the Guided Democracy period was a time of real economic stagnation and decline, foreign

26. For example, a major movement to rally anti-Communist forces named itself the Body for the Promotion of Sukarnoism.

aid could provide a continuing flow of resources to be distributed by the president in a politically advantageous way. He could buy off opponents and reward friends, using the contracts, licenses, and commodities at his disposal to reduce the level of frustration for at least a part of the political elite. Of course, to the extent that a stress on independence led to the take-over of foreign property, there would also be some spoils to be handed out by Sukarno, but this source of resources was obviously limited. Finally, foreign aid promised to yield visible results, in the form of hotels, roads, or other facilities, to which the president could point, persuasively or not, as evidence of progress in the economic development of the country.

The army leaders, however worried they may have been about excessive dependence on Western aid, had always to balance that concern against some basic political realities. American military aid, in the form of both equipment and training, was not only essential to the army's development as a modern fighting force; it also could contribute to the achievement of army unity, insofar as it provided resources to be distributed by the central army leadership in a way calculated to reward cooperative officers and punish the more independent-minded ones. Still more important, perhaps, military and economic aid from the Western powers, and the associated rise in their influence on decision-making in Jakarta, tended inevitably to strengthen the position of the army leaders vis-à-vis the PKI.

There was, then, an apparent conflict between the army leaders' perceptions and their political needs; the identity of the aid-givers was as important as the amount of aid or the degree of dependence on it. Whatever doubts they may have had about the West and however much they liked to view themselves as guardians of national independence, the army leaders could never escape the fact that the Western powers were their natural allies in the intensifying struggle with the PKI. So long as Indonesia maintained close ties with the West, Sukarno would be unlikely to allow the PKI too great a role, since such an action would certainly jeopardize Western aid.

But if the army leaders had some important political reasons for seeking to assure the flow of Western aid, they also had some political motivations for putting independence first. First, fostering their image as defenders of the national independence, and before that freedom fighters against the Dutch, was politically important as a means of justifying a growing army role in political and economic affairs. The army's actual dependence on military aid from abroad probably only heightened the leadership's feeling that they had constantly to redemonstrate the validity of their nationalist credentials.

Second, a military or quasi-military campaign staged in the name of independence would provide a clear justification for larger military budgets and expanded military influence in decision-making. Such an effort could also be manipulated as a spur to army unity. And as in the case of Sukarno, it would give a sense of revolutionary progress without the concomitant danger of a real social and economic revolution. Of course, there was always the risk that such a campaign might lead to Indonesia's isolation from the aid-givers, a danger which could be minimized to the extent that it proved possible to stage a confrontation with the Dutch or the British while continuing to receive aid from the United States. Another hazard was the possibility that the threat to national independence might be seized by the PKI as a pretext for the creation of a people's militia—in effect, the arming of the PKI.

The PKI's political interests clearly dictated a foreign policy aimed at furthering to the maximum extent possible Indonesia's independence from the Western powers. Militant anti-imperialism certainly accorded with the PKI's perceptions of what the international situation required, but it was perhaps more important that such a policy, sure to upset Washington, would probably keep Indonesia from obtaining substantial Western aid. If the possibility of securing aid were already foreclosed, Sukarno would be free from any temptation to curb the PKI's governmental role in order to satisfy Western aid-givers.

The Communists undoubtedly saw an independence-oriented foreign policy not only as a way of isolating the army leaders from their foreign sources of support but as the basis for a propaganda line that would enable the PKI to embarrass and discredit the generals, many of whom were American-trained, by portraying them as tools of the imperialists. At the same time, a foreign policy that directed attention toward nationalistic campaigns in the pursuit of independence would provide the PKI a means of demonstrating its patriotism and rebutting the allegation that the party's Communist internationalism superseded its loyalty to the Indonesian nation. By stressing the anti-Western content of the drive for complete independence, Indonesian foreign policy had the effect of helping to redefine patriotism in a way advantageous to the PKI.

The foreign policy of putting independence first was a fundamental aspect of the PKI's political strategy. The party leaders' advocacy of the "semicolonial thesis," which argued that Indonesia's dependence on the West made it a semicolonial country, was "politically indispensable," for it laid the ideological foundation needed to effect tactical alliances, or at least working relationships, with other political groups.[27] Because it led inescapably to the conclusion that the foremost problem facing the Indonesian nation was the elimination of foreign (that is, Western) influence, the semicolonial thesis drew attention away from the inherent threat which the PKI's class-based ideology posed to members of the Indonesian elite and reformulated the basic issues of Indonesian politics so as to place the PKI in the majority, opposed to foreign domination. In order to overcome the foreign enemy, national unity was of the utmost importance; any threatening moves by the PKI's adversaries thus could be denounced as a breach of national solidarity and hence a danger to the entire Indonesian nation.

Up to 1963 the semicolonial thesis and the independence-oriented foreign policy that followed from it served the PKI primarily as a shield from possible attempts to isolate the party. Subsequently it was used by the PKI in an effort to isolate the anti-Communists by branding them lackeys of the imperialists. At the same time, it lent legitimacy to the mass mobilization of PKI supporters, a move which, though ostensibly directed at the foreign imperialist enemy,

27. Mortimer, "Ideology of the PKI," ch. 3, pp. 37–39, 43. See also ch. 8, p. 17.

had its greatest impact on Indonesian perceptions of the changing balance of domestic power. But even after the PKI took the political offensive in late 1963, the party leaders were by no means free from fear of suppressive action by the anti-Communists, and an independence-oriented foreign policy remained an important defensive weapon. In all likelihood, the PKI leaders realized that the deterioration of the rightist position could spur them to try to crush the Communists before the situation grew hopeless. Indeed, when the PKI in late 1963 began encouraging landless peasants to implement the land reform law unilaterally, the reaction from the anti-Communists was so strong that by September 1964 the PKI had to retreat on the issue.[28] In any case, the PKI leaders could ill afford to forget that the anti-Communists retained the overwhelming preponderance of military power.

For that reason, the PKI, like Sukarno and the army leaders, had some political interest in a foreign policy that gave Indonesians a sense of revolutionary progress without the social and political conflict that a thoroughgoing social revolution would entail. Though one cannot doubt the PKI's ultimate commitment to such a revolution, it was certainly not in the party leaders' interests to push too hard for such a revolution at a time when the party's own position, in terms of the physical resources of power, was still relatively weak. The PKI leaders seemed to be eager to avoid actions which would needlessly alarm members of the elite on whose tolerance the party temporarily depended. At the same time, of course, the party leaders were under pressure from within their own ranks to move more rapidly toward the achievement of their revolutionary goals. An anti-imperialist foreign policy helped to reconcile, though certainly not to everyone's satisfaction, the PKI's contradictory political requirements.

Finally, the PKI favored accelerated efforts to seek aid from the Communist powers not merely to balance the influence of the West but to provide additional incentives for Sukarno to continue protecting the PKI. Soviet military aid could be used to develop the

28. *Ibid.*, ch. 7, p. 60.

navy and air force as rivals to the largely American-supplied army. Ultimately, perhaps, the promise of Soviet aid might be used to weaken the army's ties to the United States.

Though Sukarno, the army leaders, and the PKI all had important political incentives to support a foreign policy that emphasized independence, the first two, as we have seen, had also to consider the possibility that excessive emphasis on independence might give rise to serious political dangers. The army leaders were worried that isolation from the West would jeopardize their sources of foreign support, embarrass them politically, and enable the PKI to enlarge its political role. Sukarno could not have been entirely unconcerned that a domestic spill-over of his anti-imperialist foreign policy might unleash irrepressible pressures for a social revolution that could result in civil war.

Moreover, it needs to be remembered that Sukarno never abandoned the search for foreign aid, even if he did put independence first. Like every other administration since the revolution, the Sukarno government realized that it simply did not command the resources to solve Indonesia's economic problems without aid. The insistence on self-reliance really meant a downgrading of economic development, and former high officials in the Sukarno government were virtually unanimous in asserting that no one in the government, not even Sukarno, ever really believed that Indonesia could develop without foreign aid. They undoubtedly were aware that a continuing failure to make significant progress in improving living conditions would eventually pose a political danger, though not necessarily an unmanageable one.

Perceptions and Politics

If the principal competitors for power had to consider their particular political requirements, all of them were subject to an overriding political imperative to avoid appearing weak in their support of goals related to national independence, and that imperative stemmed directly from the common perception of the major powers as untrustworthy. The perception of a hostile world was a key element in each political competitor's assessment of the political ramifications of a particular foreign policy course. Because even anti-Communists shared an essential suspicion of the Western powers' motivations toward Indonesia, the allegation that reliance on Western aid would mean a diminution of independence was inherently credible to most Indonesian leaders.

From the days of the revolution, as previously noted, policies viewed as compromising the nation's independence in exchange for foreign support or the promise of it had proved politically hazardous. With the shift in the late 1950s from a form of parliamentary competition, in which the stakes were fairly low and defeat did not rule out a subsequent return to power, toward a death-struggle competition between forces fundamentally opposed to one another's existence, risks that previously could be taken were now too dangerous to bear. To be sure, an increase in the intensity of political competition might logically encourage a foreign policy aimed at acquiring from abroad resources that could be distributed so as to ease tensions. But if that aid could be obtained only at the cost of dependence on powers whose motivations were widely suspect, the political risks of advocating such a course outweighed its possible advantages. It was the deepening suspicion of the aid-givers that made independence-oriented policies politically beneficial and dependence on aid politically dangerous. The more intense the struggle for political power, the more dangerous it became to favor a foreign policy emphasizing aid at the expense of independence.

The way in which the political incentives and risks created by the interaction between attitudes and politics influenced the resolution of the aid-independence dilemma is evident in the three major foreign policy moves of the Guided Democracy period: the campaign to establish Indonesian sovereignty over West Irian; the abortive 1963 effort to fulfill the conditions for receiving substantial Western economic aid; and the subsequent confrontation with Malaysia.

The Irian campaign won the strong backing of Sukarno, the PKI, and the army leadership. Each had strong incentives to support the effort, for such a campaign, in light of the prevailing suspicion of the West, could serve important political functions. For

Sukarno, the Irian struggle was an ideal issue to justify the sort of solidarity-making leadership at which he excelled. The sense of crisis served as a means of keeping the lid on domestic conflict, lending support to Sukarno's call for national unity under his leadership and making it more difficult for the PKI's enemies to find some pretext for eliminating the Communists. And the nationalization of Dutch property gave him substantial new resources which he could distribute to his political advantage.

The Irian issue was extremely important to the PKI, for it constituted one of the "linchpins" supporting the thesis that Indonesia was a semicolonial country. With growing frequency, the party leaders sought to draw attention to the broader implications of the Irian issue, as they emphasized Indonesia's continued economic dependence on the West. Though the Irian question directly involved only the Dutch, the PKI leaders portrayed the conflict as a classic illustration of the clash between the NEFOS and the OLDEFOS. They consistently worked to focus Indonesian resentment on the United States as the principal bastion of neocolonialism, an effort significantly abetted by the UN votes on the Irian question and by the West's unwillingness to provide military aid while the Soviets did so.[29]

As Soviet military aid grew in importance, so did the PKI's role as a "political broker" between the two governments. At the same time, the PKI found its identification with Indonesian nationalism, as expressed in the Irian campaign, helpful in rebutting the accusation that it was an agent for foreign interests. The Irian campaign provided a justification for dynamic action on the part of the PKI, and the army found it difficult to restrain the party on an issue of such great national concern. The Communists even went so far as to propose that mobilization for the Irian drive be extended to in-

29. PKI chairman Aidit even talked of an American desire to maintain military bases in West Irian. This discussion of the PKI and the Irian campaign draws heavily on Mortimer's thesis. See especially ch. 3, pp. 40–42, and ch. 4, pp. 8, 35–38, 41. See also George McT. Kahin, "Indonesia," in Kahin, ed., *Major Governments of Asia,* 2d ed. (Ithaca: Cornell University Press, 1963), p. 682.

clude arming of the masses, but the army was successful in ensuring that only "reliable" elements received weapons.

The Irian campaign, however, was not without risks for the PKI, or without benefit to the army leaders. As much as Sukarno emphasized Indonesia's unwillingness to stake its claim on hopes of a "gift from the imperialists," the more militant aspects of his multifaceted strategy of confrontation were always accompanied by a hope that by creating a threat of war, Indonesia could force the United States to exert leverage on the Dutch. As we saw in Chapter 6, Sukarno was still seeking Western economic aid; though the Irian campaign clearly had higher priority, his stand against the Dutch was paralleled by a suggestion to the Americans that their help in bringing about a favorable settlement of the Irian problem would clear the way for subsequent concentration on economic development, for which American aid would be sought. Clearly, an extended agitational campaign would better serve the PKI's political interests than a quick victory, which the party and army leaders alike must have realized could well lead to closer economic relations with the West.

The army leaders, slower than Sukarno and the PKI to embrace the Irian issue, came to appreciate the political necessity of doing so. There was also the danger that the top leadership's coolness toward the Irian campaign would shake the confidence of subordinate officers in their chiefs, thus endangering army cohesion.[30] Ultimately, the army leadership came to see the Irian campaign not only as politically necessary but as a basis for the expansion and modernization of the military establishment. It provided as well a pretext for the continuation of martial law and an opportunity for the military to participate heroically in a popular national enterprise. And the nationalization proved extremely profitable to the army, which took responsibility for managing former Dutch enterprises.

The generals were, of course, disappointed at the American position and frustrated by repeated failure in their efforts to gain Ameri-

30. Some loss of army cohesion is noted by Mortimer, "Ideology of the PKI," ch. 4, p. 39.

can military aid for the Irian buildup. They sought Soviet military assistance only after it had become manifest that Washington would not cooperate. But they may well have hoped that when even anti-Communist army leaders grew outspoken on the Irian issue and joined in the effort to secure arms from the Russians, the United States would see the necessity of changing its position. After a cordial meeting between Sukarno and President Kennedy in 1961, it appeared that with a new administration in Washington such a hope might not be futile.

In any case, the army leaders clearly felt that in their hesitation they had been outflanked by the PKI.[31] Seeking to repair the political damage, the generals moved in early 1962 to capture the initiative by pressing for a full-scale invasion. Even Sukarno and the PKI had never gone that far, preferring an agitational campaign with only a minor military component. As it happened, the United States did in 1962 exert pressure on the Dutch to make a settlement favorable to Jakarta. But because the Irian victory had been achieved through agitation and diplomacy, rather than by a demonstration of military superiority, the army leaders, already blemished by their tardiness in rallying to the Irian cause, derived less political benefit from the triumph than Sukarno and the PKI.[32]

With the Irian question resolved, Sukarno now appeared free to fulfill his pledge to improve living conditions. The United States and the IMF were obviously eager to extend loans in support of Indonesia's economic development. The search for Western economic aid, submerged for years because of the priority accorded the Irian struggle, now could be pursued with vigor. Sukarno's serious interest in the Western aid package, which had begun to be assembled almost immediately following the Irian settlement, seemed to be borne out by his willingness to allow promulgation of the May 1963 regulations implementing the economic stabilization plan drawn up in consultation with Western advisers. Shortly afterwards, Jakarta succeeded in working out an accommodation with the Western oil companies, a move which was taken to reflect Sukarno's

31. Polomka, "Indonesian Army and Confrontation," p. 57.
32. Mortimer, "Ideology of the PKI," ch. 4, pp. 29, 35.

awareness of both the importance of the foreign exchange earned by oil to the country's economic development and the dependence of the army on oil for its mobility.[33] But, as we shall see, many of the same factors that led the Indonesian leaders to give priority to the Irian struggle made it politically difficult to sustain an aid-oriented policy, once the way was clear for a move in that direction.

The stabilization plan's foreign sponsorship and the belief that the stringent anti-inflationary regulations had been forced on Indonesia by the IMF and the United States as preconditions for aid left its backers exceedingly vulnerable to criticism. The May 1963 regulations had no sooner been announced than they encountered a storm of criticism led by the PKI but joined in by leaders all along the political spectrum. According to one of the plan's principal architects, all of the political parties were opposed to the stabilization program and to the dependence on outsiders associated with it.[34] Nor did the army leaders offer any support.[35] By the end of the summer it was evident that the plan was doomed.[36]

33. See Bunnell, "Kennedy Initiatives in Indonesia," for a discussion of Western aid, especially pp. 351–73 on the oil negotiations.

34. The parties had, however, gone along with a watered-down and self-contradictory version of the stabilization plan contained in the Economic Declaration of 28 March 1963. That document was said to have been coordinated by Subandrio, with sections written by PNI leaders, by Soedjatmoko of the PSI, and by the PKI's Njono, whose contribution included a reaffirmation of the importance of self-reliance.

35. A leading backer of the plan said: "We did not see the army as either an ally or an enemy of the stabilization program. It was in the middle. I knew General Yani quite well and talked with him about the stabilization plan. All he would say was, 'It's up to the cabinet.' " An American army officer well acquainted with the army leadership agreed: "I don't think the army ever had any great commitment to the stabilization program. They were never optimistic about it." And a secret memorandum from General Nasution to Sukarno in early 1963 reflected very clearly the army leadership's reluctance to accept the stringent monetary measures demanded by the IMF (Djenderal A. H. Nasution, "Nota finek Djenderal A. H. Nasution pada tanggal 19 Djanuari 1963," in Nasution, *Menegakkan Keadilan dan Kebenaran* [Jakarta: Penerbit "Seruling Masa," 1967], vol. II, p. 139). Nasution stressed the production approach and the need to cut out "unnecessary" imports and trips abroad (*ibid.*, pp. 40–49 *passim*).

36. On 7 September 1963 Sukarno agreed that the May regulations needed

The stabilization plan and the accompanying Western aid package represented a serious threat to the PKI. The deepening dependence on the West signified by the stabilization plan clearly would have ruled out Communist participation in the cabinet, a fact made abundantly clear in early 1963 when Sukarno ordered the PKI to suspend its campaign for a coalition cabinet that would include the party. The danger of political isolation, which had deeply concerned the party leaders for many years, now seemed much more ominous. Besides, like all anti-inflationary measures, the new regulations required considerable belt-tightening. It was no surprise when the PKI bitterly denounced the new course as both subservient to foreign capital and disregardful of the people's welfare.[37]

Though the army leaders undoubtedly were aware that the stabilization program's implementation would have significantly enhanced their position in relation to the PKI by ensuring that Indonesia maintained close relations with the United States, the generals had compelling economic and political reasons for withholding support. They were unwilling to absorb the budget cut required under the plan, just as they could not have relished the prospect of speaking up in defense of a foreign-sponsored program. Army cohesion was not sufficiently strong to permit the generals to run the risk of being labeled deficient in nationalist spirit. Besides, because of the heavy involvement of army officers in the management of state economic enterprises, as well as the undeniable link between growing military expenditures and rising inflation, the army was in an awkward position concerning problems of the economy.[38]

For Sukarno, the stabilization program and the aid-oriented course it represented posed some serious political disadvantages. The

---

to be altered. They were formally superseded in April 1964 (Mortimer, "Ideology of the PKI," ch. 6, pp. 47–48).

37. Mortimer, "Ideology of the PKI," ch. 5, p. 10, Ch. 6, p. 47.

38. As a member of the DPA (Supreme Advisory Council) recalled, DPA discussions of the deteriorating economic situation were dominated by attacks, coming from the PKI and its allies, on the army for its alleged corruption and mismanagement of state enterprises (interview with E. Utrecht, Jakarta, 20 May 1969).

new course would have skewed the political balance drastically in favor of the army, thus reducing the dependence of all groups on Sukarno's decisions. It would have provided far fewer opportunities for Sukarno to make use of his flamboyant exhortative skills. On the contrary, he probably would have been obliged to accord greatly expanded roles to men with more relevant, if prosaic, skills, and many of those leaders had become Sukarno's political adversaries. Moreover, not only would Sukarno have found the compromise of Indonesia's sovereignty ideologically repugnant and psychologically painful, but he would have suffered politically, since much of his political standing was based on his aggressive nationalism. His record as leader of the Indonesian revolution and foremost defender of the country's independence was an essential source of the legitimacy which automatically attached to his decisions.

If the political costs were so high, why did Sukarno permit the aid-stabilization course to be tried at all? There are at least three possible explanations. It may be that Sukarno, uncertain as to what the political costs of an aid-oriented policy would be, was prepared to drift for a time as he assessed the developing pressures and counterpressures. Some of those who knew Sukarno well emphasized that he was always an improviser who preferred to keep open several alternatives. With the Irian triumph behind him and Western aid-givers beckoning, he must have felt that he had little to lose by experimenting with the aid-stabilization approach, as long as he kept a line of retreat open.

Underlying the "uncertainty and drift" explanation were two basic facts: Sukarno, who shared the widespread belief that economic betterment was virtually impossible without aid from the Western powers, probably felt some political pressure to seek such aid in order to make good his pledge to improve economic conditions after the Irian problem was resolved; and though the Malaysia conflict was beginning to develop, there was in late 1962 and early 1963 no readily available issue which could immediately be made the cause of a new independence-oriented campaign. Besides, given the emotional pitch sustained during the last stages of the Irian campaign, Indonesia, and maybe even Sukarno, needed a breathing spell.

A second possible line of explanation is that Sukarno never seriously intended to implement the stabilization plan. Conceivably, he decided to allow the technocrats their day and wait for political pressures to build that would inevitably compel the abandonment of the plan. A variant of this argument is that Sukarno stayed with stabilization as long as he did because he hoped that the prospect of a stable Indonesia would induce the United States to intervene on Indonesia's behalf in the developing conflict with the British over Malaysia, just as Washington had done with respect to West Irian.[39]

There is certainly reason to suspect that Sukarno was never unequivocally committed to the new course. The May regulations were in fact announced by Acting President Djuanda while Sukarno was out of the country.[40] Though Sukarno doubtless approved the announcement, his failure to personally proclaim the new regulations almost certainly reflected a reluctance to be too closely identified with them. Sukarno may well have felt that by allowing the aid-stabilization approach to be pursued for a time and then repudiated, he could definitively discredit that policy and consolidate a more independent course.

The third potential explanation is that Sukarno was seriously committed to the aid-stabilization course until unforeseen circumstances made it untenable. In short, if the conflict with Malaysia had not assumed major proportions, Sukarno might have held firm for stabilization. Once it became clear that the success of the stabilization program and the delivery of the promised aid were contingent on the abandonment of confrontation, he refused to pay that political price.

Whether or not Sukarno would have been willing to pay the political costs of aid had there been no confrontation with Malaysia

39. This argument is advanced by Mortimer, "Ideology of the PKI," ch. 5, pp. 11–12.

40. Djuanda was the most important leader directly involved in the formulation of the stabilization plan.

is impossible to say. One can scarcely deny that confrontation diminished whatever chances of survival the stabilization program may have had. But given the evidence of Sukarno's coolness toward stabilization and the fact that the May regulations had already run aground on domestic political hostility even before Indonesia became firmly committed to an all-out confrontation with Malaysia, it seems unlikely the aid-stabilization course could have survived.

In any case, it is less important to know whether Sukarno was seriously committed to stabilization, or just drifting and experimenting, or setting the aid-stabilization approach up to be discredited, than to recognize that the prevailing suspicion of the West, in combination with the intense pressures of political competition, made that course politically unacceptable to all three of the principal competitors. It may be said that Sukarno, in coalition with the army leaders, could have sustained the aid-stabilization policy. But in doing so he would not only have violated his most basic political principles; he would have sacrificed the political balance which was essential if he were to remain the central figure in the political system.

By September 1963 the confrontation with Malaysia had become the paramount foreign policy issue, and Sukarno was back on the anti-imperialist course from which he had deviated following the Irian victory. The Indonesian leaders' profound distrust of the Western powers made them generally quite ready to believe Sukarno's assertion that the formation of Malaysia by the British was a challenge to Indonesia's independence. Confrontation initially had the enthusiastic support of all the principal contenders. As in the case of the Irian struggle, each saw the Crush Malaysia campaign as a means of legitimizing domestic political goals which would enhance its political position relative to the others.[41]

41. On the multiplicity of motives underlying support of confrontation, see Kahin, "Malaysia and Indonesia," pp. 253–70; Donald Hindley, "Indonesia's Confrontation with Malaysia: A Search for Motives," *Asian Survey,* 4 (June 1964), 904–13; Bunnell, "Guided Democracy Foreign Policy," pp. 37–76; Robert Curtis, "Malaysia and Indonesia," *New Left Review,* 28 (November-December 1964), pp. 5–32; Gordon, *Dimensions of Conflict in Southeast Asia;* and Arnold C. Brackman, *Southeast Asia's Second Front: The Power Struggle in the Malay Archipelago* (New York: Praeger, 1966).

The PKI eagerly welcomed the prospect of a new anti-imperialist campaign which would virtually foreclose any possibility of a return to the aid-stabilization path and greatly reduce the danger that the promise of American aid might induce Sukarno to curb the party. The PKI leaders saw confrontation as a means of keeping the army leadership on the defensive by making the generals' ties to the United States a source of embarrassment and, more important, by isolating Indonesia from the West. The Communists hammered at the theme that Washington was employing economic pressure to compel an Indonesian compromise on the Malaysia issue. Though the chief targets were the Americans and the British, the PKI also used confrontation as a basis for opposing the government's continuing efforts to attract European and Japanese investment.[42]

Moreover, it was confrontation that emboldened the PKI to take the political offensive in late 1963. In the name of strengthening the anti-Malaysia forces, the PKI carried out its most aggressive mass mobilization; similarly, confrontation served as a pretext for demanding the creation of an armed peasant militia. The party was not, however, at all enthusiastic about major military initiatives against Malaysia; on the contrary, such moves were denounced as "adventurist." At least in the early stages of confrontation, the party leaders seemed worried that an emphasis on the military aspects of the Crush Malaysia campaign would result in strengthening the army at the Communists' expense. The PKI, clearly more interested in domestic actions taken in the name of confrontation than in waging war with Malaysia, favored a lengthy agitational campaign, which it hoped would bring Indonesia closer to Communism.[43]

Confrontation provided the army leaders with justification for a large military budget, and possibly for the reinstatement of martial law, which had lapsed at the termination of the Irian crisis. By taking a vocal, militant stand against Malaysia, the generals hoped

42. Mortimer, "Ideology of the PKI," ch. 5, p. 47, 66.

43. *Ibid.*, ch. 7, p. 26; ch. 5, pp. 43, 45, 62. Mortimer reports that when he interviewed the PKI chairman and other top party leaders in November 1964 they expressed strong opposition to the recently initiated landings on the peninsula. See also *Harian Rakjat*, 14 October 1963.

to capture the initiative and keep the PKI from usurping the forefront on an issue of national independence, as had happened in the West Irian campaign; they seemed determined to be first on the bandwagon this time. As early as February 1963 army infiltrators had already been dispatched across the border, and the army commander, General Yani, had declared that his forces "only awaited the order to move" in support of "our brothers who are fighting for their freedom in North Kalimantan."[44]

Though the anti-Western course set by confrontation obviously held certain dangers for the army leaders, they were restrained from expressing whatever reservations they may have had. The combination of perceptions and political considerations that made it impossible to support the stabilization program made it even more dangerous to oppose confrontation. Of course, the army leadership did seem genuinely worried about the possible use of British bases in Malaysia to support future anti-Jakarta rebel movements, as had been the case in 1958. And the generals undoubtedly saw Indonesian nationalism at stake. They objected to having Southeast Asian affairs decided in London, and they strongly believed that Indonesia deserved to be consulted and taken seriously on matters of importance in the region. Nor can one dismiss their fear that Malaysia might ultimately fall under the domination of its Chinese population, thus extending the "Singapore problem" to Kalimantan.[45]

Confrontation's appeal for Sukarno was obvious. By directing attention toward the "external threat," it lent added credibility to his contention that national unity under his leadership was indispensable to Indonesia's survival. It helped sustain a situation in which his solidarity-making skills were in demand, provided numerous opportunities for bold presidential initiatives and heroic posturing, and promised to convey a sense of surging revolutionary momentum while avoiding any real restructuring of Indonesian society.

In fact, from Sukarno's standpoint the Crush Malaysia campaign

44. Polomka, "Indonesian Army and Confrontation," p. 93. See also Chapter 5 of this book.

45. For discussion of this, see Weinstein, *Indonesia Abandons Confrontation,* pp. 5–7.

seemed to be both a vehicle to revolutionary progress and a device to facilitate conflict management by absorbing the contradictory demands of the army leadership and the PKI. If to be a "leftist revolutionary" one had only to oppose Malaysia and denounce imperialism, then everyone could qualify, despite some rather fundamental disagreements among the "revolutionaries." Confrontation helped to obscure the inherent contradictions among the conceptions of Indonesia's future held by Sukarno, the PKI, and the left wing of the PNI, not to mention the army leadership and the Muslim party leaders, by providing a pretext for postponing the day when those hard issues would have to be faced.

By 1964, however, the army leadership was beginning to discover that the confrontation policy was actually profiting the PKI more than the army. Relations with the United States had deteriorated drastically, and even the Soviets, as already noted, had made the generals aware of their lack of enthusiasm for confrontation. Unlike the Irian campaign, in which hopes of obtaining American diplomatic assistance had kept Indonesia at least minimally attuned to Washington's concerns, there was, after the unsuccessful mediation effort by Robert Kennedy in January 1964, no serious effort to seek American diplomatic intervention, perhaps because Sukarno had concluded that such attempts would be futile. Confrontation led instead to Indonesia's increasing isolation from practically all nations except China, which backed the confrontation policy fully. This separation from their foreign allies weighed most heavily in the minds of the army leaders. When at the end of 1964 Sukarno, evidently without consulting his principal advisers, decided to announce Indonesia's withdrawal from the UN as a protest against the seating of Malaysia in the Security Council, the generals became alarmed indeed.[46]

Moreover, the army leadership, increasingly impressed with the superior strength of the British and the military futility of confrontation, was growing apprehensive that the failure to crush Malaysia might prove an embarrassment to the army.[47] At the same time, the

46. See Weinstein, "Uses of Foreign Policy," p. 593.

47. Both Indonesian and American army sources attested to the army

generals were becoming fearful that the army would have to send so many of its troops to confront Malaysia in the border regions that Java would be left vulnerable to the expansion of PKI influence;[48] their fear heightened when the PKI urged formation of an armed peasant militia. Exacerbating this difficult situation was evidence that the militance of Indonesia's anti-imperialist foreign policy was starting to spill over into the domestic sphere, as PKI-led attacks on the inefficiency and corruption of "capitalist-bureaucrats," many of whom were army officers occupying key economic positions, grew bolder.

Despite their growing dissatisfaction with some of the political consequences of confrontation, the army leaders saw no choice but to call for an intensification of the Crush Malaysia campaign. The increasingly pronounced divergence between the generals' private reservations and their vocal public support reflected their awareness that openly criticizing confrontation would have been politically suicidal. The Crush Malaysia campaign itself had the effect of setting in motion an escalatory spiral which made it ever more difficult to back away. There were in fact some indications that even Sukarno, aware of the futility of confrontation, might have accepted a graceful exit from the policy, had one been available.[49] But even

---

leadership's belief that the PKI wanted to get the army tied down in Kalimantan in a fight it could not win. In the words of one Indonesian colonel: "We felt that all the talk about crushing Malaysia was ultimately intended to embarrass the army. We knew we could not defeat the British. The people would be all aroused, would turn to the army for results, and we would not be able to produce."

48. These reports came from several army sources interviewed by the author. See also Polomka, "Indonesian Army and Confrontation," pp. 172–73, which provides the following details. According to a mid-1964 assessment by the army's strategic command (KOSTRAD), most of the army's 100 or more battalions were under strength and only about 25 were considered truly effective units. To have involved at least a third of those on the Kalimantan front, the number thought necessary for an effective military confrontation, would have left the army leadership vulnerable to Sukarno's engineering a putsch within the central army leadership, since not all units were considered reliable.

49. See Kahin, "Malaysia and Indonesia," pp. 269–70; Gordon, *Dimen-*

assuming that he entertained such thoughts from time to time, Sukarno too was locked into a political situation in which his own interests demanded that he hold to confrontation. And as confrontation provoked new acts of hostility toward Indonesia, such as Moscow's harangues and the cessation of American aid, it became impossible to arrange a retreat from the policy that would not look like a surrender to foreign pressure.

The army leadership could, and did, take steps to reduce the political risks of confrontation. The army dragged its feet in carrying out some aspects of the policy. Few army battalions were actually sent to the border areas, and those sent were taken from the areas considered safest. Overall command of military operations for confrontation was in the hands of an air force general, and the two army generals who served as his deputies were said to have been instructed by General Yani not to follow any orders that would get the army too deeply involved in confrontation. A good deal of the manpower for border operations thus had to be supplied by the air force itself. Another apparent manifestation of the army leadership's reluctance was Jakarta's failure to forward needed supplies to the army troops in Kalimantan.[50]

---

sions of Conflict in Southeast Asia, pp. 98–119; and Bunnell, "Guided Democracy Foreign Policy," pp. 65–66.

50. The information on foot-dragging is from interviews with Indonesian and American army sources. See also Polomka, "Indonesian Army and Confrontation," pp. 175–76. Polomka's account contains the allegation of Brigadier General Supardjo, made at his trial for involvement in the 1965 coup, that some troops sent to Kalimantan were, on orders of the central army leadership, placed under the command of the local army commander, who refused to deliver the troops to Supardjo for confrontation duty. On logistics, according to one report Supardjo had complained that 70 percent of the supplies due to be sent to his troops in Kalimantan were cut off in Jakarta, and that much of what he did receive consisted of spoiled medicines and other unusable items (interview with E. Utrecht, Jakarta, 10 April 1969). A foreign ministry official also informed the author that Admiral Martadinata, the navy commander, had told him after a trip to Kalimantan that the logistical situation was very bad (interview with Ferdy Salim, Jakarta, 16 May 1969). Of course, the poor logistical situation may have had more to do with corruption than with any conscious effort to sabotage confrontation.

Perhaps most significant of all was General Yani's establishment of secret contacts with Malaysia, apparently without Sukarno's knowledge, aimed minimally at keeping the level of confrontation down and ensuring that it did not weaken the army's political position any further. By mid-1965 there were Indonesian army officers living in Bangkok and Hong Kong, maintaining continuous contact with the Malaysians, exchanging intelligence data with them, and giving them information derogatory to the PKI for broadcast back to Indonesia over Radio Malaysia.[51] All these efforts on the army's part notwithstanding, political pressures on the army leadership to prove its continuing commitment to confrontation were such that General Yani felt compelled to draw up plans for an invasion of Malaysia. He even went so far as to send two battalions to North Sumatra, where they gave the appearance of being poised for action at the end of September 1965.[52]

Thus under Guided Democracy the interaction between the elite's view of the world and the existence of an intensely competitive political system created substantial incentives for all of the principal contenders to support a foreign policy that gave priority to full independence, while it made the risks of an aid-oriented policy almost prohibitive. It is hard to imagine how a foreign policy emphasizing primarily the search for aid and heavy reliance on foreign advice in the planning and execution of an economic stabilization program could conceivably have been sustained, given the prevailing mixture of attitudes and political competition. But an accelerating leftward trend in Indonesia's domestic politics led to

---

Supardjo was said to have blamed "corrupt generals in Jakarta" for selling materials due to be sent to his command.

51. For details based on the author's interviews with many of the principals, see Weinstein, "Uses of Foreign Policy," pp. 596–99.

52. According to an American army source close to the Indonesian generals, General Yani felt that "the pressures were building up, and it was necessary to do something." But the American source asserts that Kemal Idris, the general in command of the invasion force, told him that he never had any serious intention of carrying out the invasion plan. He did, however, go to some lengths at the time to convey the impression that he was serious, and he even held a briefing on the invasion plan after the 30 September attempted coup.

the attempted coup of 30 September 1965, an event which set in motion political changes that within a year produced a dramatic reversal of Indonesia's foreign policy.

Soeharto's New Order

The attempted coup ruptured the fragile political balance. The PKI's implication in the events of 30 September, in which six army generals were murdered, was seized by the army as justification for the destruction of the party, and in a matter of months most of the PKI's top leaders, along with hundreds of thousands of alleged Communists, were slaughtered or arrested. Sukarno attempted to keep alive some sort of leftist force as a counter to the army, but he failed. By March 1966, amid student demonstrations and irresistible pressure from the army, Sukarno had no choice but to yield de facto leadership to General Soeharto, who had led the army in crushing the attempted coup. Though Sukarno stayed on as president until early 1967, he was virtually powerless.

With the elimination of both the PKI and Sukarno as political forces, the army soon monopolized political power. Political party leaders who might have criticized some of the army leadership's policies were intimidated by the tense political atmosphere, in which opposition to the new government's views could lead to denunciation as an "old order" sympathizer, or if one's anti-Sukarno credentials were impeccable, as a dupe. Besides, there was a feeling that opposition would be futile; it would only raise the risk of embarrassing oneself politically without any real chance of having an impact on the government's policies.

In this new situation, striking changes in Indonesia's foreign policy became possible. Because of the diminution of political competition, the political incentives for carrying out the kind of confrontative foreign policy that Sukarno had pursued no longer existed. Though a policy of putting aid first would still leave its advocates vulnerable to allegations that they had sold Indonesia's independence, the risk of such criticism was easily bearable in view of the commanding political position held by those who favored greater reliance on foreign aid. Unlike its predecessors, the new government found that it could formulate and implement an aid-oriented foreign policy relatively unhindered by a need to consider the impact on domestic political competition.

Incentives for Putting Aid First

If the declining intensity of political competition facilitated the government's efforts to pursue a policy of putting aid first, what were the forces that actually impelled the new leaders to move in that direction? To begin with, the New Order was subject to the same pressures to seek foreign aid that had been felt by every previous regime. The diminution of political competition should not be taken to mean that those in power now possessed the political capability to mobilize indigenous resources and solve Indonesia's pressing economic problems without substantial foreign aid. The country's administrative machinery was in decay, corruption was rife, and the ability of the central leadership to effect positive action by subordinates in areas distant from the capital was limited. Having just emerged from a period of intense political struggle, the new leadership desired above all a pacified countryside and had no inclination to risk new upheavals by undertaking a massive mobilization of the population. The ruling group, protective of its privileged position, would have been adverse to any drastic measures undertaken to promote economic development with less dependence on foreign aid, since such steps could easily upset the status quo and jeopardize the rulers' own position.

In fact, pressures on the new government to seek foreign aid were considerably more intense than on its predecessors because of the disastrous condition of the Indonesian economy in 1966. According to many foreign policy elite members, there was at the outset of the New Order a strong feeling that the independence-oriented policies of the past had proved unsatisfying. Those policies had, perhaps, yielded a sense of independence, but at the cost of grinding poverty, increased human suffering, and continued underdevelopment. Just as the turn toward an independence-oriented policy in the middle 1950s had been a response to the disillusioning experiences of the preceding years, so the aid-oriented policy of the latter 1960s was a reaction against the frustrations and failures of the Guided Democracy period. Moreover, the confrontative foreign policy of Sukarno had taken a high toll in emotional energy, and by 1966 people were weary of the seemingly endless struggle for independence. Many leaders acknowledged a widespread desire for a more comfortable life even if it meant some compromise of the nation's independence.

The possibility of maintaining a greater degree of independence by balancing Indonesia's relations with the big powers was, to some extent, ruled out by the attitudes of the powers themselves. There was no way, save a withdrawal into self-reliance, for Indonesia to maintain an independent policy (as defined by the foreign policy elite) unless the contending powers proved willing to cooperate by taking an active role as aid-givers. That Indonesia would have to depend on the West for foreign aid was, in the first instance, dictated by the obvious unwillingness of the Communist powers to provide aid. China, in the throes of the Cultural Revolution, broadcast over Radio Peking vitriolic attacks on the Indonesian rulers. As for Russia, it was reliably reported that when an army general went to Moscow in 1966 to discuss debt rescheduling, some of his hosts pointed their fingers at him and called him a murderer. Given the New Order's violent anti-Communism, there could hardly have been any expectation of economic assistance from Communist powers which had not been overly forthcoming with nonmilitary aid even during the Guided Democracy years. Of course, if the PKI had won, rather than the army leadership, one may assume that the government would have sought substantial aid from the Communist powers, though it is possible (depending mainly on how and when the PKI came to power) that the Communists might have had a greater capacity to mobilize domestic resources, thus reducing the need for aid.

The non-Communist powers, on the other hand, especially Japan and the United States, were eager to give aid to Indonesia after the coup, and it was not hard to calculate what sort of image would elicit the maximum amount. Washington, the Indonesian leaders believed, saw their country chiefly as a potential bastion against the spread of Communism in Southeast Asia, while Japan sought mainly markets and raw materials—hence, the twin images of anti-Communism and stability were to be cultivated. The ending of confrontation, the return to the United Nations, the stabilization program of 1966, the assumption of a more equivocal stance on Vietnam, a "moderate" position among the nonaligned nations, advocacy of regional cooperation, and restraint in the face of Singapore's provocative hanging of two Indonesian prisoners in 1968—all these can be ascribed to diverse motivations, but taken together they were designed to create and sustain an image of stability and anti-Communism.[53] Of course, many Indonesian leaders undoubtedly preferred to think of themselves as manipulating the aid-givers to their country's advantage, but in any case, they felt they had no choice but to seek aid from the West.

If the New Order leadership was subjected, with unusual intensity, to the same kinds of pressures to seek Western aid felt by every previous regime, those who wielded direct policymaking authority had their own political reasons for favoring a policy of putting aid first. The army leaders almost from the outset of the New Order shared the making of foreign policy with the foreign minister and a group of technocrats, all of whom served at the sufferance of the ruling generals. The supremacy of the army leadership was never in doubt, not only because the president was a general but more fundamentally because the army was the only one of the three groups with an independent political base.

The subordinate participants found that the desire to maximize their own role in decision-making dictated an aid-oriented policy. The army considered the foreign minister and the technocrats useful primarily because of their technical expertise and their ability to win aid commitments from the West. Thus, their strongest political

53. The Indonesian leaders clearly did not see questions such as the morality of the 1966 massacres or of the treatment of political prisoners as issues of major concern to the two principal aid-givers, though some European governments were believed to be more sensitive (*Harian Kami,* 15 October 1973).

card was the enthusiasm they aroused in Western capitals; this naturally predisposed them toward a policy that emphasized the acquisition of Western aid, though Foreign Minister Malik's reasonably cordial personal relations with the Soviets, stemming from his prior experience as ambassador to Moscow, also gave him some political interest in a more balanced foreign policy.

Most important, of course, were the army leaders' changed political needs following the elimination of the PKI and Sukarno. A major source of pressure to seek aid was the generals' evident desire to use the promise of economic development, at which Sukarno had failed, as a basis for legitimizing their own rule. If the New Order was to have any meaning beyond anti-Communism and the ouster of Sukarno, it would have to be the promise of economic improvement. Soeharto's commitment to economic development became the principal line drawn to distinguish the New Order's policies from Sukarno's. And the acquisition of a large amount of foreign aid was seen as the only way to make that promise of development credible and thus to justify the army's right to rule.

The army leadership's reluctance to seek aid from the Communist powers reflected not only a perception that Moscow and Peking were unlikely to be responsive to an aid request, but a belief that the army's interests would be best served by reducing relations with the Communist nations to a minimum. While the army leaders no longer had to worry about the PKI as a political competitor, the generals did exhibit some concern about a possible future resurgence of Communism, which might be sparked by a desire for vengeance on the part of those loyal to the hundreds of thousands of victims of the 1965–1966 massacres. The generals feared that aid relations with the Communist powers would lend respectability to Communism generally, thus enhancing the PKI's prospects for recovery.

The army's interests as a corporate entity clearly pointed toward a restoration of close aid relations with the West. It had two principal needs: an assured supply of modern military equipment and training, and the maintenance of unity within the army itself. Western aid could directly solve the first problem and contribute to solution of the second by providing material incentives that would make it profitable for all factions to maintain cordial relations with the central leadership, through which all foreign aid, military or economic, is customarily channeled.

Finally, the personality and political style of Soeharto, the army's leader, seemed far better suited to an aid-oriented policy than to an independence-oriented one. If Sukarno's extraordinary exhortative skills naturally predisposed him toward a foreign policy that would enable him to utilize those attributes to advantage, Soeharto was a conspicuously uncharismatic figure, who projected an image of simplicity, reliability, and stability that had considerable appeal to foreign creditors and investors. Unlike a confrontative policy aimed at dramatizing the nation's independence, a foreign policy that concentrated on reassuring foreign creditors about the wisdom of their investment in Indonesia's economy did not easily lend itself to spectacular demarches and virtuoso solo performances by a superstar president. It was as hard to imagine the calm, stable Soeharto leading his people in an anti-imperialist crusade as it was to envisage Sukarno, who loved confrontation and revolutionary struggle almost as ends in themselves, deferring to his American-trained economists and presiding over an economic program attuned to the desires of the Western powers. Nor was Soeharto, a man of relatively narrow education and experience in politics or international affairs, generally regarded as a leader who would enjoy, or excel at, an active international role.[54] Few saw him as one who could successfully maneuver among the powers, as Sukarno had done, to maintain balanced relationships and at the same time establish himself as a leader of the nonaligned nations. A policy of putting aid first, on the other hand, promised to minimize the impact of Soeharto's political deficiencies and enable him to draw the greatest political benefit from his assets.

54. On Soeharto's limited education, see O. G. Roeder, *The Smiling General: President Soeharto of Indonesia* (Jakarta: Gunung Agung, 1969), pp. 86–91, 131. Roeder also notes Soeharto's lack of interest in foreign affairs. His first trip abroad was a brief mission to West Europe in 1961, and he did not leave the country again until his 1968 visit to Japan as president (*ibid.*, pp. 173–74).

Perceptions and Politics

There were, then, strong pressures on the New Order leaders to pursue a foreign policy that accorded top priority to the search for aid. But is it not also the case that the Indonesian leaders continued to perceive the world as a hostile place? We should recall that the foreign policy elite manifested a deep suspicion of those on whom Indonesia relies for aid. Taking together the responses of 65 of the 66 foreign policy elite members to questions on all of the subjects raised in the preceding chapters, we find that the Indonesian leaders on the average answered 73 percent of the relevant questions in a manner indicating adherence to the hostile world perspective.[55] Those components of the foreign policy elite closest to the center of power in the New Order—namely, the army, technocrats, and foreign ministry—were all above the average in holding to this view. The only groups that were more pronounced were the PNI and PSI leaders, and the latter, though not necessarily occupying government positions, were close to the foreign minister. The two groups that were lowest in adherence to the hostile world view were the Islamic and Catholic party leaders, and they, like the PNI, were generally remote from the center of decision-making, though some of the Catholics were close to one army faction (see Table 8.1).

Clearly, suspicion of the outside world remained high, even within the ranks of those directly responsible for Indonesia's aid-oriented policy. But after 1965 these perceptions no longer ruled out policies emphasizing aid, because the nature of political competition had so drastically changed. Political competition under the New Order was restricted to "bureaucratic competition" among army generals,

55. One leader did not provide information on enough points to permit a meaningful tabulation. There were 36 questions bearing directly on the extent to which the world was perceived as a hostile place. For most leaders, however, it was impossible to assess with confidence their views on all 36 points. Individual scores were calculated by taking the number of "hostile world" responses as a percentage of the total number of questions on which the individual's views could be discerned. The individual percentages were then averaged for each group.

technocrats, cabinet ministers, party leaders, and others for personal or factional advantage. There was virtually no public criticism of

Table 8.1. Perception of the outside world

	Average percentage of answers indicating a hostile world view
All respondents (n = 65)	73
1928 Generation (n = 11)	70
1945 Generation (n = 45)	75
1966 Generation (n = 9)	66
PNI (n = 9)	91
PSI (n = 6)	82
Foreign Ministry (n = 9)	76
Technocrats (n = 9)	76
Army (n = 12)	74
Islamic parties (n = 8)	51
Catholic Party (n = 4)	43

the army, and no overt criticism whatsoever of Soeharto. Though Soeharto was widely regarded as a leader who had few clearly defined ideas of his own and left little personal imprint on Indonesia's policies, his position as the ultimate decision-maker remained unchallenged. The political struggle took place among those who were, or would be, his advisers. At this level, there were policy disagreements and personal rivalries among, and also within, the three principal policymaking groups. Some public criticism of Indonesia's dependence on aid did surface, but unlike the previous period such criticism was easily manageable.

In the first place, none of the army leadership's bureaucratic rivals was in a position to use the widespread concern about dependence on outsiders against the army. On the contrary, the foreign ministry and technocrats were useful to the army not only because of their ability to secure aid commitments but also because they could and did absorb a good deal of the criticism that might otherwise have been directed against the army leadership.[56] In fact,

56. For example, see *Merdeka,* 7 December 1970.

both the foreign minister and the technocrats found that their chief political asset, the enthusiasm they aroused in the aid-giving countries, was at the same time a real liability because it aroused suspicions that they were serving foreign interests. The fact that Indonesian technocrats "think the same way IMF people think," as a leading economist put it, might have been an advantage in negotiating with Jakarta's creditors, but it led some of their own countrymen to question their nationalism. The technocrats, though influential in the determination of policies related to foreign economic matters, were utterly dependent on the army, for they realized that only the army possessed either the inclination or the capacity to give them the influential position they now held.

The foreign minister's weakness was time and again revealed by the president's tendency to rely on generals and technocrats as ad hoc emissaries to handle many of the most sensitive foreign policy matters. On a variety of issues, especially those relating to Asia, Malik found himself overruled in favor of generals or technocrats.[57] Army spokesmen praised the foreign minister as a "good politician" who knew enough not to disagree too strenuously with the army on any major issues; they derided his ministry as excessively cautious, even timid—"just a bunch of people hoping for another chance to go abroad." Though it was known that the foreign minister would have preferred to see Indonesia pursue a more independent course, he was essentially powerless to effect such a change.

The basic weakness of the technocrats and the foreign minister was pointed up by the partially confirmed report that newspaper editorials which in late 1970 accused the technocrats and foreign minister of "selling a nation/people" had actually been encouraged

57. Examples include: the terms under which confrontation was to be ended; the question of Soeharto's 1968 trip to Japan (Malik felt he should not have gone); Indonesia's China policy at the UN (he was less inclined to follow Washington's lead); the handling of the West Irian referendum in 1969 (he reportedly favored a more tolerant policy toward dissenters) and of the UN debate on the referendum (he would have confronted the rebels directly at the UN, instead of forbidding the Indonesian delegates to have any contact with them); the appointment of ambassadors (for example, Roeslan Abdulgani at the UN); and plans for a presidential trip to Europe in 1969 (it was planned against his advice, and later had to be cancelled).

by army leaders close to the president.[58] Their purpose was supposedly to remind the subordinate participants in the policymaking process of their dependence on the army, and at the same time to shift the burden of criticism from the army to the civilians.

The army leadership itself, of course, was by no means monolithic.[59] Army factions competed over the division of power and the generals even disagreed on some issues of substance. In fact, as late as four years after the attempted coup, prominent army generals believed to have been too sympathetic to Sukarno in the critical days of 1965 and 1966 were still being arrested. Some generals even made public statements cautiously raising doubts about Indonesia's less-than-independent foreign policy, but army officers were obviously very reluctant to question directly the nationalism of their fellow generals.[60] Nevertheless, if serious political competition returns to Jakarta it will probably take the form of liaisons between factions of the army and other political groups, and it is equally likely that the incumbents' alleged compromise of Indonesia's independence will be one justification advanced for moving against the ruling generals.

Through 1973, however, the major issues of the aid-independence dilemma figured only obliquely in the pattern of bureaucratic competition. Though particular individuals or factions were some-

58. The publisher of *Merdeka,* the newspaper which ran the most sharply critical attacks on Indonesia's foreign policy, had won a controversial election as chairman of the Indonesian Journalists Association just before the editorials were run. He had triumphed in that election thanks to the intervention of an army general close to the president.

59. Army factions divide along many lines, but for foreign policy one of the most important has been the continuing rivalry between the "institutional" generals who have dominated the army and defense ministry, especially their intelligence establishments, and "free-wheelers" who serve as personal assistants to the president and run intelligence operations that lie outside the scope of the defense ministry.

60. Shortly before President Nixon's July 1969 visit to Indonesia, General Nasution warned against any commitments that might compromise Indonesia's independent-and-active policy. In Jakarta his warning was taken as criticism of the government. Lieutenant General Djatikusumo in March 1970 criticized Indonesian participation in ASEAN as a violation of the independent-and-active policy.

times identified with different policy approaches—the foreign minister, certain army generals, and certain technocrats were thought to be more interested in moving toward an independent foreign policy than others—policy differences tended to be rather obscure and there was often considerable confusion as to which faction had triumphed in a particular decision. This bureaucratic competition for access to the president, personal prestige, and other such rewards clearly posed no threat to the army leadership's ability to carry out an aid-oriented foreign policy.

Still, on several occasions top decision-makers recognized the existence of an underlying apprehension about the compromise of Indonesia's independence, and they made gestures, however feeble, to alleviate that concern. But in the end it was always the combination of pressure to seek aid and the freedom to do so afforded by the army leadership's unchallenged political position that proved decisive. If we look at several major foreign policy decisions of the New Order years, we can see this, and we can also see how the interaction between perceptions and politics in a situation of bureaucratic competition differed from that which had prevailed under the much more intensely competitive political system of Guided Democracy.

The first important decision was the ending of the confrontation with Malaysia. In the earliest days of the New Order, there obviously lingered a concern about appearing to be "soft on independence." The 1965 coup and the 11 March 1966 transfer of authority from Sukarno to Soeharto had been followed by a torrent of reaffirmations of loyalty to confrontation, as political and military leaders, especially those leading the movement to the right, sought a hedge against the uncertain future and immunity from the still pejorative label "rightist."[61] But even as the Indonesian leaders, including Soeharto, continued to speak publicly of their commitment to confrontation, army officers close to Soeharto were using channels

61. That leaders of the militantly anti-Sukarno student action front KAMI withheld criticism of confrontation for fear of being called rightists was confirmed in an interview with KAMI leader Zamroni, Jakarta, 3 September 1969.

they had established with Kuala Lumpur before the coup to establish the basis for a settlement.[62] Within less than three months of the transfer of authority, an Indonesian delegation headed by Foreign Minister Adam Malik had met in Bangkok with Malaysian representatives to work out a formal agreement for the normalization of relations between the two countries.

There was, however, a good deal of opposition to the terms on which Malik reached agreement with the Malaysians. This opposition represented, to some extent, genuine concern that Indonesia's self-respect as an independent nation was being sold out in the rush to "restore international confidence" in Indonesia. There was also an effort to exploit this concern to embarrass political rivals.

Sharp criticism of the peace agreement was raised first by members of the Indonesian delegation to the Bangkok conference. The army participants were said to be "amazed" that Malik had agreed to the recognition of Malaysia before the holding of elections to ascertain the desires of the inhabitants of Sabah and Sarawak. All of the army delegates felt that in his eagerness to end the confrontation Malik had "exceeded his instructions."[63] On his return to Jakarta, Malik quickly discovered that ratification of the Bangkok Agreement would prove difficult to obtain.

To begin with, strong criticism came from those who had reason to be unhappy about their political status in the New Order. Sukarno, as might have been expected, was furious, though he was not in a position to say so publicly.[64] General Nasution, long viewed as the likely head of any army-dominated government, was widely presumed to be disappointed at his failure to reach the political summit. In an effort to establish a broader political base, prepara-

62. For more detailed discussion of the ending of confrontation, see Weinstein, *Indonesia Abandons Confrontation,* and "Uses of Foreign Policy," pp. 603–18.

63. That Malik felt the rug had been pulled from under his feet was evident in the complaint of one of his closest associates: "Our instructions were simply to 'negotiate the end of confrontation.' The conditions did not come until after the Bangkok Agreement had been reached."

64. In his 17 August 1966 speech, however, Sukarno did publicly declare that he had opposed the Bangkok Agreement.

tory to a possible bid for the vice-presidency, Nasution was believed to be actively wooing civilian political support. In the days both before and after Bangkok, Nasution repeatedly issued public warnings against capitulation. While there is reason to believe that Nasution was genuinely concerned about the abandonment of the principles represented by confrontation, the issue did serve his political needs.[65]

The Islamic NU party and the PNI, both of which had been split and weakened by the political turmoil of the preceding months, found a critical stance toward the Bangkok Agreement a relatively safe means of registering their disapproval of any drastic disavowal of the past which might in the process completely destroy the political parties. For the PNI in particular, the capitulation issue, on which the contending factions of the party could agree, was viewed as useful to leaders desperately struggling to hold the PNI together.[66] For all of these "opposition" leaders, criticism of the Bangkok Agree-

65. Weinstein, *Indonesian Abandons Confrontation,* pp. 47–49, 64–65. In a written interview on 11 March 1970, Nasution, unlike many other leaders, made no effort to conceal the fact that he had strongly supported confrontation. He even expressed the view that he still thought it best if Sabah and Sarawak were given independence individually, and then allowed to decide whether or not they wished to enter Malaysia. According to an Indonesian living in Malaysia, Nasution's real fear of the consequences of accepting Malaysia was expressed in a letter, written in May or June 1966, to a friend in Malaysia. In that, Nasution allegedly stated that he did not want peace with Malaysia until Indonesia had grown stronger. Nasution himself has informed the author that he was very concerned, back in June of 1966, about obtaining a guarantee that British bases in the area, especially the one in Singapore, would be abandoned.

66. On the NU and PNI positions, see Weinstein, *Indonesia Abandons Confrontation,* pp. 49–51, 63–65. The NU's genuine unhappiness with the Bangkok Agreement was emphasized by NU leaders K. H. Dahlan (interview, Jakarta, 28 August 1969) and Chalik Ali (interview, Jakarta, 27 January 1970). Their objection was that the agreement made it look as if Indonesia, not Great Britain, had been wrong. But another NU leader, Subchan (interview, Jakarta, 13 August 1969), insisted that the NU leaders' criticism of the Bangkok Agreement had been "dictated by political demands." That a key consideration in determining the PNI's position on the Bangkok Agreement had been the need to unify the party was stressed by the secretary-general of the party, Usep Ranawidjaja (interview, Jakarta, 25 November 1969).

ment was a way of delivering with impunity a mild rebuke to the new leadership, something which they had wanted to do for reasons unrelated to confrontation. In a sense, the lingering perception of confrontation as an issue involving the nation's independence may be said to have legitimized their dissent.

Though none of these critics had the power to threaten the politically dominant position of the new leaders, Sukarno, and to a lesser extent other leaders, retained some capacity to embarrass a government that was still unsure of itself. Fear of such political embarrassment, among other considerations, led the government to abandon its original plan to seek parliamentary ratification of the Bangkok Agreement.[67]

As it happened, however, even Soeharto and his army advisers were unhappy with the settlement Malik had negotiated; the appearance of capitulation was too humiliating. According to one general who had been a member of the delegation at Bangkok, it was "essential to prove, for the sake of history, that confrontation had been launched with good reason—that it was not all just a mistake, something done for no reason." The army leaders were also concerned that the Bangkok Agreement would expose the army to ridicule, in view of the army's prominent role in the Crush Malaysia campaign. "After all," asserted a source close to the army, "what kind of people would we look like to wage war one day, peace the next, just like that." When a delegation of student leaders asked Soeharto why it was taking Indonesia so long to ratify the Bangkok Agreement, he reportedly replied: "What do you want us to do, sell out our national honor?"

Apart from this concern, army leaders apparently hoped to ensure that the foreign minister grasped the fact that his position in foreign policymaking was subordinate to that of the army leadership. As a source close to the generals said: "Speaking frankly, there was real competition between Malik and the army to see who could be

67. This was acknowledged by foreign ministry, army, and parliamentary sources. In October, after a secret annex had been added to the agreement and leaked, the Bangkok Agreement won parliamentary ratification without difficulty.

the hero in ending confrontation, and Malik was just too eager. He wanted to steal the show." It would have been impossible for Malik to withdraw his initial proposals at Bangkok, which became the basis of the agreement, without destroying his authority, it was said. "If we wanted to continue using him as foreign minister, we had to protect his authority," observed the spokesman cited above. Thus, the army sought to reprimand Malik, but it could not afford to strike too hard.

The impasse was finally broken in late July when Jakarta and Kuala Lumpur agreed to take note, in a secret annex to the Bangkok Agreement, of Indonesia's stipulation that general elections in Sabah and Sarawak precede diplomatic relations. When the Bangkok Agreement was signed in Jakarta on 11 August 1966, the secret annex was also signed, and in a matter of days leaked to the public. Even with the annex, however, the agreement clearly was a capitulation. Diplomatic relations were established before the holding of elections, which did not really constitute a referendum on Malaysia anyway.[68]

What does the ending of confrontation tell us about the interaction between perceptions and politics? First, by insisting on the secret annex, the army leadership did make a minor concession to the widely shared view that Indonesia should not "sell out its national honor" just to impress potential aid-givers. Second, practically every major political actor, except the foreign minister, tried to exploit that view to gain political advantage. But the decisive fact of the situation was that no one was in a position to challenge the leadership's basic decision to end confrontation even though it did in fact amount to a capitulation. Because of the low intensity of political competition, support of confrontation had become irrelevant to the army leadership's political needs. The political risks of

68. The Sarawak elections which the Indonesians had expected in 1967 were postponed. In the Sabah elections of April 1967, to which Indonesia sent observers, not a single one of the seventy-nine candidates called for a withdrawal from Malaysia, so there was no way in which opponents of the Malaysia idea could have expressed their view (Weinstein, *Indonesia Abandons Confrontation,* pp. 85–87).

capitulation, which would have been serious in a more competitive system, were outweighed by the need for foreign aid to improve the economic situation.

Nowhere was the changed relationship between perceptions and politics more evident than in the adoption and implementation of the economic strategy first enunciated in October 1966. In 1963 a basically similar plan had been attacked from all sides (save the technocrats who produced it) as a compromise of Indonesia's independence. The New Order's economic policies also attracted considerable criticism, as we have seen, from a broad spectrum of Indonesian leaders. But there was never any danger that such criticism would force the abandonment of those policies.

The principal architects of Indonesia's stabilization and aid policies were, in fact, well aware that it was only the low level of political competition that enabled them to carry out a set of policies which conflicted with the views of a majority of the Indonesian elite. Though they could sympathize with many of the critics' concerns, the top policymakers asserted that they, as the men responsible for dealing with Indonesia's overwhelming problems, had no alternative but to follow this course.

They were simply grateful that they had been able to do what they felt necessary unhindered by political opposition. One economist acknowledged that "there really was no one in favor of [the government's economic policies] outside the government. . . . We were fortunate to have an emergency situation in which we could steamroller them through."[69] As another technocrat explained: "Frankly, there was no reason for us to worry about trying to persuade them [the critics]. Oh, people may say this is ignoring the voice of the people, but we simply had more important things to do with our time. We had clear support for our policies from the government, and that was really all that was necessary. When you are

69. A similar evaluation was expressed by Frans Seda, finance minister in 1966 (interview, Jakarta, 27 December 1969): "The parties opposed the stabilization plan in 1966 as they had in 1963. What had changed was the fact that there was a government committed to the program and possessed of the authority to carry it out."

in the government, you can do certain things." The economists were particularly appreciative that Soeharto, aware of the unpopularity of the new policies, had told them back in 1966 that he was "more interested in improving Indonesia's economic situation than in seeking popularity."[70]

Despite their unpopularity, the government's economic policies did serve the political interests of the ruling generals. Those who suffered most severely from the tight money policy were businessmen associated with the Islamic parties and the PNI. Best able to withstand the effects of the government's policies were the stronger local Chinese businessmen. Because the position of the Chinese, as a despised ethnic minority, was always insecure, they could most easily be induced to pay protection money to the army. Though many generals were anti-Chinese, they thus found political and financial profit in policies that strengthened the local Chinese. Moreover, the army leadership had no desire to strengthen the economic community which supported the Islamic parties. Though they were politically weak and disorganized at the time, the Muslim politicians, many of whom had opposed Sukarno and favored an aid-oriented policy when Soeharto and his fellow generals were thriving on Guided Democracy, posed a potential threat to the army because of their broad mass support. The generals clearly preferred, furthermore, to rely on the technocrats, who had no political base of their own, rather than on economic experts who because of their ties to a political party would not be totally dependent on the army for their position.

To be sure, government spokesmen did make efforts to dispel the impression that Indonesia had fallen under the thumb of the IMF. The government emitted a good deal of rhetoric that aid would

70. Interview with Widjojo Nitisastro, Jakarta, 30 December 1969. Soeharto's attitude was that once the decision had been made, it was necessary to stay with it and see it through. According to key army sources close to the president, Soeharto listened to the words of Sarbini and other critics, but he never seriously contemplated changing Indonesia's policies in response to such criticism. In any case, the economists and generals alike dismissed most of the criticism as "politically motivated."

never be permitted to play more than a supplementary role in Indonesia's development. As we have seen, Indonesian negotiators sought to avoid terms and conditions regarded as excessively exploitative. Especially after 1969, there were attempts to repair economic relations with the Communist nations and to distribute the burden of aid more evenly among the Western nations. But those were, for the most part, hollow and halfhearted gestures.

Soeharto's unsuccessful 1968 trip to Japan illustrates the same basic pattern. The trip was proposed in order to secure an aid commitment; some officials protested that its probable failure would detract from Indonesia's image of independence; and aid considerations ultimately prevailed, though a gesture was made in the name of independence after the mission encountered difficulties.[71]

The visit had been suggested in the hope that the personal intervention of Soeharto would make it awkward for the Japanese to reject Indonesia's 1968 aid request, which Tokyo had thus far been reluctant to accept. Army generals close to the president consulted with their contacts in Japan, especially with business and parliamentary members of the so-called "Indonesia lobby," and they assured Soeharto that an aid commitment would be forthcoming during the presidential visit. But the foreign minister, among others, had concluded from conversations with Japanese diplomats that Tokyo would not be in a position to make any commitment at the time of Soeharto's visit. The foreign ministry view was that the trip was demeaning and in violation of an elementary rule of diplomacy—namely, "never expose your chief of state to insult." Nevertheless, acting on the optimistic advice of both his army advisers and the technocrats, one of whom referred to the trip as Indonesia's "trump card" in the aid negotiations, Soeharto decided to go. When the Japanese declined to commit themselves, the Indonesian side refused to sign the pro forma joint communique that had been prepared for release at the conclusion of the visit.

71. Based on interviews with virtually all of the generals, economists, and foreign ministry officials involved at the top level on the Indonesian side and with several on the Japanese side. For more details, see Weinstein, "Uses of Foreign Policy," pp. 633–38.

Subsequently, the generals and technocrats who had counseled the president to go to Japan claimed that the trip's real purpose had been to administer a "shock treatment" to the Japanese and to show them that, much as their country needed foreign aid, the Indonesians could not be "pushed around." The trip was, however, widely recognized as an embarrassing failure for the government, but because there was no one to challenge the military rulers, virtually no political ill effects were felt.

A final, rather dramatic, example of how much difference the intensity of political competition can make in the extent to which perceptions find expression in policy comes from the events surrounding Singapore's October 1968 execution of two Indonesian marines convicted of sabotage activities during the days of confrontation. The Singapore government, rejecting Soeharto's personal plea for clemency, was viewed even by the highest Indonesian officials as deliberately flaunting Indonesian sensitivities in order to put the Indonesians "in their place," and presumably to demonstrate to Singaporeans and Indonesians alike that Jakarta was not free to retaliate in any significant way.

With the issue cast as a test of Indonesia's independence, the marine corps and the navy were said to be eager to launch an invasion of Singapore, and some army generals were believed ready to support such a move. Others, including leaders of most political parties, vigorously urged that some strong action be taken, for example, a break in diplomatic and economic relations.[72] Emotions reached a high pitch with student demonstrations and the burning of the Singapore embassy. But the government, aware that any serious response to the demand for retaliatory measures would be viewed as irresponsible by the IGGI nations, essentially ignored the popular outcry. In fact, neither the foreign ministry nor the top army leadership ever seriously considered strong retaliatory meas-

72. For typical editorial commentary, see *Suluh Marhaen,* 22 and 25 October 1968, and *Sinar Harapan,* 21 October 1968. Reports of wide support for an invasion, or at least a break in relations, came from interviews with army generals, technocrats, and navy admirals.

ures.[73] It is, however, highly doubtful that the government could have resisted such pressures in a more intensely competitive political situation.

What, in summary, was the impact of the interaction between perceptions and politics on Soeharto's foreign policy? The hostile world view stimulated considerable criticism of the government's policies. But because the intensity of political competition remained low, the ruling group had considerable latitude in responding less to that criticism than to economic and political pressures to pursue a foreign policy that put aid first; the government had to make only minor gestures in the direction of independence, despite the persistence of a view of the world that strongly encouraged an independence-oriented foreign policy. The Indonesian leaders seemed well aware, however, that Jakarta's aid relationships were widely viewed with suspicion, and they knew that should the political system grow more competitive, they would find their freedom to pursue an aid-oriented policy narrowed and would begin to feel strong political pressures to move once again toward a policy emphasizing independence.

Recent Trends and Projections

How long can such a relatively noncompetitive situation be maintained in a political system that faces economic and social problems as difficult as Indonesia's, especially when the country's elite has a high degree of political consciousness? Continuation of the present pattern depends, above all, on the army's ability to sustain a reasonably high degree of internal unity. This requires that conflict within the army be contained at the level of fragmented personal or factional rivalries and not be permitted to develop into a sharply defined, issue-oriented polarization linking civilian critics with army dissidents. The intensity of political competition can be kept low only so long as rival army factions can agree that socioeconomic conditions are not deteriorating so badly as to undermine

73. Interviews with army and foreign ministry sources, as well as with technocrats and political party leaders.

the present leadership's mandate to rule. Given the general suspicion concerning Indonesia's presumed benefactors, an apparent failure to approach the anticipated degree of economic progress would surely be attributed to the country's dependence on foreign aid and the corrupting effects of that dependence. Because that suspicion is so widely shared and deeply felt, the allegation that Indonesia's problems are due to policies permitting excessive foreign influence would be inherently credible and probably would demolish the legitimacy of the responsible leaders.

A widespread perception on the part of the politically articulate public that the government's policies are failing badly could encourage dissatisfied army officers to challenge the present holders of power and provide them the necessary justification for their action. Thus, from the frustration born of yet another round in the cycle of failure that has plagued Indonesian's development efforts since the revolution, there could well come a revival of serious political competition. While we cannot predict with confidence how the incumbents would respond, were they to observe such a challenge developing, they would surely have new incentives to follow a more independent foreign policy course.

Developments of the early 1970s suggest that the New Order may already be evolving in that direction. There is evidence of deepening pessimism about the government's capacity to achieve its economic and social goals and sharpening criticism of the leaders for their willingness to make Indonesia's development so dependent on foreign aid. To be sure, there has also been evidence of a further concentration of power in the hands of a narrowing circle of leaders. By 1970 army generals who had demonstrated signs of independence had been exiled to distant command posts or ambassadorial positions abroad. In preparation for the 1971 general elections, political parties and professional associations were purged of leaders considered too independent by the generals closest to Soeharto. In the process, the Islamic parties, already weak but always a potential threat because of their mass following, were crippled as an autonomous political force.

The 1971 elections produced an overwhelming victory for the government, and the army leaders began talking of a twenty-five-year plan for development, as if to suggest that they interpreted their electoral triumph as a mandate to rule for the next quarter century. By 1972 the foreign minister found his position vis-à-vis the army leadership appreciably weakened, a change symbolized by the exile of his closest assistant, a man with strong PSI connections, as ambassador to an East European country. In the cabinet reshuffle of March 1973, the one technocrat in the cabinet with political experience and (it was believed) ambitions was transferred to a post outside the economic policymaking apparatus. But this apparent consolidation of power was in large measure offset by the tensions caused by the leadership's policies and by events beyond the government's control.

The heavy-handed manipulation which the government employed in its efforts to assure an overwhelming electoral victory alienated a large part of the political elite, which was feeling increasingly excluded from meaningful participation in the country's political life. In early 1973 the mood of many of the government's critics was bitter and frustrated, almost without hope. One leading spokesman for the 1966 Generation declared: "This is the most alienated government in the history of Indonesia. Everyone is very depressed. . . . I'm afraid we demonstrated against the wrong fellow." Another young leader stated flatly: "It's not our country any more, at least not for the next twenty-five years." Politics was "dead," concluded several foreign policy elite members.

Disillusion with the prospects for economic and social development increased dramatically during the course of 1973. The 1972 rice crop failure created critical food shortages, sent the price of rice soaring, and set off a new inflationary spiral.[74] As the Five Year Plan begun in April 1969 approached its final months, there was

74. *Pedoman,* 16 August 1973, reported that the inflation rate was 25 percent in 1972. In fiscal year 1973/74 consumer prices increased at a rate of nearly 50 percent, dropping to a 20 percent increase in 1974/75 and an annual rate of 17.5 percent in the first four months of 1975 (*BIES,* vol. 11, no. 2 [July 1975], p. 18).

increasingly vocal disappointment with what had been achieved. Pointing to surging inflation, rising unemployment (extending even to the middle class), failure to reach food production targets, the collapse of many indigenous businesses, the "destruction of the Islamic middle class," stagnation in traditional exports (as opposed to oil and logs), and rising educational costs, critics claimed that for most people life was getting harder and harder—approaching, in many cases, the point of "desperation."[75] Some declared that Indonesians were now worse off than they had been in colonial days, when they were "a nation of coolies and a coolie among nations."[76]

Foreign policy elite members interviewed in 1973 contended that stagnation and corruption were worse than they had been in 1970. Skepticism about Indonesia's economic accomplishments was vividly expressed in posters carried by university students in Bandung late in 1973: "The GNP goes up but the people's pants go down"—"A thousand yen are invested and a thousand Majalayas [a town

75. See *Indonesia Raya,* 16 August 1973, 12 November 1973; *Harian Kami,* 13 August 1973, 8 November 1973; *Pedoman,* 8 November 1973; *Nusantara,* 8 November 1973; *Kompas,* 31 October 1973; and *Sinar Harapan,* 29 October 1973.

76. *Nusantara,* 8 November 1973. While there is room for argument about the long-range impact of the government's development policies, there is at least some evidence that tends to confirm this bleak assessment. Though self-sufficiency in food production had been the central goal of the Five Year Plan, rice production in 1973, even with a record harvest following the disastrous shortfall of 1972, was estimated at 14.5 million tons, well below the goal of 15.4 million tons set in 1969 (*BIES,* vol. 5, no. 2 [July 1969], p. 71). More important, the increase in rice production, which may in any case be difficult to sustain at a rate equal to population growth, came largely from the use of irrigation and fertilizer to produce a second rice crop on land formerly used for other crops. Production of the major secondary food crops remained stationary or declined, with the result that total per capita output of foodstuffs actually declined between 1968 and 1973 (*ibid.,* vol. 10, no. 2 [July 1974], pp. 31–33). In a similarly discouraging vein, some foreign diplomats concluded from their studies that the bottom half of the Indonesian population was worse off in 1974 than it had been in 1968. The same observers concluded that Indonesians were growing shorter due to deteriorating nutrition and noted that human laborers reportedly were replacing draft animals in certain parts of Java.

where many textile factories had been forced to close] die."[77] If the first Five Year Plan had "mostly come to nothing," Indonesians were asking, what hope was there for the second?[78]

Increasingly, attention was being drawn to the widening disparity between rich and poor—and to the fact that foreign investment seemed to benefit most those who were already strong. People could not see the benefit of IGGI credits or foreign investment for any but the wealthy few, it was argued. Moreover, the result of foreign aid had been to encourage extravagant international standards of consumption, which given Indonesia's stage of development, were premature and likely to produce an even more damaging degree of dependence on other countries.[79] The ever stronger position of foreigners and overseas Chinese in Indonesian economic affairs led a once militantly anti-Sukarno newspaper to warn of a "new colonialism via the economic sector."[80] There was growing talk of the need to reevaluate Indonesia's development strategy, and to consider seriously the relevance of China's labor-intensive, low technology, and self-reliant approach for Indonesia.[81]

Besides sharpening their public attacks on the negative results of

77. *Mahasiswa Indonesia,* 11 November 1973. There were reports that in the area of Majalaya alone some 50,000 were thrown out of work (*Indonesia Raya,* 24 August 1973). In the batik industry of Tasikmalaya, it was said that of 1500 enterprises registered in 1968, only 38 remained in 1973, and the same trend was found in other areas (*BIES,* vol. 9, no. 3 [November 1973], pp. 13–14). Even more dramatic was the impact of the introduction of Japanese rice hullers in Java. It was estimated that by displacing the traditional hand-pounding method, the rice hullers eliminated 1,200,000 jobs. In fact, the number of man-hours of employment lost just as a result of the introduction of labor-saving rice hullers in Java was 125 million, which dwarfed the 44 million man-hours of employment believed to have been created throughout Indonesia by the government's major employment creation effort in the rural areas, the *kabupaten* program (William A. Collier *et al.,* "Choice of Technique in Rice Milling on Java," BIES, vol. 10, no. 1 [March 1974], pp. 106–20).

78. *Indonesia Raya,* 14 November 1973. See also 13 November 1973.

79. *Indonesia Raya,* 13 November 1973, 29 August 1973, and *Tempo,* 17 November 1973.

80. *Mahasiswa Indonesia,* 11 November 1973.

81. *Pedoman,* 21 November 1973, and *Indonesia Raya,* 23 November 1973.

government development efforts, emboldened critics also assailed the loss of political independence. Noting their government's failure to lodge any real protest at the passage of American naval vessels through the Straits of Malacca without Jakarta's permission, one newspaper lamented Indonesia's meekness, which it blamed on the country's entry into the "IGGI orbit," while another asked: "How long will we allow ourselves to be regarded as a weak people that can be disregarded at will?"[82]

How far the critics intended to go toward challenging the position of the ruling group was unclear. Though some of the dissatisfied leaders seemed resigned to their fate, others had warned the author back in early 1973—before critics of the government dared to speak as boldly as they did later in the year—not to mistake their discreet silence for inactivity. One spokesman said they were following a "submarine strategy," by which they hoped to torpedo the present leaders without exposing themselves fully. Included among the "submariners" were certain strategically-located army officers, who were developing links with civilian critics focusing on the lack of strong presidential leadership, the alleged corruption of Soeharto and his closest associates, especially his wife, and the "selling" of the country to overseas Chinese and foreigners. Significantly, they noted that even though they were all strong anti-Communists, there was an anti-U.S. component to their criticism, because of Washington's willingness to assist the present corrupt powerholders. "When things explode," it was asserted, "the Americans will be hit not by the Communists but by the anti-Communists."

Dissatisfied army officers were reluctant, however, to contemplate a coup, mainly because of the precedent it would set. Later in 1973, civilian sources publicly intimated that coercing the leaders to change their policies was not out of the question. The student-led coup in Thailand prompted some newspapers to invite the Indonesian leaders to reflect on the Thai experience. One warned that if the Indonesian rulers did not stop living so luxuriously amid such widespread suffering, the "Bangkok affair" could be repeated in Jakarta.

82. *Merdeka,* 2 November 1973, and *Indonesia Raya,* 5 November 1973.

If the Indonesian leaders did not begin to orient their policies toward providing greater equity and social justice, "other forces" which might "not be under control" would do the job.[83]

By the end of 1973, it was indeed clear that civilian critics were counting on support from dissatisfied army elements. The rapid escalation in the boldness of public criticism undoubtedly reflected the critics' belief that influential army leaders sympathized with them and would afford them a degree of protection. To be certain, there was little evidence during the course of the year of any inclination on the government's part to consider a major shift of policy, though some official spokesmen did acknowledge the seriousness of the unemployment problem.[84] But the apparent erosion of army unity pointed toward a possible revival of the kind of political competition which could transform the existing criticism into real pressure for a more independent foreign policy.

In January 1974, however, anti-Japanese demonstrations occasioned by the visit of Prime Minister Tanaka turned violent, and the Indonesian government claimed that the demonstrators had actually aimed at the overthrow of Soeharto. The president moved quickly to crush his critics, many of whom had no connection with the demonstrations. He ordered the arrest of some of the most outspoken intellectual and student leaders, shut down most of the critical newspapers, and forced the exile or retirement of army leaders who had seemed to be aligning with dissident civilians.

In the aftermath of the January demonstrations, the government made some modest gestures to meet the criticism that had been expressed so sharply. Policies concerning foreign investment were changed to increase the Indonesian share in ownership of joint ventures and the indigenous component of the Indonesian share. Though the new regulations were viewed by some as evidence of rising economic nationalism, they clearly were not intended to discourage further foreign investment. In fact, an unusually large number of applications for new investment won government ap-

83. *Mahasiswa Indonesia,* 28 October 1973, 4 November 1973, and *Indonesia Raya,* 15 November 1973.

84. See, for example, *Analisa Previsionil,* p. 25.

proval during 1974 (see Appendix C). And as already noted, Indonesia received a record commitment of foreign aid in 1975, with the World Bank projecting that the country's annual aid needs would rise to $4 billion by 1980. There was, however, a sharp drop in investment applications in 1975.[85]

Though public criticism has been muted since the newspaper closings and arrests of early 1974, there is no reason to assume that the widespread concern about Indonesia's dependence on outsiders has diminished. Given the intractible problems which Indonesia faces, it probably will not be too long before new challengers begin to arise. And as noted in Chapter 7, it may well be that the oil bonanza, if it lasts long enough, will heighten political tensions by raising high, but unfulfillable, expectations in many people while affording opportunities for extravagant living for a conspicuous few.

But even if pressures for a more independent policy and a more equitable distribution of wealth continue to build, it will not be easy for this government, or a successor regime, to swing dramatically away from the present course. Both the incumbent leaders and their potential challengers find themselves caught in the contradiction between, on the one hand, their suspicious view of the world and their desire to be nationalists, and on the other hand, their sensitivity to the many attractions of foreign aid. The Indonesian leaders, even the critics, may have become to some extent prisoners of their own dependent psychology: if problems grow more difficult to solve, there seems to be an irresistible urge to seek more foreign aid, not less.[86] Nor can we rule out the possibility that a new regime, even one

85. The new regulations required 51 percent Indonesian ownership of joint ventures within ten years and Indonesianization of all but top executive positions within three to five years. They also imposed a tax on foreign employees to be placed in a fund for training Indonesians, reduced investment incentives such as tax holidays, and closed some sectors to further foreign investment (*BIES*, vol. 11, no. 2 [July 1975], pp. 23–24). The problems of implementing such regulations are discussed in Franklin B. Weinstein, "Multinational Corporations and the Third World: The Case of Japan and Southeast Asia," *International Organization*, vol. 30, no. 3 (Summer 1976). For a discussion of foreign investment, see *Far Eastern Economic Review*, 7 November 1975.

86. Even critics who contend that Indonesia should rely less on foreign

that seeks to legitimize its seizure of power as an action intended to reclaim the national independence sold by the previous rulers, would, on finding itself in a position to control the distribution of incoming foreign resources, pursue policies similar to those of its predecessor.

To the extent, though, that the present leaders retain a weakened hold on power, or a new regime feels its control to be tenuous, there will be substantial incentives to use the independence appeal as a means of placing opponents in an awkward position. In any case, the developments described in the above paragraphs—the sharpening criticism of dependence on foreign aid and rising social inequality, the frustration and alienation of a large segment of the political elite, and the intimations of political action to compel a change—represent the kinds of processes which, sooner or later, seem likely to lead to an intensification of political competition, and ultimately to a foreign policy that accords greater priority to independence.

---

investment, which tends to be capital intensive, and more on intermediate technology end by asking that foreigners provide Indonesia with the necessary intermediate technology. See Soedjatmoko, "Technology, Development, and Culture," pp. 4, 7.

9 | Conclusion: Implications of the Indonesian Case

What does our analysis of the way Indonesia has confronted the dilemma of dependence suggest about the relationship between foreign policy and underdevelopment? We have seen how the Indonesian leaders came to view the international order as exploitative and the big powers as threats to their country's independence. Their view of the world as a hostile place arose out of the colonial predicament, found reinforcement in their frustrating experiences with the major powers during and after the struggle for independence from the Dutch, and was sharpened by the discovery that economic aid could impair their independence without bringing development. The leaders of Soeharto's New Order, like the men who dominated Sukarno's Guided Democracy, have seen more exploitation than genuine assistance in their relations with the big powers; leaders in both periods have viewed the risks of dependence on foreign aid as excessively high. But in spite of those perceptions, the basic weakness of Indonesia's economic and political institutions placed both regimes under strong pressure to continue seeking such aid.

Though the two regimes have perceived the dangers of dependence in roughly similar terms, they have responded to the aid-independence dilemma in very different ways.[1] The intense political

1. Most studies of attitudes and foreign policymaking seek to show the influence of attitudes by demonstrating that they fit or correspond to the policies adopted. (For example, see Burgess, *Elite Images and Foreign Policy Outcomes*, and Brecher, *India and World Politics*.) In Guided Democracy, the dominant attitudes and policies did fit, but in the New Order, the underlying perception of the world has not found significant expression in foreign

competition of the Guided Democracy years, together with the prevailing perception of a hostile world, created strong incentives for carrying out a foreign policy that put independence first; it made the liabilities of an aid-oriented policy formidable. In the much less competitive political situation of the New Order, a suspicious view of the aid-givers did not create any insurmountable obstacles to a policy of maximizing aid, while the political attractions of an independence-oriented policy were diminished.

Of course, many other factors have affected the way the dilemma of dependence has been resolved: the tendency to react against the failure of past policies, the condition of the economy, the availability of aid and the attitudes of the aid-givers, and the presidential personality and political style. Moreover, the question of dependence can never be considered in a wholly abstract way; it makes a great difference to each political competitor whether the proposed aid-giver is an ally or a supporter of domestic adversaries. But we have focused on the interaction between perceptions and political competition because that relationship greatly limits the scope for expression of a president's personal idiosyncracies and the freedom of governments to respond to economic conditions, to react against past failures, and to take advantage of available aid. Similarly, it may be true that when the PKI and the army leadership were locked in a death struggle, dependence on Western aid would have hurt the PKI and helped the generals; but the combination of intense political competition and deep suspicion of the aid-givers made it impossible for the generals to advocate such a policy.

Stressing the importance of political incentives and risks in the determination of foreign policy should not, of course, be construed as suggesting that the policies Indonesia has followed have been insincere or merely politically expedient. Both the policy of emphasizing independence and that of stressing aid represented genuinely felt impulses, but in both periods the two impulses coexisted, and the degree of political competition helped to determine which would be dominant. The essential point is that it was not the attitudinal

policy. Thus, we are in a position to see both the importance of perceptions and their limitations as a determinant of policy.

base alone—the dominant perception of the world as hostile—that determined Indonesian foreign policy; nor was it the presence or absence of serious political competition alone. It was the interaction of attitudes and political competition, the effect that the one had on the other, that played a major role in shaping the Indonesian response to the aid-independence dilemma.

The conclusions drawn from this study may be reformulated in more general terms as a hypothesis for other less developed countries. When there is a strong underlying suspicion of the aid-givers, we may expect that the more narrow the ruling elite's margin or more tenuous the coalition, the greater the sensitivity to the dangers of becoming dependent on foreign aid. Or the proposition may be restated as follows: Where the foreign policy elite of an underdeveloped country perceives the world as hostile, intense political competition will lead the country toward a foreign policy that puts independence first, while a less competitive situation will permit a policy that accords priority to the search for aid.

One last point deserves comment. In the first chapter, we noted a strong theme running through much of the writing on foreign policy in underdeveloped countries: the irrelevance of foreign policy to the real needs of these countries. Often, emphasis is placed on the importance of idiosyncratic factors and the consequent irrationality of the policies. Does the Indonesian foreign policy elite's view of the world as a hostile place mean that there is a basic element of irrationality in Indonesia's foreign policy? Are the Indonesians xenophobic or paranoid? Can it be said, as some writers referred to in Chapter 1 seem to suggest, that the Indonesian perspective on the world is merely a manifestation of psychological disorders lingering after the trauma of colonialism and the revolution?

In the case of some Indonesian leaders, the perception of a hostile world did seem to reflect an inferiority complex spawned by the trauma of colonialism; the existence of such a complex was mentioned by the foreign policy elite members with enough frequency to suggest that it probably does account, at least in part, for the attitudes of some leaders. Younger men claimed that some of their elders, obviously deferential and uncertain in the presence of foreigners, seemed obsessed with a need to prove that Indonesians were the equal of Westerners. The demand that Indonesia be recognized as an international leader was described as stemming from the same insecurity that motivates some Indonesians visiting Holland to insist that Dutchmen shine their shoes—"just to prove that they are superior to the Dutch."

Most of the 1928 Generation leaders themselves agreed that Indonesian society was afflicted by an inferiority complex. There was, they said, evidence of a "slave mentality" and a feeling that "other countries can do things better." The independent-and-active policy, according to one leader, was essentially "an effort to regain our self-confidence, which was destroyed by colonialism." The same man attributed the Indonesians' persistent feeling of inferiority to the attitude of racial superiority displayed by the white powers and to the arrogance of the Chinese and Japanese: "They [the white powers] really recognize only three Asian countries as civilized—China, India, and now Japan. . . . If we have an inferiority complex, they have a superiority complex. They consider all nonwhite people to be inferior. Even stupid farmers who don't know anything about international relations are considered to be superior. . . . Every white man is considered superior to every nonwhite." Another 1928 Generation leader still bothered by racially inspired feelings of inferiority recalled how much his later thinking about the West was influenced by the racial segregation practiced in theaters and restaurants under the Dutch: "The younger generation just cannot understand what it means to be discriminated against in that way."

Though some suggested that the two younger generations of leaders also showed manifestations of an inferiority complex, by and large the younger men were much more reluctant to admit such feelings. They tended to argue that other Indonesians, especially their political adversaries, lacked confidence in dealing with foreigners, but not "mature people like us." A few 1945 Generation leaders did, however, give evidence of their own self-doubts in dealing with the outside world. For example, one 1945 Generation leader declared:

The only people we can really relax with are the Malaysians and the Filipinos, because we don't feel inferior to them. We go to Europe and say, "I am an Indonesian," and people say, "so what? . . ." Everyone respects an American, but it means nothing to be an Indonesian. . . . That's why Indonesians so often try to make themselves look more important than they are, because of their feeling of inferiority. Sukarno's foreign policy was definitely a reflection of this. . . . When he sat with Kennedy or told the United States to go to hell with its aid, it made us feel proud that we were independent enough to tell the United States to go to hell. The Filipinos or Malaysians would never dare to do that.

Leaders who boasted of relationships with white women, and others who felt pressed to outperform white classmates to overcome their embarrassment at the condescension with which they were treated by white women, were consciously attempting to compensate for their sense of insecurity. Even a member of the 1966 Generation recalled his pleasure when, at a conference abroad, he found himself "scolding all those Europeans and having them take me seriously."

If feelings of inferiority have made certain Indonesian leaders suspicious of foreigners, some of those who saw the present ruling group as insensitive to the many dangers from abroad probably were expressing their own frustration at being excluded from power. There were frustrated men in all three generations, but the problem seemed especially pronounced among older leaders who had been first to oppose both Sukarno and the PKI, who had always conceived of themselves as the legitimate heirs to governmental power if Indonesia were ever to oust Sukarno and give priority to economic development, and who have been left out completely by the New Order leadership. In looking for ways to explain their disappointment, perhaps it was natural that they should claim that those in power, because of their inexperience, were being manipulated by foreigners. In the words of one leader:

I have seen all my dreams for Indonesia smashed. Everything we fought for has been lost. The spirit of the revolution is practically dead. The present government is run by traitors. . . . I just cannot understand how it has come to pass that those people are now running things, and those of us who dedicated our lives to struggling for our people's independence have been shunted aside. . . . Young people don't know the meaning of independence. . . . The government is much too interested in being praised by foreigners. They are so naive. . . . These technocrats are like the doctor who performs a perfect operation and is amazed to find that the patient has died. They just want to be patted on the back by their former teachers.

It may be, then, that inferiority complexes and personal frustrations lent an element of irrationality to the perceptions of some Indonesians. But to dismiss the hostile world perspective as mere xenophobia or paranoia is to overlook its broader basis. In the conclusion of Chapter 3 we hypothesized that there might be a positive correspondence between increased exposure to the outside world and a heightened perception of the world as hostile to Indonesia. In other words, a suspicious view may not be just a product of ignorance and maladjustment but rather the result of an accumulation of knowledge about the world and experience in international relations.

The data drawn from our investigation of the foreign policy elite's view of the world support that hypothesis. In the first place, there is a reasonable degree of correspondence between the groups that had high exposure and the ones that were most likely to view the world as threatening. The two groups lowest in perception of a hostile world were the two with by far the least exposure, as measured by the extent to which they had undergone the five key experiences described in Chapter 3. The other groups were all high in both exposure and the perception of hostility, though the correspondence is not precise.[2]

2. The PNI, fourth in exposure, was first in seeing threats to Indonesia's independence, while the foreign ministry officials and technocrats, virtually tied for first in exposure, were tied for third in viewing the world as a hostile place. However, the tendency of foreign ministry officials and technocrats to describe the world as hostile was inhibited somewhat by a reluctance to make statements which would reflect unfavorably on the wisdom of policies for which they were directly responsible. On the other hand, the PNI leaders' extraordinary enthusiasm for the hostile world view undoubtedly reflected their quasi-Marxist ideology. For that matter, it is quite conceivable that some Catholic and Islamic politicians, who were lowest in perceiving a

More evidence of the link between exposure and the perception of a hostile world emerges when the foreign policy elite is broken down into leaders with high, moderate, and low exposure to the outside world. The high exposure leaders answered an average of 81 percent of the questions in a manner indicating a hostile world perspective, while leaders with a moderate degree of exposure averaged 68 percent, and the low exposure leaders averaged only 37 percent. Though the numbers are too small to be of statistical significance, it is interesting to note that within each of the generations and other groups except one, the higher exposure leaders were more pronounced in the perception of hostility than the other members (see Table 9.1).[3] In every major group except one, the leader who was most aware of threats to Indonesia's independence was someone who had had all five experiences. It tended to be the most intellectual members of each group, the ones generally singled out by their countrymen as excelling in intelligence, sophistication, and experience, who were most emphatic in their espousal of the hostile world view. Finally, the 55 leaders who saw the world as predominantly hostile (that is, those who answered more than 50 percent of the questions in a way reflecting a perception of threats to Indonesia's independence) had had, on the average, 81 percent

---

hostile world, were so vehemently anti-Communist that they were practically incapable of seeing any anti-Communist power as a threat. But these ideological predispositions do not explain variations within the Islamic and Catholic groups, while differences in exposure do. For example, as we shall see, Catholic and Islamic leaders with greater exposure were much more likely to see the world as hostile than were other Catholics and Muslims. Moreover, the one area in which the Islamic leaders were most suspicious of the outside world was economic policy and the role of the IMF. This may well reflect the fact that the Islamic party leaders, either through their own business activities or those of people close to them, had a much greater degree of personal knowledge and experience in this field than in foreign relations generally.

3. The exception was the PSI, which had only one leader without high exposure. This highly unusual individual has, for reasons which cannot be specified without identifying him, become one of the best informed Indonesians on international affairs, though he had only three of the five exposure experiences. Also, no tabulation was possible for the technocrats because all of them had high exposure.

Table 9.1. Exposure and the perception of a hostile world

Exposure*	Average percentage of answers indicating perception of a hostile world	Index of exposure by groups
All respondents (n = 65)	73	71
High (n = 38)	81	
Moderate (n = 22)	68	
Low (n = 5)	37	
1928 Generation (n = 11)	70	73
High (n = 7)	83	
Moderate (n = 2)	65	
Low (n = 2)	27	
1945 Generation (n = 45)	75	76
High (n = 30)	80	
Moderate (n = 14)	67	
Low (n = 1)	58	
1966 Generation (n = 9)	66	45
High (n = 1)	80	
Moderate (n = 6)	73	
Low (n = 2)	38	
PNI (n = 9)	91	78
High (n = 6)	92	
Moderate (n = 3)	88	
PSI (n = 6)	82	87
High (n = 5)	80	
Moderate (n = 1)	88	
Foreign Ministry (n = 9)	76	92
High (n = 8)	78	
Moderate (n = 1)	60	
Technocrats (n = 9)	76	91
High (n = 9)	76	
Army (n = 12)	74	75
High (n = 7)	83	
Moderate (n = 5)	60	
Islamic parties (n = 8)	51	50
High (n = 2)	72	
Moderate (n = 3)	45	
Low (n = 3)	43	
Catholic Party (n = 4)	43	50
High (n = 1)	61	
Moderate (n = 2)	45	
Low (n = 1)	21	

* "High exposure" means at least 4 of the 5 key experiences; "moderate exposure" means 2 or 3 of the experiences; "low exposure" means fewer than two experiences.

of the five key experiences, while the other 10 leaders averaged only 38 percent.

If those Indonesians who knew the outside world best were the ones most disposed to see it as threatening, perhaps this perception is less a manifestation of paranoia than a reflection of reality. Though studies of the attitudes of Americans have suggested that the more they know about the outside world, the less they tend to see it as threatening,[4] the underdeveloped countries certainly face dangers that do not exist for the strong.

After all, even many European states have given ample evidence of their uneasiness at being dependent on a superpower patron; they have scarcely hidden their anxiety that Washington and Moscow might settle the fate of Europe without consulting them. For that matter, even Americans, citizens of the mightiest nation in the world, have heard their president speak of the dire consequences of dependence on Middle Eastern oil and of the need to end this intolerable infringement on the independence of the United States as quickly as possible. If these powerful nations have cause to fear that foreigners may exploit them or ignore their vital interests, how much more reason there must be for a weak underdeveloped state, whose leaders believe that their country's development depends overwhelmingly on aid from untrustworthy nations, to fear the consequences of dependence.

The Indonesian leaders' view of the world as a hostile place has emerged as the product of much bitter experience acquired over many years. Considering its bases, especially its espousal by younger Indonesians highly conscious of their country's weakness, this view of the world seems likely to persist for some time.[5] For the underdeveloped nation, there is no easy road to independence and no

4. See, for example, Herbert McClosky, "Personality and Attitude Correlates of Foreign Policy Orientation," in Rosenau, ed., *Domestic Sources of Foreign Policy,* pp. 51–109. Though McClosky's study deals explicitly with "isolationism," he actually appears to be talking about a general attitude of suspicion toward foreigners. See also Michael Roskin, "What 'New Isolationism'?" *Foreign Policy,* 6 (Spring 1972), 122–23.

5. See Table 9.1.

sure path to development; but perhaps leaders who are aware that they live in a world dominated by powers which are not disposed to help them achieve their goals will eventually face, more directly than they have thus far, the implications of their view of the world. It may well be that the only way for them to develop in a hostile world is to seek their own more autonomous path.

Statistical Appendixes, Index of Sources, and General Index

Appendix A | The Underdeveloped Countries in International Trade

Table A-1. Value of exports and imports in current prices, 1950–1970 (million $)

Exports	1950	1970
Developed market economy countries	37,200	223,900
Socialist countries	4,930	33,390
Developing countries and territories	18,930	55,000
Indonesia	800	810
Imports	**1950**	**1970**
Developed market economy countries	41,600	236,100
Socialist countries	5,000	34,660
Developing countries and territories	17,500	56,200
Indonesia	440	883

Source: UNCTAD, *Handbook of International Trade and Development Statistics* (United Nations, 1972).

Table A-2. **Declining share of the underdeveloped countries in world exports, 1950–1970 (in percentages)**

	1950	1951	1952	1953	1954	1955	1956	1957	1958	1959
Developed market economy countries	60.9	63.0	65.4	64.9	64.3	64.7	66.3	67.2	65.9	65.4
Developing countries and territories	31.0	29.0	25.9	25.5	25.7	25.3	24.0	22.7	22.9	22.3
Socialist countries	8.1	8.0	8.7	9.6	10.0	10.0	9.7	10.1	11.2	12.3

	1960	1961	1962	1963	1964	1965	1966	1967	1968	1969	19
Developed market economy countries	67.0	67.5	67.2	67.4	68.2	68.8	69.5	69.6	70.3	71.0	71
Developing countries and territories	21.3	20.7	20.5	20.4	20.1	19.5	19.1	18.8	18.4	18.1	17
Socialist countries	11.7	11.8	12.3	12.1	11.8	11.6	11.4	11.6	11.3	10.9	10

Source: UNCTAD, *Handbook of International Trade and Development Statistics* (Unit Nations, 1972).

Appendix B | Foreign Aid to Indonesia

Table B-1. Foreign debt as of 31 December 1965 (million $)

Country	Debt
Communist	
USSR	990
Yugoslavia	115
Poland	100
Czechoslovakia	77
East Germany	72
Hungary	19
Rumania	16
China	13
Other	2
Total	1,404
Western	
U.S.	179
West Germany	122
France	115
Italy	91
United Kingdom (including Hong Kong)	42
Netherlands	28
Switzerland	3
Other	7
Total	587
Asian	
Japan	231
Pakistan	20
India	10
Total	261
African	
UAR	4
International agency	
IMF	102
Grand total	2,358

Source: *Bulletin of Indonesian Economic Studies,* no. 4 (June 1966), p. 5.

Table B-2. Commitments since 1966 (million $)

	U.S.	Japan	IBRD/ ADB*	West Germany	Holland	France	Aust'lia	UK	Other†	Total
1966–68	353	225	51	61	37	10	–	5	2	687
1969	236	120	60	27	40	16	21	5	9	534
1970/71	225	140	89	35	35	15	19	7	7	571
1971/72	215	155	105	41	37	21‖	20	23	8	627
1972/73	203	185§	145	47	44	21	24	26	29	724
1973/74‡	150†	180†	164	57	52	26	24	30	34	877
1974/75	176	150	330	73	66	37	33	na	34†	899#
1975/76	50	140	520	43	52	na	34	25	56	920
Total	1,608	1,325	1,464	384	363	146	175	121	179	5,839

* IBRD includes both regular World Bank loans and those administered through the IDA, the World Bank's "soft loan window." ADB is the Asian Development Bank.

† Includes Denmark, Belgium, Canada, Italy, New Zealand, and Switzerland.

‡ The individual country figures do not include food aid, which was expected to total $160 million. No country breakdown on food aid was available.

§ In 1972 Japan also agreed to provide a $200 million loan for development of oil, but this was outside the framework of the IGGI.

‖ This $21 million commitment was extended jointly with Belgium and Italy; the breakdown among the three is unavailable, so for the sake of convenience the entire commitment is listed under France.

The 1974/75 aid commitment was actually expected to total between $899 and 913 million. Japan was considering an additional $5 million and the ADB an additional $10 million.

Source: *Bulletin of Indonesian Economic Studies,* July editions, 1969–1975, and March 1970.

ppendix C | Foreign Investment in Indonesia

Table C-1. Projects Approved by Indonesia, 1967–1974 (million $)*

	1967–1973		1974		1967–1974	
	Number of projects	Intended investment	Number of projects	Intended investment	Number of projects	Intended investment
sector						
anufacturing	56	$ 436.8	12	$ 250.4	68	$ 687.2
Textiles	81	101.7	12	190.0	93	291.7
Chemicals	35	58.7	4	11.5	39	70.2
Electronics	235	447.9	27	362.0	262	809.9
Other	407	1,045.1	55	813.9	462	1,859.0
griculture	66	113.0	5	12.5	71	125.5
restry	82	495.5	4	10.9	86	506.4
ining	19	860.5	–	–	19	860.5
onstruction	44	51.9	10	10.3	54	62.2
otels, tourism	12	101.8	3	71.4	15	173.2
eal estate	13	94.1	11	129.3	24	223.4
ther services	43	66.4	4	3.2	47	69.6
rand total	686	$2,828.3	92	$1,051.5	778	$3,879.8
country						
pan	149	633.4	32	450.0	181	1,083.4
.S./Canada	118	959.6	6	14.4	124	974.0†
ong Kong	94	267.4	18	178.8	112	446.2
ngapore	42	100.0	3	25.6	45	126.1
ther Asian	89	485.3	8	39.9	97	525.2
ustralia	35	151.0	7	23.1	42	174.1
etherlands	40	72.9	8	98.0	48	170.9
'est Germany	27	33.5	2	139.2	29	166.4
ther European	53	77.7	4	70.4	57	148.1
nited Kingdom	38	46.5	4	18.4	42	64.9
frica	1	0.5	–	–	1	0.5
rand total	686	$2,828.3	92	$1,051.5	778	$3,879.8

* These figures do not include oil and banking. According to the Pertamina office in San Fran-sco, $1,854,200,000 was approved for investment in oil under the production-sharing contract stem between 1966 and the end of 1974. This does not include investments by some of the largest mpanies (including Caltex and Stanvac) under the work contract system both before and after 966; no figures are made available for that form of investment. Most investment in oil comes om the United States.

† Though no exact breakdown is available, the Indonesian consulate in San Francisco estimates anadian investment at about $80 million, with the rest coming from the United States.

Source: *Bulletin of Indonesian Economic Studies,* vol. 11, no. 2 (July 1975), p. 25.

Appendix D | Indonesian Trade Statistics

Table D-1. Exports, 1960–1973 (million $)

	1960	1961	1962	1963	1964	1965	1966	1967	1968	1969	1970	1971	1972	1973
Japan	34	56	41	67	122	113	121	195	180	256	297	530	902	1707
U.S.	193	185	93	85	173	153	138	103	119	129	111	182	265	465
Western Europe	179	131	166	197	174	178	224	148	141	139	128	171	247	345
Singapore	194	163	146	103	3	6	18	66	118	147	153	143	134	341
Eastern Europe	9	14	14	16	15	14	17	11	4	4	7	2	6	10
USSR	28	32	35	25	21	26	26	15	18	16	19	10	7	6
China	4	36	34	42	52	40	9	1	0	0	0	0	0	0.4

Sources: Bank Indonesia, *Indonesian Financial Statistics: Monthly Bulletin* (February 1973), for 1960–1971, and IMF/IBRD, *Direction of Trade* (May 1975), p. 76, for 1972–1973.

Table D-2. Imports, 1961–1973 (million $)

	1961	1962	1963	1964	1965	1966	1967	1968	1969	1970	1971	1972	1973
Japan	142	135	88	143	159	142	182	159	226	263	390	532	800
Western Europe	234	181	154	245	167	136	197	195	175	214	280	322	519
U.S.	136	117	59	10	66	49	52	123	154	158	176	243	513
Singapore	17	13	5	0	0	1	17	34	40	49	73	102	134
China	40	48	44	61	99	41	54	38	43	31	31	39	49
Eastern Europe	27	15	19	26	36	22	12	8	7	10	8	7	24
USSR	11	9	15	11	13	6	5	6	5	6	14	6	3

Sources: Bank Indonesia, *Indonesian Financial Statistics: Monthly Bulletin* (February 1973), for 1961–1971, and IMF/IBRD, *Direction of Trade* (May 1975), p. 76, for 1972–1973.

Index of Sources

To assist the reader in checking citations, an index of most of the primary and secondary sources used in this book has been compiled. Newspapers and magazines have not been included. Documents are listed alphabetically by title or short title. The number after an author's name or document indicates the page where the full citation appears. Where more than one article or book by an author is cited, a short title indicates the appropriate reference.

General Index

Library of Congress Cataloging in Publication Data
(For library cataloging purposes only)

Weinstein, Franklin B
Indonesian foreign policy and the dilemma of dependence.

(Politics and international relations of Southeast Asia)
Includes bibliographical references and index.
1. Indonesia—Foreign relations. I. Title.
II. Series.
DS638.W44 327.598 75-36998
ISBN 0-8014-0939-X